Cover design: Luis Baldomir & Julia Lokkova
Content & production development and editing; visual resources: Miriam Ramos

ISBN: 978-84-09-83446-4

Trauma-Informed Relational Approach for Dissociative Parts

(TADP)

Dolores Mosquera

To Giovanni Liotti,
whose work continues to illuminate the path of many clinicians.

His thinking transformed our understanding of trauma,
attachment, and dissociation, and this book stands
on the foundations he built and his enduring legacy.

A Note of Gratitude

To **Miriam Ramos**, for the extraordinary work you have done editing, formatting, and designing this book—the charts, the graphics, all of it. You are truly amazing. Thank you for helping me refine how I present my work and ideas, and for your thoughtful questions, suggestions, and practical guidance. I am deeply grateful to have you in my life. You always make me better.

To **Natalia Seijo**, for encouraging me to write this book, and for always feeling proud of what I achieve. Thank you for being who you are and how you are. As you once said, nothing would be the same without you in my life. I feel profoundly grateful, and I cherish all the moments and projects we have shared and those we continue to build together. You are family.

To **Emilio Vercillo**, for being such a fantastic supervisor, colleague, and friend. The more I know you, Emilio, the more grateful I am to have met you in Venice so many years ago. I always learn from you, not only professionally, but personally as well. Thank you for reviewing the entire book, especially the sections on motivational systems. It has been a great honor to think alongside you. This book would not be the same without your feedback and suggestions.

To Onno van der Hart, Kathy Steele, and Suzette Boon, I consider you mentors on many levels, and I feel deeply privileged to have you in my life. Beyond your influence on my thinking and my work, I am grateful for the shared history, the generosity, and the many moments of connection along the way. And thank you, too, for the fun. It is always a joy to be together. **Onno**, thanks for reviewing the entire book and for the ongoing exchange of ideas, feedback, and suggestions. Thank you for reviewing almost everything I do. It is an honor and a privilege to think alongside you. And, of course, thank you for writing the back-cover blurb. **Kathy,** thanks for reviewing this book and for the many ways we think, work, teach, and supervise together. Our collaboration has shaped my clinical thinking in profound ways, and it is always an honor and a privilege to work alongside you. Thank you for writing the back-cover blurb, and for your generosity, clarity, and the shared commitment that runs through all that we do. Your friendship and steady presence mean more to me than words can easily say. **Suzette,** I am so glad we have come to know each other over the years. Your support has been a constant presence in my professional and personal life, always offered with clarity and directness, and at the same time with generosity and heart. You are one of the most authentic people I know. Thank you for the many ways we have collaborated, teaching together, exchanging ideas, and thinking side by side over the years.

To Andrew Leeds, for your friendship, for the many projects we have written and presented together over the years, and for always being there when I ask you to read, review, or think through my work. Your careful eye, thoughtful comments, and quiet work in the background have been invaluable. I feel deeply grateful to think alongside you.

To Paula Baldomir, my sister in every way that matters: family, colleague, and friend. Your presence in my life and in my work is essential. Thank you for always being there reading everything I write, thinking alongside me, asking the right questions, and bringing your extraordinary intelligence and clarity to everything we do together. You are a beautiful human being, and sharing work, ideas, and life with you is one of the greatest gifts I have.

To Jim Knipe, Roger Solomon, Colin Ross and Ana Gómez, whose influence and collaboration have been part of my professional life for many years. **Jim**, your work has been a constant inspiration, and our shared writing and exchanges have deeply shaped how I think clinically. Your unwavering support for my work and ideas has meant more to me than you know. **Roger**, your friendship and collaboration over more than two decades have been a true gift, from writing and teaching together to translating, co-presenting, and continuing to think side by side year after year. **Colin**, collaborating with you through writing and presenting has been both stimulating and genuinely enjoyable, and our exchanges have contributed in meaningful ways to my clinical thinking. **Ana**, your friendship, our shared teaching, and the many ideas we have exchanged over the years have been a valued and sustaining part of my professional life.

To **all my teachers**, across different fields and approaches: my integrative way of working has been shaped and enriched by all of you.

To **my team**, those who do the clinical work, those who collaborate in training, research, and projects, and those who support everything we do behind the scenes. Thank you for your trust, commitment, and shared responsibility in building INTRA-TP into what it is today, especially to those who have walked alongside me for decades. This work is sustained not only by ideas, but by people—by care, reliability, and collaboration—and I am deeply grateful to each of you for what you bring.

To **my family**: to my parents and brother who have passed, I carry you with me always. To my wonderful husband, for your steady presence, your constant support, and for believing in me and in every project that I choose to take on. Living and building a life with you makes everything easier. To my parents-in-law, Loli and Pancho, and to my sisters and brothers-in-law: I feel I still have a family thanks to all of you.

To **my nieces and nephews**, I am deeply proud of each of you. Watching you grow into such beautiful human beings fills my heart. In this book, I want to acknowledge in a special way the oldest, who has been in my life the longest and who, to my surprise, has chosen to follow a path close to mine. Having become a psychologist and part of my team, your path is marked by thoughtfulness, responsibility, and a depth of clinical sensitivity well beyond what one might expect so early in a professional journey. I am so proud of all that you are doing—your curiosity, your investment in learning and sharing, and your readiness to help in any way that is needed.

To the **clients who have trusted me**, thank you. Every page of this book has been shaped by what you have taught me about survival, courage, resilience, and complexity. To my colleagues, friends, and fellow travelers in the field, thank you for your support and encouragement.

And finally, to the **parts inside the people who do this work**—the protectors, the skeptics, the ones who struggled to ask for help or to trust it—this book is for you, too. And to the clinicians who sit in the quiet of session after session, showing up with steadiness and compassion: you are doing deeply meaningful work.

Foreword

In the medical-philosophical tradition of the Renaissance, inspired by the ideas of Plato's Timaeus, the idea of the *microcosmic man*, that the human being is in fact a small universe mirroring within itself the wider order of nature, was successful. This book could represent a striking clinical re-actualization of that concept. The old idea that the human person incarnates in their inner world the same web of forces, laws, and tensions that sustain the cosmos is here given a modern contour: no longer the harmony of the spheres, but the dense weave of early experiences, guided by the naturally available narrow catalogue of Motivational Systems, and dissociative parts that silently shape the inner architecture of some traumatized subjects.

With the meticulousness and rigor that characterize all her work, Dolores Mosquera offers in these pages a true phenomenology of dissociative parts, locating them within Giovanni Liotti's Multimotivational perspective. Parts are not mere *personifications* of inner states nor fashionable psychological metaphors: they are configurations organized around basic motivational systems (attachment, defense, caregiving, rank, cooperation, sexuality, exploration) that, in histories of disorganized attachment and early relational trauma, become entangled to the point of generating unsolvable knots.

Following Liotti, this book reminds us that what is at stake is not simply a conflict between systems, as if they alternated in linear opposition. In disorganized attachment, there is a *tangle*—an entanglement—of motivational systems that activate *simultaneously*. Attachment and defense, caregiving and rank, sexuality and the search for safety are switched on together, in chronically incompatible ways. The child cannot seek protection without, at the same time, fearing the very figure who should provide it; cannot long for closeness without awakening, in the same instant, circuits of alarm, submission, rage. Dissociation then becomes the only possible way to survive an inner world where the motivational code is short-circuited.

In Mosquera's reading, this has a decisive clinical consequence: the function of a *part* can never be reduced to a single label or a single drive. Each part must be read on several planes at once.

On one plane, we ask which Motivational Systems are organizing its logic: attachment or defense, rank or caregiving, sexuality or cooperation.

On another plane, we look at the role of this part within the overall internal system, in its relationships with the other parts: persecutor, guardian, scapegoat, sacrifice, mediator.

On yet another plane, we consider its position in the external relational field: how it shapes the person's way of approaching others, of entering therapy, of repeating or resisting old relational contracts.

Thus, even an aggressive, hostile, or seemingly destructive part—even a suicidal part—reveals, when seen through this multimotivational lens, a fundamentally protective intention. Behind the wish to annihilate, we may recognize the attempt to silence unbearable shame; behind the threat to destroy the self, the desperate effort to avert some other, more feared catastrophe; behind the attack on the body, the attempt to regain control where power was once entirely lost. Teleologically, the aim is still survival, even when the strategy is tragic. It is this layered reading —simultaneously motivational, intrapsychic, and relational—that justifies and requires the complexity of Mosquera's approach.

The book revisits and deepens several theoretical nuclei that Mosquera has been developing for years:

- the rigorous distinction between *ego states*, *modes*, and true *dissociative parts*, showing how simple and effective interventions in structural dissociation can become harmful if applied indiscriminately to ego-state work;
- the reframing of *inner voices* as potential expressions of dissociative parts rather than psychotic symptoms, within a firmly trauma-informed framework;
- the centrality of disorganized attachment, divided loyalties, and betrayal trauma in the genesis of protective, persecutory, sexualized, hostile, and self-destructive parts.

Alongside Mosquera, the thought of Giovanni Liotti provides the deep theoretical scaffolding. His research on disorganized attachment, on Interpersonal Motivational Systems and their tragic entanglements in complex trauma, is here fully assumed and elaborated from within not as ornament, but as load-bearing structure. The Liottian idea that trauma-related psychopathology arises from a short-circuit among motivational systems—above all between attachment on one side, rank and defense on the other—is translated by Mosquera into a precise clinical cartography: every kind of part, every internal dynamic, becomes legible as the expression of conflicts and tangles among motivational systems frozen in trauma time.

The true innovation of this volume lies precisely in this unifying approach: the relational dynamics that Liotti had described between persons and motivational systems are brought *inside* the individual. What, in attachment relationships, was experienced as dangerous closeness, ambivalent care, humiliating power, or betrayed cooperation, is re-enacted among dissociative parts. The inner world becomes a relational stage, a theatre in which the motivational choreographies learned in trauma are repeated and, gradually, transformed.

In the face of the contemporary spread of a *pan-dissociative* reading, where every fluctuation, every inner conflict, every mental state is hastily named as a *part*, Mosquera maintains a rare critical lucidity. Just as in *pan-traumatic* readings, where everything becomes trauma, the risk is the loss of clinical precision, and therapeutic harm: mental states that might be understood as psychological reactions, ego states, or modes are reified into fully-fledged *parts*. The naively literal use of metaphorical language —often encouraged by oversimplifying models in the style of Internal Family Systems— ends up obscuring the far more complex and painful reality of dissociative structures in actual dissociative disorders. This book is also a firm warning not to confuse metaphor with ontology, therapeutic language with psychopathological structure.

At the same time, the *Trauma-Informed Relational Approach for Dissociative Parts* (TADP) displays a surprising didactic clarity. It is not a text that simplifies by flattening. On the contrary, it preserves the full theoretical complexity, from the Theory of Structural Dissociation to the Multimotivational framework, from rank dynamics to betrayal loyalties, while making it workable, inhabitable, and thinkable in everyday clinical practice. Mosquera's meticulousness, the care with which she describes the different kinds of parts, their protective functions, their relational risks, their countertransferential traps, prevents every hasty generalization: the reader is guided to see nuances, not to take refuge in labels.

In this sense, the book has a profoundly formative function: it does not train the clinician in a protocol, it educates a *way of seeing*. The therapist learns to distinguish where it is appropriate to speak of ego states, and where, instead, one must recognize the presence of true dissociative parts; when work on modes is sufficient, and when the multimotivational tangle requires radical caution; when mapping parts sheds light and when, by contrast, it risks confusing, suggesting, or over-structuring.

This work also stands as a necessary prologue to Mosquera's previous volume on Voices. Those who learn here to read dissociative parts through the lens of motivational entanglements will find it easier, in the book on Voices, to grasp the continuity between a *part that speaks* and a *voice that imposes itself*. This text prepares the theoretical and clinical ground: it defines the lexicon, sharpens the boundaries, warns against abuses of language, and opens the possibility of a truly respectful dialogue with inner multiplicity.

Ultimately, the importance of this book lies in at least three essential points:

1. It restores theoretical and clinical dignity to dissociation, rescuing it both from diagnostic trivialization and from cultural fashions that dilute its meaning.
2. It integrates in an original way the Theory of Structural Dissociation and Liotti's Multimotivational model, offering a fine-grained grammar for understanding parts as expressions of tangled motivational systems, active on multiple levels at once.
3. It proposes a deeply relational and non-reductionistic therapeutic stance, in which conceptual precision coexists with a quasi-philosophical vision of the traumatized mind: a fractured microcosm that is nonetheless still capable, if listened to with respect, of rediscovering within itself a more fluid and more human order.

This is not a generic book *about trauma*, nor simply a manual on parts, but an invitation to think the traumatized psyche as a complex system of inner relationships, supported by the narrow natural modes offered by Interpersonal Motivational Systems, where every fragment carries within itself the memory of a bond and of an attempt to survive.

Emilio Vercillo
Psychiatrist, Trauma Therapist trained in Liotti's Evolutionary Cognitivism

Table of Contents

PART I:
Establishing the Foundation for Relational Work

Introduction and Framing

This book was born out of hundreds of conversations with clients, with parts, with colleagues, and from the quiet moments in between. It is rooted in the belief that dissociative systems are not broken, but deeply adaptive. They do what they must to survive.

The intention of this book is to offer clinicians a relational map, not a rigid protocol, for engaging with the internal complexity of dissociative systems. While techniques matter, it is the therapeutic stance that shapes the healing: presence over pressure, respect over interpretation, attunement over control.

This work builds on the Trauma-Informed Approach to Dissociative Parts (TADP) described in *Working with Voices and Dissociative Parts*, a trauma-informed lens for understanding inner voices and multiplicity. As the work was applied in clinical settings, an important question repeatedly arose: does this approach apply only to parts that speak? This new book is a response to that question. It expands the frame to support work with all parts, speaking or silent, felt or hidden.

This volume is conceptually and clinically linked to *Working with Voices and Dissociative Parts*, which presents detailed clinical procedures, trauma-processing tools, case conceptualization and treatment planning guidelines, and extensive case material with session transcripts. The Trauma-Informed Relational Approach for Dissociative Parts (TADP) articulated in the present book provides the relational and organizational foundation for that clinical work.

Working with Voices and Dissociative Parts shows how the work unfolds in the therapy room, through five extended clinical cases that explicitly identify interventions and therapeutic steps. This volume clarifies, organizes, and deepens the clinical logic that supports those interventions. TADP builds, dissects, and connects the elements of clinical work so they can be understood, integrated, and applied flexibly across cases. Read together, the two books are complementary: TADP offers the framework that makes clinical practice coherent, while *Working with Voices and Dissociative Parts* demonstrates its application in detail. Together, they guide clinical judgment, pacing, and therapeutic stance.

SCOPE AND LIMITS

This is a book about dissociative parts. Throughout, *parts* refer specifically to dissociative parts that emerge from fragmentation in complex trauma, not to ego states, common conflicted positions, or ordinary intrapsychic dialogue.

The focus is on the multiplicity that accompanies structural dissociation, towards the end of the spectrum. The interventions described are not meant to be applied broadly to every presentation of conflicts, self-harm, suicidality, or aggression. In non-dissociative populations, those issues should be assessed and treated according to standard clinical practice. The strategies offered here are adjunctive, designed for cases where dissociation and fragmentation are central.

This is a guide to think and listen clinically and conceptually: to hear beyond words, to recognize function, and to address the system's multiplicity without reenacting it and especially without making it worse. Some ideas may translate to less complex cases, but only when they clarify rather than confuse; applying a dissociative-parts frame where it does not belong can cause more harm than help.

Part I sets the groundwork: how to distinguish dissociative parts from ego states, and how to navigate contemporary presentations, including *trendy dissociation* and identity confusion or disordered identities (Mosquera, 2024) that can blur the picture. The aim is diagnostic clarity and practical discernment, so interventions fit the phenomenon in front of you. Part II describes the origins and functions of the different types of parts; Part III explores the dynamics between dissociative parts; Part 4 focuses on facilitating integration. Taken together, the book offers tools for the preparation phase of trauma therapy: cultivating safety, stability, and internal cooperation required before direct trauma processing can proceed.

WHAT YOU WILL FIND IN THIS BOOK

This is not a step-by-step manual or rigid treatment protocol. It is a relational map: a guide through the terrain of dissociative inner worlds, grounded in trauma theory, clinical practice, and what I have learned from clients who live this reality every day.

You will find grounding principles, clinical reflections, respectful language, and a trauma-informed frame. Each chapter explores a core theme: establishing safety, understanding protective parts, supporting younger parts, working with shame and grief, and helping systems move toward cooperation.

Rather than pushing for integration or compliance, the center of gravity is curiosity, steadiness, and trust. Healing is not about fixing the system, it is about listening to it, and helping it listen to itself.

A central aspect of this work is maintaining clear, humane boundaries. In dissociative personality systems shaped by relational trauma, over-availability can feel soothing in the moment yet destabilizing over time. Rescue, caretaking, or excessive contact outside the therapeutic frame often strengthens dependency, escalates internal conflict, and reinforces the belief that safety comes from an external regulator rather than from internal cooperation.

In TADP, limits are not a withdrawal of care but a form of containment. Predictable session structures, thoughtful pacing, and clearly held boundaries support parts in learning that connection does not require collapse, urgency, or fusion. Collaboration happens within a stable frame; without it, dependency quietly replaces cooperation.

LANGUAGE CHOICES

In this book, the term *parts* will be used rather than *subpersonalities* or *identities*. While some clients relate to the term *voices*, others do not. The choice is intentional: it allows for a wide spectrum of inner experience, from clearly articulated parts to subtle felt presences, emotions, behaviors, images, or silence, but always with the characteristics of structural dissociation phenomena.

In other contexts, I would write *dissociative parts* to explicitly distinguish from ego-state models; in this book, parts always mean dissociative parts unless otherwise specified. Clinicians are always encouraged to follow the client's own language, rather than imposing a theoretical frame. The goal is attunement, not categorization

The term disorganized attachment will also be used throughout the book. The construct originates in observational research using the Strange Situation paradigm (Main & Solomon, 1990), and its direct application to clinical populations has been debated (Granqvist et al., 2017). In this book, the term refers to relational contexts in which the attachment figure becomes simultaneously a source of comfort and fear, creating what has been described as fright without solution. When referring more broadly to the developmental impact of chronic caregiver-related trauma, the concept of attachment trauma may at times provide a more precise description.

WHO THIS BOOK IS FOR

This book is written for therapists who work with trauma and dissociation, whether in private practice, community settings, or specialty clinics. You need not be a dissociation specialist to find value here, but you do need to prize safety, humility, and relational pacing, and to seek consultation when complexity demands it.

My hope is that this book will help you feel less alone in the work and that it will help your clients feel the same.

Chapter 1: Foundations of the Work with Dissociative Parts

THERAPIST REFLECTION

I notice my urge to understand and fill in gaps, to keep moving forward, but I remind myself that curiosity is the map. I pause and lean into not knowing: What is this hesitation really holding? What is the system trying to communicate here? I ask open questions and listen to every form of communication, not just the words. In these moments, my wonder, rather than any answer, models the stance I'm inviting my client to practice. Each time I stay curious, I open space for parts to be seen, heard, and understood.

When working with individuals who experience dissociation, clinicians are invited into a complex internal world shaped by trauma, resilience, and adaptive survival. Many clients living with dissociative parts have learned to compartmentalize experience to endure overwhelming circumstances. Our role as therapists is to understand how the internal system has organized and reorganized itself to protect the whole.

A central aim of the approach described in this book is to help clients explore and relate to each part with deep respect, openness, and curiosity. This chapter lays the foundation for that orientation, one grounded in trauma-informed care, therapeutic humility, and relational attunement. By prioritizing safety and trust, we foster internal cooperation and, eventually, a form of integration, not necessarily as fusion, but as a respectful, fluid internal dialogue.

Crucially, the way the therapist relates to the client and to the client's parts is not neutral: it actively models a relational template. Through the therapist's stance —marked by consistency, clarity, curiosity, and respect— the client is offered an experiential reference for how parts can relate to one another without coercion, fear, or collapse. In time, these evolving relationships help shift internal dynamics toward healthier, more adaptive functioning in the here and now.

It is important to remember, however, that work with dissociative parts is rarely linear and almost never predictable. A part may emerge clearly one week and seem to vanish for many sessions afterward. Dissociative parts are not continuously present; they become active when triggered or when conditions evoke them and then may retreat again. Information often seeps through the system because defensive walls are never complete separations. This is why some parts remain unnamed, unnoticed, or unacknowledged for long stretches. It is not that they are gone, they are simply not activated.

Parts are not like tenants who permanently live in their own apartments, choosing to come or go. Rather, they function more like facilitated neural circuits, patterns of brain activity that become more easily activated over time, like highways laid down within the neural network. When a trigger lights up that circuit, the part appears with a sense of consistency and autonomy. Yet even though they may seem like completely independent parts, they remain deeply embedded in the broader system, inseparable from the whole.

Although clinicians may feel the urge to check in with quieter parts when they do not come up for a while, this is not the goal. In general, we work with what is active in the moment. The absence of a part is not a problem to solve. We do not need to check in with every part every time. We do not try to evoke or search for parts that are not emerging. Naming or searching for a part when they are not present can create confusion or internal tension. These are internal representations shaped by dynamic internal processes and shifting triggers, not static personalities waiting to speak. What matters is that we hold all parts of the system in our broader awareness.

What follows are some of the essential ingredients for beginning this work; not a step-by-step protocol, but a relational stance and orientation clinicians can return to repeatedly.

A THERAPEUTIC STANCE OF CURIOSITY, RESPECT, AND SAFETY

Effective work with dissociative parts begins with the therapist's stance. When clinicians approach the internal system with curiosity, consistency, and respect, they help create a therapeutic space where parts begin to feel seen and heard rather than judged. This will often lead to calmer moments that allow space for clients to explore and understand. The goal in the initial contact is not to rush toward integration or force insight, but to build the conditions for inner trust, cooperation, and collaboration. Through this approach, therapy becomes a collaborative process where even the most protective or withdrawn parts can begin to safely engage.

At the heart of this work is a commitment to honoring each client's internal experience with compassion and curiosity. The therapeutic stance outlined here is not one of control or correction, but of co-exploration. Clinicians are encouraged to approach dissociative parts with reverence for how they came to be, recognizing that each holds a purpose rooted in protection. Trust, collaboration, and stability become the scaffolding for deeper healing. This orientation helps create a foundation for transformative work, not by forcing change, but by inviting understanding.

Regardless of the client's experience, it is important to keep in mind that dissociative parts are doing what they have learned to do, either through poor relational modelling or through long-term adaptation to internal conflict shaped by threatening, chaotic, or unsafe family and environmental contexts. Even dissociative parts that might seem mean, hostile or driven by evil intentions have good reasons to exist. As we will see through the book, one of the central clinical challenges lies in the client´s experience of other parts, which is often profoundly negative due to fear, mistrust, and the legacy of living in environments where safety, predictability, and protection were unreliable or actively dangerous.

OPTIMAL CONDITIONS FOR INNER COLLABORATION

Rather than targeting individual symptoms or striving for rapid change or integration, this model focuses on helping clients establish a safer, more collaborative relationship with their internal system. Each part is viewed as carrying a valuable role, even when its strategies may appear disruptive. The clinician's task is to nurture safety, attune to shifting internal dynamics, and foster respectful dialogue among parts. Importantly, collaboration does not imply that all parts share the same aims. Rather, cooperation emerges when parts can work alongside one another, each oriented toward its own protective or survival goals, while gradually discovering points of alignment that allow movement toward shared safety and functioning in the present. Over time, this process supports a more integrated and less fragmented experience of self.

1. **Keep structure in mind without being rigid about it.** To begin creating the conditions for inner collaboration, clinicians must remain structurally attuned without becoming rigid. While it is important to hold an internal map of the system's complexity, this structure should guide the therapist's awareness, not be imposed on the client. Especially in early work, avoid the appearance of following a scripted protocol. Clients should feel they are being met as individuals, not analyzed through a lens.

2. **Acknowledge parts in the client's language.** Language plays a central role in this work, and clinicians are encouraged to use the client's own terminology as much as possible when referring to parts. If a client says, "the angry one" or "the little girl", reflect that language respectfully. Avoid asking for names or encouraging the creation of identities where the client has not mentioned them. Clients with dissociative parts are highly sensitive to suggestion, and we must avoid unintentionally shaping the client's inner world. The primary exception to this guideline arises when the language used is pejorative, contemptuous, or frames parts as autonomous persons, supernatural entities, or external agents (for example, angels, demons, or independent beings). In such cases, gentle reframing may be clinically indicated. Rather than correcting the client directly, the therapist can model a different stance or invite curiosity about what has led the part to be spoken about in such an externalized way, for instance, by saying:

    ★ "What you describe as a person (or an angel) I would understand as a part of you."

- ★ "I notice you experience it almost like a separate person; I would understand that as a part of you, but we can keep both perspectives in mind."
- ★ "I'm curious what it's like to think of it as an angel. I would usually think of that experience as a part of you. How does that land for you?"
- ★ "If we imagined this as a part of you rather than an external being, what might change?"

This approach maintains respect for the client's experience while supporting coherence, safety, and a trauma-informed understanding of internal multiplicity.

3. **Invite respect, this is key for building curiosity, safety and trust.** Respect is foundational, not just between therapist and client, but within the client's internal system. Many clients begin therapy profoundly afraid of some of their own parts. They may describe them as dangerous, evil, or out of control. The aim is not to force comfort, but to invite respect as a starting place. One guiding principle is: You do not have to like your parts to begin this work, but you do have to respect them. Every part has developed as a means of protection, no matter how disruptive or distressing its strategies may seem. Helping clients understand this is one of the most powerful early interventions. Start from the assumption that each part has helped the client survive and is still trying to help. Validate that purpose before inviting change. Be open to exploring with the client and parts but set boundaries to communication that can feel unsafe.

4. **See the system, not just the symptom or problematic behavior.** Seeing the system as a whole rather than focusing on isolated symptoms is essential. Instead of zeroing in on specific behaviors like self-harm or avoidance, look systemically trying to see the whole picture. What is this part protecting and why? When does it emerge? What dynamics are unfolding between parts? It is a systemic approach, so paying attention to how they interact and asking these kinds of questions helps shift therapy from symptom management to relational integration.

5. **Support cooperation and collaboration not forced integration**. Importantly, integration is never something we push. The initial goal

is cooperation, not fusion. Language matters here. Instead of suggesting that parts should disappear or merge, we might ask:

★ "Can this part work with you, even a little, today?"

These small, respectful invitations help preserve the system's autonomy and reduce internal threat.

Integration, if it happens, is a gradual and relational process, not a therapeutic requirement. It is an option, not a goal imposed, and when it occurs, it should reflect the system´s readiness and choice. Integration often unfolds when parts are no longer needed in the way they once were. They may take on new forms or soften into the background. For instance, what was once a distinct voice might now be experienced as the person´s own thought or reflection; the part no longer needing to speak separately. It is not a *dissociative part* anymore.

Throughout all of this, the therapist's stance remains one of steady curiosity. It is not the sophistication of our techniques that opens doors, but the reliability of our presence, consistency, calmness, and genuine interest. When parts sense or notice a therapist is grounded, nonjudgmental, and consistently attuned, they are more likely to soften and engage. This trust, once earned, becomes the foundation for deeper healing work.

ENGAGING PARTS WITH RESPECTFUL DIALOGUE

Much of the early work with dissociative systems centers around how we invite parts into relationship, which can be no easy task considering they usually have been involved for years in an internal conflict that entails fights, disdain, rejection, fear, etc. Rather than demanding access, clinicians learn to offer gentle invitations, with an emphasis on consent, safety, and flexibility. These invitations are not meant to provoke immediate disclosure or insight, but to create space. A space where parts begin to sense they can be seen without being overwhelmed, pushed, or judged.

Simple, open-ended language can go a long way:

★ "Would it be okay if we got to know this part a little more?"

- ★ "It makes sense that another part might feel scared about this work."
- ★ "What do you think that part is trying to protect?"
- ★ "You can just describe what it feels like being near this part."
- ★ "If there's hesitation, that's something we respect, not something we push through."

These kinds of statements convey empathy, curiosity, and a willingness to go at the client's pace. Over time, this helps establish a shared culture of inner consent: one where each part knows it will not be coerced into speaking or changing.

BUILDING TRUST, NOT CONTROL

Instead of focusing on fixing or organizing the internal system, early work is about listening consistently and without judgment. Every part carries a story, even if it cannot yet be spoken. We begin by listening for tone, emotion, presence, and triggers, not just words.

We shift from a symptom lens to a relational one. Rather than seeing a panic attack, we help the client notice. What got triggered? Which part was activated? What is being protected, and from what? We begin to think in terms of both responses and relationships. This helps reframe the work away from pathology and toward meaning.

Above all, it is important to resist the urge to fix. Many clients understandably arrive with a desire to solve or get rid of what feels overwhelming. In this sense the clinician can validate their desire and motivation for change while gently guiding the client toward pacing, helping them understand that true change comes not from urgency, but from learning to adapt to and include all parts. What distrustful and protective parts often need most is a steady presence: someone predictable, who does not push for insight, and who is not afraid of their intensity. This steadiness becomes the anchor for trust and exploration.

Metaphors can also support the work. Describing the system as a team, committee, or network offers language that feels less clinical and more human. These can be personalized to fit the client: a soccer team, an orchestra or any group dynamic that requires collaboration and respect and does not feel triggering for the client. When chosen appropriately, such metaphors reinforce the idea that every part matters, even if they disagree or do not yet feel safe with one another.

Consistency, reliability, and predictability in the structure of the session, in the tone, and in the therapeutic boundaries are the ingredients that build trust. Without these, parts often remain guarded, retreat entirely or interfere in therapy, trying to interrupt this process through different symptoms and complications. For example, in some of the more complicated cases, parts may try for the client not to come back to therapy, and if the client wants to come to session, they may go to the extreme of self-harming as punishment.

COMMON CLINICAL PITFALLS

Despite good intentions, therapists may inadvertently misstep in ways that destabilize the system or reinforce internal fear. One of the most common errors in early work is **over-labeling parts or trying to get information too soon**. While the clinician may feel eager to map out the system, assigning roles (protector, persecutor, inner child) or pressing for names has the potential of feeling invasive and overly simplistic. The system may perceive this as an attempt of control, not real curiosity in understanding. For clients with developed dissociative parts this can be very scary too. It is important to note that, since the pandemic, some clients have started coming to treatment and presenting with distinct parts, each with its own name, role, and characteristics, all carefully mapped out. However, this differs from what we usually see in clients with genuine dissociative structures. We will delve into this further in chapter 4.

Another frequent misstep is **interpreting or judging parts**—even subtly. Referring to parts as *manipulative*, *resistant*, or *bad* reinforces the very shame and rejection many clients already carry internally. While it is central to this approach to recognize that parts exist for a reason, naming a part's protective function too quickly or too definitively can itself become a form of interpretation. For this reason, protective intent is best approached as a *shared inquiry* rather than a label: something to be wondered about, explored, and gradually discovered, rather than assigned from the outside.

It is also essential to avoid **siding with one part against another,** even when a client appears to do so themselves. For example, if an adult part expresses disdain for a younger or reactive part, the therapist should remain neutral and invite both perspectives without taking sides. Our role is to mediate understanding, not try to solve problems quickly.

Therapists must also avoid **rushing into trauma** memory exploration or work before sufficient stabilization has occurred. Clients need internal cooperation and collaboration before accessing traumatic memories. Premature deep dives into trauma content can retraumatize, leaving the system overwhelmed, reinforcing avoidance and fragmentation.

Finally, it is equally important to let go of the expectation that clients will have easy or **immediate access to a cohesive or grounded capacity for reflective functioning and self-regulation,** often referred to as the Adult Self (Gonzalez & Mosquera, 2012), competent self or internal leader. In many internal systems, this capacity is not yet available or has never been allowed to emerge. Rather than forcing access, we support its development through relationship, attunement, and time.

CLOSING THOUGHTS

Beginning this work is not about doing more, it is about doing less. When we approach with curiosity and humility, the pressure to fix gives way to the space for understanding. At this stage, what matters most is not insight or cohesion, but safety, steadiness, and trust, the foundation for everything that follows.

This work requires us to adapt our expectations, slow our pace, and lean into the relational field with openness. It is not a step-by-step formula. It is a beginning, not a blueprint. A respectful dialogue that, over time, can lead to insights and eventually become transformative.

Clinical Anchors

What to remember...

- Our role as therapists is to understand how the internal system has organized and reorganized itself to protect the whole. Every part has a story and a reason for existing, so begin by listening.
- Parts are internal representations shaped by dynamic internal processes and shifting triggers, not static personalities waiting to speak.
- The goal in the initial contact is not to rush toward integration or force insight, but to build the conditions for inner trust and cooperation by honoring each client's internal experience with compassion and curiosity.
- Clients do not have to like parts to begin this work, but do have to respect them. Every part has developed as a means of protection, no matter how disruptive or distressing its strategies may seem.
- See the system, not just the symptom or problematic behavior. We shift from a symptom lens to a relational one.
- It is not the sophistication of our techniques that opens doors, but the reliability of our presence, consistency, calmness, and genuine interest.
- At this stage, what matters most is safety, steadiness, and trust, the foundation for everything that follows.

What to avoid...

- Over-labeling or over-structuring and trying to obtain information too soon in the process.
- Interpreting, judging or pathologizing parts; referring to them as *bad*, *crazy*, *resistant* or *manipulative*.
- Siding with one part against another within the internal system.
- Rushing into trauma memory work too soon, before there is sufficient stabilization.
- Expecting immediate access to a cohesive or grounded sense of adult-self leadership.

Chapter 2: Understanding Internal Multiplicity. From Ego States to Dissociative Parts.

THERAPIST REFLECTION

When I first began exploring internal multiplicity with clients, I found myself getting entangled in definitions, trying to figure out if a shift in tone was an ego state, a mode, or a dissociative part. Early in a client's journey, it's far more important to understand process than content; much more important than to pin down a theoretical term.

Concepts and definitions can be extremely useful, but they can also become barriers rather than bridges. In the broader field of psychotherapy, we encounter multiple frameworks for speaking about the many facets of Self. While each has interesting and useful information, they encompass differences and mixing them up can lead to detrimental interventions.

In this chapter, we will attempt to untangle the differences in the most common descriptions of parts, ranging from ego states, aspects of self or different ways of being me, to schema modes, and dissociative parts. One of the goals is to explain key differences in the applicability of interventions so you can understand why some very useful and simple interventions with ego states phenomena can backfire when applied to dissociative parts. We will also explore when part-work can be helpful or recommended and when it can distract, confuse and even overwhelm.

PSYCHOTHERAPEUTIC MODELS INVOLVING PARTS

Several contemporary psychotherapeutic approaches explicitly work with the idea that the mind is composed of parts, subpersonalities, or internal voices. While their underlying theories and clinical goals differ, each model acknowledges the multiplicity inherent in human experience, and the therapeutic potential in engaging with that multiplicity directly.

1. **Ego State Therapy.** Developed by John and Helen Watkins (Watkins & Watkins, 1997), Ego State Therapy is a psychodynamic and hypnosis-informed approach that conceptualizes the mind as made up of ego states, distinct aspects of personality present in all people. These states may reflect roles, moods, or developmental stages, and while typically integrated, they can become increasingly divided in cases of trauma or dissociation. Drawing on family systems and group therapy principles, this model aims to improve communication and cooperation between ego states, particularly when they are in conflict or operating in isolation.

2. **Internal Family Systems (IFS).** IFS, developed by Richard Schwartz in the 1980s is an integrative model that views the psyche as an internal family of parts, each with its own emotions, beliefs, and goals (Schwartz, 1995; Schwartz & Sweezy, 2019). Parts fall into three main categories: Managers (responsible for control and prevention), Firefighters (reactive and impulsive protectors), and Exiles (holders of pain, shame, and trauma). A central tenet of IFS is that all parts have a positive intent, even when their strategies are harmful. The model centers around the emergence of the Self, a calm, compassionate internal leader, capable of healing and harmonizing the system without exiling or suppressing any part.

3. **Schema Therapy.** Developed in the 1990s by Jeffrey Young for working with personality disorders, Schema Therapy blends cognitive-behavioral techniques with psychodynamic and experiential interventions (Young et al., 2003). It identifies enduring cognitive-emotional patterns (schemas) and organizes client experiences into *modes*, temporary states reflecting coping strategies, unmet needs, or emotional vulnerability (Arntz & Jacob, 2013). Examples include the Vulnerable Child, the Punitive Parent, and the Detached Protector. While modes are not dissociative parts, they offer a structured way to explore how early experiences shape current functioning and provide accessible language for clients to link past pain with present patterns.

4. **Theory of Structural Dissociation of the Personality.** Introduced by Van der Hart, Nijenhuis, and Steele in the early 2000s, this theory

proposes that dissociation is not merely a symptom, but a structural response to overwhelming trauma (Van der Hart et al., 2006). It distinguishes between *Apparently Normal Parts* (ANPs), which handle daily functioning and avoid trauma, and *Emotional Parts* (EPs), which remain fixated in defensive states and relive traumatic experiences. These parts are often amnesic to one another and operate from different action systems (e.g., attachment vs. defense). Subsequent work has further refined and clinically elaborated this model, particularly regarding assessment, phase-oriented treatment, and the differentiation of dissociative phenomena (Steele, Boon, & Van der Hart, 2017). Together, these contributions provide a trauma-informed framework for understanding voice hearing, inner conflict, and identity fragmentation, emphasizing the need for careful, phased treatment in complex dissociative cases.

5. **Trauma-Informed Relational Approach for Dissociative Parts (TADP):** Drawing on the Theory of Structural Dissociation, systemic family perspectives and trauma-informed interventions, Dolores Mosquera (2019) has expanded our understanding of voice hearing by framing many voices not as psychotic symptoms, but as dissociative parts that speak, particularly in clients with complex trauma and dissociative disorders (Mosquera, Moskowitz, & Longden, 2017, Mosquera, D. 2019). This approach identifies the origins and protective functions of various speaking parts (e.g., hostile, fearful, suicidal, critical), emphasizing that even the most aggressive or disturbing voices often serve adaptive roles within the system. By fostering respectful, non-pathologizing dialogue with these voices, this model helps clients reframe internal conflict as meaningful communication between dissociative parts. This trauma-informed perspective is especially valuable for bridging interventions across psychosis and dissociation-informed models, supporting differential diagnosis, and promoting integration through relational rather than suppressive strategies.

MAPPING THE MODELS OF MULTIPLICITY

When we first invite a client into the landscape of their inner experience, we often speak of *parts* as if they were interchangeable metaphors; different ways of describing shifting emotions, perspectives, or roles. Yet in complex trauma work, it is crucial to be precise about what we mean by *parts* and when the language of parts facilitates integration or risks confusion.

As seen in the previous section, our field has offered multiple models to describe *subpersonalities*. Each model carries its own conceptual map and vocabulary for the conflicted perceptions (selves) that clients notice inside. Some people speak of ego states, brief self-states like Bossy Me or Nurturing Me, which flow in and out without significant barriers. Others describe modes, as in Schema Therapy, where patterns of feeling, thought, and behavior cluster into roles such as the Vulnerable Child or the Detached Protector. In Internal Family Systems, parts are grouped into Managers, Firefighters, and Exiles. Still others simply talk about aspects or sides of me, language that is loose enough to embrace any inner quality.

However, dissociative parts differ in degree and kind. They are not mere states or moods but represent distinct self-representations with their own autobiographical memories or fragments of memories, their own first-person perspective, and often amnesic barriers between them (Van der Hart et al., 2006). One part may guard a memory of terror so that the rest of the system can function; another may freeze the body in moments of unbearable overwhelm. Unlike an ego state, which a client readily accepts as "me in a particular mood", a dissociative part may feel foreign. "It wasn't me who shouted; it was her." This separation signals fragmentation and therefore the need for careful, trauma-informed relational work rather than using casual metaphors.

In this context, it becomes essential to distinguish dissociative voices from psychotic hallucinations (Van der Hart et al., 2006; Mosquera, Moskowitz, & Longden, 2017), as both can manifest as multiple voices but arise from very different mechanisms. In schizophrenia and related psychotic disorders, voices are generally auditory-sensory hallucinations perceived as coming from outside the self (phrased as "They told me to do it") and are embedded in a broader psychotic syndrome characterized by cognitive disorganization, delusional logic, and impaired insight. In contrast, in dissociative disorders, voices are experienced as emerging from within the internal system. They belong to dissociative parts with recognizable identities, histories, and relational dynamics. Clients often retain intact reality testing even when an internal voice expresses hostility toward another part.

Research by Martin Dorahy and colleagues (Dorahy et al., 2009) underscores these distinctions. Individuals with dissociative disorders tend to report a greater number of voices, an earlier onset of voice-hearing, and the presence of child voices, rarely seen in schizophrenia. While imperative voices (those issuing commands) can occur in both conditions, in psychotic disorders they are typically accompanied by broader disturbances in perception and thought. Dissociative presentations, by contrast, show structured internal organization and preserved reflective awareness.

It is important to acknowledge that reality testing is not a perfect differentiator (Moskowitz, 2008), since some individuals with psychosis maintain coherent dialogue and appear lucid. Nevertheless, in dissociative phenomena, the relational quality of the voices, the coherent internal logic, and the awareness of multiplicity are key markers of distinction (Van der Hart et al., 2006; Steele, Boon, & Van der Hart, 2017; Mosquera, Moskowitz, & Longden, 2017). The focus here, when using the term *psychosis*, is primarily on schizophrenia. Other psychotic presentations (such as organic psychoses, paranoid delusional disorders, or bipolar psychoses) tend to involve hallucinations less prominently, and imperative commands are rarer still. Drug-induced psychoses may produce similar experiences, but these usually occur within states of cognitive compromise.

Ultimately, the distinction lies not merely in where the voices seem to originate—inside or outside—but in the *structure and meaning* of the experience. Dissociative voices are very often parts that speak, expressions with their own protective roles and intentions (Van der Hart et al., 2006; Steele, Boon, & Van der Hart, 2017; Mosquera, 2019). Recognizing this allows clinicians to engage with them relationally, not as symptoms to be silenced, but as communications within a fragmented system seeking coherence.

HOW DISSOCIATIVE PARTS COME TO BE

Dissociative parts arise from an unsolvable dilemma in disorganized attachment. The child must both seek attachment and defend against threats with the same caregiver. These actions involve different physiologies, emotions, thoughts, behaviors and goals that are fundamentally incompatible. A different sense of self evolves from each of these two different tendencies, resulting in parts that hold relational strategies and parts that hold defensive strategies (Steele et al., 2005; Van der Hart et al., 2006).

These opposing tendencies correspond to distinct biological action or motivational systems, such as attachment and defense, which are designed to function independently. In safe environments, they operate flexibly and sequentially. But under chronic threat, especially in disorganized attachment, these systems become rigid, distorted, or simultaneously activated, leading to internal fragmentation (Van der Hart et al., 2006). Viewed through Giovanni Liotti's (2004, 2017) multimotivational lens (see chapter 3), the contradictions are not limited to attachment and defense: caregiving, rank/competition, cooperation, sexual bonding, and exploration/play can also be pulled in opposing directions. When that happens, experience is segregated into parts organized around different aims and feeling states. Chapter 3 maps these systems in detail and shows how they illuminate why parts develop, how they behave, and what they need in therapy.

Some models describe searching for the core self as if it had been hidden due to trauma. However, we must consider whether this is applicable to more severe cases. Children are not born with a sense of a unified identity; it develops gradually through coherent experiences and caregiving, from many sources and experiences. In cases of early trauma or severe neglect, that integration never fully occurs. The mind instead develops through compartmentalization, creating separate islands of experience to preserve survival functioning. In these cases, there is no unified core to recover, only the possibility of gradually building integration where it was never safely allowed to form. In such cases, integration must be gradually built rather than recovered (Van der Hart et al., 2006; Bromberg, 1998).

WHAT ARE EGO STATES?

Ego States are transient self-states such as Angry Me or Nurturing Me, that flow in and out of consciousness and are experienced as recognizably *me*. There are no amnesic barriers between them, and they ordinarily function in the background of our awareness. People experiencing ego states usually do not express a sense of disownership; they may indicate not liking how they respond but they do not even think for a moment "That is not me". There is no investment in separateness and hardly ever an intense phobia towards inner experience or those states.

These states are best understood as different perspectives that coexist within a cohesive self, with permeable boundaries, shared autobiographical memory, and a sense of belonging to the whole self (Bromberg, 1998). They are not indicative of fragmentation but of natural inner multiplicity.

CLINICAL VIGNETTE

The Angry Me

During a session, Maria described snapping at her partner: "It got really bad this weekend, I lost it, I went crazy! What the hell?"

The therapist asked if she could describe what was happening inside when this occurred, and Maria replied: "When I saw him look at some girls that were on the beach, I got scared, I felt he was going to leave me like everyone does. That made me so angry, I just couldn't control it."

After understanding the trigger, the therapist invited Maria to stay with the feeling: "Tell me what 'angry you' wants me to know." As they spoke, Maria recognized that her anger served as a boundary-setter when she felt overwhelmed.

Clinical Reflections

This would be an example of a reaction, a side of me; an ego-state. This angry me experience flowed in and out, keeping the *Me* at all times despite not liking the reaction. *Not Me* experience is absent; there is no phobia or disowning the action. She was surprised but could link it to her early experiences of abandonment, a trauma trigger.

Conceptualizing this as a part and working with it as a part would probably confuse Maria and if her identity was not very clear, she might start reading about parts and identifying all her feelings, thoughts and reactions with parts.

Terminology like *aspects* or *sides of me* can be used as softer, client-friendly alternatives to *ego states.* These terms avoid clinical jargon while still communicating inner complexity without implying separateness. This language can also be a point of entry for clients who may have dissociative parts but are not yet ready to describe them in those terms. Metaphoric language is not really needed but can be used without backfiring. If what we say does not fit, the person might just say, "Not really."

In some Complex PTSD and OSDD cases, ego states may show less permeable boundaries, some amnesia especially for past events) and a greater sense of *Not Me* (Steele et al., 2017, Van der Hart et al., 2006). These may be better understood as **cases with overlapping features between ego states and dissociative parts**—more elaborated than typical ego states but not necessarily requiring the same therapeutic approach as more distinct dissociative parts (Watkins & Watkins, 1997; Mosquera, 2019). Some common statements that may help us differentiate this overlap:

- "I know these parts are me, but they don't feel like me."
- "I know these are my voices, I know that I am producing them, but they don't feel like mine."
- "When I react like that it feels as if I was acting like someone else/like my mother."

Notice how these statements reflect a first-person perspective and greater conflict around some of the emotions that may be more difficult for the client to regulate, tolerate or accept. As mentioned before, in these cases, it can be more challenging to distinguish ego states from dissociative parts. However, if we listen carefully to the previous statements we will not pick up on the phobic avoidance that is often present in more elaborate dissociative parts that have increased autonomy (Steele et al., 2005; Van der Hart et al., 2006).

WHAT ARE SCHEMA MODES?

Modes are integrated states of functioning. A mode refers to the way a person presents at a particular moment, encompassing a specific constellation of thoughts, motives, emotions, bodily sensations, and behaviors (Young et al., 2003). Shifts between modes can be illustrated by differences in how someone responds across contexts and relationships. Depending on whether a mode is maladaptive or healthy, it may block or facilitate the meeting of core emotional needs.

The Schema Therapy model helps explain the rapid shifts in emotion and mood commonly observed in individuals with early trauma histories or chronic mental health difficulties who present with markedly different ways of responding. In the therapy room, this may be seen when a client moves quickly from emotional overwhelm to a numb, cut-off state (Young et al., 2003; Arntz & Jacob, 2013; Farrell et al., 2014).

Schema modes, as described in Schema Therapy (Young et al., 2003; Arntz & Jacob, 2013) are organized coping patterns that include thoughts, feelings, and behaviors shaped around particular roles, such as the Vulnerable Child or the Detached Protector. These modes are typically grouped into broad categories including child modes, coping modes or critical modes, and healthy modes. While they resemble ego states in that they are not structurally separate or fragmented, the model places greater emphasis on the function each pattern serves in regulating emotion and behavior.

Clients may experience confusion about their reactions, often expressed as "I don't understand why I responded like that", yet generally they still maintain a continuous sense of self. The *Me* experience remains a connecting thread even when responses feel automatic, contradictory, or difficult to make sense of.

Metaphoric language can be useful and relieving for clients when discussing schema modes, as it helps explain entrenched patterns without implying internal fragmentation. Although these modes include learned defenses and distortions, they remain functionally integrated within the person's identity. There is no Dissociative Disorder implied or required for this conceptualization.

Modes, like schemas, primarily develop in childhood, emerging through repeated experiences in which a child's core emotional needs are unmet and coping strategies are required for emotional survival. Modes can be understood as the state-based activation of schemas combined with specific coping responses (Young et al., 2003; Arntz & Jacob, 2013). Rather than targeting each schema separately, the mode model organizes these activations into patterns of functioning that emerge in real time. This allows therapy to focus on what is happening now—which mode is present, what function it serves, and how it interferes with or supports the meeting of needs.

Schemas are broad, enduring patterns of belief, emotion, memory, and bodily expectation about the self and relationships, rather than discrete internal parts or states. In Schema Therapy, maladaptive schemas are understood as themes that organize experience across situations, such as expectations of abandonment, defectiveness, mistrust, or emotional deprivation (Young et al., 2003).

CLINICAL VIGNETTE

It is Easier Not to Care

Amir, 29, enters the session with a flat tone and minimal eye contact. The therapist gently comments on the shift from their last session, where Amir had been expressive and connected. Amir shrugs: "I don't know. I just feel like nothing matters this week. I stopped caring." When asked what triggered this, Amir recalls a moment at work where his boss criticized his project. "I messed it up. Of course I did", he says, his voice dull.

The therapist recognizes the activation of a **mode** (Detached Protector mode), a learned coping style Amir developed to numb pain and avoid further humiliation. Instead of exploring emotions directly, the therapist reflects, "It sounds like a part of you shut down to protect you from feeling like a failure." Amir nods. "It's easier not to care than to feel stupid."

Together, they explore how this mode helps him avoid shame, but also how it leaves him disconnected and alone. The therapist introduces the idea of the Vulnerable Child Mode, the part of Amir that holds early feelings of inadequacy and abandonment. As they build trust, Amir slowly starts to recognize how the Detached Protector helped him survive school and family expectations, but also how it gets in the way of his current goals. Over time, therapy focuses on helping Amir step out of rigid protector roles and begin caring for that vulnerable part rather than abandoning it.

Clinical Reflections

In this example we can conceptualize what happens as Modes. There is no *Not Me* experience: Amir is aware of what happened, does not disown it. No amnesia or fragmentation. Schema modes are conceptualized as patterns, not personalities. Mode language helps normalize defenses while opening space for deeper healing.

Unlike dissociative parts or ego states, schemas do not represent separate aspects of self, but rather enduring interpretative lenses through which experience is filtered. When activated, schemas shape perception, meaning-making, and emotional response, often outside of conscious awareness, and influence which schema modes come online in a given moment. and how a person responds, often outside of conscious awareness. Schema modes organize patterns of responding to oneself, others and the world; however, they are not experienced as separate or autonomous aspects of the personality. Rather than constituting distinct parts of self, they function as subsystems of organization within the personality, reflecting activated schema-driven states rather than dissociative structures (Moskowitz & Van der Hart, 2020).

WHAT ARE DISSOCIATIVE PARTS?

Dissociative parts as described in the Structural Dissociation Theory involve actual structural fragmentation of the personality. These parts hold autonomous first-person perspectives, that is, a sense of "I, me, and mine", unique self-representations, and distinct autobiographical memories (Nijenhuis & Van der Hart, 2011; Van der Hart et al., 2006). They are often separated by amnesic barriers and may remain hidden from the person's primary identity.

When individuals are aware of these dissociative parts or of their actions, they are frequently experienced as *Not Me*, often accompanied by deep internal conflict, fear, or outright phobia toward inner experience or the parts themselves (Van der Hart et al., 2006; Steele et al., 2005). In other cases, particularly where amnesia is prominent, the person may have little or no awareness of the parts' existence at all. Clients may say,

- "I did not try to kill myself; this has been an attempt of murder." (By a part.)
- "I cannot leave my house; I am afraid of what the monster inside of me can do; I can't control when it shows up or what it does."
- "What do I do if this man shows up again and does not allow me to move?" (Referring to a part inside that the client confuses with the real perpetrator.)

These statements reflect not just discomfort, but a sense of alienation and danger associated with the part. Some clients want to eliminate these parts, showing the intensity of the disconnection. Such reactions are understood within trauma treatment as expressions of phobic avoidance of dissociative parts, a central clinical feature in more structurally dissociated systems (Steele et al., 2017). Dissociative parts can even mimic perpetrators or carry out roles like freezing or attacking from within, often to protect the system or suppress overwhelming emotions or memories.

Clients often describe internal conflict that goes beyond disliking behavior—it is a denial of ownership. There may be phobic avoidance of certain parts while others are more accepted, yet the system remains fragmented and in need of trauma-informed therapeutic work.

CLINICAL VIGNETTE

The Locked Door

During an early EMDR preparation exercise, James, 35, describes a sudden image of a locked door leading to his childhood home. As he leans in to explore, his breath catches: "I can't go there, something bad will happen." The therapist shifted to grounding, "Can you try to look at me?" James looked up. The therapist said, "You are here with me, you are not there."

As they both tried to understand what happened, James said: "A dark figure came up, like a warning. I couldn't move; he didn't want me to get close to any of that." The therapist validated this part's help, and James felt a mix of fear and relief: "I understand what you mean, but you know, this is not the first time I notice this dark figure, and when he shows up, I get really scared."

Once they understood what happened better, the therapist said: "It's good to know this figure is there. It seems he is protecting, but we can help him protect you in ways that are not so scary for you. How does that sound?"

James said: "That would be good."

The therapist asked: "What do you notice when I suggest this idea?"

James said: "He says he is not trying to scare me, that what is behind the door is much scarier."

The therapist concluded: "Let's thank him for letting us know and let him know it's very good to have him protect whatever might be there. He can be the guardian of the door and let us know when it's okay to get close to it."

Clinical Reflections

This is clearly a dissociative part. As James became the guardian of the door, things got calmer inside, especially since he was not trying to yank it open anymore. Both James' Adult Self and the dark figure understood there was room for cooperation. Over subsequent weeks, James learned to approach the door with curiosity, but trusting the dark figure's timing, "I know he will let us know when it's okay to explore that," laying the foundation for eventual reprocessing of the trauma behind it.

CLINICAL IMPLICATION FOR INTERVENTIONS

The distinctions outlined in this chapter directly determine therapeutic stance. When working with ego states or schema modes—where personality remains organized within a single sense of self and experiences are recognized as *Me*—experiential techniques, metaphors, and direct dialogue can enhance awareness and regulation. Identity in these clients may be conflictual, developmentally uneven, or lacking integration; however, experience remains experientially owned. Because there is no structural division of personality, the interventions are less likely to destabilize or interfere in the work that is needed. They can deepen reflective functioning without disrupting identity or adding confusion.

In contrast, dissociative parts involve structural division of the personality, phobic avoidance of internal experience, and sometimes amnesia or discontinuities in agency. Here, interventions that assume unity, such as rapid exposure, casual part-mapping, or premature dialogue, may intensify fear, amplify internal phobia or increase confusion. A trauma-informed relational approach is therefore essential in these cases. Pacing applies not only to trauma processing but also to history taking and treatment planning. Validation of protective functions, and the gradual development of cooperation must precede trauma work and even exploring some information about parts of the system.

Part-work is helpful when it increases reflective awareness and fosters internal collaboration. It becomes confusing or overwhelming when introduced unnecessarily, for example, with disordered identity clients who do not have dissociative parts but are searching for explanations for a still-forming or unstable sense of self, or with dissociative clients when sufficient safety, diagnostic clarity and structural assessment have not yet been established.

When applied to clients whose personality organization remains singular (even when potentially conflicted or unstable), overly literal or premature parts language may inadvertently increase internal polarization or reduce ownership of affect. Ordinary fluctuations in mood, role, or perspective do not in themselves indicate structural division of personality and do not require structural mapping or parts work. Precision in language prevents the unnecessary reification of transient states into fixed internal entities.

In summary, when dissociative parts are present, the clinical risk lies in destabilization through assuming unity where structural division exists. With non-dissociative structures, where personality remains singular but conflictual, the risk lies in artificially addressing regular everyday conflicts as something to be understood separately, where ambivalence is the core issue. Careful assessment and a process-oriented approach will be much more useful in all the types of presentations to discern what is really there and what type of work is needed.

CLOSING THOUGHTS

Dissociative parts are not separate personalities or independent people, but adaptive representations of a single individual, formed in response to overwhelming or contradictory experiences that were unescapable. They reflect the mind's attempt to preserve functioning and survival when integration was not developmentally possible due to conditions of threat. They should not be treated as separate individuals, but as expressions of the client´s internal survival strategies.

Working with parts is therefore not an optional add-on in therapy. It is often the core of trauma-informed care when fragmentation runs deep.

Throughout this chapter, we have explored the differences between ego states, schema modes, and dissociative parts, not only conceptually but also in how they manifest in therapy sessions. These distinctions are not merely theoretical. Clear and shared definitions shape therapeutic stance, pacing, and clinical judgment.

Precision protects the client. When we accurately understand the structure of multiplicity present—whether conflict within a singular personality structure or division of the personality—our interventions become better calibrated, and the work can move toward integration rather than increasing confusion or division.

Clinical Anchors

What to remember...

- Early in a client's journey, it is far more important to understand process (how) than content (what), particularly the ongoing interactions between parts and the patterns through which the internal system organizes itself.
- Some very useful and simple interventions with ego states phenomena can backfire when applied to dissociative parts.
- In cases of early trauma or severe neglect, the integration of a unified sense of identity never fully occurs. The mind instead develops through compartmentalization, creating separate islands of experience to preserve functioning.
- Ego states, modes and dissociative parts differ significantly in structure, function and treatment needs. Ego states are transient self-states that flow in and out of consciousness and are experienced as recognizably *Me*, without amnesia or disownership. While modes resemble ego states in that they are not structurally separate or fragmented, they place more emphasis on the function each pattern serves in behavior regulation. Unlike ego states, dissociative parts are often experienced as *Not Me*, involve fragmentation and phobic avoidance toward inner experience or the parts themselves.
- Dissociative parts are often experienced with a stronger sense of *Not Me* experience if there is no amnesia.

What to avoid...

- Concepts and definitions can be extremely useful, but they can also become barriers rather than bridges.
- Using different languages for parts as if they were synonymous. The presence of fragmented dissociative parts signals the need for careful, trauma-informed work rather than using casual metaphors.
- Introducing parts language or mapping too early, especially when the client is frightened or highly suggestible.
- Seeing parts as separate people or independent personalities.

Chapter 3: Why Parts Do What They Do: Action Systems and Motivational Conflicts

THERAPIST REFLECTION

When I first started working with dissociative clients, I tended to focus more on content than process; focused on the behaviors, trying to reduce self-harm, manage shutdowns, or calm hostile parts. I often found myself stuck, unable to reach what was really happening underneath. It wasn't until I began to recognize the action systems driving each part, the fight that masked fear, the seduction that disguised care-seeking, the compliance that served survival, that I understood how deeply biological these roles were. Each part wasn't just "acting out". It was following the internal code of an action system still stuck in trauma time. My stance shifted: I stopped trying to fix behaviors and started trying to understand what each part was trying to solve.

Internal multiplicity can take many forms: ego states, schema modes, dissociative parts (Watkins & Watkins, 1997; Young et al., 2003; Schwartz & Sweezy, 2019, Van der Hart et al., 2006; Moskowitz & Van der Hart, 2020). But to truly understand why dissociative parts emerge, behave the way they do, and often come into conflict with each other, we need to look beneath the surface, into what drives them. To understand why parts do what they do, we must look at action systems and motivational systems working—often colliding—under trauma

The Trauma-Informed Relational Approach for Dissociative Parts (TADP), building on Mosquera (2019), integrates action systems from the Theory of Structural Dissociation of the Personality (Van der Hart et al., 2006; Steele et al., 2017) with Liotti's Interpersonal Motivational Systems (Liotti, 2010, 2014, 2017). Both models describe biologically rooted systems that organize behavior and experience, and both include motivational domains such as attachment, caregiving, cooperation, and sexuality.

In TADP, these frameworks are used in complementary but non-equivalent ways. The Theory of Structural Dissociation provides an organizing map, clarifying how traumatic experiences lead to a fundamental division between action systems dedicated to daily living and those organized around defense and attachment alarm. This division underlies the emergence of dissociative parts, organized around action tendencies and defensive or attachment-related states, often separated by amnesic barriers. Liotti's multimotivational model, by contrast, is used to illuminate why particular patterns of conflict, entanglement, and relational contradiction arise, especially in contexts of disorganized attachment, where multiple motivational systems are activated simultaneously in incompatible ways.

From this perspective, action systems can be understood as state-dependent patterns of activation that express broader motivational systems. At a fundamental level, these action systems are organized around two broad domains: those dedicated to daily life and those organized around defense and survival, a distinction already present in primary structural dissociation. Under conditions of attachment alarm or relational danger, action systems prioritize defensive and survival-oriented organization. Under conditions of sufficient safety, action systems support exploration, play, caregiving, cooperation and collaboration, rest, energy regulation and the practical demands of functioning in the world including, when not compromised by abuse, sexuality. In TADP, defense is described both as a core action system (TSDP) and as a (basic or evolutionary older) motivational organizer that can override interpersonal systems when threat cues dominate.

Liotti's model adds a crucial relational and developmental lens, making visible how these systems become tragically entangled and how such entanglements are later replayed both in relationships and among dissociative parts.

Together, these often conflicting relational perspectives show that dissociative parts are neither random nor willful, but organized adaptations to complex relational demands; sometimes reflecting broader motivational entanglements across the personality system, and other times appearing as child parts that are developmentally frozen and organized around specific action systems (e.g., fear or attachment), rather than the broader identity-based organization seen in more complex protector roles.

This integrated understanding lays the groundwork for the approach developed throughout this book: one that views dissociative parts not as problems to be solved, but as meaningful configurations to be understood, included, and engaged within a trauma-informed and relational framework.

STRUCTURAL DISSOCIATION AND ACTION SYSTEMS

Human beings, like all mammals, are born with built-in action systems, organized patterns of behavior that support survival in a broad biological sense, maintaining life, development, and reproduction across changing conditions (Van der Hart et al., 2006). These include attachment (seeking closeness), defense (fighting, fleeing, freezing), exploration (learning, curiosity), hierarchy and rank establishment, caregiving, and sexual bonding. These systems are phylogenetically ancient, meaning they are deeply embedded in our evolutionary inheritance. In this book, survival is used in two related but distinct ways. At times, it refers to this broad evolutionary function shared by all motivational systems. At other times, it refers more narrowly to situations of acute threat, where defensive systems dominate in response to danger to life or bodily integrity. Where relevant, this distinction will be made explicit.

In healthy development, these systems operate flexibly. A child who feels safe will explore; a child who feels in danger or alone, will seek protection or defend himself. Most of these systems activate when needed and deactivate when the goal is met. However, in cases of chronic trauma, with disorganized attachment, specific action systems can become rigid, distorted, or chronically activated. When this happens, the mind often forms dissociative parts to manage internal contradictions that cannot be resolved within a unified sense of self.

The Theory of Structural Dissociation of the Personality (TSDP; Van der Hart, Nijenhuis, & Steele, 2006) proposes that dissociative parts emerge when incompatible action systems such as the need for attachment and the need for defense, are simultaneously activated and cannot be integrated. In such cases, structural dissociation becomes a survival adaptation, allowing the mind to manage conflicts that would otherwise be unlivable.

TSDP describes five primary action systems, each linked to specific survival needs and corresponding dissociative adaptations:

1. **Attachment System:** Promotes proximity to caregivers and safety through closeness. Some examples are crying, clinging, protest at separation, and reunion behaviors. When this system becomes distorted, it may coactivate with fear or shame, leading to parts that pursue unsafe connection or fear intimacy.

2. **Defense System:** Protects the organism from threat or harm. There are four major subtypes, present in most living beings:

    - Fight – Confront or overpower threat
    - Flight – Escape from threat
    - Freeze – Immobilize to avoid detection
    - Collapse / Submit – Surrender to minimize damage

    When defensive responses become fixated in *trauma time,* they create dissociative parts that are hypervigilant, collapsed, aggressive, or absent and lacking present time orientation.

3. **Exploration System:** Drives learning, curiosity, and play in safe conditions. Some examples could be spontaneous play, creative expression and discovery. When the system is inhibited: the child may suppress playfulness or curiosity due to fear; exploration becomes dangerous or shameful.

4. **Caregiving System:** Supports nurturing and protecting others perceived as vulnerable. Soothing, protecting, or providing care are examples of this system. When distorted, some parts may become overly responsible, parenting the system or others as a survival role.

5. **Sexual / Reproductive System:** Drives mating and adult pair bonding. Sexual interest, attraction and intimacy are good examples of this action system. When distorted, it may merge with attachment or defense systems, leading to parts that use seduction or submission to seek safety or control.

Among these five, the most clinically significant source of internal conflict lies in the first two: attachment and defense (Van der Hart et al., 2006; Liotti, 2004). In complex trauma, especially when the caregiver is also the source of threat, these two systems are often activated simultaneously. Their goals are fundamentally incompatible (one seeks closeness, the other escape) leaving the child with no way to resolve the conflict within a single, coherent identity. The result is structural dissociation: a division between Apparently Normal Parts (ANPs) and Emotional Parts (EPs).

- **Apparently Normal Parts (ANPs):** These parts are responsible for navigating daily life, functioning socially, and often avoiding traumatic material. They are typically driven by attachment, caregiving, or social cooperation systems.
- **Emotional Parts (EPs):** These parts remain fixated in trauma-time and are dominated by defense-based action systems such as fight, flight, freeze, or collapse. They hold traumatic memories, bodily reactions, and unmet survival needs.

Within the framework used in this book, it is important to distinguish ANPs from what can be described as the Adult Self. The Adult Self is not conceptualized as a separate dissociative part, nor as equivalent to an ANP. Rather, it refers to a set of integrative and metacognitive capacities (such as reflective functioning, affect regulation, perspective-taking, and internal cooperation) that can organize experience across parts and contexts. From this perspective, there might be more than one ANP, each managing different domains of daily life, while the Adult Self represents a unifying capacity rather than a role or state. Much of the therapeutic work described here can be understood as supporting the development and strengthening of Adult Self capacities so that ANPs can operate with greater flexibility, awareness, and relational coherence rather than relying primarily on avoidance or compartmentalization.

MOTIVATIONAL SYSTEMS AND EMOTIONAL DRIVES

Building on Bowlby's ethological attachment theory, and the subsequent research and discoveries of Mary Ainsworth, Mary Main, and Judith Solomon (Bowlby, 1969, 1982; Ainsworth, 1978; Main & Solomon, 1990), Giovanni Liotti argued that disorganized attachment, where the caregiver is both haven and source of fear, is the key mediator between early relational trauma and dissociation. This "fear without solution" sets up the chronic co-activation of incompatible action systems And it is these incompatible simultaneous activations, with the resulting conflicts experienced at the level of consciousness, that prevent the process of integration that characterizes normal development, thus forming the basis of structural dissociation. Developmental research is consistent with this bridge: quality of early care predicts later dissociative phenomena across development, supporting the view that disrupted care organizes vulnerability rather than acting as a single causal event (Ogawa et al., 1997; Dutra et al., 2009). Leeds (2012) similarly emphasizes developmental pathways in which early relational conditions shape dissociative risk, particularly when later trauma is present.

Liotti (2017) expanded Bowlby's research on the internal attachment system, incorporating it into a broader multimotivational model in which innate systems (attachment, caregiving, rank with its dominant and submissive subroutines, cooperation, sexuality, exploration/play and defense) interact. Trauma and neglect entangle these motivational systems and drive psychopathology when incompatible systems are chronically co-activated.

Building on the work of Giovanni Liotti (2005, 2017), dissociative parts can be understood not only through basic action systems but also within this broader multimotivational framework rooted in evolutionary biology and attachment theory.

These motivational systems are biologically embedded and hierarchically organized across brain structures: from the reptilian brainstem, through the limbic system and into the neocortex (Panksepp, 1998). While basic systems help respond to survival needs like defense, homeostasis, or exploration, mammals also evolved interpersonal systems guiding attachment, caregiving, competition, cooperation, and sexual bonding.

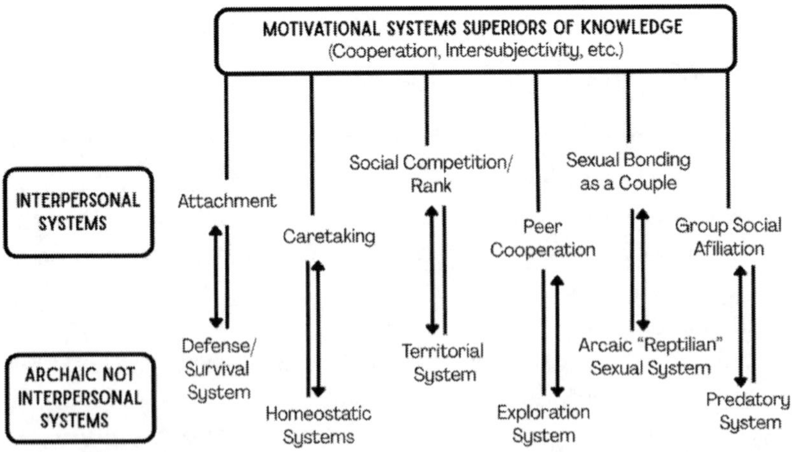

Fig. 3.1. Interpersonal and archaic not interpersonal motivational systems. Modified from Liotti, G., & Monticelli, F. (2008). *Il sistemi motivazionali nel dialogo clinico*. Raffaello Cortina, Milano.

Motivational and action systems (rank/power, defense, caregiving/loyalty, and attachment) are not parts; they are programs any part can recruit in response to specific internal or external conditions. They are like modules in our brain, with their own relative independence and interactions. Each system has its own activating cues—such as need for proximity, opportunities for care, social challenge, curiosity, play, or danger—and its own patterns of affect, attention, and action.

Some motivational systems are phasic: they come online in response to specific conditions and deactivate when those conditions resolve or the need is met. Others — such as exploration, cooperation, group affiliation, and intersubjectivity — function more tonically, shaping experience in the background and becoming suppressed primarily when defense or threat dominate. Defense is meant to be phasic, mobilizing rapid survival responses to danger. In PTSD and other trauma-related conditions (particularly in complex trauma) it can become quasi-tonic, repeatedly overriding interpersonal systems. When defensive systems are chronically activated and defense remains dominant, tonic systems stay inhibited, narrowing consciousness and compromising intersubjectivity, reflective functioning, and relational attunement.

By identifying the predominant system organizing a part´s behavior, we gain insight into its role, logic, and needs, allowing for a more attuned and adapted therapeutic response.

In dissociative personality systems, trauma and neglect entangle or distort these circuits, explaining the logic behind how dissociative parts think, feel, and relate—both to others and within the internal system.

Different parts often specialize around one dominant system; trauma co-activates incompatible ones.

These systems include:

1. **Attachment**: The attachment system is an evolutionary solution to threat, that in mammals, often modulates or re-channels raw defense by seeking a protective figure. When a child feels threatened, not just by external danger, but also by loneliness, pain, or fatigue, the innate response is to activate the search for a protective figure. This system drives proximity seeking, protest at separation, and reunion behaviors. Its primary goal is to search for safety through closeness.

It is worth emphasizing that attachment does not equate to the general capacity to form bonds; rather, it is a system that serves the evolved function of seeking proximity to a figure capable of providing protection and safety. Attachment is not bonding in general, nor is it love different interpersonal motivational systems establish different kinds of ties—sexual bonding, rank/dominance, cooperation, intersubjectivity, and social bonding. Attachment, specifically, is the pursuit of protection and security through proximity, and it is deactivated once that objective has been attained.

In the case of a disorganized attachment, this system is not compatible with normal life management; since the caregiver is also a source of threat, creating internal conflict. When this is the case, typical attachment behaviors break down. To stabilize the relationship, children often develop the so-called **controlling strategies** (caregiving the caregiver, dominating, or appeasing) between ages 3–5 (Main & Cassidy, 1988; Liotti, 2017). These strategies temporarily impose order and compactness; under stress or further trauma they collapse, and the original disorganization re-emerges as dissociative phenomena.

When these adaptations fail, especially after actual trauma events or relational ruptures, the underlying disorganization resurfaces. At that point, dissociative responses may emerge, fragmenting consciousness as the system struggles to manage the collapse of both attachment and defense.

Emotional signals: *when blocked (due to separation or loss):* fear, protest-anger, sadness, despair, emotional distancing; *when fulfilled (due to reunion and closeness):* comfort, joy, felt safety, trust/filial love.

2. **Caregiving**: The caregiving system is activated in response to separation call for attachment seeking; and in response to others' vulnerability, especially attachment signals like distress or helplessness. It drives empathy, protection, soothing, and repair, and forms the basis for compassion and prosocial behavior. In healthy development, it emerges from consistent, attuned caregiving experiences and becomes internalized as the foundation for self-care and care for others.

In chronic trauma and neglect, especially when early caregiving was absent, unsafe, or reversed, this system can become underdeveloped, distorted, or prematurely activated. Some parts may attempt to care for others (or for internal parts) from a place of hyper-responsibility, control, or appeasement, rather than true attuned caregiving. Other parts may reject caregiving altogether, due to having associated providing care with enmeshment, obligation, or harm.

Many clients lack an internalized caregiving system, making the development of an Adult Self—capable of empathy, regulation, and internal leadership—a central therapeutic goal. Clinically, engaging this system supports internal compassion, protection of vulnerable parts, and greater tolerance for vulnerability. Therapists can facilitate this by modeling safe, attuned care without rescuing or over-identifying.

Over time, in normative development, the caregiving system provides essential infrastructure for integration: it supports repair, protection, and connection, and creates the conditions under which a coherent sense of self can emerge. In contexts of trauma and disorganized attachment, however, these functions cannot be recreated through direct caregiving or by stimulating attachment bonds in therapy. On the contrary, assuming a caregiving role or encouraging dependency may intensify disorganization and undermine safety. In therapeutic work with dissociative personality systems, integration is supported instead through consistency, boundaries, and reflective presence, maintaining sufficient relational distance so that caregiving capacities can gradually emerge internally rather than being enacted externally.

Emotional signals: *when strained:* anxious over-diligence, compassion tinged with guilt; *when fulfilled:* protective tenderness, joy, parental love.

3. **Competitive/rank (dominance/subordination):** This system regulates every evaluation or judgment of right-wrong, greater-lesser, valid-useless; it regulates how we navigate power, status, and hierarchy in relationships. It is activated by perceived threats to self-worth, autonomy, or social standing.

It has two subroutines: 1) Dominance, linked to control, assertion, the pursuit of higher rank linked to emotions like pride, anger or a sense of triumph. in case of success. 2) Subordination, linked to withdrawal or appeasement of the dominant when faced with perceived inferiority or defeat, often accompanied by shame, humiliation, feelings of uselessness and incapacity.

In trauma-related dissociation, this system can become rigid or distorted, especially in parts shaped by early coercion or punitive dynamics. It shows up in perfectionistic, punitive and self-critical or perpetrator-identified parts, where dominance serves as protection and submission as survival. These parts impose internal rules, attack other parts, or collapse under perceived failure, all in an effort to manage unbearable affect through rank-based logic.

Emotional signals: *when downranked/judged:* fear, shame, humiliation, sadness (defeat), envy; when *dominant/successful:* challenge-anger, triumph/power, pride, contempt, superiority.

4. **Sexual Bonding:** This system supports adult intimacy, pair bonding, and sexual connection. In healthy development, it activates in appropriate relational contexts, typically in adulthood, serving both reproductive and emotional bonding functions. Unlike the older, phylogenetically ancient sexual system—an automatic, reproductive drive focused on species propagation and conserved across many animals—the sexual bonding system integrates complex social behaviors. It underpins sustained pair formation, long-term caregiving, and emotional attachment, enabling cooperation in raising offspring and deepening relational bonds.

   However, in individuals with developmental trauma—especially involving boundary violations, sexual abuse, or caregiver seduction—this system may become prematurely activated or distorted. When the attachment system is unsafe or unavailable, sexuality may be co-opted to meet needs for connection, safety, or control. Sexualized parts may use flirtation, seduction, or provocative behavior not for intimacy, but as protective strategies: to avoid abandonment, assert control, or survive confusing relational dynamics. These parts often hold early, unresolved experiences where closeness and danger were fused.

Therapeutically, it is essential to approach this system with curiosity, clarity, and compassion, avoiding shame or moral judgment. Reclaiming a more regulated experience of sexuality, as a consensual, adult, relational system, can be a powerful part of integration. This process begins by understanding how the sexual bonding system may have been misused by the system to survive attachment confusion.

Emotional signals: *when blocked:* modesty/shyness, fear of rejection, jealousy; *when fulfilled:* erotic desire, pleasure, erotic love.

5. **Exploration/Play:** These tonic systems—unlike others that turn on and off in response to specific stimuli—are constantly active by default, unless suppressed by more urgent or dominant systems (such as those related to threat, danger, or rank conflict). They drive curiosity, learning, creativity, and spontaneity. Exploration helps navigate environments; play fosters flexibility and emotional expression. Though not inherently interpersonal, they prepare the individual for adaptive adult functioning.

   In trauma, these systems are often suppressed by dominant survival systems like defense or rank. As a result, clients may lose access to spontaneity, curiosity, or joy, which are essential for self-discovery and integration.

   Therapeutically, reactivating these systems is a strong sign of progress. Encouraging imaginative engagement, experimentation, and playful internal dialogue can help rebuild flexibility, agency, and healing within the self-system.

   Emotional signals: *when suppressed/blocked:* flatness, boredom, anxiety about novelty; *when active:* curiosity/interest, spontaneous joy/playfulness.

6. **Peer cooperation.** This system activates when individuals recognize a shared goal that benefits from collaboration. Unlike the rank system, it operates on mutuality, not hierarchy—"We are different, but equal in this task or for this scope." It enables perspective-taking, joint attention, turn-taking, and co-regulation, forming the basis of reciprocal relationships. The emotions associated with this system include a sense of loyalty, satisfaction

derived from joint work, and resentment in response to betrayal or disloyalty.

In therapy, strengthening reflective adult functioning is foundational to the therapeutic alliance. It allows the client to collaborate with both the therapist and dissociative parts, fostering metacognitive awareness and internal cooperation. However, in clients with relational trauma, this capacity may be underdeveloped or overridden by control, fear, or mistrust.

Therapeutically, modeling cooperation and inviting shared decision-making can help restore mutuality, activate the Adult Self, and support integration through relational safety and co-creation. Most importantly: it is the main tool we have for replacing a dysfunctional and inoperable attachment mechanism.

Emotional signals: *when cooperation breaks:* guilt/remorse, isolation, mistrust, resentful/lasting anger; *when it works:* empathy, mutual loyalty, shared joy, trust, friendly love. (Social play and group affiliation share this palette).

7. **Social Belonging:** This system drives the need for group inclusion, social acceptance, and safety within a larger community. As an evolved interpersonal system, it plays a critical role in survival for species that depend on social bonds, not just one-on-one attachment, but integration into a group. It supports identity through shared norms, roles, and rituals, and fosters cooperation and relational stability. In contrast to peer cooperation, social belonging functions as a *tonic* motivational system: it is continuously active when not inhibited by more urgent systems such as defense or attachment. The need to belong to a group remains present even in highly traumatized or dissociative personality systems, although it may be expressed through distorted or costly strategies.

   In trauma—especially in environments marked by emotional invalidation, shame, or chaos—this system often becomes overactivated or warped by threat. While the need to belong remains intact, clients may adopt survival-based strategies such as fawning, people-pleasing, hyper-adaptability, or self-abandonment to avoid rejection or maintain approval. These patterns are often mistaken for personality traits but reflect deep survival strategies developed in relationships where acceptance was conditional.

In therapy, this may show up as over-accommodation, reluctance to express disagreement, or guilt for needing space and support. Healing involves helping clients differentiate authentic connection from performative belonging and supporting the Adult Self in creating internal conditions of inclusion—where all parts are welcomed without having to earn their place. Therapists can attune to this system by recognizing false compliance, validating the healthy drive to belong, and modeling non-contingent, mutual connection both relationally and internally.

Emotional signals: *when belonging is conditional or threatened:* shame, loneliness, social anxiety; *when belonging is secure:* security, pride in membership and affection.

8. **Intersubjectivity (Theory of Mind, Metacognition, Mentalization):** This higher-order system enables us to understand and reflect on the inner worlds of ourselves and others—mental states, intentions, and beliefs beyond observable behavior. Although these terms originate in different theoretical models and emphasize partially distinct domains, they are used here together for pragmatic and integrative purposes, following Liotti's view of intersubjectivity as a unified higher-order capacity. This system builds upon the peer cooperation system and is crucial for self-awareness, emotional regulation, and relational depth.

   In dissociative personality systems, intersubjectivity is often disrupted by trauma, unmet attachment needs, or chronic survival responses. Clients may struggle to mentalize their parts, reflect on their reactions, or distinguish past from present in relational contexts.

   Strengthening this system is fundamental to develop the Adult Self—capable of internal leadership, curiosity, and reflection. As it matures, clients gain more flexibility, insight, and capacity to hold complexity within themselves and their relationships.

   Emotional signals: *when ruptured*: confusion, shame, mistrust/misreading; *when functioning:* reflective calm, empathic interest, compassionate understanding.

SYSTEM	WHEN FAILED/ BLOCKED/CHALLENGED	WHEN FULFILLED/ACHIEVED
Attachment	Fear, protest-anger, sadness, despair, emotional distancing	Comfort, joy, felt safety, trust/filial
Caregiving	Anxious over-diligence, compassion tinged with guilt	Protective tenderness, joy, parental love.
Competitive/Rank (Dominance/ Subordination)	Fear, shame, humiliation, sadness (defeat), envy	Challenge-anger, triumph/ power, pride, contempt, superiority
Sexual Bonding	Modesty/shyness, fear of rejection, jealousy	Erotic desire, pleasure, erotic love
Exploration/Play	Flatness, boredom, anxiety about novelty	Curiosity/interest, spontaneous joy/playfulness
Peer cooperation	Guilt/remorse, isolation, mistrust, resentful/lasting anger	Empathy, mutual loyalty, shared joy, trust, friendly love
Social Belonging	Shame, loneliness, social anxiety	Security, pride in membership, gratitude/affection
Intersubjectivity (Theory of Mind, Metacognition)	Confusion, shame, mistrust/ misreading	Reflective calm, empathic interest, compassionate understanding

Table 3.1. Summary of the emotional signals that flag whether a system is blocked or fulfilled. (Rank often recruits defense; mixed phenomenology is common in parts dynamics

This multimotivational model offers therapists a powerful lens for decoding the internal logic of dissociative part behaviors. Each part may be organized around dominant motivational systems but may also carry co-opted elements from other systems. When parts operate in isolation, the natural coordination and compromise between these systems, possible in an integrated individual, is affected. By identifying which systems are active, and how they have been distorted or misused for survival, therapists can attune more precisely to the underlying motivational logic behind even extreme or confusing behaviors (Cortina, 2018; Liotti & Cortina, 2010). It helps us see why the part exists, what the part is trying to achieve, what tends to trigger its activation and what it needs to deactivate or soften. This kind of clarity is about tracking the survival-based logic behind it, not about categorizing behavior.

It can be helpful to think of dissociative parts as motivational specialists, each one organized around a dominant action or motivational system since these systems influence how parts act and relate to others. For example:

- A care-seeking child part may be driven by the attachment system, longing for proximity and safety.
- A hypervigilant protector might reflect the defense system, constantly scanning for danger.

- A punitive or critical part may embody a distorted rank or dominance system, enforcing internal control through shame or judgment
- A self-harming part may turn rage inward, rooted in unmet caregiving needs or unmanageable guilt
- A withdrawn or compliant part may be shaped by the social belonging system, formed in response to exclusion, rejection, or pressure to conform

Through repeated interactions with real people in our lives, interpersonal motivational systems consolidate into internal working models (IWMs)—childhood-formed schemas of self, other, and "self-with-other". In the context of trauma, these IWMs frequently encode danger/loyalty conflicts, biasing parts toward protection rather than contact and shaping perception well into adulthood. These unique experiences explain the idiosyncratic variations in the schemas encoded within IWMs across individuals.

CONFLICTS BETWEEN SYSTEMS = INTERNAL CONFLICT BETWEEN PARTS

In secure contexts, IMSs activate in an orderly, hierarchical way: when attachment needs are met by caregiver availability, other systems (play, exploration, cooperation, and later, sexuality) can emerge without conflict. In **disorganized attachment**, the caregiver is both protection and threat. Short-circuits follow:

- The child seeks safety (attachment) while simultaneously feeling terror and defeat (rank/agonistic).
- Role inversion appears: the child cares for the caregiver (caregiving distorted).
- Early, chaotic sexualized elements intrude into the attachment bond.
- Cooperation with peers is undermined by mistrust and fear of betrayal.

This lens explains the logic behind how parts think, feel, and relate—both externally and internally.

Many core internal conflicts in dissociative clients can be understood as clashes between incompatible systems:

- Attachment vs. defense: one part reaches; another attacks or shuts down.
- Caregiving vs. rank: one soothes; another monitors with perfectionism or punishment
- Exploration vs. flight. one wants to play or create; another fears visibility and inhibits.

Therapy often progresses when the therapist can identify and validate both systems at play, rather than siding with one or pathologizing the other.

Motivational Entanglement in Disorganized Attachment

When these collisions repeat in caregiving contexts, they consolidate into a chronic pattern: attachment and defense fire together. Over time this motivational tangle co-activates systems in contradictory ways, undermines affect regulation, and increases dissociative vulnerability.

Liotti (2017) proposed that disorganized attachment is not simply one style among others, but a fundamental failure of integration in which the attachment and defense systems are activated simultaneously. This disorganization is not pathology in itself, but the developmental precursor that predisposes the individual to dissociative splitting as well as other adult disorders, as shown by research. Prospective and longitudinal findings support a developmental pathway in which early relational care quality—particularly chronic neglect and disrupted responsiveness—predicts later dissociative symptoms, especially when later trauma occurs. In this view, neglect is often an early driver of rudimentary dissociative shutdown and a marker of compromised integration, increasing vulnerability to structural dissociation when subsequent traumatic experiences are added (Ogawa et al., 1997; Dutra et al., 2009; Leeds, 2012). Importantly, disorganization is not dissociation: disorganization reflects a failure of coherent integration that can lead to multiple adult outcomes, with dissociation emerging most reliably when disorganization is compounded by traumatic threat, particularly in caregiving contexts (Liotti, 2004, 2017).

Structural dissociation functions as an adaptive partition that allows the child to meet irreconcilable demands by segregating competing aims (e.g., approaching for care vs. fleeing for safety). Conceptually, however, its emergence reflects an initial failure of integration, followed by the establishment of structural dissociation as

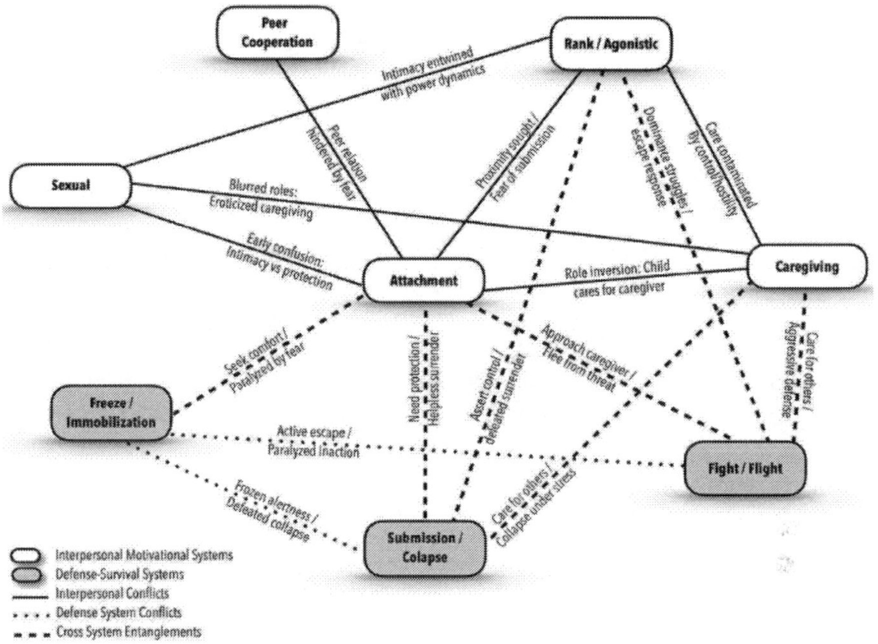

Figure 3.1. Motivational Systems Entanglement in Disorganized Attachment: Interpersonal and Defense-Survival Systems (Liotti, 2017). This figure maps how attachment and defense co-activate and spill into other motivational systems; dissociation acts as a temporary partition that lets incompatible action tendencies run in parallel.

a lower-order substitute solution that preserves survival at the cost of coherence. Clinically, mapping which systems are co-activated and why, prevents pathologizing and guides de-activation strategies (Cortina, 2018; Liotti & Cortina, 2010).

These divisions are not arbitrary, they reflect the child's solution to impossible relational and emotional demands, like needing to seek a source of security (attachment) from someone who is simultaneously a source of threat. This is the core situation of disorganized attachment, the underlying condition of dissociative disorders. For example:

- A child who both loves and fears a caregiver must split or divide the experience. One part maintains the bond (attachment system), while another mobilizes defense (fight, flight, or freeze).
- A part stuck in defense may freeze the body, hide, or shut down emotion to avoid danger.

- Another attachment-based part may pursue connection, even with people who resemble past perpetrators, because attachment is still biologically wired as necessary for survival.

Understanding which action system is active, and what the part is trying to achieve, helps therapists respond in a way that does not unintentionally deepen internal conflict and fragmentation. It also allows for a more attuned, non-pathologizing approach that understands and respects the part´s original protective function.

With that survival scaffolding in view, motivational systems show the relational *why* behind a part's strategy and the emotions that signal whether the system is activated and its goal is blocked or fulfilled.

WHY THIS MATTERS IN THE WORK WITH DISSOCIATIVE PARTS

Effective therapy is organized to build **Adult Self** capacities such as metacognition, reflective distance, internal leadership and choice, which gradually grow as integration progresses. The motivational systems most directly involved in supporting these capacities are cooperation/ collaboration, caregiving, and social affiliation. These systems are not activated all at once, nor do they develop linearly; rather, they are cultivated over time through relational experience and therapeutic modelling.

- **Peer-to-peer cooperation and collaboration systems:** Support mutual recognition, turn-taking, empathy, the capacity to work *with* others. and have shared goals. It is central to the development of intersubjectivity and forms the backbone of the therapeutic alliance, especially useful in clients with attachment wounds in which activation of the attachment system should be avoided. When sufficiently activated, they allow engagement without submission, domination, quest for protection or seduction Internally, cooperation enables collaboration among parts—the ability to coexist, negotiate differences, and coordinate action without erasing distinct aims or roles. Collaboration does not require harmony or consensus other than for goals or tasks. It allows shared participation in the service of safety and functioning.

- **Caregiving system:** Orients us toward responding to vulnerability with protection, soothing, and repair. In therapy, it provides the emotional foundation for compassionate internal leadership in the Adult Self.
- **Social affiliation / group belonging system:** Motivates inclusion in groups and avoidance of social exclusion. It overlaps with cooperation and attachment systems but with a broader focus on community, safety in numbers, and shared identity.

CLINICAL VIGNETTE

The Affectionate Teen

Sofia, 31, enters therapy with confusing mood swings. One part of her longs to connect with her therapist, asking personal questions, dressing up for sessions, and making flirtatious comments. Another part interrupts with icy silence, internal threats, and eventual shutdown. When asked what the silence was about, Sofia says, "He (a watchdog part) does not trust you. He says this is a trap."

Through exploration, it becomes clear that one part is organized around the attachment by the sexual bonding system, trying to gain closeness through seduction. The other is rooted in defense, warning against vulnerability based on past betrayal. Instead of seeing this as manipulation or trying to convince the part that it is not a trap and therapy is safe, the therapist names the intent on both sides: "It makes sense that part of you longs for warmth and connection, and that another part would feel terrified, or even angry by that. Both are trying to keep you safe in different ways."

Naming the conflict and the protective intent allows Sofia to feel less ashamed and more curious. Over time, both dissociative parts begin to tolerate the therapist's presence without having to do what was needed in other relationships, and a third position, the Adult Self, starts to emerge as a potential internal mediator.

Clinical Reflections

Naming both strategies as protection, keeping clear boundaries and a steady presence. Modeling another way of relating gradually invited the Adult Self to show up, pace contact and eventually turned a polarized push–pull into a permissioned, slower proximity that both parts could tolerate.

As described earlier in the chapter, this pattern is classic in disorganized attachment: when direct care-seeking feels unsafe, proximity gets routed through controlling strategies (seduce/perform/dominate or shut-down/submit). Identifying action and motivational systems helps de-shame both roles, align with protection (not blame), and reintroduce choice, contact can happen by permission, with brakes, and without reenacting the old contract.

By identifying which action systems are activated and the internal working model (IWM) each part is enacting, therapists can attune more precisely to function, likely triggers, and deactivation needs. This shifts us from pathologizing behavior to tracking survival logic and directly guides stance, pacing, and language. In practice, this helps therapists: make sense of behaviors that appear contradictory; step out of power struggles with parts; offer targeted interventions that address the motivational logic behind a part's strategy; and validate protective intent—even when strategies are extreme or self-destructive.

It also helps clients recognize that dissociative parts are creative adaptations to early survival demands and that internal conflict is not irrational but rooted in biological and evolutionary logic. There is meaning, not madness, in their internal chaos.

CLOSING THOUGHTS

Parts do not develop at random; they emerge as organized survival adaptations to overwhelming and contradictory demands. By understanding which action systems and motivational circuits are active within different parts, we gain access to the logic beneath the existing internal conflict. Rather than viewing parts as irrational or problematic, we begin to recognize them as highly organized but divided responses to competing needs generated within contexts of disorganized attachment. Liotti's (2004, 2017) key contribution was to show how disorganized attachment functions as the bridge between early neglect and trauma and later structural dissociation. During early traumatic experiences—particularly those involving caregivers—the process of dissociation of the personality is already set in motion, even though the resulting parts are initially rudimentary and loosely organized. Over time, and through repeated exposure to incompatible motivational demands, these early dissociative configurations become more differentiated, elaborated, and structurally stabilized.

By linking Bowlby's (Bowlby, 1969/1982) secure base concept to the multimotivational model, Liotti provided clinicians with a map for understanding dissociative parts as organized around biologically rooted yet conflicted motivational systems, shaped developmentally by trauma rather than emerging suddenly or arbitrarily later in life.

This framework does not replace relational work, it deepens it. When we use motivational systems-based accessible language, we offer clients a map for understanding their inner world, not a pathologizing one, but a compassionate, biological grounded, and meaning-making one.

In the next section, we will apply this understanding to specific types of parts, those shaped by defense, shame, hostility, caregiving, appeasement, sexuality, and more. These are among the most frequent internal representations in clients with fragmentation. By recognizing the action systems and motivational forces that organize each of these parts, we can better attune our stance, language, and interventions to meet them where they are; this will help us build bridges instead of more walls.

Clinical Anchors

What to remember...

- To understand why parts do what they do, we must look at action systems and interpersonal motivational systems working—often colliding—under trauma.
- Parts are not random or willful; they are organized adaptations to complex relational demands.
- ANPs and EPs reflect different priorities (avoidance vs. activation) and often clash.
- Dissociative parts often reflect dominant action systems (defense, attachment, caregiving, sexual bonding). and emerge when incompatible action systems such as the need for attachment and the need for defense, are simultaneously activated but cannot be integrated.
- Understanding which action system is active, and what the part is trying to achieve, helps therapists respond in a way that does not unintentionally deepen internal conflict and fragmentation.
- By understanding which action systems and motivational circuits are active within different parts, we gain access to the logic beneath the existing internal conflict. It also helps therapists know how to engage, what to validate, and when to wait.

What to avoid...

- Assuming all parts have the same goals or need the same kind of relational response.
- Pushing for connection when defense dominates.
- Interpreting seduction, hostility, or collapse as interpersonal maneuvers.

Chapter 4: Why and When to Work with Parts

Therapist Reflection

There was a time early in my work when I felt excited every time a client mentioned an inner voice or anything that sounded like a potential conflict. I saw it as an invitation to dive into parts work. Sometimes, that instinct served the client well. But other times, therapy became more chaotic than before.

Now that we have laid the foundation for understanding parts and the protective roles they serve, we turn to the crucial question of timing and appropriateness. When is it helpful to work with parts and when is it not?

Not every client, and not every moment, is right for parts work. While this approach can be deeply healing when introduced with care, it can also destabilize or confuse when applied prematurely or without proper attunement (Steele et al., 2017). As we have seen, dissociative parts differ from ego states or modes not only in structure but in the level of fragmentation, disownership, and internal phobia they often reflect. This has relevant implications for treatment. Well-timed, respectful parts work can become a path to integration, while premature or misapplied interventions can inadvertently worsen confusion or overwhelm.

This chapter explores the clinical rationale for working with parts, the necessary conditions for doing so safely, the warning signs that suggest the system is not yet ready, and the risks of imposing a parts-based lens where it does not belong. Through clinical vignettes, we will examine how to recognize readiness, and support internal dialogue, without creating artificial systems or reinforcing identity confusion.

WHY WORK WITH PARTS?

With the groundwork in place, we return to our central question: why engage in parts work? Its power rests on three intertwined aims. First, by honoring each part's survival wisdom, we validate the very strategies that once helped the client endure overwhelming conditions, even when those strategies were only partially effective or carried significant costs, building the trust essential for healing. Second, as parts learn to cooperate, internal intrusions soften and the client's capacity for emotion regulation deepens. Third, we gently invite collaboration and integration, offering a relational space in which parts can gradually lower their walls, enter into dialogue, and, when the system itself is ready, weave into a more unified self (Mosquera, 2019; Steele et al., 2017).

For many clients with dissociative disorders, life is experienced as a relentless inner battle, fragmented, confusing, and often terrifying. Effective treatment therefore begins with a shared exploration of that internal landscape. Which parts are active, and under what circumstances? What survival strategies do they rely on, and what protective goals drive their behaviors? Are they willing to consider new ways of keeping the client safe? Together, therapist and client explore these parts as allies whose hard-won strategies carry invaluable wisdom.

By learning to notice and track these internal parts, and to approach them with curiosity rather than fear, clients discover that overwhelming emotions can be welcomed instead of avoided, and that painful memories can be integrated rather than walled off. Indeed, every part arises from an adaptive response to overwhelming experience, once necessary to survive, now invited into a different partnership. In shifting from symptom suppression to collaborative healing, parts work unlocks the path toward genuine integration and lasting resilience.

WHEN TO WORK WITH PARTS AND WHEN NOT

Parts work is not just about having the right tools; it is about knowing *when to use them.* Some clients light up with relief when we explore their inner system, but others get frightened. And some adopt the parts language in a way that feels performative or disconnected. I have learned that the presence of parts' language does not always mean the system is ready, and that curiosity must be tempered by clinical judgment.

Parts work can be deeply transformative, but only when the client and their system are truly ready. Introduced prematurely, it can overwhelm, destabilize, or lead the therapy into territory the client is not equipped to navigate. Just because someone uses the language of parts, or seems interested in inner exploration, does not mean they are ready to engage with fragmentation in a therapeutic way. Discernment is essential.

It takes patience to wait. To stay with the client's day-to-day struggles; to build trust and to return repeatedly to safety and regulation, especially when we know how powerful parts work can be.

Assessing Readiness for Parts Work

Before initiating parts work, the therapist must assess whether the system has sufficient stability and internal capacity to tolerate it. Readiness is not determined by the client's use of parts language or apparent curiosity about inner experience, but by structural and functional indicators.

At a minimum, the client should demonstrate a baseline level of grounding, affect regulation, and safety, both internally and in their external environment. Clients who are actively suicidal, self-injuring without control, experiencing severe dissociative episodes, or displaying psychotic symptoms need symptom containment and stabilization first.

Equally important is the client's relationship to their inner world. Clients who dissociate or space out when asked about feelings, or express fear, disgust, or confusion when internal experiences are gently invited, often reflect deep phobia of their inner world. In these cases, parts work, especially when it includes mapping, naming, or direct dialogue, can be premature and even counterproductive. These systems need more readiness, more trust in the therapeutic relationship, and often more internal cooperation before parts work can safely begin (Steele et al., 2005; Steele et al., 2017; Van der Hart et al., 2006).

A New Phenomenon: *Trendy* Dissociation

With the development and expansion of social media, clinicians have increasingly noted presentations shaped by cultural or social trends, particularly in adolescents and young adults (Mosquera, 2024). Clients may arrive already using parts language, talking about alters, inner children, or systems. They may offer polished *cast lists* of names, roles, and internal rules, but without relevant distress, conflict, or avoidance. Often, these presentations reflect identity exploration, social modeling, or developmental instability rather than fragmentation.

CLINICAL VIGNETTE

When Multiplicity Becomes the Mask

Diana, age 15, was referred to therapy with a mix of diagnostic labels: borderline personality disorder, ADHD, DID, and a recent history of self-harm and gender questioning. In the first session, she sat forward with animated urgency. "I hear voices. Do you want to talk to any of them?" The therapist responded with warmth and curiosity, "Thanks for offering. For now, I'd really like to get to know you first. Is that something you feel you can do?" Without hesitation, Sofia replied, "Oh, yeah! Whenever you want, just tell me, and I'll switch into that part."

What followed was a cascade of information: names, ages, aesthetics, favorite colors, phobias, music tastes, each part sharply defined and instantly accessible. There was no visible hesitation, no internal conflict. It all felt a little too rehearsed, too immediate, a system without struggle, without the emotional complexity typically seen in dissociative parts. The therapist began to notice that the more they tried to explore the inner system, the more confusion and contradiction emerged. Claims of amnesia were vague, voice hearing lacked distress, and internal conflict appeared more theatrical than disruptive.

Rather than challenge or dismiss Diana's narrative, the therapist shifted focus: What's school like? What gets overwhelming during the day? What helps? Gradually, therapy became anchored in her daily experience: difficulties with attention, peer relationships, and emotional reactivity. Without directly confronting the parts narrative, the therapist made room for a different kind of contact.

Over the next few sessions, something shifted. Sofia stopped mentioning the voices. She began using "I" instead of "we". Her clothing changed. She talked about being bullied for being *weird* in middle school and how she started watching videos about systems and alters around that time. She spoke of feeling "more like a girl again", though unsure what that really meant. By session ten, the elaborate system of parts had quietly dissolved, replaced by a more grounded, curious adolescent beginning to explore her real-life pain.

Clinical Reflections

This case speaks to the growing clinical trend previously mentioned: adolescents who adopt dissociative language or parts-based frameworks based on what they hear or see in social media. It can also be a desire to fit in with others, through peer identification and, very often, unmet relational needs.

In such cases, parts work risks reinforcing a fragile or confused sense of self, especially if it is applied prematurely or without sufficient diagnostic clarity. Careful assessment models of dissociation emphasize the importance of distinguishing between true dissociative phenomena and other presentations (Boon, 2017). From a therapeutic standpoint, rather than invalidating or confronting the client´s narrative, the work remains anchored on the client's real-life experience, day-to-day functioning, emotional regulation, skills, relational dynamics, and underlying wounds.

As the client builds real-world identity and regulation, the parts narrative often fades on its own, not because it was purposely made up, but because they were genuinely confused and it was serving a temporary organizational need. The language of parts gave them a way to express what was happening, a way to be seen, understood, and held. And some might even have complex internal dynamics that they do not speak about because the new representations serve as a distracting strategy.

The Risks of Suggesting Parts

Some clients may not arrive with parts' language, but quickly adopt it when suggested, especially those who are fantasy-prone, gifted, imaginative, or highly attuned to perceived therapeutic expectations. These clients may over-identify with metaphor, turning internal impulses into fixed identities to please, perform, or create coherence. Well-intentioned interventions, such as inviting names or inner maps, can solidify structures that would not have emerged on their own.

What was initially symbolic becomes reified, and therapy may veer off course, away from real emotional work and into a proliferation of roles, journals, and inner systems. Here, the therapist must stay grounded in function, not form; process, not content. The question is not, "What is this part's name?" but "What is this impulse trying to protect?" or "What does this shift say about what's hard to feel right now?"

CLINICAL VIGNETTE

Naming Too Soon

Christina, 32, came to therapy feeling stuck between two powerful impulses. One part of her was desperate to grieve her father's death, while another seemed equally determined to avoid it. "Part of me wants to scream and sob, she said, and another part is like, 'Don't you dare'."

During an exploration exercise, the therapist noticed her voice shift slightly as she toggled between these positions. "It sounds like there are two very distinct sides pulling on you", the therapist offered. "Would it help to give them names?" Christina nodded. They called one the Explorer, who sought emotional release, and the other the Guardian, who protected against overwhelm. Together, they sketched a simple diagram. In the moment, it helped, the visualization softened the internal conflict and allowed Christina to acknowledge both drives without needing to pick a side.

But by the next session, something had changed. Christina arrived with three new *parts*, each with names, backstories, and complex motivations. A week later, the number had doubled. By month two, Christina insisted she had 15 distinct personalities each with a color-coded journal entry, a preferred food, and a list of emotional triggers. Therapy sessions became consumed with organizing her system rather than processing her grief. The original conflict, the push-pull around loss, was now obscured under layers of invented inner roles.

Clinical Reflections

What began as a well-intentioned metaphoric intervention had inadvertently suggested that every internal impulse was a separate entity. Rather than building capacity to hold emotional tension, the intervention fragmented it. The therapist, upon reflection, realized that inviting names and maps too early had transformed a normal internal conflict into a pathologized narrative of multiplicity. The naming, meant to externalize the tension for exploration, had instead created a false internal architecture.

From a Janetian perspective (Janet, 1945), this proliferation of named parts can be understood as a substitute action: an activity that replaces a more demanding adaptive process when the latter feels inaccessible. In this case, organizing, cataloguing, and elaborating parts substituted for the more difficult task of staying present with grief and ambivalence. The symbolic activity provided a sense of control and coherence, but at the cost of emotional integration.

This case highlights an important clinical caution: naming invites permanence. Once something is named, it can become real in the client's internal world, even if it was originally introduced as a metaphor. Clinicians must stay alert, especially with clients who are fantasy-prone or highly identified with clinical labels. These clients may unconsciously adopt parts language to impose coherence on emotional chaos. In such cases, it is crucial not to rush the mapping process.

In all these cases, regardless of whether the client is unready, over-identified, or overly suggestible, the path forward is the same: stay close to the lived experience. Support emotional regulation, build trust, and gently deepen contact with the present moment Internal conflict, while distressing, does not necessarily point to structural dissociation. Instead of asking, "What is its name?" we can ask, "What role might this voice or impulse be playing?" Focusing on function allows us to stay with the felt experience without prematurely assigning identity. And finally, more parts do not mean more insight. System inflation can reflect confusion, avoidance, or even therapist overreach, not therapeutic progress. Naming should be used with caution, and always in service of the client's integration, not their fragmentation.

CLOSING THOUGHTS

Working with dissociative parts can be extremely useful and clarifying. In fact, in complex cases, it might be the only viable point of entry into therapeutic work. But as emphasized throughout this chapter, not every client is ready for parts work, and not every expression of internal conflict reflects structural dissociation or fragmentation.

Some clients may adopt parts' language from cultural narratives or therapeutic suggestions; others may use it to organize internal chaos, achieve unmet relational needs, or seek belonging. In such cases, our task is not to challenge the language itself, but to return to the client's inner experience and to anchor the work within the therapeutic relationship, gradually grounding the process in lived reality.

In the next chapter, we will build on these foundations by exploring how to foster first initial contact between parts: creating safety, containing conflict, and supporting the emergence of an Adult Self that can guide the system toward more integration.

Clinical Anchors

What to remember...

- Parts' language is powerful but should only be introduced when the client is ready and can benefit from it.
- Parts often reflect protective strategies, even when they seem chaotic or maladaptive.
- Use the client's language but do not assume that naming or mapping always helps.
- Clients may use parts language without actual fragmentation; focus on process, not content.

What to avoid...

- Introducing terms referring to parts to indicate conflicting impulses or tendencies in the client.
- Starting parts work too early, especially in clients that need stabilization.
- Assuming that every reference to parts or voices implies the existence of dissociative parts.
- Encouraging mapping, naming, or dialoguing with parts before discerning if this can be helpful or contraindicative.
- Treating parts as separate people or independent personalities.

Chapter 5: Developing the Adult Self. Supporting Internal Leadership

Therapist Reflection

I notice my impulse to teach *the Adult Self, to rush towards inner coherence. But I remind myself that leadership in such complex systems is a felt capacity learned through new interactions and experiences. I slow my questions, point out hesitations, and validate new responses and interactions. I keep in mind that my steadiness is the first lesson in internal leadership. Each time I stay curious and honor ambiguity, I'm modeling the very capacity I'm inviting my client to discover.*

Rather than viewing the Adult Self as a single figure or a fully formed leader part, we understand it as a relational capacity—one that often has not had the chance to fully develop—and as a network of ways of relating to oneself and one's parts. While the term *Adult Self* can be clinically useful, it also carries the risk of being heard as a distinct internal entity. Framing it as an identity that must emerge and take charge can inadvertently create additional pressure for clients who already feel inadequate, overwhelmed, or fragmented.

Importantly, this is not about reification in a strict sense, but about how language is received and internalized in therapy. For this reason, *Adult Self* is best understood as conceptual language for therapists, rather than a label that must be explicitly introduced to clients. The therapeutic task is not to instruct clients to "develop an Adult Self", but to support the gradual emergence of integrative capacities, such as reflection, regulation, and cooperation, through relational experience. It would therefore be a mistake to identify the Adult Self with the Apparently Normal Part, whose role is primarily to manage everyday functioning. At the same time, some ANPs may, over the course of therapy, increasingly develop and express the integrative capacities associated with the Adult Self, allowing them to function at higher levels of reflection, regulation, and cooperation.

In many dissociative systems, this internal leadership has been blocked, undeveloped, or hidden beneath layers of fear and protection. It is not missing; it is waiting for space and support to emerge.

This chapter explores what it means to nurture this capacity for grounded internal leadership. We do not do this by asking clients to "be an adult", or by pushing for coherence. We support its emergence by modeling regulation, inviting reflection, and offering relational experiences that awaken steadiness from within.

THE ADULT SELF AS A CAPACITY

The Adult Self is not a performance or a static role; it refers to a *felt sense* of presence, curiosity, and grounded care; an emergent capacity to pause, reflect, care for other parts, and make decisions with awareness.

This capacity may be anchored in one part, shared across several, or developed gradually between parts. Sometimes it emerges only in fleeting moments, a hesitation before reacting, a choice made with awareness. It may begin as a whisper, a flicker of perspective that vanishes just as quickly as it came. But even those small moments matter. They are not failures of constancy; they are the seeds of internal leadership.

The goal is not to maintain a constant Adult Self initially, but to increase access to those relational capacities over time. With care and practice, those moments stretch, becoming a bridge between parts, a calming presence in the storm, and eventually, an anchor for the system as a whole.

Therapists can name and support this emerging capacity:

- ★ "I noticed how you paused and checked in with your system just now. That felt like leadership."
- ★ "Even when it's messy or difficult, the fact that you're noticing and wondering is an adult capacity."

These moments correspond to what Pierre Janet (1938) described as reflective actions, as opposed to immediate or automatic actions—

responses that allow pause, consideration, and choice rather than reflexive discharge. It is precisely these reflective actions that therapy seeks to support and expand.

We want to frame the Adult Self not as control or perfection, but as the ability to remain curious, connected and attuned, even in distress. Through cooperative engagement, this capacity scaffolds higher-order processes such as intersubjectivity and shared metacognition. When development has been marked by disorganized attachment (and especially by dissociation), these capacities tend to be state-dependent and partitioned, held in isolated parts within their own operational scopes. Therapy helps bring them into shared awareness and coordinated use.

WHY THE ADULT SELF MAY BE HARD TO ACCESS

For many clients, there is no internal model of what safe, competent leadership looks like. Caregivers may have been chaotic, absent, or abusive. The word *adult* may be associated with danger or performance. For others, the experience of being an adult is chronologically new. The client may be in their twenties, thirties, or older but internally organized around child or adolescent parts.

Clients may say,

- ❖ "There is not an adult here."
- ❖ "They don't trust me."
- ❖ "When I try to lead, someone inside gets angry or disappears."

Rather than challenging this, we validate it,

- ★ "That makes sense. If no one ever showed you how, how would you know what it feels like?"
- ★ "It's okay that it's hard, we're not asking you to be in charge, just to stay curious about what leadership might look like."

This reframing opens space for growth, not from pressure, but from permission. Importantly, these reflections are often voiced not from a fully developed Adult Self, but from Apparently Normal Parts (ANPs) that are beginning to cooperate, reflect, or experiment with curiosity. In early phases of therapy, the capacities associated with the Adult Self frequently emerge within ANP functioning, before they can be experienced as a more stable, integrated stance. From this perspective, the work is not about accessing a pre-existing leader, but about supporting parts that function in daily life in developing and sharing capacities for reflection, regulation, and cooperation, which over time may coalesce into what we describe as the Adult Self.

CLINICAL VIGNETTE

When the Adult Self Begins to Emerge

A client with a highly divided system presented with frequent switching and little internal communication. No part identified as *in charge*, and early sessions were often chaotic, marked by distrust, confusion, and survival-based responses.

Rather than pushing for coherence, the therapist focused on grounding and containment. Slowly, she began gently naming moments of adult capacity: when the client paused before reacting, expressed concern for another part, or noticed multiple perspectives.

Over time, the client began referring to "the one who can slow things down." This presence wasn't fully formed, but it offered enough steadiness to begin mediating conflict. With support, it evolved into a shared leadership function—a space within the system that others could trust as a holding environment.

Clinical Reflections

Therapy becomes the space where these blocks can be named, explored, and gradually softened. We don't push for leadership. Instead, we help make space for it by modelling, within the therapeutic relationship, ways of intervening with and relating to other parts of the system. Through this interpersonal modelling, clients are offered an experiential reference for how internal relationships can become more cooperative, curious, and regulated over time.

Leadership can be distributed across parts or arise situationally. Some clients develop a *collaborative team* model where different parts share responsibility. This absence is not failure. It reflects the beginning of cooperation and collaboration, and it invites a different kind of work: co-regulating first, leading after. We can support this with questions

- ★ "Is there a part that feels calm enough to help right now?"
- ★ "Is anyone inside open to working with others on this?"
- ★ "Could two parts work together, even if they don't fully trust each other yet?"

These small relational moves invite collaboration and cooperation instead of control. They make room for the possibility that multiple parts can co-hold responsibility—a more realistic, effective and flexible model of internal leadership.

THE THERAPIST AS A MODEL OF INTERNAL LEADERSHIP

Therapists model what internal leadership might feel like, through steadiness, regulated pacing, and non-judgmental attunement. In practice, this looks like pausing when needed, naming mixed emotions and holding multiple perspectives without pushing for resolution.

We show that being in charge does not mean being perfect. It means being curious, flexible, and grounded enough to stay in relationship. This helps the Adult Self emerge as a felt sense, not just a cognitive ideal. Examples of sentences you can use:

★ "I'll hold this steady while you feel into it."
★ "You don't have to figure it all out right now. We'll understand more, over time."
★ "This feels confusing; we can slow it down and explore it together."

Over time, the client begins to internalize these steady, compassionate responses. Internalization then becomes the seed of adult presence inside: quiet, growing, and relationally grounded.

SUPPORTING THE DEVELOPMENT OF THE ADULT SELF

As therapists, we cannot force the development of the Adult Self, but we can invite it consistently. Often, this happens in small, meaningful moments of awareness, choice, and care. Here are a few ways we can support this process:

One of the most powerful interventions is to **name and affirm moments when adult presence is already happening**:

★ "You slowed down and checked in. That's leadership."
★ "You were able to feel the fear and still choose a response."

- ★ "That part of you that wants to understand. I think that's the beginning of adult presence."

By reflecting these moments, we help the client recognize that the Adult Self is not something to become, but something to notice and grow.

When triggered, dissociative parts can intrude on the Adult Self's capacities, hijacking attention and generating fear-based reactions. The therapist supports the Adult Self in **interrupting these reactive impulses with reflection**. We can cultivate this capacity by offering prompts such as:

- ★ "Can we slow this down and notice what's happening inside?"
- ★ "Is there another way to respond to this part, even just a little?"
- ★ "What would it be like to listen instead of fight here?"

These questions support internal differentiation and help the client **shift from immediate response to reflective choice**—a hallmark of adult capacity. Let us see other ways of facilitating the development of Adult Self:

1. **Model it in the therapeutic relationship.** Because early caregiving was chronically misattuned, the child had limited exposure to modeled reflective functioning and metacognition. Treatment therefore requires an explicit modeling intervention: a co-regulated, corrective relational and cognitive experience within the therapeutic relationship. Before the Adult Self can emerge internally, clients often need to feel it from you. Your regulation, clarity, boundary-setting, and tone provide a template. The way you stay steady when things get chaotic, the way you name what is happening without shaming, is all part of that modeling.

    - ★ Be consistent. Predictable structures build trust.
    - ★ Be curious, invite reflection without pushing too much. Wonder aloud about what might be happening, even when it's unclear.
    - ★ Speak to all parts while anchoring in the present: "Right now, I'm talking to the part who's overwhelmed, and I also want to support the part that feels unsure about what to do next."

    Over time, the client internalizes your tone, your presence, not as obedience, but as *relational memory*.

2. **Name adult capacities when they show up.** Often the Adult Self is present in subtle moments: choosing not to react, asking for a pause, caring for another part. Clients may not recognize these as meaningful. Therapists can reflect back these shifts:

    ★ "You just helped that younger part feel safe. That's leadership."
    ★ "You paused before reacting. That's the Adult Self beginning to guide."

    This helps clients reframe what adult capacities look like: not always having answers but showing up with care.

3. **Invite without insisting.** As with all parts work, we do not push. We might ask:

    ★ "Would it feel okay to ask if anyone inside feels calm enough to listen for a moment?"
    ★ "Is there a part who might be willing to help support the others right now?"

4. **Honor resistance and protection.** Some systems have parts who actively block the emergence of an Adult Self. These parts may fear loss of control, exposure, or failure. Rather than confronting these parts, we try to understand:

    ★ "What do you worry might happen if someone else leads?"
    ★ "It makes sense that no one feels adult right now. What would it look like to take one small step toward steadiness?"

    By respecting these parts, we create space for eventual collaboration.

5. **Support internal communication about leadership.** As the system stabilizes, you can help parts explore leadership together:

    ★ "What would it mean to have more than one part to help guide?"
    ★ "Is there someone who could hold perspective, even if they're not the strongest?"
    ★ "Could this be a shared effort instead of a solo one?"

    For many systems, leadership becomes a collaborative function, a collective agreement.

BARRIERS TO ADULT SELF DEVELOPMENT

In many dissociative systems, the Adult Self is not absent, it is unavailable. It may be blocked by fear, overwhelmed by chaos, or simply undeveloped because no one modeled what internal leadership could feel like. Common barriers include:

- **Protector parts who fear vulnerability:** Some parts may equate leadership with exposure or risk. If the Adult Self is associated with contacting feelings, slowing the pace, sharing control or tolerating uncertainty, protector parts may interpret this as dropping defenses and will block access to keep the system safe.
- **Shame-based systems:** Clients may feel "not grown enough", "not real", or fundamentally incapable. They may say things like, "I can't respond like an adult" or "There's no one that can do this". These beliefs often reflect early neglect or enmeshment.
- **Internal hostility or ridicule:** In systems with polarized parts that interact according to the rank system, any attempt at leadership may be mocked, attacked, or undermined internally. The idea of someone guiding the whole may feel threatening to other parts who have held control for survival.
- **Lack of relational experience:** Some clients have never experienced safe, attuned leadership from the outside. Without this modeling, it is hard to build it inside.

CLOSING THOUGHTS

Developing the Adult Self is not a prerequisite for healing; it is a result of healing. It emerges not from force or performance, but from repetition, relationship, and safety. It is cultivated through small, relational moments: a pause, a choice, a moment of care. It develops from moments of collaboration, with the therapist and between the parts, showing how the system of peer cooperation is the foundation for developing an Adult Self capable of metacognition and reflective awareness.

Therapists cannot assign leadership, nor can we make it happen. But we can model it. This modeling is not based on caretaking or the stimulation of attachment bonds, which in disorganized systems often increases dependency, confusion, or collapse. Rather, it relies on cognitive empathy, cooperative engagement, and metacognitive stance: staying curious without intrusion, responsive without rescue, and present without collapsing distance. These capacities allow the therapist to offer a relational experience that supports integration while maintaining the safety necessary for disorganized attachment to gradually reorganize.

It may not be polished or constant, but when even a brief experience of grounded presence becomes accessible inside, it marks the beginning of internal trust—not just between therapist and client, or part and part—but within the self, as a whole.

CLINICAL ANCHORS

WHAT TO REMEMBER...

- The Adult Self is a capacity to develop, not a part. It does not need to be identified or named to be supported.
- Integrative leadership is relational. It can be held by one part or shared across many.
- Notice and name small moments. Pausing, checking in, or reflecting are signs of emerging leadership.
- Validate difficulty. Many clients have no model for safe internal leadership. It is not resistance, it is unfamiliarity.
- Model calm, flexible presence. You are the client's first internal template.
- Support internal communication. Leadership often grows through collaborative reflection, not singular control.

WHAT TO AVOID...

- Idealizing or over-emphasizing the rapid development of the Adult.
- Using Adult Self language with clients.
- Shaming parts who interfere with leadership. They are usually protecting something vulnerable.
- Assigning leadership or labeling a part as the Adult Self without consent. This must come from the system, not from you.

Chapter 6: Attuning to the System's Many Languages

THERAPIST REFLECTION

At times, I find myself wanting to fill every silence or smooth discomfort with answers, yet I know the true expert in their inner world sits across from me. I remain open to all modes of expression: posture, tone, imagery, words, and silence; I serve as a translator, not a fixer. I shift from seeking answers to helping understand signals, weaving together the multiple languages of body and mind. Each time I honor these expressions, I help the system learn to speak, to listen, and to be understood.

Many clinicians feel confident engaging with parts once they appear in conversation, speaking clearly, offering insight, naming fears or needs. But what happens when a part does not speak at all? When the room fills with silence, tension, or confusion? When something is present, but not verbal?

One of the most important shifts in working with dissociative systems is understanding that not all parts use language and not all communication is verbal. Some parts never speak. Others cannot. Still others communicate through sensation, behavior, drawing, impulse, image, or relational dynamics.

This chapter explores the many ways parts communicate beyond words and how we, as therapists, can learn to listen with more than our ears. Learning the language of the system means expanding our awareness to include tone, movement, silence, imagery, affect, and relational shifts. It means letting go of pressure and making room for presence.

WHEN PARTS DO NOT SPEAK IN WORDS

Parts speak in many ways, not just words, and they may express themselves through:

- Body language: freezing, turning away, shifting posture.
- Somatic symptoms: pain, nausea, shaking, numbness.
- Impulses: fleeing, self-harming, hiding, needing to move.
- Images or symbols: internal spaces, colors, metaphors, fragments.
- Feelings or mood shifts: sudden shame, anger, collapse, or fear.
- Silence: refusal to speak, dissociation, absence.
- Drawings or writing: images that come through when words fail.

The therapist's role is to attune and help in translating inner experience. It is not about interpreting but about helping clients pay attention and figure out what the system is trying to communicate. We name what we observe with curiosity, and we make room for meaning to unfold.

★ "I noticed your posture changed just now. Does it feel like another part/aspect might be close?"
★ "Sometimes parts communicate through feelings or pictures instead of words. That's okay."
★ "Even silence can be communication. Maybe something needs more time or safety to emerge."

When we show that all communication is welcome, the system begins to trust.

Many clients come into therapy believing they must "do therapy right". Especially in dissociative systems, where being articulate or attuned to others' expectations was once a survival strategy, clients may try to perform what they think is expected. They might offer insights that sound mature but feel learned or repeated, or they might speak on behalf of parts they do not yet fully trust or understand.

Our task as therapists is to shift the focus from performance to presence. This means slowing down the pace, helping the client tune into what is happening inside, not what they believe should be happening. We can support this shift by:

- Inviting awareness of immediate sensations and emotions rather than cognitive interpretations.
- Modeling curiosity about vague, partial, or even contradictory experiences.
- Respecting that not all inner experiences can (or should) be verbalized right away.

Sometimes it is good to begin with simple acknowledgments:

- ★ "You don't have to explain it if that doesn't feel right. We can just sit with what's here."

WORKING WITH SILENCE AND SHUTDOWN

In many dissociative systems, silence is not resistance—it is communication. Silence can mean a part is watching, another might be assessing for danger and another feeling scared. It can also reflect a system's uncertainty about how their inner experience will be received. In these moments, process and presence matter more than content.

Therapists can hold space for the silence itself. Naming it respectfully, helps these parts of the system feel seen:

- ★ "I notice it feels quiet right now. It´s okay, this can be more silent work."
- ★ "It's okay if no one wants to speak. We can take a moment and share the silence together."

Sometimes, simply acknowledging silence as a valid form of participation is enough to reduce internal fear and soften defenses. When verbal communication feels too risky or complex, nonverbal forms of expression can offer a safer pathway into the work. Many systems find it easier to communicate through art, gesture, writing, or movement. These modalities bypass shame, allow for distance, and often access deeper emotional truth.

- ★ "Would it feel okay to draw how this part feels?"
- ★ "Could we use color or shape to show what it's like inside right now?"
- ★ "Sometimes people write letters to or from parts. No pressure, just a possibility."

These forms of expression allow the system to engage at a safer distance, especially early in treatment. Keep in mind that even when nothing is being said, the system is often communicating. Subtle shifts in posture, gaze, voice, energy, or emotional tone can signal the presence or influence of a part.

We might notice a change in the client's affect or tone of voice, a moment of sudden stillness, a flicker of emotion that seems unconnected to the current conversation, or perhaps a small physical gesture or shift in breathing.

Rather than interpreting these moments, we acknowledge or stay with them:

★ "Something seemed to shift. I wonder if that's worth noticing?"
★ "You looked away when we mentioned that. Should we slow down?"
★ "Are you okay if we notice and check in with that part inside?"

This kind of nuanced attunement builds trust, not only between therapist and client, but within the system itself. Over time, these small moments of reflection create a safe enough context with room for curiosity.

CLINICAL VIGNETTE

Listening Beyond Words

In early sessions, a client sat in near-total silence. Her posture was tense, gaze lowered, hands gripping the chair. When the therapist asked if something felt hard to speak about, she shook her head slightly but didn't respond. Rather than pushing, the therapist acknowledged, "It feels really quiet here. I wonder if someone's watching or waiting to see what happens." The client's eyes welled up. She whispered, "Someone's scared you'll get mad."

Clinical Reflections

This moment marked a turning point. The therapist's respectful naming of the silence, without interpreting or rushing, opened a door for a young part to feel seen. Over time, silence became less about shutdown and more about listening from within.

In the work with dissociative systems, what we offer through our presence often matters more than what we say. Clients may not remember our questions, but they will remember how we sat with their silence, how we responded to their uncertainty, and whether we stayed steady when things became unclear. A grounded therapist can become an internal model of safety — not through words alone, but through how we hold the space.

The most powerful intervention in this kind of work is often our presence: calm, curious, open to ambiguity, willing to stay without answers, reassuring and validating. You might say:

- "No rush here. Even if you don't have words, I'm still listening."
- "We can hold this together. You don't have to carry it alone."

COMMON CLINICAL PITFALLS

When a session falls into stillness, it can feel like an empty void, but often that silence carries more than words can bear. In those moments, a client's quiet may mean they are flooded with sensation or memory, unable to translate inner chaos into speech. Rather than trying to fill the gap, we invite that rich, unspoken terrain into the room and honor it as a doorway to deeper work.

Instead of insisting, "Tell me what you're feeling", we lean into a shared presence. We can suggest what usually helps clients, such as taking a deep breath and tracking shifts in posture or offering externalizing tools such as drawing instead of dialogue. This attunement reminds every part of the system that connection can happen beyond language.

When a part pushes back, refusing to engage, withdrawing, or acting out, it is important to remember that this points out difficulties, it is not *manipulative* or *resistant*. Those strategies were forged in moments when survival depended on shutting down or pushing away. By approaching each reaction with compassionate curiosity, we uncover the protective story beneath the behavior rather than colluding with shame.

Rather than expecting clarity, especially when the person can hardly think due to overwhelm, we keep in mind that some parts speak with images, sensations, or metaphors.

Although validation is important, we can unintentionally invalidate other parts when we single out certain parts as *helpful*. Every fragment of the personality, no matter how extreme, once carried and still carries an intention to protect or adapt. It is important not to dismiss a part's hard-earned role. Instead, we acknowledge each part's positive intent and welcome its voice with equal respect.

CLOSING THOUGHTS

Communication in dissociative systems is layered, symbolic, and often slow. What appears as silence or confusion on the surface may hold profound meaning underneath. When we let go of the need to interpret or fix, and instead offer steady presence, the therapeutic relationship becomes a bridge. Parts that were once hidden begin to show up in subtle ways. Emotions that once overwhelmed begin to soften. And trust starts to take root.

This chapter reminds us that words are only one form of language. Attunement is another. The more we honor the system's natural pace, the more we invite honest expression in whatever form it takes.

CLINICAL ANCHORS

WHAT TO REMEMBER...

- Begin with presence, not pressure. Connection precedes communication.
- Silence is not resistance. It often signals caution, protection, or observation.
- Language is not always verbal. Tune into posture, tone, rhythm, image, and pause.
- Trust shows up in small moments. Respect every effort, even if it is not spoken.
- Invite, do not interpret. Stay curious about what is showing up, not what is missing. There will be other moments for that.
- Parts may speak through behavior, gesture, metaphor, or absence. All are valid.
- Co-create new ways of relating. Include nonverbal options—drawing, writing, movement—and let the system lead the way.

WHAT TO AVOID...

- Assuming silence means absence rather than overwhelm.
- Forcing verbal expression instead of co-regulating nonverbally.
- Labeling defenses as manipulation or resistance.
- Expecting immediate, coherent explanations.

Chapter 7: Initial Contact with Inner System and Dissociative Parts

THERAPIST REFLECTION

I notice the client's rush to know all the answers and their discomfort with the unknown, and I notice my own pull for clarity—yet I welcome silence and follow cues to guide my pace. I remind myself this work is about process, not content. I stay present and patient, tuning into shifts in posture, voice, or energy. My curiosity makes space for the system's own. Letting contact unfold at its pace eases the need for quick answers and plants seeds for genuine exploration.

So far, we have explored how dissociative parts communicate in layered, often nonverbal ways, through posture, silence, sensation, image, or emotional shifts. Before parts speak, they often signal their presence, sometimes subtly and cautiously, other times more abruptly. This chapter turns to what happens next: those first moments of clearer contact.

FACILITATING INITIAL CONTACT

Once the therapeutic foundation has been laid with safety, respect, and steady presence, the next step involves facilitating initial contact with dissociative parts. These early encounters set the tone for how the system will experience therapy, not only the therapist, but also the idea of internal dialogue, collaboration, and change.

First contact is not always dramatic or verbal. It may come as a change of energy in the room, a shift in voice or gaze, or a sudden wave of emotion. It may emerge through a drawing, a pause, a phrase. Sometimes the client notices; other times, they are unsure, and many times, they try to ignore, reinforcing other ways of communicating from parts that are not so subtle. This is one of the main difficulties we will encounter.

Meeting parts for the first time can be a delicate and layered process. Some parts may step forward quickly, while others remain hidden or defensive. Some may appear eager to engage; others may mistrust the therapist, some parts or the client entirely. Rather than expecting clarity or full presentations, clinicians are encouraged to notice subtleties: shifts in posture, changes in tone, silences, images, sensations, or sudden changes in affect. These signals often point to the presence of a part, even when clients themselves are unsure of what is happening.

Our task is not to prompt or push, but to accompany. We meet what shows up with calm, grounded curiosity. These early moments lay the groundwork not only for the therapeutic alliance, but for the client's growing ability to witness and relate internally.

When we meet these encounters with steadiness and respect, we begin to earn the trust that makes deeper internal work possible.

RECOGNIZING THE PRESENCE OF A PART

The presence of dissociative parts is often subtle and nuanced. Parts do not usually introduce themselves with fanfare or clear names, and clients may avoid referencing them due to internal avoidance, shame, or fear. In fact, many clients are unaware that a shift has occurred. They may describe "feeling weird", "not like myself", or "blanking out". Others may notice a sudden emotion, thought, or urge that feels unfamiliar or disconnected from their usual sense of self. In more pronounced dissociative presentations, some clients may develop partial or full amnesia for the emergence or actions of another part, becoming aware only of the aftereffects or of gaps in experience.

The therapist's role is to attune to these moments, not to define or interpret, but to invite observation:

- ★ "I wonder what's happening inside right now. Sometimes when there's a shift like that, something inside might be stirring. What are you noticing?"

The goal is not to confront too directly or to introduce anything that the client has not already mentioned or experienced. Instead, we offer space. This becomes an invitation to notice, without pressure or assumption. Some clients may have difficulty talking about their inner experience because they worry about "being crazy" or fabricating what they feel. Rather than offering premature interpretations, therapists can affirm the validity of the experience itself:

- ★ "That sounds like it was really confusing. Let´s try to understand; what is happening inside."
- ★ "You're not doing anything wrong. We can stay with what's here, even if it's uncertain."

By validating the client's internal perception without labeling or defining it, we validate their experience while reducing shame. Presence and curiosity—not immediate explanation—become the first bridge to trust. Psychoeducation can be introduced once we have a clearer understanding of the system´s dynamics and where the client or the parts may be getting stuck.

Some parts may reveal themselves more directly, through speech, a shift in voice or posture, or the sudden expression of a distinct emotion or agenda. When this happens, our job as clinician is to remain calm, respectful, and grounded. No urgency. No alarm. Just a steady presence.

Even if the part appears angry, disruptive, or skeptical, our stance should remain consistent and curious. Rather than moving into open welcoming statements like, "I'm glad you're here. I'd like to get to know you, if that's okay", which may sound kind but can unintentionally encourage switching, we can respond with a grounding inquiry that keeps the broader system in view:

- ★ "What just happened? Why do you think *[client's name]* can't be here right now?"

This kind of questioning keeps the therapist oriented to the system as a whole and supports shared awareness, rather than reinforcing part-specific engagement. If a part seems cautious or reluctant, it is important to validate that experience:

- ★ "It makes sense you might be watching from a distance."
- ★ "You don't have to talk today. Just knowing you're here is important."

These responses help parts feel acknowledged in their autonomy and pace. The goal is not to make contact happen, but to allow it to unfold respectfully.

INTERNAL DYNAMICS

When other parts begin to emerge, parts functioning in daily life may experience discomfort, confusion, or resistance. They may feel embarrassed, frightened, overwhelmed, or even dismissive. These reactions are not barriers to the work; they *are* the work. Rather than pushing for acceptance, therapists are invited to explore these internal responses with compassion and curiosity.

You might say:

- ★ "It sounds like this part showing up is difficult for you."
- ★ "Do you notice what happens in your body when you feel that shift inside?"

Language like *host* or *main personality* is increasingly seen as outdated and can reinforce hierarchy within the system. Instead, we can refer to "the part that usually manages daily life", or "the one who spends the most time out front", always using the client's preferred language when available.

Rather than trying to harmonize the system too soon, early work often focuses on helping parts simply notice one another, to tolerate each other's presence without panic, rejection, or fusion. This process can be disorienting, even scary, and may surface grief, fear, or shame. The therapist's job is not to fix these dynamics, but to name them and hold them with patience and neutrality.

First contact with parts can be powerful and moving, but it also requires clear, consistent boundaries. When therapy is anchored through the Adult Self, it is less likely that parts will try to take over the session. Still, there may be moments when a part steps in more forcefully to test the therapist, to protect the system, or simply because internal regulation has not yet been established.

Rather than seeing this as resistance, therapists can meet it with grounded curiosity:

★ "I noticed something shifted. I wonder what this part needs right now. Is it okay if we slow down and check in with the part of you that's usually here too?"

Warm, steady structure helps create safety for the whole system:

★ "I'd like to hear from you, and I also want to make sure this feels okay for everyone inside. We'll go slowly. There's no rush, and you don't have to do anything alone."

If the session begins to feel overwhelming or disorganizing, the therapist's job is to anchor. Not to shut things down, but to create a safer frame. Invite a pause. Bring attention to the here and now. Use grounding tools such as, objects, breath, movement, or orientation, to support containment.

This is not avoidance; it is relational stewardship. Protecting the system from flooding or reenactment is not about control, it is about building trust through consistency, attunement, and pacing.

THERAPIST'S EMOTIONAL REACTIONS

First contact with parts can stir unexpected emotional responses in the therapist. You may feel protective, unsettled, confused, moved, even excited or overly engaged. These reactions are entirely human, but in this work, they must be tended to with care. Dissociative systems are exquisitely attuned to tone, subtle shifts, and unspoken dynamics. If the therapist becomes emotionally reactive in ways that are not named, it can reinforce internal distrust. Other parts may perceive it as pressure or threat.

The work calls for steadiness, and attunement over action. Maintain reflective awareness of your internal responses. Use supervision, consultation, and personal grounding practices to support your own regulation. It is not your job to rescue, convince, or interpret. Your task is to remain present and focused from moment to moment, even in moments of uncertainty or discomfort. In doing so, you become a reliable presence the system can begin to trust.

To put this into practice, notice how your emotional responses emerge in specific moments and how small adjustments in your stance can foster safety and trust. The following scenarios of protectiveness, over-identification, confusion and excitement illustrate typical therapist reactions alongside more regulated, reflective responses that uphold the Adult Self's leadership rather than override it.

- **Protectiveness**: A younger part emerges expressing fear and shame. The therapist feels an urgent wish to comfort and reassure: "I just want them to feel safe." While this instinct is compassionate, too much emotional intensity can overwhelm the system or bypass other parts who are wary. Remember that in disorganized attachment the person offering protection is the same person who generates the feeling of danger. A better response that reinforces safety without overreaching might be:
    - ★ "Thank you for sharing that. We'll go slowly, and I'll stay here with you."
- **Over-identification**: A part speaks with anger and insight that resonates strongly with the therapist's own personal history. The therapist feels pulled to join this part's perspective. This may unintentionally create imbalance and alienate other parts. A grounding reframe could be:
    - ★ "I hear how strongly you feel about this. I also want to make space for other parts, when and if they're ready."
- **Confusion or disorientation**: There's a sudden shift in the client's tone and posture, and the therapist is not sure what just happened. Instead of rushing to interpret or hiding confusion, therapists can name it with humility:
    - ★ "I noticed something shifted just now. I'm not sure what that is, but I'm here with you. We can notice it together."
- **Excitement or emotional investment**: A part who has never spoken before starts to engage. The therapist feels a wave of enthusiasm and hope, and responds with, "This is amazing! You're doing so well!" While well-meaning, this may feel too fast or too much to the system. A more regulated stance might be:
    - ★ "I appreciate your willingness to be here. We can take this moment slowly."

Therapists do not need to be perfect, but they do need to be attuned. Your role is not to rescue, convince, or interpret parts into coherence.

Your task is to witness, accompany, and remain available, even in moments of uncertainty or complexity. In doing so, you become a reliable presence the system can begin to trust.

SUPPORTING THE SYSTEM AFTER CONTACT

After a part shows up in session, even briefly, it is important to check in before closing. These encounters can leave the client feeling confused, disoriented, vulnerable, or ashamed. Some may have little or no memory of what occurred; others might quickly minimize it, unsure of how to make sense of what happened.

Use grounding language to help orient the client:

★ "How are things feeling inside now? Sometimes parts step forward and then step back; that's okay."

Closing the session with containment and reassurance helps regulate the system and builds trust over time. Invite the client to re-ground with small, familiar rituals: movement, breath, orienting to the room, or simply noting what feels most present now.

Offer validating, normalizing language that supports understanding:

★ "This is part of the process. You're not doing anything wrong. Even when it feels confusing, your system is responding in the ways it knows how."

It is essential to remember that therapy with parts is not linear. Some sessions may include clear moments of contact; others may feel quiet or distant. That does not mean nothing is happening. Some dissociative parts are always listening, always watching, as long as this is needed. Consistency in your presence—calm, respectful, attuned—speaks louder than any technique.

COMMON CLINICAL PITFALLS

One of the most frequent pitfalls in early work with dissociative parts is **moving too quickly**. Whether driven by the therapist's curiosity or the client's eagerness to "get better", this rush can lead to premature attempts at contact or dialogue before the system feels stable or safe.

When this happens, what may look like therapeutic engagement can be **surface-level compliance**. On the other hand, interpreting or trying to define too soon can interfere with the client's opportunities to curiously notice what happens. Building collaborative awareness happens gradually with questions such as,

- ★ "What are you noticing inside right now?"

Therapists must also stay aware and be able to appreciate defensive strategies from parts; these should be understood as a way of pacing and protecting. Trying to speed up the process, bypass protector parts or trying to convince them, will activate or deepen distrust.

CLINICAL VIGNETTE

I'm Afraid You'll Think I'm Crazy

A client arrives visibly anxious, hands clenched, eyes darting. She speaks quickly, apologizing repeatedly before saying anything of substance. "I almost didn't come today", she says. "I don't know how to explain what's happening. It sounds... weird."

The therapist notices a subtle shift, her shoulders lift, her breath shortens, as she says this. Rather than asking for details, the therapist slows the pace.

"We don't have to explain anything yet", they say. "Can we just notice what it's like inside right now, as you say that?"

The client hesitates. "There's this pressure in my chest. And then I kind of go blank."

She looks embarrassed. "This is the part where people think I'm making it up."

The therapist does not introduce parts language, nor reassure excessively. "That sounds confusing and uncomfortable." "Let's stay with the pressure for a moment. You are doing great."

As the session continues, the client's voice softens briefly, then tightens again. She does not name a part, and the therapist does not ask her to. Instead, the therapist tracks the rhythm of approach and retreat, occasionally reflecting: "It seems like something wants to be noticed, and something else is worried about that."

By the end of the session, no clear part has spoken. There is no breakthrough moment. But the client leaves saying, quietly, "This is the first time I didn't feel rushed to explain."

Clinical reflection:

Early contact did not require identifying or engaging a dissociative part directly. Safety was built through pacing, validation of uncertainty, and adapting to the client's pacing, allowing the system to register that curiosity and lower the alert.

Another subtle but significant misstep is **encouraging or reinforcing switching** without realizing, statements like "I'm glad you're here" may sound adequate and welcoming but can inadvertently send the message that this is expected and positive, when switching is a response of the system when the client cannot cope. Orienting the Adult Self towards noticing and being curious about the inner system as a whole, asking more general inclusive questions helps build trust.

- ★ "What just happened?"
- ★ "Is it okay if we slow this down together?"

Language itself is an essential part of therapeutic pacing. Terms like *host*, *main personality*, or *real self* are not only outdated but can reinforce hierarchy or internal conflict and separation. Using client-preferred inclusive terms helps all parts feel respected, especially those watching from the sidelines.

Finally, therapists must **not assume that meaningful contact will look verbal or overt**. Dissociative parts often communicate through energy, posture, sensation, or images. When therapists expect words, they may miss the other levels of communication that are already taking place.

CLOSING THOUGHTS

Meeting dissociative parts is not a one-time event; it is the beginning of a relational process. Each part is like a guest approaching a door, uncertain whether they will be welcomed, rejected, or misunderstood. The therapist's task is not to open that door forcefully, but to keep it gently open, offering steadiness, respect, and patience.

First contact is not a breakthrough, it is a start. When met with calm presence and curiosity, these early moments lay the foundation for internal collaboration. Even the quietest, most hesitant parts may one day move toward connection, not because they were pushed, but because they felt safe enough to emerge.

Clinical Anchors

What to remember...

- Attune to subtle communication: parts often speak through shifts in posture, energy, tone, or sensation rather than words.
- ·Invite noticing, not interpreting; stay curious about what is emerging without assigning meaning too soon.
- Go slow: presence matters more than progress. Trust builds through pacing and consistency.
- Use inclusive, system-oriented language. Ask, "What just happened?" or "Is this okay for everything inside?"
- Normalize uncertainty. Not knowing is part of the process, for both client and therapist.
- End with care. Leave time to check in and ground before closing the session.

What to avoid...

- Rushing can activate protectors or create surface-level compliance.
- Overinterpreting. Defining parts too soon can short-circuit the client's own meaning-making.
- Forcing collaboration. Respect parts' right to observe, decline, or remain silent.
- Eager welcoming that encourages switching. "I'm glad you're here" may bypass system safety.
- Taking sides. Avoid labeling parts as good/bad, cooperative/resistant.

Chapter 8: Exploring and Mapping the Internal System

THERAPIST REFLECTION

Whenever I catch myself wanting to pinpoint parts, I remind myself this work unfolds slowly and relationally. I invite the client to explore from within, noticing shifts in emotion, posture or voice without rushing to name or fix. I pay attention to any changes, no matter how subtle they might seem. I explore guided by curiosity, patience and openness, trusting that discovery unfolds in its own time. By modeling this stance, I help the client learn to approach their internal world with genuine care and curiosity.

As clients begin to notice distinct internal experiences, through shifts in emotion, behavior, posture, or voice, the therapeutic work can gradually expand to include exploring the system from within. This is not a hunt for parts or a push for clarity, but a slow, relational unfolding—discovering what is there without rushing to name or fix it.

EXPLORING VS MAPPING THE SYSTEM

Exploring the system means becoming curious about internal patterns, protective responses, emotional rhythms, and the roles different parts may play. It is a process guided by attunement and led by what the system is ready to reveal. In some clients, parts come forward clearly and distinctly. In others, the inner world remains more diffuse, cautious, or hidden. All of it is welcome, it is information to keep in mind and understand.

Mapping may emerge organically as a secondary step—not so much to define the system, but to help both client and therapist orient within it. Think of mapping as creating a gentle outline, a sketch that brings just enough shape to support awareness. This might look like noting familiar patterns ("The one who always interrupts when I cry"), building metaphors ("They feel like they're in different rooms"), or sensing internal relationships ("He watches but does not talk").

We are not charting terrain to tag it; we are holding space so the client can begin to inhabit it more fully. Rather than pushing for answers, we help clients notice:

- ★ "What part tends to show up when I feel unsafe?"
- ★ "What happens inside when I feel emotionally close or connected to someone?"
- ★ "Why does this reaction feel so out of proportion or not mine at all?"

These inquiries mark the shift from conflict to curiosity and from chaos to internal relationship.

When held with flexibility and warmth, exploring, and gently mapping the internal system becomes a form of internal respect, being curious about all that is present while gradually organizing an often contradictory and confusing inner experience. It is less about getting every detail *right* and more about making room for what is emerging. Every part holds a history. Every role developed for a reason. Our work is to walk alongside that unfolding, with patience and care. It is about getting a glimpse into how clients represent their inner experience and making sense of it gradually, without needing all the answers.

INTRODUCING THE MAPPING PROCESS

Mapping the system is less about figuring out who is inside or how many parts are exactly there, and more about making space for parts to be seen, named, or described if and when they are ready. For some clients, this may come naturally. For others, the idea of having parts may still feel strange, shameful, or unreal. Rather than introducing the concept as a task, we begin gently:

- ★ "I wonder if there are familiar patterns or ways of being that show up in different situations."
- ★ "Does it feel like there's a part of you that always wants to shut things down? What would we call that part, just for now?"

★ "Sometimes people notice an inner team, or different parts of them that show up in different moments. Does that feel at all familiar?"

We follow the client's language and pacing. Some may name their parts; others may describe roles, energies, images, or simply "the one who always...". We are not correcting or analyzing, we are listening for how clients experience themselves.

Not every system is ready to be mapped—and not every system needs to. Early exploration may look more like getting to know the terrain than plotting it. The client begins to recognize that certain responses, behaviors, or emotions may belong to different internal parts, even if those parts are unnamed or blurry.

This exploration can include:

- Naming feelings or patterns without pressure to link them to specific parts.
- Noticing internal responses to certain people, themes, or memories.
- Gently wondering about shifts in tone, body, or emotion.

Mapping can begin informally: a drawing, a journal entry, or a simple chart with phrases like:

❖ "The one who watches everything."
❖ "The one who panics when I get close."
❖ "The quiet one who does not speak but is always there."

These dissociative fragments, when gathered over time, offer both therapist and client a sense of the system's inner architecture, not as fixed, but as living and relational.

USE OF CREATIVE AND SYMBOLIC TOOLS

Exploring and mapping the internal world does not have to be verbal or cognitive. Many systems respond better to metaphor, symbol, or nonverbal expression. Clients might draw a house, a landscape, a control panel, or a set of figures. They might use animals, colors, or elements to represent different parts.

These representations can become:

- Anchors for internal communication.
- Soothing alternatives to direct dialogue.
- Ways to visualize distance, roles, or relationships.

The therapist might ask:

★ "If your inner system were a room, who might be near the door? Who stays hidden?"
★ "What image comes to mind when you think of the one who shuts things down?"
★ "Would it feel okay to give that part a symbol or name that only you understand?"

There is no single or correct method. Systems express themselves in highly personal ways, and the mapping process should reflect that diversity. What is most important is that the approach feels accessible and safe to the client. The aim is to support internal recognition, in whatever language feels safest.

Some possibilities include:

- **Descriptive lists.** Clients may create a simple list of known parts, aspects, roles, or internal experiences using their own language and tone.

- **Drawings or diagrams.** Some clients find it helpful to sketch how parts relate: who feels close, who stays distant, who interacts, and who remains unknown or in the background.

- **Metaphors or internal system.** Clients may describe an inner house, a set of rooms, a battlefield, or a school, each representing aspects of the internal system. These metaphors often emerge spontaneously and can become anchoring tools for exploration.

- **Timelines.** Occasionally, it is helpful to map when different parts developed, especially in relation to specific life events or survival needs. Use timelines only when they serve a clear purpose. In complex systems, they can overwhelm or oversimplify if introduced too early.

- **Action figures (e.g., Playmobil), puppets, or other symbolic objects.** For clients who feel deeply phobic of their inner experience, selecting figures to represent different parts can be safer than looking inward. This method externalizes the work and provides a buffer that protects against emotional flooding.

As clients grow more comfortable with exploring the system tools, we can resort to more interactive ways of exploring such as inner meetings where parts can begin to communicate in different ways. This can be guided by the therapist and staged as needed.

One approach to explore is the Meeting Place Procedure (Gonzalez, Mosquera, & Solomon, 2012), a guided imagery procedure developed to foster internal communication and understanding dissociative systems. Building on earlier proposals like Internal Group Therapy (Caul, 1984), the Dissociative Table Technique (Fraser, 1991, 1993), and the Conference Room (Paulsen, 1995, 2009), this method differs in a key way. The Adult Self remains outside the meeting, acting as an observer and mediator. All interventions are directed through this Adult Self, rather than through a part within the system.

The process begins with the client visualizing a comfortable, safe internal meeting space, which could include a table and chairs or any setting that feels welcoming. Through guided imagery, all parts or inner voices are invited to enter. Participation is optional; parts may speak, observe, or remain silent. No one is forced to engage. The therapist supports this by asking questions such as:

- ★ "What is this space like?"
- ★ "How many seats do you see?"
- ★ "Who is occupying them?"

These tools are meant to be flexible, adapted to client and moment, not used as fixed templates. They shift as the internal world becomes more accessible and as trust deepens, both within the system and in the therapeutic relationship. We are not trying to define the system, but to accompany it with curiosity, care, and a willingness to follow rather than lead. The map is not the goal, understanding is.

FROM MAPPING TO SHIFTING INTERNAL AWARENESS

As understanding happens, maps can begin to take shape and represent inner dynamics, not only the ones that were known but the changes that have started to happen with this work. Clients may begin to notice:

- Protective patterns (who steps in and when).
- Conflicts or alliances between parts.
- Isolated or silent parts who do not yet feel safe to engage.
- Repeated triggers or relational themes.

This increased awareness helps reduce confusion. A client who once felt "all over the place" may begin to see that their responses make sense, once understood through the lens of parts and protection.

Mapping also helps the Adult Self or internal leadership begin to take shape, as clients start to observe and notice what happens inside rather than being overwhelmed by it and trying to ignore it.

REVISITING THE MAP OVER TIME

As therapy progresses, the system may shift. Parts who were once silent may begin to engage; others may step back. Internal relationships evolve, and this is expected.

Revisiting a map over time can become a powerful clinical anchor. Visual changes—such as shifts in posture, proximity, or how parts are represented (lighter, clearer, smaller, or larger)—often reflect meaningful movement toward integration. Even subtle changes in the inner system can offer both therapist and client a shared sense that something is unfolding, often before it can be fully named.

In general, it can be useful to ask for a new drawing—or whichever tool is being used—rather than working directly with older representations. This protects against unintentionally introducing ideas that may no longer reflect the system's current reality. However, later in the therapy process, it can be valuable to revisit earlier representations with the client, especially to explore how they now make sense of what has changed.

Some prompts might include:

- ★ "Has anything changed inside since we first explored this?"
- ★ "Are there parts who feel differently now about being seen?"

★ "Is there anything new showing up, even if it's just a feeling or sensation?"

This reinforces the idea that the system is alive, not a puzzle to be solved, but a set of relational dynamics to be understood, accompanied, and respected.

Keep in mind that for some clients, even the idea of mapping may feel invasive or overwhelming. It can trigger protective parts, invite shame, or raise fears of being *figured out*. In these cases, we slow down. There is no rush to define who is inside.

We respect:

- Parts who do not want to be seen yet.
- Clients who say, "I don't know who's here... it just feels like chaos."
- Parts who fear being exposed.

The invitation remains open. This normalizes uncertainty and prioritizes safety over clarity.

★ "We don't need to know who, just that something is happening inside. That´s a meaningful place to start."

COMMON CLINICAL PITFALLS

In the effort to foster connection and cooperation, we may fall into patterns that undermine the very safety we are trying to build. One of the most frequent pitfalls is **trying to make things happen too quickly**, prompting dialogue, encouraging internal cooperation, or orchestrating encounters before the system is ready. While this may come from a place of therapeutic hope or urgency, it can backfire, intensifying mistrust or prompting shutdowns.

As mentioned before, another common error is **taking sides**, even subtly, in internal conflicts. When one part expresses distress and another reacts protectively, or even harshly, it is easy to align with the part that appears more vulnerable. But this dynamic reinforces hierarchy within the system and risks alienating protectors who are often acting from a place of trauma-informed caution. All parts need to feel heard, not managed.

CLINICAL VIGNETTE

Clinical Moments that Signal the Need to Slow Down

The following brief clinical moments illustrate how attempts to explore or map the internal system can inadvertently move ahead of readiness. They are examples of signals that the system is protecting itself. These moments help us slow down, step back, and adapt pacing and language to the client´s needs.

1) Performance instead of presence

A client eagerly presents a detailed internal map after only a few sessions, naming multiple parts and roles. While describing it, she repeatedly checks the therapist's reaction and asks, "Does this make sense?" When invited to notice how it felt to create the map, she pauses and says, "Not sure I did it right, I think this is what I'm supposed to do, it´s what my previous therapist asked me to do too."

Clinical reflection: Apparent clarity may reflect compliance or performance rather than genuine internal contact. Returning to felt experience helps restore authenticity.

2) Protective refusal to map

When invited to draw or describe her internal system, a client shrugs and says, "There's nothing there. It's just chaos." Her body stiffens and her breathing becomes shallow.

Clinical reflection: Refusal is meaningful information. The system may not yet feel safe enough to be explored. Mapping is deferred while trust and regulation are strengthened.

3) Premature naming that freezes exploration

After a client describes a sudden surge of anger, the therapist suggests, "That sounds like an angry protector." The client becomes quiet, averts her gaze, and says, "I don't want to do this anymore."

Clinical reflection: Naming too quickly can interfere with curiosity and activate protective withdrawal. Staying with description rather than definition keeps exploration open.

4) Assuming internal familiarity

A client describes two conflicting impulses when trying to explain the conflict she notices inside, one pushing forward, another pulling back. When asked how those parts relate to each other, she looks genuinely confused and replies: "They don't know about each other."

Clinical reflection: Internal separation and lack of awareness are often protective. Therapists should not assume communication or familiarity between parts.

These moments remind us that mapping is not a goal to be achieved, but a process that unfolds in the therapeutic relationship. When the system hesitates, resists, or goes quiet, the work is not to push forward, but to listen more carefully to what that response is saying or protecting.

Another common trap is **misreading difficulties** in mapping or describing parts. This may reflect limits in awareness, or the presence of one or more parts that refuse engagement, withhold information, or actively oppose communication. If we interpret this as obstruction or intentioned avoidance, we will be missing the point. It is an expression of loyalty, duty, or survival. Instead of pushing through protection, the work is to understand and honor it, inviting trust through pacing and presence rather than persuasion.

Similarly, confusing silence for absence can lead us to overlook moments of contact that are nonverbal but deeply meaningful. In this type of work, we may also feel compelled to *fix* conflict between parts, especially when strong emotions or impasses arise. Instead, the task is to understand why the conflict is showing up and what for, i.e. what it is protecting. If we try to move too quickly to resolve internal disagreements, this might override the trust-building process that was beginning to take place, which is the goal of these interventions.

CLOSING THOUGHTS

Mapping the internal system is not about certainty, it is about making space for exploration. When clients begin to see their inner world with more clarity and less shame, something fundamental shifts. Chaos gives way to coherence. Fear makes room for recognition. And relationships, both internal and external, begin to improve.

This work is not about discovering who is in charge or labeling who is who. It is about honoring the internal experience and building trust with the parts that exist, even those still in hiding. With patience, presence, and permission, the map becomes clearer and more coherent. And the system becomes just a little more known to itself, and to you.

Clinical Anchors

What to remember...

- Mapping is a relational process, it is not static.
- Use the client's language, images, symbols, and pacing.
- Stay curious, we are exploring to understand, not to find certainty
- Model internal respect and support Adult Self leadership gradually.
- Pacing *is* the intervention. When multiple internal reactions are activated, clients often need time for regulation and meaning-making before any further movement is possible.
- Externalizing tools such as drawing, journaling, action figures, or inner meetings can support safer access.
- Invite clients to notice different internal perspectives without needing to take sides.
- Expect changes in representation. Parts may shift, change roles, merge, or go quiet over time. That is part of the process.
- Welcome and validate resistance; trust the system's protective timing.
- Watch for performance in confused individuals.

What to avoid...

- Pushing for names. Some parts do not have names or clearly developed first person perspectives. Do not complicate it more than necessary.
- Trying to capture every part or every dynamic.
- Assigning roles and labeling instead of understanding the function.
- Do not assume familiarity between parts, some parts are unaware of each other due to protective barriers or amnesia.
- Mistaking silence or avoidance as resistance. Some clients and parts need time to communicate differently. This is one way of communicating too.

Chapter 9: Building Relationships Within the System

THERAPIST REFLECTION

I notice the pull to orchestrate which parts should meet or collaborate, to rush the system toward harmony. But I remind myself that the Adult Self must lead, staying curious, patient, and open to whatever emerges in the moment. When I feel the urge to label or classify, I shift my focus to function over form and invite dialogue only when it arises naturally or when we've hit an impasse that calls for cooperation. My aim is to witness and describe what I observe without doing too much, holding a neutral, steady presence even as conflict flares so that trust and collaboration can grow from the inside out.

As clients begin to map their inner system and notice who is present and what roles or functions they hold, a natural next question arises. How do these parts relate to one another? Naturally, the therapeutic focus begins to shift from identification to relationship. Recognizing a part is one thing. Learning to relate to that part, or supporting parts in relating to each other, brings a new layer of complexity, vulnerability, and potential for growth.

In this chapter, we move from understanding the client´s representation of their inner world to helping them communicate, navigate conflict, and eventually be held and lead by an emerging Adult Self. We will explore how to cultivate those emerging relationships; offering invitations to notice each other, pay attention and listen, even when understanding feels far away. This will become the essential process of fostering respect, communication, and collaboration over time.

NOTICING INTERNAL RELATIONAL PATTERNS

As clients begin to recognize and connect with their dissociative parts, the therapeutic work gently shifts from establishing contact to cultivating relationship and cooperation. First appearances, such as a flash of emotion, a sudden urge, or a change in voice, eventually give way to something deeper: internal presence, mutual awareness, and, when safety allows, communication.

These relationships are complex. Some parts know each other or of each other; others remain completely unaware or intentionally hidden. Some are fiercely protective, others tentative and silent. The therapist's role at this stage is not to orchestrate these connections, but to hold space for them; helping clients notice, name, and eventually relate to the many internal voices and needs that exist within.

This work unfolds slowly. It is not about getting all the parts to get along but about creating enough safety and respect inside the system for each voice to gradually be heard, even if the message is painful, confused, or full of fear.

Early relational work involves helping clients begin to sense the dynamics between parts, who knows who, who is close or distant, who watches but does not speak. Many clients describe having a vague awareness of other parts being "somewhere in the background", or they may speak of internal figures they try to avoid. Some may be surprised when a part they have come to know is unfamiliar to another part in the system.

Gently and without pressure, therapists can support this exploration. It may begin with a question as simple as:

- ★ "I wonder if this part knows about the one that came up last week?"
- ★ "Are there parts who don't feel safe being around each other yet?"

This is not about classification, but about listening. It can be subtle and nonverbal noticing how a client's tone shifts when talking about different parts, or how their posture tightens when one is mentioned. These reactions often tell us more than words.

Understanding internal relationships also means understanding disconnection. Sometimes, a protector part may deliberately block a more vulnerable part. Other times, amnesia barriers make it impossible for parts to know each other's experiences. Keep in mind there are good, protective reasons for that.

FOSTERING RESPECTFUL INTERNAL DIALOGUE

When internal communication begins to feel possible, the therapist can support safe, contained ways for parts to *talk* to one another. This does not always mean a verbal conversation. It might start with noticing or allowing one part to feel that another is nearby. It might take the form of imagery, journaling, symbolic gestures, or body sensations. The method is less important than the tone: respectful, curious, and non-intrusive.

Metaphors can be useful here, a roundtable, a walkie-talkie system, a set of rooms in a house. These images help externalize internal dynamics, making them easier to explore.

Consent is key. Just as we do not force a client to speak before they are ready, we do not push parts to engage with each other before trust is present. The question is always:

- ★ "Would it be okay to let this part know that another part is feeling scared?"
- ★ "Could this part be willing to just listen, nothing more?"

By keeping the invitations small and respectful, we reduce the threat and reinforce the system's curiosity and cooperation.

MANAGING INTERNAL CONFLICT

It is not uncommon for parts to dislike each other, sometimes intensely. Clients may report arguments, interruptions, or parts trying to erase each other's presence. Some protector parts may dismiss or ridicule younger parts; others may try to shut down therapy altogether.

The therapist's stance is to hold space with steadiness, curiosity, and consent. Remember not to take sides but to help each part feel heard, knowing that every part is trying to help, even if their strategies clash.

You can hold any conflict that arises with curiosity:

- ★ "It sounds like this part does not trust what the other is trying to do."
- ★ "Maybe both parts want safety, but they have very different strategies."

Conflict often softens when parts begin to feel truly seen. Sometimes, helping each one understand that the other is not trying to harm, but to protect, can shift the energy inside. Other times, it takes weeks or months of containment and repetition before this can be noticed or introduced or for trust to begin to form.

CLINICAL VIGNETTE

Naming Without Taking Sides

A man in mid-treatment, aware of multiple parts but overwhelmed by conflict between them. During a session, one part expressed disgust toward another that "falls apart all the time", and the client began to get blocked.

The therapist slowed the session and reflected, "It sounds like one part is very upset with another, and maybe another part is pulling away altogether."

The client nodded and said, "Yeah... it's like there's a war in here, and I'm the one stuck in the middle." The therapist replied, "And maybe noticing that without having to fix it, is already a way of staying connected to all sides."

Clinical Reflections

This intervention helped the client stay engaged without collapsing into one position or another and created a shift. Over time, naming the tension became safer, and parts became more willing to acknowledge each other's roles and function, even when they still disagreed.

WHEN PARTS RESIST COLLABORATION

Not all parts want to work together. Some fear exposure, betrayal, or annihilation. Others believe that therapy threatens the very function they have been carrying for years. Such parts may resist collaboration out of loyalty to early attachment figures, to internalized relational rules, or to the survival roles they assumed in response to danger. They may also feel a sense of duty toward protecting younger parts, maintaining family secrets, preserving bonds, or preventing anticipated catastrophe.

From this perspective, resistance is a sign of trauma wisdom, the system's way of ensuring survival. As commented in other chapters, rather than pushing through it, we identify and put words to it:

- ★ "It sounds like this part isn't sure that working together is safe."
- ★ "We can go slowly. Nothing needs to happen today."

Just as clients need time to build trust with the therapist, parts need time to build trust with each other. Forcing connection too soon can backfire. Instead, we keep returning to steadiness, patience, and the invitation to move at the system's pace.

CLINICAL VIGNETTE

Respecting the No

A young woman with a highly protective part who refused all internal dialogue. When the therapist asked if it might be okay to let a part know she was safe, another part responded abruptly: "That's not going to happen. She'll ruin everything."

Instead of trying to mediate, the therapist simply said, "Thank you for letting me know. It makes sense you'd want to protect things by keeping them separate. That feels important."

For the first time, the protector part didn't shut down or interrupt the work. The client later shared, "He stayed, even if he didn't say much more."

Clinical Reflections

That moment—being respected in his "No"—built a foundation of trust for future work.

SUPPORTING THE CLIENT AS A BRIDGE

As internal relationships begin to emerge, the client is increasingly invited to take an active role as a bridge, not just the one experiencing parts, but the one capable of holding perspective and presence within the system. This is where the Adult Self begins to participate more fully: observing without being pulled, staying near without needing to control.

Again, this role is not about taking sides or managing conflict. It is about making space for complexity, noticing when parts are in distress, when others react protectively, and offering an internal tone of steadiness that mirrors the therapist's stance.

Bridging moments can be subtle: a client pausing to reflect on two internal perspectives; noticing a younger part's fear while also sensing another part´s urgency; choosing to stay present rather than distancing.

These might seem like small acts but are foundational steps in cultivating internal relationship.

Internal contact is rarely neutral. As parts notice and respond to one another, the emotional impact can be intense; grief, shame, tenderness, or fear may surface. These are signs that the system is alive and listening. Our task is not to soothe or direct, but to stay alongside, affirming that these moments matter, as they quietly support the process of integration.

CLINICAL VIGNETTE

A Bridge Begins to Form

A woman with a complex dissociative system, early in therapy, who had recently begun recognizing distinct parts after months of groundwork. A younger part expressed sadness in session, and shortly after, a protector part interrupted, saying the sadness was pointless and weak.

Rather than siding with one part or trying to mediate the conflict, the therapist turned to the client and asked, "Is there a part of you that can notice both what just happened, the sadness, and the reaction to it, without needing to take sides?""

The client paused, then said quietly, "I think there's a me who gets why she's sad... and also gets why the other one is scared of that." The therapist reflected, "That sounds like a bridge, a part of you that can stay close to both without getting pulled under."

Clinical Reflections

This moment was subtle, but it marked a turning point. Over the next few sessions, the client began referring to the one who watches and cares, a part that did not fix or control, but helped hold space. What emerged was the early voice of an Adult Self, hesitant but present enough to begin linking the system from within.

COMMON CLINICAL PITFALLS

One of the most frequent missteps is the **urge to push for harmony too soon**, to push towards an early use of the peer cooperation System. Whether driven by therapeutic intention or discomfort with internal conflict, this rush can override the system's pacing, missing opportunities to understand. Collaboration between parts cannot be forced; attempts to elicit dialogue or consensus prematurely may provoke withdrawal, shutdown, or escalate tension between parts who do not yet feel safe or are still needing help with time orientation.

Another subtle pitfall is **framing conflict as something to be solved rather than something to be understood.** When therapists move too quickly to mediate or fix, they may inadvertently align with one part's agenda. This disrupts neutrality and can reinforce existing internal hierarchies (rank) or fears (defense) What helps instead is affirming and reminding that all parts are trying to protect, even when strategies conflict, and holding a steady presence that allows each voice to be heard in its own time.

Therapists may also underestimate the power of silence, **misreading a lack of overt communication as resistance or disengagement**. Yet often, early internal contact is nonverbal, felt in tone, posture, or energy; all these cues offer valuable information about the system's readiness and relational dynamics. Speaking too much, interpreting too quickly, or rushing to name what is unfolding can interfere and inadvertently impose meaning where reflection is still forming.

At times, **the therapist's own emotional responses** can become another source of pressure. The desire to rescue, soothe, or resolve may emerge when faced with a client's internal distress or polarization (Caregiving System activated in therapist). But acting on these urges, rather than noticing and regulating them, can subtly shift the focus away from the client's own development, and possibly activate fears related to disorganized attachment.

Finally, therapists may **conflate disconnection with defiance**. When parts resist contact or deny each other's presence, it may be tempting to interpret this as obstruction. In truth, such difficulties just reflect protective strategies shaped by trauma. Approaching these dynamics with respect for internal timing and autonomy is essential; therapists being able to say "no" to these impulses can be one of the most important pieces of our work.

CLOSING THOUGHTS

Helping a client build internal relationships is important work that must first be modeled by the therapist. It is about more than communication. It is about trust, repair, and reclaiming connection after fragmentation. This process rarely unfolds quickly, and it does not always happen smoothly. Yet each respectful encounter between parts lays a brick in the foundation of cooperation, collaboration, and healing.

Our job as therapists is not to make these relationships happen but to support the conditions in which they might emerge. We model Adult Self capacities for mindful noticing with steadiness, patience, and guidance. We become a trusted presence in a system that has often learned to expect danger. And over time, that presence becomes something the system can lean into, and eventually, internalize as a new way to relate to self and other parts.

Clinical Anchors

What to remember...

- Internal relationship work is relational, not procedural. Connection grows through presence, not pressure.
- Treat every interaction between parts with consent and care, nothing is required, everything is invited.
- Use external metaphors to support internal exploration (roundtable, walkie-talkies, rooms, teams).
- Validate internal conflict as meaningful. Every part is trying to help, even when strategies clash.
- Support the client in bridging, not fixing.
- Return repeatedly to safety, pacing, and permission. Trust takes time, especially inside.

What to avoid...

- Fixing or letting your own discomfort drive the pace.
- Pushing for cooperation or dialogue too soon. Respect why parts might resist or fear connection.
- Filling the silence or rescuing.
- Rushing towards clarity. Let it unfold.
- Ignoring nonverbal signs.
- Interpreting lack of collaboration or conflict as resistance.

Chapter 10: Building Trust with Fight-Based Protective Parts

THERAPIST REFLECTION

I notice tension rising when a protector part challenges the pace or questions my intentions. I pause, breathe, and check whether I am holding space without judgment. I remind myself that this part's control grew from a history of threat and that my steadiness, calm presence, and genuine curiosity are the first acts of inclusion I can offer. Only then can I clarify my true intentions, so they are heard and understood.

All dissociative parts serve a protective function. However, some parts, particularly those inclined toward fight, control, dominance, hostility, or aggression, can be more difficult for both therapists and clients to understand. This is often because their strategies closely resemble the environment in which the person grew up, or because their very formation is rooted in that context.

In this final chapter of Part 1, our focus is how to develop trust with all parts, emphasizing clinical stance, which forms the foundation of therapeutic work. Therapists can learn a variety of tools, techniques, and protocols, but what ultimately makes these effective is our stance and the quality of our management of transference and countertransference. Later, in Part 2 of this book, one by one we will examine the similarities and differences among these parts, exploring their origins, characteristics, and functions.

The first aspect to keep in mind for our work to be effective is that these protective parts are not obstacles to healing, they are central to it. Their strategies may seem disruptive, but their presence signals wisdom: they remember danger. They have learned that vulnerability can lead to harm. and they often expect therapy itself to become a threat.

The therapist's task is not to override these parts, but to understand them and, in time, earn their trust. Protective parts hold keys to stability, safety, and long-term collaboration within the system. When they feel included, therapy moves forward. When they feel bypassed or blamed, therapy stalls.

UNDERSTANDING THE FUNCTION BEHIND A STRATEGY

Protective parts do not act out of spite. They act out of memory, of chaos, betrayal, threat, and helplessness. Their strategies may look aggressive or rigid, and their modes of interaction are those aimed at dominance and control, distrust and contempt, typical of the rank system; yet underneath is usually a message like: "If I don't stop this, we'll get hurt again."

And that *again* is not metaphorical. For many protector parts, the threat feels present and immediate. They are often stuck in trauma time: a felt sense that the danger has not ended, that the system is still under siege, and that safety is an illusion. In that context, their strategies, even when extreme, are attempts to survive.

These parts may punish, silence, avoid, or control. They might use substances, provoke shutdowns, or override other parts. What looks like sabotage is often a desperate form of protection.

Some protector parts are even modeled after abusers or neglectful caregivers. They may take on critical or shaming voices, not because they are inherently abusive, but because they have internalized these roles as ways to stay in control. This internalized violence is not a sign of cruelty; it is a survival script replaying itself.

When therapists recognize that protector parts act from a time loop of survival, we respond differently. We stop trying to correct behavior and begin tending to the fear underneath. That shift in posture changes everything.

EARNING TRUST THROUGH INCLUSION

Protector parts organized around the fight and control-rank systems are often the last to trust. They scan constantly for signs that therapy is unsafe, not just in what is said, but how it is said, what is remembered, what is promised, and what is avoided. These parts are attuned to tone, timing, body language, and, above all, consistency.

CLINICAL VIGNETTE

You're Not Going To Trick Me

A mid-30s adult woman with a complex dissociative system, in therapy for just over a year. She recently began sensing the presence of multiple parts but had little verbal contact between them.

After a few sessions where a younger part had briefly emerged, a strong, contemptuous tone filled the room. The client's posture stiffened. The client's voice deepened and flattened. "What is this even supposed to do? You think we're just going to fall apart so you can fix us? You don't get it. You therapists never do."

The therapist responded calmly, "Sounds like there's a part here who's watching closely. Maybe not so sure this is safe." The protector part, mistrustful, exclaimed, "You're trying to make me say things. I know how this works. You act nice, then you twist it."

"I'm not here to trick you", said the therapist. "And I'm not trying to take anything away. If there's something you want me to know, I'm listening. But if you'd rather stay quiet, I'll respect that too."

Silence followed. Then the client's shoulders eased slightly. She glanced up for the first time in minutes, quietly stating, "We don't trust this. Not yet." The therapist agreed, "That makes sense. I am sure you have good reasons for that."

Clinical Reflections

This brief interaction was not a breakthrough, but it was a turning point. The protector part felt seen without being exposed; acknowledged without being pressured; and met with steadiness, not control.

That small shift, from full resistance to tentative observation, opened a doorway. Over the next sessions, the therapist noticed more flexibility, fewer shutdowns, and brief moments of co-presence between parts.

Many protector parts whose job is to keep things as they are, fear being overpowered, exposed, or discarded. They may worry that therapy will strip them of their function or unearth what they've worked so hard to suppress. Some distrust the therapist; others distrust some parts. Some distrust everyone.

To build trust, these parts must be included, not just tolerated or appeased, but genuinely invited into the process. They need to feel consulted, respected, and taken into account. That might sound like:

★ "It sounds like this part is trying really hard to keep things under control."
★ "You've been carrying a big job. I don't want to take that from you; I just want to understand it."
★ "Would it feel okay to hear how this part sees things, even if it's different from the others?"

This kind of acknowledgment helps protector parts feel seen and respected on their own terms. They may not soften right away, and that is okay. What they *do* notice is when the therapist does not flinch. When you do not push. When you stay steady, even in the face of resistance. Over time, they begin to test that safety, not always with words, but with small permissions.

NEGOTIATING BOUNDARIES WITHOUT POWER STRUGGLE

Some fight-based protector parts may try to take control of sessions by interrupting, refusing contact, taking over the body, or shutting down communication altogether. These behaviors are often tests of safety. Many of these parts want to know: "Can you hold steady when I push back? Will you stay respectful even when I'm disruptive?"

This is where the therapist's consistency and calm presence matter most. Rather than engaging in a power struggle, we respond with warm, attuned boundaries and firm without force:

★ "I hear that you're not comfortable with this part of the work, that's okay, it´s good to know."
★ "I want to check in with you, too, so everything inside feels safe with what we're doing."

These statements offer containment without rejection. The aim is not to override the part, but to show, through action and tone, that safety does not come from control, but from respect.

If a session becomes flooded or chaotic, it is not a failure. It is communication. The system is telling us something is too much, too fast, or too exposed. In those moments, the most therapeutic move is to pause, reflect, and reorient, showing the system that even overwhelm can be met without judgment.

MEETING FEAR OF CHANGE WITH VALIDATION AND TRUST

Fight-based protector parts can be easy to misunderstand, even for seasoned therapists. They may push others aside or shut down the session just as something vulnerable begins to emerge. It is natural to feel stuck or even frustrated. But treating protector parts as obstacles only deepens the mistrust they already carry.

This is where the therapist's own regulation and humility matter most. Feelings of urgency, helplessness, or defensiveness often signal that a fight-based part is activated, and doing exactly what it believes is necessary. Rather than being reactive, we return to a steady, non-judgmental presence.

Repair is possible and deeply meaningful. Fight-based protector parts notice when the therapist acknowledges them and re-engages with curiosity and care. Even small statements make a difference: "I realize I missed something important last time, and I want to hear it now. Moments like this show these parts that the therapist can stay connected even when things get hard. Over time, this becomes a relational blueprint for trust.

Perhaps the most challenging and essential aspect of working with fight-based protector parts is addressing their fear of change. These parts often experience their survival strategies as non-negotiable, having been shaped in contexts where flexibility meant danger.

- ❖ "If I stop doing this, everything will fall apart."
- ❖ "They'll take over again, and we'll be hurt."
- ❖ "No one else can keep us safe, not even you."

Rather than countering these beliefs, therapists are invited to approach them with genuine curiosity.

- ★ "What would it mean for this part to stop protecting in this way?"
- ★ "What has it seen happen when others tried?"

For fight-based parts, change often feels like surrender, not relief. They are not necessarily afraid of healing; they are afraid of letting their guard down and what healing might cost. That is why we go slowly, honoring not just the function of the part, but the fear beneath it. In Part II of this book, we explore in greater detail the distinctions among critical, hostile, and perpetrator-identified parts, and how their differing functions call for distinct therapeutic responses.

GIVING PROTECTOR PARTS A NEW JOB

As trust builds, some protector parts may begin to question their long-held strategies. A quiet hesitation might emerge: "What if there's another way?" This moment, though often subtle, is deeply significant.

Rather than pushing for change, the therapist stays alongside with curiosity:

★ "If you didn't have to protect in this exact way, is there something else you might want to do?"
★ "Would it feel okay to imagine a different role? One that keeps the system safe, but in a less exhausting way."

Some fight-based protector parts eventually become allies in boundary-setting, grounding, or internal coordination. Of course, these transitions take time. For many fight-based protector parts, their role is synonymous with survival. Change only becomes possible when safety, trust, and internal collaboration begin to outweigh fear.

COMMON CLINICAL PITFALLS

When working with fight-based protector parts, one of the most common missteps is **seeing their behavior as sabotage or resistance** rather than protection, thereby entering a competition for dominance with the part, accepting the rules of the rank system through which it manifests. Even when strategies appear disruptive or oppositional, they often carry a protective logic rooted in trauma time, moments when these parts had to step in and take control to ensure survival. They are not simply remembering what happened; many are responding as if the threat is still present. This means our task is to understand their purpose and the fears that drive them (i.e., triggers).

Rather than waiting for difficulties to emerge, it is crucial to include these parts from the very beginning. Acknowledging their presence early, inviting their input, and validating their role in keeping the system safe helps build trust.

A second aspect to keep in mind is that these parts are not trying to derail therapy, they are testing for relational safety. Their challenges are less about pushing people away and more about seeing if they truly mean what they say or if it is just another trick, sometimes it is about seeing who will really stay. In these moments, our steadiness and coherence is what matters most. It is not just what we say but how we say it.

A third aspect to keep in mind is that many fight-based protector parts operate in *trauma time*, a state in which the danger never really ended. Their urgency, control, or defensiveness makes sense in the world they still inhabit. This work is not easy. We will run into complications, this is expected, but they are excellent opportunities to understand better. Repair is one of the most powerful interventions we can offer. Misattunement is inevitable, but what matters most is how we respond to ruptures. Protector parts are often more focused on what we do after things go wrong than on what we do when things are going well. Our willingness to acknowledge missteps is what earns their trust. And all of this takes time. Going as slow as needed, at the pace that maintains connection, is often the fastest path to change. When fight-based protector parts feel respected and understood, the internal dynamics begin to shift.

CLOSING THOUGHTS

Fight-based protector parts are not obstacles to overcome; they are the system's frontline responders, vigilant, loyal, and often forged in profound isolation. Their strategies may look like resistance, but beneath that surface lies a deep devotion to survival. What we often call control is actually care. What looks like reactivity is memory in motion, a part or more living as if the danger never ended, because in their experience, it has not.

When we meet these parts with steadiness and respect, we offer something different than correction, we offer presence, and inclusion. We signal, not through words alone but through relational consistency, that this moment might really be different. That safety, however unfamiliar, is no longer a theory but a possibility, one that begins in the small, sacred space of a trusting therapeutic relationship.

With time, something remarkable can unfold. Fight-based protector parts may begin to sense they are no longer alone. Not because they have been pushed aside or quieted, but because a new internal presence is forming inside, the Adult Self, an emerging feeling or cooperation and collaboration that does not seek control, it offers company. It does not demand trust, it earns it.

This shift from fear to trust does not happen quickly. But when fight-based protector parts are welcomed as allies to include, the whole system begins to breathe differently. What was once rigid becomes responsive. And in that space, healing becomes a shared unfolding.

Clinical Anchors

What to remember...

- See strategy as protection, not sabotage.
- Include protector parts from the start. Actively acknowledge their presence, ask for their input, and honor their role as essential to the system's survival.
- Stay steady when challenged. Your regulation and tone matter more than your words.
- Honor the fear beneath control. Most protector strategies are rooted in fear, not power.
- Their function is tied to survival.
- Use boundaries, not power. Firmness does not require force.
- Assume trauma time.
- Let the Adult Self emerge organically.
- Repair matters more than misattunement.
- Misattunement is an opportunity to learn and adapt.
- Slower is faster.

What to avoid...

- Taking sides. Labeling as sabotage. Calling behavior *defensive* or *resistant* deepens mistrust.
- Over-reassuring or overpowering.
- Rushing change or rushing protector parts toward a new role.
- Pushing too much for cooperation. Pressuring parts to get along or yield control replicates the coercion they learned to survive.

PART II:
Working with Specific Parts

Chapter 11: Shared Origins and Protective Logic of Dissociative Parts

Therapist Reflection

When I began this work, I tried to categorize each part by what it did. One was angry, another avoided, another was self-critical or sexualized. Over time, I realized they shared something deeper: each part was trying to protect, to survive something that felt unbearable. Even when the methods seemed harmful, the motives were not. Once I began listening to what they were protecting, therapy shifted.

Up until now, we have been building the foundation of the Trauma-Informed Approach for Dissociative Parts (TADP): creating safety, pacing contact, and forming collaborative relationships with and within the personality system as a whole. We have established that trust is earned slowly through attunement and consistency, and that what we refer to as the Adult Self reflects a set of emergent capacities—such as reflection, cooperation, and metacognitive awareness. These capacities develop through forms of cooperation and leadership that are grounded in curiosity, non-judgmental observation, and gentle exploration of possibilities, rather than control or directive authority.

With this groundwork in place, we can move from a whole-system stance to a unifying lens for understanding *why* dissociative parts behave as they do.

Rather than asking, "What's wrong with this part?", we begin to ask:

★ "What happened that made this part necessary, and what is it still protecting right now?"

This shift dissolves shame and opens an engaged curiosity that invites relationship instead of escalation. Throughout this chapter, *leadership* refers not to directing parts, but to the capacity to remain present, curious, and responsive while holding multiple perspectives at once.

As laid out in chapter 3, dissociative roles are best understood at the intersection of action systems (how state programs organize behavior in the body) and motivational systems (why a strategy persists). In this chapter, we will use these systems to point out the shared origins and protective logic that unite parts across presentations.

SHARED ORIGINS: HOW DISSOCIATIVE PARTS EMERGE

Dissociative parts do not appear in response to a single event; they emerge by degrees, against a background of early non-organization in the attachment system. When the first year of life is marked by neglect, misattunement, frightening or unpredictable caregiving, the infant lacks the co-regulation and reflective feedback needed to knit together experience into a coherent self. This early disorganization is the primary issue, not the dissociative parts yet, but the absence of a stable organizing frame.

As noted in chapter 3, between roughly ages 3–5, many children in these contexts adopt controlling strategies (e.g., controlling-caregiving, controlling-punitive) to impose some consistency on an inconsistent environment to ensure some form of bonding. These strategies provide a provisional organization that keeps everyday life manageable.

When trauma and betrayal accumulate, or when new stressors overwhelm that provisional organization, the system may segregate experience and organize it into functionally distinct parts to preserve continuity (compartmentalization): some manage reality and relationships; others hold fear, shame, rage, or sensory fragments. This parts-based structure can remain quiet for years, only becoming visible when adult demands outstrip the capacity of managing reality and forcibly prompts the activation of a malfunctioning attachment system (Liotti, 2011).

This sequence also explains variability in outcomes: not all abused children develop dissociative parts or dissociative disorders. Without the underlying disorganized attachment, later adversity may not crystallize into a dissociative parts organization.

Contributing conditions

- **Early non-organization**: lack of reliable protection, reflection, or soothing in the first year prevents integration of self and affect.
- **Provisional control**: preschool controlling strategies create a manageable but brittle coherence.
- **Overload events**: chronic coercion, grooming, sexual/physical abuse, or repeated betrayal surpass the system's coping capacity.
- **No reflective mirror or buffer**: persistent absence of containment and mentalization (no one to help make sense of internal states).
- **Adult triggers**: later stress exceeding the reality-managing part's bandwidth unmasks dissociative phenomena.

How Parts Take Shape: Conditions That Raise Risk

While dissociative parts typically emerge by degrees (from early attachment non-organization to provisional controlling strategies), the ground conditions also shape how these parts develop. The following experiences in later years of development increase risk for more developed compartmentalized presentations:

- Chronic emotional or physical neglect.
- Chronic misattunement, unpredictability, or enmeshment.
- Lack of protection, reflection, or validation at key developmental moments.
- Psychological coercion or betrayal by attachment figures.
- Sexual or physical abuse.

When such supports are absent, the system improvises to keep life manageable by narrowing awareness, suppressing expression, or adopting roles that preserve proximity. Later, under cumulative stress or betrayal that overwhelms provisional organization, experience may continue to be partitioned across parts to preserve continuity. Depending on the jobs these parts have to take on, some will be more developed than others.

The division of the personality tends to become more complex when:

- Emotions are too intense or contradictory to integrate.

- Vulnerability cannot be expressed safely.
- Reality is too painful to acknowledge directly.
- Connection to unsafe caregivers must be maintained.
- No one provides containment, reflection, or regulation.

Dissociative parts do not take shape in calm or supportive contexts; they are forged in chaos. In the absence of protective adults or relationships, someone to help the child process feelings or tolerate distress, the mind adapts as it can: by suppressing, compartmentalizing, and creating roles to survive. These adaptations do not make the environment safe, nor do they create a coherent or continuous experience of self. Instead, they allow aspects of functioning and survival to persist despite ongoing danger, fear, and pain, at the cost of internal discontinuity.

Rather than calling these parts maladaptive or dysfunctional, it is more accurate (and more respectful) to recognize them as intelligent, creative survival strategies. Each part formed in response to a specific danger or absence. Each one is the mind's attempt to survive when safety, protection, and integration were not possible.

Seen in this light, we shift from judgment to understanding. Protective parts are not obstacles; they are the system's best attempt to endure unbearable conditions. Their strategies may now be rigid, extreme, or even harmful, but they did not begin as obstacles; they began as adaptations. Clinically, the task is to honor their purpose and update their methods (same purpose, more adaptive method) while rebuilding organization through permission, pacing, and present-day co-regulation.

Relational Trauma as the Blueprint for Protective Parts

While trauma can arise from many sources, the protective parts we focus on in this context are shaped primarily by relational trauma—wounds that occurred within attachment, not isolated events.

Because these injuries occurred in relationship, the parts that formed in response are likewise relational in nature. They carry an internal logic shaped by the original dynamics of closeness and danger, often scanning for betrayal, appeasing to maintain connection, anticipating rejection, or recreating early distorted attachment patterns.

These parts were not only organized by trauma; they were organized by relationships that hurt when they should have healed. As a result, they often expect pain in intimacy, danger in vulnerability, and obligation in connection. Their logic becomes clearer when seen through the lens of their origin, the type of relationship that gave rise to the disorganized attachment.

These early relational wounds or breaking points (Steele et al., 2017) often over activate or distort key action systems—particularly attachment, rank and defense, and recruit specific motivational systems. When caregivers were unsafe or unresponsive, the child may have relied on submission (rank), dominance (rank), perfectionism (care-seeking distortion), or people-pleasing (group affiliation) to preserve connection. These strategies become encoded in parts that continue to organize behavior and beliefs long after the threat is gone.

Every part carries imprinted experiences, voices, rules, emotions, and roles absorbed from caregivers, institutions, or cultural messages, according to internal working models specific to their relational experience. Some parts mirror abusers. Others hold roles the child had to play to survive. Some parts enforce rules like:

- "You must be perfect to be loved."
- "It's your fault."
- "Don't trust anyone."

These are not always conscious beliefs but felt truths embedded in the part's way of being. Until these truths are named and recontextualized, they continue to shape both internal and external relationships.

KEY SHARED FEATURES OF PROTECTIVE PARTS

These relational origins not only explain why parts formed but also help us understand how they operate. Across systems, parts tend to share key structural and emotional features, hallmarks of their protective design.

Because these parts formed under the dominance of one or more survival-based systems, particularly defense or disrupted attachment, they remain stuck in that system's logic. A part driven by the flight response does not realize the threat has passed. A part organized around appeasement still believes connection must be earned through submission or performance. Recognizing which system the part is operating from allows us to respond not with confrontation, but with precision and attunement.

Recognizing these shared traits helps us move from surface behavior to attuned therapeutic contact. Instead of asking, "Why is this part doing this?", we begin to ask: "What is it protecting?" "What would it need to stop protecting in this way?"

The most important shared features are the following:

- **Protective by design:** Regardless of their surface behavior (aggression, collapse, self-criticism), each part exists to protect the system from something worse: overwhelm, danger, rejection, or annihilation.
- **Stuck in trauma time:** Parts act as if the original threat is still present and often lack access to the Adult Self or present-moment awareness.
- **Emotionally isolated:** Each holds something too painful for others to carry—grief, terror, shame, rage—and therefore often feels alone, mistrusts connection, and hides pain beneath rigid roles.
- **Change feels dangerous:** When they let go of protective strategies, even harmful ones, they risk vulnerability that once came at a high cost.
- **They need curiosity, not control:** These parts do not respond to logic or pressure; they respond to relational safety. They want to know: "Is it safe to show up?" "Will I be understood?" "Can I stay in control?" "What happens if I soften?"

These features guide our approach with respectful curiosity. When we understand their protective logic, we begin to ask a deeper, more transformative question: What is this part trying to do for the system?

SHARED FUNCTIONS OF PROTECTIVE PARTS

Every part, no matter how confusing, extreme, or painful its behavior may appear, serves a protective, organizing function. Many parts act like internal first responders, operating with urgency and clarity, even when their methods cause harm. These parts are not trying to sabotage healing. They are trying to prevent collapse, overwhelm, or further betrayal. At the deepest level, they are protecting the system from a feared disintegration; one in which even the parts that normally organize experience fall apart, leaving only raw, uncontained sensation and affect.

Dissociative parts offer a kind of structure, even if fragmented, which otherwise would give way to the chaos of total disintegration. One way to imagine this is through the metaphor of an orchestra: at times, it may sound like there is a string quartet playing together, there is a group interpreting a Vivaldi piece, while elsewhere, a lone piano may carry a Beethoven sonata. This is the experience of a dissociative system—different but still organized around some form of musicality. By contrast, when each instrument plays on its own, tuning and improvising without coordination, what emerges is not music but dissonance, reflecting the most painful inner experience of clients—the descent into chaos of disorganization when parts lose all connection and coherence in themselves and with others. This metaphor helps us appreciate that—even when the music is disjointed or fragmented—it is still music, because protective parts are not the chaos; they are attempts at creating order within overwhelming conditions.

While the tone and strategy of each part may differ, they often share core functional goals:

- **Prevent exposure to external threats:** Protect against relational danger (criticism, abandonment, humiliation, or violence) by striking first or disappearing. Examples: rejection of others, perfectionism, self-criticism, avoidance.

- **Control internal chaos:** When the system becomes overwhelmed by trauma activation, intense emotion, or inner conflict, some parts suppress, redirect, or take over to prevent collapse. Examples: shutting down emotional expression, dominating other parts or self-harming to regain control.

- **Maintain bonding (even when unsafe):** Preserve proximity through loyalty, blame, or submission. Examples: shame-bound parts, perpetrator-identified parts, sexualized attachments.

- **Avoid vulnerability:** Where vulnerability once led to danger, parts protect by shutting it down or attacking it. Examples: hostility, compliance, detachment, ridicule of emotional needs, or aggression used to override vulnerability.

- **Silence unbearable truths:** Hold or hide traumatic realities that are too dangerous to fully know. Here are some examples: rewriting history, masking abuse as love, hiding dissociated material.

- **Regulate unbearable affect:** Manage shame, grief, rage, or terror through numbing, compulsive control, collapse, aggression, or ritualized behaviors.

- **Preserve internal structure or coherence:** Enforce rules and hierarchies to create predictability in the absence of safe external regulation.

These are not conscious strategies. They are embodied survival adaptations. Understanding these functions helps us see through behavior to unmet needs, hidden fear, or frozen logic. When we say, "I think you are protecting against *this*", parts often soften. The task is not to win an argument with strategy, but to honor the mission and update the method.

CLOSING THOUGHTS

What unites dissociative parts is not their form, but their function, which, as we have seen, developed in traumatizing circumstances. Each emerged in response to pain, absence, or contradiction; each adapted to protect the system in the best way it could. While these parts may appear irrational, resistant, or extreme, each carries a protective logic waiting to be understood. Some parts may even take on the tone or behaviors of caring figures, imitating protection, guidance, or reassurance when such experiences were scarce or unreliable. These, too, reflect adaptive attempts to meet unmet needs.

In the chapters that follow, we will explore specific part types through this lens, not as pathologies to fix, but as survival strategies to honor, unpack, and gently update through relational work. With shared function established, chapter 12 examines how different action systems show up as recognizable roles and what motivational goals they pursue.

Clinical Anchors

What to remember...

- Dissociative parts emerge by degrees in the absence of a stable organizing frame in the attachment system
- Parts are relational, adaptive responses to early conditions.
- Controlling strategies provide a provisional organization that keeps everyday life manageable.
- When trauma and betrayal accumulate, the system may segregate experience more and organize it into functionally distinct parts to preserve continuity. It is not a matter of all or nothing.
- Internal conflict often signals competing Action Systems (e.g., attachment vs. defense).
- Naming motivational logic reduces shame and strengthens alliance.
- The Adult Self grows through repeated experiences of accurate reflection, predictable limits, and cooperative engagement, first with the therapist, and gradually among parts themselves.

What to Avoid...

- Treating protector strategies as *resistance*.
- Pushing for insight or emotion while defense is active.
- Turning roles into rigid categories.
- Pathologizing internal aggression/control that once prevented worse harm.
- Framing *integration* as the only valid outcome.

Chapter 12: Behind the Behavior

Therapist Reflection

I used to think of therapy with dissociative clients as uncovering trauma or increasing insight. Over time, I've learned it's far more relational: recognizing which part is present, what for, what it needs, and responding without pressure, fear, or rescuing. Often the most profound movement comes not from the content of an interpretation or hypothesis, but from how we work together—through a shared, reflective process that gradually strengthens metacognitive capacity and internal coordination.

Earlier chapters emphasized whole-system safety, containment, and therapeutic stance. As contact deepens, internal distinctions begin to emerge. Many clients do not start with clearly defined parts. Even when they do, those distinctions ripen slowly as parts of the system move gradually from trauma time to relational connection and interpersonal connection in the presence of safety. At this stage, our focus becomes more specific: Which part? Why now? What for?

Building on chapter 11's logic of survival, we now shift from shared origins to part-specific engagement. We ask how parts show up in the room and what they are trying to accomplish *today*. In this chapter, common parts are described not as fixed identities, but as internal representations organized by Action Systems (how a state pattern runs) and guided by Motivational Systems (why a strategy persists), as introduced in chapter 3.

Parts are lenses, not boxes. They help us recognize function so we can adjust stance with precision and care.

For each part, we will list:

- **Action system expression:** how the emotional state organizes behavior in the therapy room.

- **Motivational goal:** what the strategy is pursuing.
- **Protective function ("what for"):** the danger it prevents or the need it preserves.
- **Why now (triggers):** what tends to trigger it or call it forward?

The aim is practical: to translate the foundational lenses into clear stances, consent-based language, and micro-interventions that honor each part's mission while updating its methods.

THE ROLE OF ACTION SYSTEMS IN SHAPING PARTS

As mentioned in chapter 2, the Theory of Structural Dissociation (Van der Hart, Nijenhuis & Steele, 2006) offers a helpful frame for understanding how dissociative parts form—not as random fragments, but as organized adaptations around innate action systems. These parts emerge when two fundamentally incompatible systems (such as attachment and defense) are simultaneously activated in response to the same caregiver. This contradiction cannot be resolved within one unified identity, so the child splits experience across different parts, each shaped by distinct physiological and motivational states. These systems are like biological programs that guide core human behaviors like attachment, defense, submission, and collapse.

When chronic neglect and trauma overwhelm or distort one of these systems, the result is often fragmented parts, frozen in time, shaped by the demands of survival, and still operating from the logic of trauma time.

Each of the part types we encounter in therapy can be better understood by identifying the motivational or action system that organizes its behavior, goals, and emotional tone.

To translate theory into practice, it can be helpful to organize common inner representations of dissociative parts by the predominant action or motivational system shaping their behavior. While no part fits perfectly into a single category, and many are shaped by the combination or co-opting of multiple systems, this framework offers a starting point for understanding the internal logic behind their strategies. The following descriptions are an initial overview of how different types of dissociative parts may be shaped by specific motivational systems, their typical goals, and clinical clues. This is not meant to reduce complexity but to support attuned, individualized therapeutic work.

- **Child parts:** Mainly mediated by attachment and survival defenses (flight, freeze, submission). They carry vulnerability, dependency, and early unmet needs. Often rooted in attachment ruptures and developmental trauma, these parts preserve innocence, fear, longing, and shame, and may hold preverbal or sensory memory states.

- **Adolescent parts:** Mainly mediated by fight, flight, and emerging rank/dominance dynamics. They often carry protest, defiance, idealism, or shame, reflecting the developmental struggle for autonomy while still depending on attachment figures. These parts may oscillate between rebellion and vulnerability, frequently replaying unresolved conflicts from adolescence.

- **Fearful and avoidant parts:** Mainly mediated by freeze, flight, and submission. These parts often emerge in response to overwhelming threats where neither fight nor connection is possible. Their primary goal is to escape emotional or relational danger, either by disappearing (freeze), staying invisible (flight), or appeasing perceived threat (submission).

- **Critical and punitive parts**: Mainly mediated by dominance, fight turned inward, dominance, and control. Typically rooted in the rank system. These parts often internalize early experiences of power imbalance, assigning roles of dominance and submission inside the system. When submission fails, the predatory system may activate, particularly in cases of self-harm or suicidal dynamics.

- **Hostile and aggressive parts**: Mainly mediated by fight, control, and dominance. May reflect different systems depending on function. Protest and rage often arise from attachment ruptures. Competitive or controlling parts reflect the rank system (dominance/submission). Cold, calculating aggression may stem from the predatory system.

- **Self-harming parts:** Mainly mediated by fight turned inward, submission, and collapse. They often serve to regulate unbearable emotional states, reenact early punishment dynamics, or restore a sense of control through pain. These parts may draw on both the rank system (through internalized dominance/submission) and shutdown-based defensive responses. At times, elements of the rank or competition system are recruited, though not in the sense of asserting dominance over others. Instead, control is directed inward, functioning as an *escape hatch*: a way to end intolerable helplessness, arousal, or tension when no other option feels available. Within this internal logic, self-harm is less about hierarchy and more about reclaiming a minimal sense of agency when all other routes to regulation or relief feel blocked.

- **Suicidal parts**: Mainly mediated by fight and/or flight and control. Often linked to a collapsed or shutdown defense system. When all other strategies fail (fleeing, fighting, appeasing) disappearance can become the only perceived escape.

- **Internally focused homicidal parts:** Mainly mediated by fight, control, and predatory systems. Can reflect defensive logic ("Eliminate threat before it eliminates me") or rank-based dominance. These parts often arise from identification with the aggressor, carrying scripts of retribution or pre-emptive violence.

- **Perpetrator-identified parts**: Mainly mediated by fight and control, with submission distorted into survival through mimicry. These parts reproduce the abuser's role internally, not primarily to harm, but to maintain survival through domination and control.

- **Sexualized parts**: Mainly mediated by the sexual system to achieve attachment and dominance/control related goals. Often shaped by distorted activation of the sexual bonding system as a substitute for attachment, especially in betrayal trauma. These parts may also be influenced by the rank system: seduction as control (dominance) or appeasement (submission).

- **Shame-bound parts**: Mainly mediated by flight, submission, and freeze. Structured by the rank system's submission subroutine. These parts carry the sense of defeat, humiliation, and inferiority. They may activate caregiving when the system believes it has failed to protect someone vulnerable.

PART	ACTION SYSTEM EXPRESSION	MOTIVATIONAL GOAL	PROTECTIVE FUNCTION	WHY NOW (CUES)
Younger/ Child Parts	Disorganized attachment; defense (flight/freeze); sometimes exploration/play	Connection; safety; soothing.	Keep need visible or hidden to preserve bonding and avoid danger.	Proximity needs/ separation; anniversaries; therapist absence; misattunement.
Adolescents/ Teenage Parts	Social Belonging (ingroup affiliation), Exploration/ Play (identity experiments), Peer Cooperation (mutuality/ alliances), Rank (status/ defiance).	Belonging with peers, autonomy, identity formation; closeness through mutuality rather than care-seeking.	Manage status threat and exposure/shame. Protecting younger pars.	Status threat, correction by authority, perceived unfairness/hypocrisy.
Fearful / Avoidant Parts	Defense (freeze/flight); rank (submission/appeasing).	Safety; predictability; arousal control. Avoid challenge and confrontation.	Reduce contact with threat (internal/external); keep activation manageable.	Novelty; uncertainty; time pressure; sensory/memory cues.
Critical / Punitive Parts	Rank (dominance); defense (fight turned inward)	Coherence; control; preserve attachment via self-monitoring. Submission to the perpetrator leads to internalization of rules..	Enforce rules to prevent rejection, chaos, or punishment.	Errors; exposure; perceived failure; praise (triggers unworthiness).
Hostile / Aggressive Parts	Defense (fight); rank/control.	Safety and consistence through dominance; autonomy/control.	Pre-empt threat by attacking or controlling; keep vulnerability unreachable.	Shame activation; closeness; correction; power imbalance.
Self-Harming Parts	Defense systems (collapse/shutdown (inward turn of fight).	Arousal regulation; release of unbearable affect; re-establish control.	Convert overwhelming inner pain into somatic, controllable pain; enact punishment to avoid external punishment or abandonment.	Shame; rejection; perceived failure; relational rupture; dissociative flooding.
Suicidal Parts	Defense (collapse/ shutdown; fight turned inward); faint (escape via give up).	Rapid relief; control over pain; end of exposure.	Provide a perceived exit when all else fails.	Overwhelm; defeat; entrapment; loss of control.
Homicidal Parts	Defense (fight); rank/control; predatory system.	Safety through pre-emptive dominance; eliminate perceived threat; restore order.	Neutralize danger by externalizing aggression; enforce survival by controlling or eradicating the source of harm.	Flashbacks involving persecution; perceived humiliation or loss of control; threat to vulnerable parts; exposure of secrets or shame.
Perpetrator-Identified Parts	Defense (fight); rank/control	Safety via power; coherence with trauma rules. Submission (identification with aggressor)	Mirror the source to pre-empt harm; enforce trauma logic internally.	Helplessness; intimacy; boundary setting; shame.
Sexualized Parts	Sexuality	Connection; belonging; predictable access; power balance. Attachment, rank (seduction as influence); defense (appease).	Regulate closeness when attachment cues feel dangerous; manage asymmetry.	Intimacy themes; admiration; separations; shame.
Shame-Bound Parts	Defense (flight/freeze); rank (submission)	Belonging via invisibility; safety through smallness.	Prevent rejection or attack by self-erasure.	Praise; attention; errors; closeness; cultural/identity threat.

Table 12.1. From Action System to Role: A quick reference for clinical formulation

This lens helps us avoid mislabeling protector parts as resistance or dysfunction. When we follow the logic of the action systems and motivational systems, we can better attune to the part's survival role and adjust our therapeutic stance accordingly. It is important to remember that these parts and the systems that mediate them do not operate in isolation; they often overlap or activate simultaneously when this serves their function.

The most reliable clue for understanding which system is at play lies in the emotions themselves. By carefully exploring which emotions are present, and attending to their quality, intensity, and nuance, we can trace the underlying motivational system and its organizing logic. In the context of disorganized attachment, however, motivational systems are often recruited in a fragmented or conflicting manner and emotions may arise with confusion or mixed signals. Holding this perspective helps avoid rigid classifications and supports a more flexible, compassionate understanding of the dynamics at work. Each of these typical representations will be described in detail in the following chapters.

ORGANIZING FROM THE PERSPECTIVE OF THE ADULT SELF AND COOPERATION

From this framework, organization and integration emerge through the development of the Adult Self or collaborative parts. These parts are primarily mediated by the motivational systems of cooperation, intersubjectivity, and caregiving. They tend to arise gradually within relational safety and an attuned therapeutic stance that supports trust and co-regulation.

As cooperative and collaborative parts strengthen, they provide leadership, consent, and coordination among parts, bringing greater compactness and coherence to the system. They support collaboration rather than dominance, allowing multiple parts to be present without takeover. This internal organization fosters stabilization, trust, and more reliable regulation, both internally and within the therapeutic relationship.

As the Adult Self builds capacities, it can also extend caregiving inward, offering protection, guidance, and comfort to parts that lack these capacities. This internal caregiving makes exploration possible, including play and curiosity with younger parts, without overwhelming the system.

Through future orientation, coherence, and sustained collaboration, cooperative parts gradually remedy the failures of the attachment system, allowing the person to experience continuity, agency, and relational safety where it was once missing.

LISTENING BEYOND THE PRESENTATION

When a part appears, identify the action system(s) (the emotional state active now) and motivational goal (purpose, sometimes veiled), name the protective function, and choose a stance that honors the mission while updating the method. The Adult Self is invited to co-lead, not override. This phase of therapy is defined by increased discernment. We are learning to ask what are the functions of this part's behavior, what internal dynamics are present, and what kind of stance will allow this part to feel included, not exposed?

Many parts do not fit neatly into categories. Some parts overlap, combine, or transform over time. Perfectionistic parts may carry shame. Suicidal parts may also self-punish. Sexualized parts may protect frightened child parts. Shame-bound parts might present through sexualized behavior. Others may carry both self-loathing and a desperate need for care. And the same part may serve different functions at different times.

What matters is not that we name them, but that we listen beyond the presentation. That we translate learned coping strategies into new ones, with the guidance of the Adult Self, and a sense of time. We will offer clinical language, case vignettes, therapeutic postures, and common pitfalls. They are not prescriptive rules, but invitations to open doors the client has found difficult to approach.

CLOSING THOUGHTS

This shift, from general system work to part-specific engagement, marks a significant turning point in therapy. The core remains the same: respect, regulation, reaching agreements, cooperation, and collaboration through the Adult Self's developing leadership.

Each part that emerges is an opportunity, not only to understand history, but to shift how that history lives in the present. Through attuned engagement and the growing leadership of the Adult Self, parts can transform from isolated survival strategies into integrated participants in the client's internal world.

Clinical Anchors

What to remember...

- Parts are not categories, they are relational, adaptive responses to early conditions.
- Behavior reflects survival logic shaped by underlying action and motivational systems.
- Each part is trying to solve something the system once could not.
- Internal conflict often reflects competing action systems (e.g., attachment vs. defense).
- Asking "What is this part protecting?" or "Why now?" helps shift confusion into curiosity.
- The Adult Self is enhanced through external and internal experiences of cooperation, caregiving, and relational safety among parts.
- Naming a part's motivational logic can reduce shame and strengthen alliance.

What to Avoid...

- Assuming all protector parts function the same way, their motivational roots (e.g., rage, shame, care, control) matter greatly for how we engage them.
- Assuming consistency across parts with similar presentations (i.e., not all critical parts are alike).
- Pushing for emotional connection, insight, or change when defense systems are still active; premature engagement may increase internal conflict or shutdown.
- Describing the client's experience in rigid categories, many parts are fluid, overlapping, or evolving in therapy.
- Pathologizing internal aggression or control, these strategies often reflect parts mimicking the trauma environment.
- Framing integration as the only goal. For many clients, safety and cooperation between parts is already a major achievement.

Chapter 13: Child Parts

THERAPIST REFLECTION

I notice the pull to step in and comfort the vulnerable part, or to rush to understand its story as if it were a literal child. I make room for them, pause, and remind myself that genuine safety is built slowly. Instead of filling silences or rescuing, I stay alert to subtle shifts in posture, tone, or energy. Steadiness and patience open space for child parts to express themselves in their own time.

Child parts are often the most vulnerable members of a dissociative system, holding raw, unintegrated fragments of fear, helplessness, longing, confusion, and shame that were too overwhelming to process when they occurred. Clinically, they are organized around the attachment care-seeking system, yet their signals are frequently entangled with defensive strategies because closeness once brought danger.

This chapter looks at how these parts originate, their central features and functions, and how to hold space for them; emphasizing therapeutic stance, pacing, and the countertransference awareness that make interventions effective.

ORIGINS OF CHILD PARTS

Child parts typically arise when repeated overwhelm meets insufficient protection. When a child's bids for care (attachment) are met with neglect, inconsistency, humiliation, or abuse and maltreatment, the system cannot reconcile "I need you" with "You hurt me". To keep connection and survival possible, experience is segregated: what longs, cries, hides, or reaches out is pushed out of daily awareness and held in these parts.

Common formative patterns

- **Attachment–defense collision.** Care-seeking reliably triggers danger; attachment signals pair with fight/flight/freeze and are stored in separate parts to reduce conflict and dissonance.
- **Disorganized caregiving.** The same figure is alternately comforting and frightening; incompatible truths ("safe/ dangerous") are divided to preserve proximity and connection.
- **Chronic misattunement and silence.** Feelings arrive without a regulating other; vulnerable affects are hidden to protect the bond and avoid shame, punishment, or retaliation.
- **Coercion, secrecy, betrayal** These dynamics arise in abuse, not in neglect alone. Loyalty rules ("Don't tell", "Be good", "It's your fault") require the child to hide their experience; secrecy becomes internal law.

Across these conditions, time-anchored divisions form. They hold age-linked sensation, affects, and meaning; not literal ages, but developmental positions encoded when protection fails (e.g., pre-verbal terror, toddler panic, school-age confusion). Some clinicians confuse child parts with *regression,* but it is much more complex than that. Child parts do not know that the danger is over, that the body is older, or that safer options exist (this is why some time-orientation grounding interventions can backfire, such as asking them to look at their hand).

Often these parts have little to no awareness of what is happening in the present and may feel terrified when contact is attempted, with other parts, with adults in the client's life, and, of course, with the therapist. Many associate all adult figures with danger. When child parts are aware of other parts that are trying to protect or help (like some teenage parts described in the next chapter) prognosis is usually better. When child parts are extremely isolated (hiding, immobilized), it often reflects severe maltreatment and abuse. In such cases, preparatory work needs to be done before they can even hear that the danger is over and other options exist.

These parts carry unmet attachment needs and unprocessed threats, organized by survival strategies. Our task is not to rescue. Direct caregiving by therapists often backfires, either reinforcing the frequent emergence of child parts or triggering protector parts determined to avoid any connection. The goal is to support the system through the Adult Self: ask permission, adapt pace, and use present-time orientation so their experience can be included without overwhelm.

MAIN FEATURES OF CHILD PARTS

Child parts are early internal representations of disorganized attachment, but they are not literal children and do not map neatly to chronological age. Some feel three, others eight, and some are nonverbal. Clients may name ages or simply describe "someone very little". What unites them is what they carry and how they relate to the present.

- **Trauma-time anchoring.** Limited sense that time has passed, "it's happening now"; the body might feel small.
- **Developmental childlike reasoning.** Concrete, global, self-referential logic ("it's my fault", "good/bad").
- **Modes of communication.** Gaze down, breath-holding, somatic cues (stomach drop, trembling), or small/younger voice.
- **Attachment sensitivity.** Approach–avoid flips in response to warmth; bids for closeness followed by shame, freeze, or retreat.
- **Trigger-linked activation.** Separation, authority tone, closeness, or touch often as triggers; especially at night or in settings that resemble past scenes. In short, any trigger that activates attachment or fear systems can reawaken these parts.
- **Protector elicitation.** Visibility triggers teenagers, critics, enforcers, or hostile/perpetrator-identified parts to avoid, guard, or monitor access.
- **Emotional load.** Concentrated fear, grief, confusion, longing, and shame.
- **Orientation gaps.** Little awareness of present-time options, other parts, or the therapist as safe. Direct time-orientation attempts may intensify fear rather than reduce it. At this stage, safety is supported indirectly through pacing, containment, and working with protective parts, until present-time awareness can be tolerated.

Sometimes, their presence is subtle: an impulse to self-soothe or a yearning that feels disproportionate or inexplicable to the client. Other times, it is not so subtle, like a drawing left behind or an interaction with someone else in the client´s life. These expressions may feel confusing or even shameful to the Adult Self.

If you pick up on some of these moments, your attunement matters more than interpretation. Rather than naming or drawing attention to the shift too quickly, we slow down and gently make room for the experience.

Clients may feel embarrassed or conflicted: "I feel childish" or "This doesn't make sense". Our task is not to rescue but to normalize and contain. These moments are often described or perceived as regressions, but they are openings. Openings that require steadiness, curiosity, and acceptance, not quick solutions. As we move forward in treatment, these moments will bring fantastic opportunities. However, only when we know enough about the internal dynamics of the system can we adapt the work with these parts accordingly.

Some of the most common outer/inner cues that will help us recognize these parts are the following:

- Hiding, trembling, curling inward.
- Childlike speech or sudden silence.
- Marked fear of rejection/abandonment.
- Sudden shifts in tone, affect, vocabulary.
- Confusion or freeze: "I don't know where I am".
- Communication through drawings, posture, or emotional floods rather than narrative.

Here are some examples of typical descriptions of inner representations:

- ❖ "She's in a dark room/corner", "in a closet", "under the bedcovers."
- ❖ Inconsolable: "She won't stop crying".
- ❖ Compliant/appeasing: trying hard to "get it right".
- ❖ Lonely or clinging: "She needs something from me", "She's waiting for me to do something".

A note on access and consent: Not all child parts want contact. Many are shielded by protector parts (including hostile or perpetrator-identified roles) or remain hidden behind shame/fear. Approach should be done gradually through the Adult Self and with explicit permission to reduce backlash and strengthen internal leadership.

FUNCTIONS OF CHILD PARTS

Child parts are childlike states that hold early experiences within the system. Though they may appear or be experienced as fragile, vulnerable or needy, they serve essential functions in the internal system:

- **Carrier of the abuse related unbearable pain and unmet attachment needs.** Holds terror, confusion, grief, loneliness so the rest can function. Often appears as sobbing, collapse, pleading, or numb overwhelm. This part absorbs what would otherwise flood consciousness.
  Systems: Attachment (inhibited/distorted), defense (division through hiding and ignoring needs).
  Survival logic: "If I hold the pain here, the rest can keep living. If the terror stays inside me, they can go to school, work, survive."

- **Alarm for unresolved trauma.** Signals "this feels like then". It detects similarity cues and triggers protective distance before danger repeats. Often shows up as sudden panic, body tightening or fear of being seen.
  Systems: Defense (threat detection), interoceptive monitoring.
  Survival logic: "If I warn you early, you won't be trapped again. If I react fast, maybe we can escape before it happens."

- **Proximity seeking for safety and soothing.** Reaches (directly or indirectly) for protection, warmth and understanding. May appear as clinginess, pleading, idealization, or helplessness.
  Systems: Attachment (proximity/care-seeking).
  Survival logic: "If I can stay close to someone safe, we won't be abandoned or hurt. If I am lovable enough, they will protect us."

- **Keeper of emotional truth.** Preserves feelings and meanings that could not be expressed then (rage, grief, betrayal, innocence, longing) and often waits for a safe witness. It carries the truth the family system could not allow.
  Systems: Attachment (recognition/mirroring, being mentalized). defense (sealing until safe).

Survival logic: "If I keep the truth alive, we won't lose ourselves. If someone finally sees it, things can change."

- **Storehouse of nonverbal memory.** Encodes posture, gesture, voice tone, physical sensation, and procedural memory from experiences that occurred too early for words or that were too overwhelming to be put into words. Often expressed through shrinking, flinching, tension, or sudden shutdown.
  Systems: Defense (hiding procedural/implicit memory).
  Survival logic: If I keep it in the body, I don't have to speak. If it stays nonverbal, it won't trigger danger from others."

- **Holder of shame labels ("too much", "not enough").** Takes on blame, defectiveness and submission to preserve connection. It often presents as self-hate, hiding, apologizing, or wanting to disappear.
  Systems: Rank/power (submission/shame schema), attachment (deactivation).
  Survival logic: "If it's my fault, I can fix it. If I take the blame, I won't lose them. Being bad is safer than being alone."

- **Compliance and appeasement.** Pleases, submits or becomes "good" to limit harm and preserve connection. Often shows perfect behavior, similes, agrees or stays invisible.
  Systems: Rank/power (fawn, submission).
  Survival logic: "If I obey, they won't hurt me. If I am good, the danger passes and I still belong."

- **Internal siren that mobilizes protectors.** Distress recruits hostile or punitive parts to manage exposure.
  Systems: Defense (escalation/mobilization), attachment (indirect proximity-seeking activates protector parts).
  Survival logic: "If I activate the guard, I won't be alone with what is happening."

Their presence signals areas where the system still needs to build adaptive information, realistic information about what is right and wrong. These parts are stuck in very complicated moments of the client's life, without awareness of having grown up or that the present is safe now and often very few experiences or repair and real relational attunement.

When child parts are active, other parts, especially hostile, punitive, or perpetrator identified parts, often show up. Contact with these parts should therefore be approached gently, with steadiness and consent from the system. When protector parts show up, it is a sign that the system is trying to manage proximity to vulnerability and here is where those other parts need modeling from the therapist to respond in new healthier ways.

Keep in mind that intervening with child parts without checking with the system can evoke powerful internal responses, not just from these fight-based, ranked-based parts, but also from the parts responsible for managing daily life. Parts that function in daily life often hold intense phobic reactions toward younger or more vulnerable parts, expressed through fear, hate, disgust, frustration, guilt, or blame for what the system, as a whole, has endured.

The Adult Self, as an integrative capacity, emerges precisely through the gradual softening of these phobic responses and the development of reflective distance, compassion, and cooperation toward internal experience.

RELATING TO CHILD PARTS

Child parts are very sensitive to subtle internal and external cues such as shifts in tone from the therapist, changes in posture, or perceived emotional availability. When they become activated, they often respond in ways that may appear disproportionate from an adult perspective, reflecting the part's orientation to trauma time: a state in which threat, abandonment, or harm still feel imminent. Clients may be confused or ashamed by these shifts, wondering, "Why do I feel like a little girl crying?" or "Why am I suddenly terrified for no reason?" These responses are traces of overwhelming experiences that remain alive in the system. Often confusing interactions in therapy with other interactions that were dangerous.

Creating a Safe Relational Space and Alliance

A safe relational frame with clear boundaries and norms is a good way to begin since we are working with these parts as we keep in mind their protectors. What helps is grounded presence and attuned pacing, not rescuing, infantilizing or fostering dependency. Therapists model a connection that is respectful, non-intrusive, offering space without engulfment or demand.

Simple, respectful phrases can support this:

- ★ "Something feels close, let's make space for it."
- ★ "You don't have to explain anything right now."
- ★ "This part of your experience matters, and we'll move at your pace."

Metaphors like inner hideaways, rooms, or gentle containment may support orientation when the experience is overwhelming, but should be introduced with care, and only when needed. Remember these parts are not literal children to interact with; they are representations of past experience held in emotional memory. This is why it is so important to keep in mind that the therapeutic stance is not one of interacting with a literal child, but of supporting the system, especially the Adult Self, in recognizing, orienting to, and creating conditions of safety for these internal experiences.

Therapist Stance - Aspects to Keep in Mind with Child Parts

When child parts emerge, the therapist's stance matters more than the intervention. They might not be literal children, but they carry the embodied memory of being one. Remember they do not need rescue, they need steady relational ground.

Some guiding principles:

- **Pace through the Adult Self**: Engage with child parts only after checking with the system. This preserves internal boundaries and reinforces safety.
- **Signal safety through presence**: A quiet tone, relaxed posture, and consistent attunement do more than words.
- **Normalize trauma-time perspective**: When a client says, "Part of me feels like a child", we might respond,
  - ★ "That makes sense. Sometimes there are parts that didn't get to grow up."

- ★ "It makes sense, there might be parts that still don't know you grew up."

- **Keep these parts in mind even when they are hidden**: A part does not need to speak to be included. We can say,
    - ★ "Even if we don't hear from them today, we are keeping her/him/they in mind."

- **Repair relationship, not extract content.** Showing up, communicating or participating in any way, must always be introduced as a choice.

Finally, remember that working with child parts is not about finding out what happened, it is about repairing relationship. These parts do not need to be drawn out or included if they are not active. We keep them in mind and remember to cultivate a way of relating and a safe space where showing up is a choice, not a demand.

At the same time, child parts may become activated outside of sessions, often in moments of loneliness, vulnerability, or exhaustion, such as during the night. In these situations, the task is not to pursue them or analyze their content, but to support whatever capacities are available in the system to offer presence, grounding, and care from parts that function in daily life. Preparing the client to respond with gentleness, containment, or to seek external support when needed helps ensure that activation does not become overwhelming or isolating.

Maintaining Therapeutic Boundaries

The presence of younger parts often evokes emotional responses in the therapist, protectiveness, tenderness, or a pull to soothe. While these are natural reactions, they must be held with care. It cannot be overstated: younger parts are not literal children in need of external caregiving; they are internal expressions of overwhelming experience, shaped by distress, threat, and unmet needs. Moving too quickly to comfort or take over can disrupt the system's own capacity for internal connection and unintentionally reenact dependency dynamics.

What builds safety is not intensity, but steadiness. The therapist models a grounded, adult stance that is:

- Clear and warm, without overstepping.
- Responsive without rushing in.

- Able to witnesses pain without needing to resolve it.

This often sounds like an invitation to a cooperative work between client and therapist, not a rescue:

★ "You don't have to do anything right now, I'm here. Even if this is hard to stay with, we can go slowly together."

Rather than directing care toward the younger part, the therapist supports the client's capacity to relate inwardly, especially through the Adult Self. This strengthens internal trust and avoids pulling the therapist into a central rescuing role. In disorganized attachment, direct bids for rescue can flip the system through the classic victim–rescuer–persecutor triangle; if the therapist is cast as *rescuer*, backlash often arrives quickly as attack or withdrawal.

To prevent reenactment, the stance shifts from attachment-activation to cooperation. In disorganized attachment, interactions tend to oscillate among persecutor, victim, and rescuer positions; activating attachment directly often intensifies alarm and role-switching. For this reason, an attachment system organized around threat and deficit should not be further stimulated but gently redirected toward cooperative engagement. Using inclusive, non-demanding language supports the client in functioning at a higher level of integration, inviting reflection, shared attention, and choice. Rather than activating a distinct Adult Self, these moments facilitate access to integrative capacities as they become available in the here and now. Over time, this cooperative stance replaces urgent calls for rescue with shared agency and choice.

★ "What if we look at this together?"
★ "Shall we see what happens next?"

Keep in mind that cooperation signals safety; attachment activation signals danger and alarm.

Obtaining Permission from the System

As introduced in previous sections of this chapter, before turning therapeutic attention toward younger parts, it is essential to check in with the broader system. Many internal reactions, such as withdrawal, switching, or shutdown, are not signs of resistance, but protective strategies. They often reflect concern that therapy is moving too quickly, becoming too exposed, or bypassing internal agreements that have kept the system functional.

It cannot be emphasized enough that, whenever possible, this work should be mediated through the Adult Self. Direct engagement with younger parts without internal consent can inadvertently disrupt internal structure, increase dependency, or escalate disorganization. Working through the Adult Self, which is the most integrative way of doing the work, reinforces internal leadership, respects relational boundaries within the system, and supports long-term autonomy.

Some examples of this kind of internal inquiry include:

★ "Would it feel okay to acknowledge that this younger experience is present right now?"
★ "Is there anything I need to understand before we bring attention to this part of the system?"
★ "Can we check together if this is the right moment, or if more support is needed first?"

If the response is no, we honor that fully. That "no" is not a failure, it is meaningful information. In practice, this often leads to a second, equally important inquiry:

★ "What would need to be in place for this to feel safer or more possible later?"

The capacity of any part of the system to express limits, caution, or hesitation is itself a form of healing. It reflects movement away from reenactments of voicelessness or coercion and toward internal trust.

This approach also models how the Adult Self, and eventually other internal roles, can relate to younger parts with clarity, steadiness, and respect. Rather than seeking immediate access or emotional display, the focus is on conditions: creating the internal and relational ground in which younger parts may gradually become present in awareness and in the therapeutic relationship, if and when it feels safe for them to do so.

Remember: the goal is not to *get to* younger parts. It is to create the internal climate in which their experience can be acknowledged, included, and held, without urgency or demand.

Clinical Vignette

I Think She Likes Animals

A woman in her 30s was seated across from the therapist in an office that included a few shelves with toys, books, and drawings. During the session, her gaze wandered toward the shelf. Within seconds, she looked away and lowered her head. She tried to continue the conversation, but her attention drifted back to the shelf again, followed by the same reaction: looking down, as if ashamed.

The therapist gently observed, "It seems something on that shelf is catching your attention. It's okay to look". The client remained silent. The therapist added, "We can even take some of those things if they seem interesting". After a longer pause, the client pointed to a wooden animal puzzle and quietly asked, "What are those for?"

It seemed like a younger part was more present. The therapist took the wooden puzzle and offered it to the client. There was a visible inner struggle to engage and look away. The therapist validated this again: "Maybe something inside is curious, that would be okay too." After a brief pause, the client nodded and admitted, "Maybe, yeah, I think she likes animals".

With quiet permission, the therapist offered the puzzle as a bridge. Together, they used it gently to orient the younger part in time. Using the pieces, the therapist invited the client to ask the younger part what she noticed, and whether she could look at the puzzle through the Adult's eyes. "She says she hopes it can help", the client responded.

As they explored what that meant, it became clear that this simple wooden puzzle was helping the younger part orient to feel the safety of the present moment in the therapy room.

The therapist said, "It's good to know she can look through your eyes and see what's in this room. Can she see me?" The client nodded. "Fantastic", the therapist replied. "That means she's beginning to grasp that she's not there anymore." The client looked surprised. "Why?" she asked. "Because this puzzle, and what's in this room, wasn't there. And neither was I", the therapist answered.

After a long reflective pause, the client said quietly, "It's like some light just entered the dark room where I always see this part".

Motivational and Action Systems at Play

Note on shame: In this scene, shame fits better under rank/power (fear of negative judgment) than under defense. Defense is the inhibitory move (freeze); shame is the evaluation threat (judgement) from a hierarchy internalized elsewhere (and may belong to another, non-child part). Also, shared play itself is not cooperation, but here it enables cooperation. The true cooperation shows up when Adult and Child align perspectives to view the room as safe enough and to hold the puzzle as a bridge.

SYSTEMS	WHERE IT SHOWS UP	FUNCTION	CLINICAL IMPORTANCE
Exploration/Play System	Gaze drawn to the wooden animal puzzle; quiet questions; tentative engagement with pieces.	Reopens curiosity and learning in a safe-enough context; signals a shift from pure survival toward engagement and spontaneity.	Permissioned invitation ("it's okay to look") nurtures this system; a hopeful marker that defense is easing and integration can grow.
Defense System (Flight/Freeze)	Head lowering, looking away, difficulty sustaining eye contact or play; internal pull to hide visibility/ vulnerability. Emotion: Fear	Reduces perceived risk by inhibiting movement and expression; keeps the system from "being seen."	Go slow. Use brief, reversible steps with a practiced stop-signal; validate the function ("keeping you safe") while updating method (pacing vs. shutdown).
Rank System Negative Evaluation	Downcast posture and self-consciousness that anticipate being judged or scolded for "curiosity/play." Emotion: Shame	Avoids humiliation or status threat by self-limiting before an imagined evaluator does it.	De-shame explicitly: normalize curiosity/play; remove "courtroom" language; emphasize "no wrong way to notice" to reduce rank threat.
Attachment System Safety-Seeking	Acceptance of the therapist's offer; allowing the object to be a bridge; "she hopes it can help." Signals (subtle)	Seeks safe-enough engagement and recognition rather than overt rescue; tests whether play/curiosity can exist without punishment.	Provide steady, non-intrusive presence; mirror recognition ("someone inside is curious") without pushing proximity.

Table 13.1. Motivational and action systems at play in the vignette

Clinical Reflections

When we lead with permission, treat curiosity/play as a safety-tilt signal, offer gentle, reversible invitations ("It's okay to look", "We can stop any time") and adapt pacing (with practiced stop-signal when needed), changes begin to take place, defenses seem to decrease or soften. Notice each micro-step, name when useful, and re-orient to now when needed. De-shame by addressing rank/evaluation threat, name that the fear is of being judged, not "being bad", and remove any tone that might sound judgmental, harsh or infantilizing ("no wrong way to notice", "curiosity is welcome here").

If a critical part appears, engage it with curiosity about its concerns, make cooperation explicit. Highlight Adult–Child alignment ("two parts inside are looking together") and invite the Adult Self to set pace and words; repair misreads promptly to build trust and intersubjectivity.

With non-dissociative clients we often cultivate collaboration through *We* language and curiosity about others' intentions and the client's own reactions. In dissociative systems the same stance is directed inward, between parts. The work is done on two parallel tracks: (1) therapist–client co-regulation to establish safety, and (2) Adult Self–parts dialogue that grows internal metacognition about each part's aims and functions. Use time-orientation concretely. The object is a bridge to now: "This puzzle wasn't there then, neither was I". Repeat until the part can begin to believe it as a possibility (full belief cannot be when conflict is so high and parts are stuck in trauma time).

Close cleanly and prevent future obstacles by planning aftercare. Leave time to regulate (breath/grounding), name what helped, and anticipate backlash ("If shame or doubt shows up later, we will treat it as protection, useful information, and review here together"). Track progress markers: easier re-engagement after brief pauses; less rank-threat tone. What was avoided: insisting on direct eye contact or performing play, debating the content of shame, or rushing proximity because engagement appears. Instead, therapists let permission and pacing do the work.

Building Relationship Over Time

Work with child parts is rarely linear, and almost never predictable. A part may emerge clearly one week and seem to vanish for many sessions afterward. This is not necessarily avoidance. Parts are not continuously present; they become active when triggered or when conditions evoke them. That is why some parts remain unnamed, unnoticed, or unacknowledged for long stretches. They are not gone; they are simply not activated.

Although clinicians may feel the urge to check in with quieter parts when they do not come up for a while, this is not the goal. In general, we work with what is active in the moment. We do not try to evoke or search for parts that are not emerging or do not make their internal presence noticeable. As stated in chapter 1, these are not fixed entities waiting for airtime, but internal configurations shaped by ongoing processes and changing triggers.

When a part is not present, nothing is missing. There is no requirement to summon or reference every part in every session. Actively searching for a child part who has not emerged can introduce unnecessary strain or internal confusion. What matters is that we keep them—along with the rest of the system—within our field of awareness, even when they are quiet.

Do not push for more access, remain steadily present and process oriented. Safety grows from consistency, not intensity. We show the system, especially child parts, that they are not remembered only when expressive or distressed. Their existence does not depend on visibility.

When it seems a child part may be near, but the Adult Self has not noticed, consider checking in a gentle and indirect way. For example:

- ★ "I wonder how the little one inside (or whatever name they use) is doing today."
- ★ "Even if we don't hear from them, we are still holding them in mind."
- ★ "They don't have to come forward; we just want them to know they're welcome."

These gestures reinforce the foundation of safety. They remind the system that connection does not depend on performance or disclosure. That relationship can exist even in absence. Over time, this stance is internalized, not just by child parts, but by the entire system. The goal is an enduring, respectful relationship that can hold presence and absence without rupture.

This is also where the therapeutic space, shaped by consistency, tone, and attunement, becomes an internal reference point. When the therapist stays present without pushing for contact, younger parts begin to test the environment in new ways. They may linger longer, even silently, observing. They begin to notice what is different: danger is not happening now and safety might be real.

Curiosity About How These Parts Express and What it Means

As mentioned in the features section, some of these parts take time to express directly, others emerge quickly, especially when a safe therapeutic space begins to take shape. And when they do come close, it is not necessarily a sign that direct engagement is helpful or safe; or that the Adult Self is ready to engage. Remember that these parts are often deeply entwined with complex internal dynamics, including aggressive parts, punitive voices, or parts aligned with perpetrators. Their presence can stir internal chaos and even trigger backlash after the session. Careful with doing too much.

The therapist's task is not to move in too quickly, but to observe, attune and listen closely. The emergence of a younger part is not a call to intervene, but an invitation to understand what is happening in the system, and to notice how other parts are responding. Understanding internal dynamics and modeling safe observation is the foundation of this work, only from there can real contact and exploration take place. Safety, not access, must remain the guiding principle.

Practically, this means:

★ Using *we* language and co-designed micro-steps: "What if we look together for ten seconds and then stop?"
★ Checking conditions with protectors first and keeping proximity optional: "You set the distance; I'll match it)."
★ When the system pulls for rescue, we name and decline the role without shaming: "I feel the pull to swoop in; instead, let's help your Adult take the lead while I stay with you both."

CLINICAL VIGNETTE

A Child Part in Crisis Time

A young adult client arrived at the clinic visibly dysregulated: pacing in the waiting area, agitated, and on the verge of tears. When the therapist invited her into the room, she immediately said she needed to leave and go to the emergency room.

The therapist remained grounded, calmly reminding her that they still had an hour together and that there was no need to rush. "If by the end of the session you still feel you need to go, of course you can", the therapist reassured. "Let's try to understand what is happening." After a few moments, the client sat down. Her distress continued.

The therapist explored what might have triggered the panic. "Nothing", the client replied. "Nothing important happened."

"How is everything inside?" the therapist asked. "You mean the little girl who's crying?" the client responded. "For example, yes", the therapist said. "So, there is a little girl crying. Do you hear her, or do you also see her?" The client hesitated, then said, "I see her". "Where do you see her?", asked the therapist. After a pause, the client replied, "She's in bed, hiding under the covers". The therapist remained curious. "What bed is that?" The client's expression shifted, her eyes widening. "It's my bed... from when I was little."

This marked a clear moment of realization: the part that had taken over was not in the present. It was a younger part, stuck in trauma time. From there, the therapist gently supported the Adult Self in differentiating past from present, grounding in the safety of the here-and-now and extending compassionate curiosity toward the child part.

They spoke about how the younger part might be feeling, what she was afraid of, and what she might need now. The therapist helped the client orient the younger part to the current moment: that she was no longer alone, no longer in that bed, and that what awaited her now was support, not punishment or danger.

As the session progressed, the client's breathing slowed. Her posture softened. The child part settled. Near the end of the session, the client said quietly, "She's not crying anymore." The urge to flee to the emergency room had faded. Something had shifted. Safety had reached the system, not through medication or crisis management, but through attuned presence, time orientation, and relational repair.

Motivational and Action Systems at Play

Note on entanglement: The urge to go to the ER reflects attachment distortion. The system seeks safety by appealing to an omnipotent Protector (doctor/hospital) rather than turning toward cooperation with the therapist in the here-and-now.

For the child part, shared regulation feels too risky (entrusting someone else with that need could expose them to rejection or failure). By outsourcing safety to an all-powerful authority, the system avoids the danger of needing the therapist directly.

SYSTEMS	WHERE IT SHOWS UP	FUNCTION	SURVIVAL LOGIC
Defense — flight/collapse	Arrives panicked; urgent wish to leave for the ER; agitation, pacing, near-tears.	Escape overwhelming internal arousal; outsource danger management to an external setting.	If I leave now, the feelings can't swallow me; a hospital will stop what I can't stop.
Rank/Power — submission to authority	"I need to go to the ER" framed as the only solution; difficulty considering co-regulation in-session.	Seek control/safety by transferring responsibility to a higher authority/setting.	If someone in charge takes over, I won't be blamed or left to fail at calming down.
Attachment — care-seeking (blocked/ disorganized)	No direct request for comfort from therapist; "nothing important happened"; child part is hidden/crying "under the covers."	Protect proximity by avoiding exposure; test safety indirectly.	If I don't ask here, I can't be shamed or refused; distance feels safer than asking.
Caregiving — internal/ Adult-Self engagement	Therapist invites the Adult Self to notice, name, and speak with the child part; differentiates then/now.	Provide containment and soothing from within the system; reduce dependency on external crisis fixes.	If the Adult can care for the child inside, we don't have to run to be safe.

Table 13.2. Motivational and action systems at play in the vignette

Clinical Reflection

First, it is important to read the ER impulse accurately. It is not simple care-seeking; it is defense (flight), entangled with attachment (distorted/ outsourced). Safety is handed over to an external authority rather than risked in the therapeutic relationship. Validate the need for rapid relief without colluding with escape: "If by the end you still want to go, you can. Let's first understand what's happening together". That stance keeps choice intact, lowers threat, and slows the flight reflex.

Next, make permission and pacing explicit. Rehearse the stop-signal; invite tiny, reversible moves (naming what the Adult sees, one breath, one orienting glance) rather than pushing content. Use concrete time-orientation ("That bed isn't in this room, or in your actual room now in 2025") to differentiate then/now at the body level. As reflective capacity returns, consult protectors so the Adult's caregiving can proceed without backlash.

Finally, close predictably and plan aftercare (brief grounding, "what helped", normalize possible post-session wobble). Progress markers include: the urge to bolt giving way to pausing and re-engagement; the ER-as-only-option softening to "maybe we can try a few minutes"; protectors becoming consultable; and the child part being held by the Adult Self without immediate collapse or flight.

Why attachment is not primary here: "Going to the hospital" is resorting to a specific form of disorganized attachment, which moves between the three positions of the *drama triangle* (persecutor, rescuer, victim). In this case, it is the search for a powerful rescuer who will free the client from her problems.

The therapist recognizes the client's emotional state but proposes a completely different emotional solution: trying to work together to understand. In other words, she shifts the emotional dialogue from attachment, a compromised system, to a cooperative and collaborative system between peers.

Cooperation emerges later and more subtly, once defense eases and the system tests whether it can be seen, soothed, and believed in the room. This is not a direct bid for co-regulation with the therapist, but a defensive exit that outsources safety; genuine cooperation emerges only after defense eases. At the beginning of the session, the therapist is clearly not seen by the client as a powerful protector or savior. This is possibly due to the therapist's previous attitude, which did not promote the use of attachment in the therapeutic relationship. In fact, the characteristic of disorganized attachment is its extreme instability, the ease with which one passes from savior to persecutor or victim.

The therapist still offers warmth and steadiness, but channels care through collaborative procedure (permission before proximity, stop signal honored immediately, brief approach and reliable return). Cooperation becomes the safety signal; attachment can follow once the body trusts the process.

You might invite:

- "Would it feel okay to sit beside this part for a moment?"
- "Could you let them know they're not alone, in whatever way feels possible?"

These are gentle, non-demanding invitations. They offer options, not instructions. Over time, this approach helps clients discover that they can remain present with vulnerability, without being overtaken by it.

CLOSING THOUGHTS

Child parts offer one of the clearest windows into the division of care-seeking and submission systems and the legacy of early relational trauma. They also carry the original longing for connection, comfort, and safety that never happened. When they are welcomed, understood, and respected, other dynamics can unfold in the system; the past begins to lose its grip.

Our role is to introduce a new reality where the present is no longer perceived as dangerous, and they no longer feel isolated. We stay present, consistent, predictable, ask for preferences and listen. We remind them repeatedly, as many times as needed.

Clinical Anchors

What to remember...

- Younger parts do not need to be *accessed* to be taken into account. Sudden shifts in affect, posture, or tone may signal proximity. Stay curious about emotional or somatic cues.
- Always check the system's readiness. Permission matters. Hesitation is not resistance, it is protection.
- Containment is relational. Your tone, pacing, and steadiness offer safety which is more important than technique.
- Boundaries matter. Be warm and responsive without stepping into parental or rescuing roles.
- Child parts often carry grief, shame, and unmet longing. These are not symptoms to solve; they are truths to witness.

What to avoid...

- Child-like language or tone that treats parts as literal children rather than inner representations of emotional experiences.
- Rushing to interpret or analyze fragments of memory instead of simply holding the space.
- Moving into a parental or rescuing role that undermines the client's Adult Self leadership.
- Invalidating vulnerability rather than acknowledging difficulties and survival strategies.
- Filling the space for silence with comfort or reassurance.

Chapter 14: Adolescent Parts

Therapist Reflection

When a teenage part shows up with a stare that says, "Try me", it's easy to become either the strict parent or the overly nice friend. Neither helps. If we can meet them without power-struggling—respecting their opinion, explicitly asking for it, offering real choice, and keeping our word—protest softens into collaboration.

Adolescent parts sit at a hinge in development, and often at a hinge in treatment. Following chapter 13 on child parts, we continue to focus on trauma-time states organized around attachment and defense. Like child parts, adolescent parts carry unmet care-seeking needs, unprocessed threat, and time-anchored meanings that have not yet updated to the present. They may also hold sensory fragments, shame, or despair tied to betrayals by attachment figures. For this reason, it could make sense to group child and teen presentations together. And yet, many systems benefit from recognizing adolescent organization specifically.

Where child parts seek proximity and protection more directly through appeasing, hiding, freezing, or clinging, adolescent parts often add another layer: rank, status, and identity. Adolescence is the developmental moment when the rank/power motivational system comes online, alongside peer affiliation and sexual or romantic bonding. Teens test limits to locate self, rules, and place. In trauma-organized systems, that same thrust is redirected toward survival, showing up as sharp right/wrong lines, rapid threat appraisal, group belonging as a shield, and protest to control proximity and ward off shame.

Teenager years also bring a social-cognitive shift. The child begins to turn into an adult who makes meaning through their own ideas and through peers. They no longer look only to family for answers but compare family norms with peer norms (and their families). For many clients, this is when they first realize that what happened or happens at home is not happening in all families. They may not yet have the tools to act on that discovery, but the intent—and the awareness of discrepancy—are already present.

Finally, adolescence often brings a sense of bigness. For many clients, adolescence was the first time the body felt "big enough to push back". That new sense of strength makes boundary-setting and status protection central tasks for teen parts. What can look oppositional in the therapy room such as sarcasm, eye-rolling, rule-testing, blunt challenge, may actually be an effort to prevent re-submission to a caregiver who should have protected and empowered them but instead deceived and harmed them.

Adolescent parts form the early architecture from which more complex protector roles may later consolidate. Early intervention is key before these strategies harden into fixed patterns.

ORIGIN OF ADOLESCENT PARTS

While rooted in the early conditions described in chapter 13 (attachment-defense collision, disorganized caregiving, chronic misattunement and coercion, secrecy, or betrayal), adolescent parts often crystallize later, around first feelings of agency, peer rank, and identity sorting. When safety remains uncertain, protest becomes a new way to try to change things; to set boundaries: set rules, keep exposure down, and prevent shame. Over time, if conditions do not change, these can consolidate into more coercive strategies (see chapter on *Hostile and Aggressive Parts*). Certain developmental amplifiers accent the tone of these parts, which can turn brief sparks into repeated strategies:

- Early experiences of shame and humiliation.
- First awareness of physical power or size differences.
- Peer hierarchies and belonging pressures (school, teams, online groups).
- Moral sorting as identity glue (right/wrong, loyal/disloyal).
- Public exposure or reputational injury.

These amplifiers give adolescent parts a distinct flavor in the therapy room.

MAIN FEATURES OF ADOLESCENT PARTS

Compared with child parts, teen parts bring a different tone: language shifts toward rank and fairness; respect and consistency become decisive. While therapists are crucial relational figures, initial attention is often pulled toward peer dynamics, image management, and fitting-in.

Looking for these common presentations in session will help us recognize these parts:

- **Fight-tilted signals and stance.** Sarcasm, refusal, or a defiant glare may surface, along with challenges such as, "Don't you dare" or "Try me". Spikes of sarcasm or abrupt hard limits often follow moments of softness.
- **Exposure control.** Topic-shifting, selective non-answers, or hedging/withholding appear as ways to manage visibility ("I don't know", "Maybe", "Could be"). As child states near exposure, rapid protector recruitment is common.
- **Procedural control and rank monitoring.** Hypervigilance to the therapist's tone and posture is common, as is scanning for judgmental language.
- **Peer/status focus.** High attention goes to belonging, group norms, fashion, and slang. Active image management is central, alongside ongoing evaluation of the therapist's credibility.
- **Aftermath markers.** Post-session backlash often shows up as "I messed up" or "This is stupid", functioning as self-protection after perceived exposure.

FUNCTIONS OF ADOLESCENT PARTS

The adolescent presentations below are not just styles of interaction; they are embodied functions. Although some of the descriptions can also fit with ego states, use the rationale in chapter 2 to assess real developed dissociative parts. Teen parts can flip modes as context shifts; a protector can move from supportive to cutting when not heard. Each fulfills a distinct job:

- **Protester-Boundary-Setter.** Direct and outspoken, often calling out unfairness or hypocrisy. Its function is to keep adults honest, preserve fairness in the frame, and block humiliation.
  Systems: Rank/power (status protection), defense–fight (territorial boundary), and attachment deflected (proximity guaranteed by the action of standing guard).
  Survival logic: "If I hold the line and set the rules, the small one won't be shamed or hurt again."

- **Detached Teen.** Presents with a flat or ironic tone, frequent "whatever", and minimal disclosure. This stance reduces visibility, controls exposure, and lowers the stakes.
  Systems: Defense–deactivation/flight, rank/power (refusal of evaluation), and attachment denied (distance regulation).
  Survival logic: "If I don't show need, you can't use it against me."

- **Parentified Teen.** Hyper-competent, crisis-managing, and quick to minimize personal needs. Its role is to keep the system functioning and preempt criticism by outperforming it.
  Systems: Caregiving (reversed attachment), rank/power (competence superiority), and defense (avoidance of attack).
  Survival logic:" If I carry the load perfectly, no one will hurt or humiliate us."

- **Achiever.** Perfectionistic, rule-literate, and self-disciplining. This part converts vulnerability into advantage, gaining status to reduce exposure.
  *Systems***:** Rank/power, using Exploration/ achievement at its service, and deactivate the need of attachment (belonging through competence).
  Survival logic: "If I'm top-rank, I'm safer and less exposed."

- **Risk-Tester.** Sensation-seeking and limit-pushing. It asserts agency where helplessness once dominated and works to prove "I'm not small anymore".
  Systems: Exploration/novelty, rank/power (agency assertion), and defense (anti-collapse).
  Survival logic: "If I take the risk, I decide the terms, fear doesn't. I'm no more submissive, I'm capable in the extreme."

- **Chameleon.** Adaptable, tuned to group norms, fashion, and slang, curating image with care. Its purpose is to secure belonging as armor and to avoid outsider shame.
  Systems: Attachment through Affiliation (peer bonding as source of security), rank/power (status signaling), and search of self-empowering through Sexual/Romantic bonding (early experiments).
  Survival logic: "If I belong visibly, I won't be singled out and shamed."

Across these presentations, protest functions as protection. Teen guardians often stand between others and a younger part with the implicit message: "I'll take the heat. Back off." The aim is proximity management and humiliation-prevention, not hostility for its own sake. Structurally, adolescent parts shield vulnerability.

FUNCTION (PROTOTYPE)	DOMINANT MOTIVATIONAL/ACTION SYSTEMS	CLINICAL STANCE / WHAT HELPS
Protester / Boundary-Setter	Rank/Power; Defense—fight; Attachment (guarded)	Name function first; co-set rules; keep every agreement; avoid moralizing
Detached Teen	Defense—deactivation/flight; Rank/Power (refusal of evaluation)	Lower evaluation threat; allow low-disclosure engagement; invite tiny, reversible steps
Parentified Teen	Caregiving (reversed); Rank/Power (competence); Defense	Respect competence without over-relying; invite burden-sharing; protect against shame
Achiever	Rank/Power; Exploration/achievement; Attachment (belonging via competence)	Decenter performance as worth; widen identity; normalize rest and error
Risk-Tester	Exploration/novelty; Rank/Power (agency); Defense (anti-collapse)	Offer safe "tests"; set clear edges; debrief outcomes; honor agency without glamorizing risk
Chameleon	Attachment/affiliation; Rank/Power (status signaling); Sexual/Romantic bonding	Validate belonging needs; separate safety from image; track consent and pacing

Table 14-1. Adolescent Part Functions, Dominant Systems, and Clinical Stance. *Note on motivational entanglement in adolescent parts*: When the caregiver (and sometimes the therapist frame by transference) is read as both haven and hazard, attachment and defense co-activate. With adolescence, Rank/power and peer affiliation add layers: protest guards dignity; image management guards belonging; rule-setting guards proximity. Mapping which systems are active clarifies function (what the part is solving) and guides de-activation conditions: explicit fairness, reversible steps, real choices, and Adult-led cooperation.

Keep in mind that when protest escalates into intimidation, punishment, or control (even after rank threat has lowered and rules are clear) the work has moved beyond typical adolescent organization. At that point, the material links forward to hostile and aggressive parts, (see following chapters where strategies for those presentations are addressed in more detail). This chapter's task is to stay with the adolescent frame: protest as protection, stance as survival, and collaboration as the opening toward repair. With that frame in place, the next step is learning how to meet adolescent parts in practice.

RELATING TO ADOLESCENT PARTS

Protest at the doorway is communication, not mere resistance. When therapists recognize protest as a boundary tool, the teen part can be engaged as a collaborator to co-design the frame of work. Stance adjustments from work with child parts:

- **Honor rank sensitivity.** Be clear about how decisions are made, what is negotiable, and what is not. Offer realistic choices and keep every agreement. Fairness steadies the rank system.
- **Name function before content.** When a part pushes back, reflect the job before debating details. Naming the role highlights purpose rather than fueling argument.
  - ★ "I see this as your way of keeping the frame honest and protecting the smaller one. Let's work with that."
- **Invite co-construction of rules.** Teen parts often settle when they help shape the terms of contact and what will be worked on and how. In some cases, decisions about where to sit, how close to go, what should be considered as "too much", how important it is to express opinion and communicate anything that does not fit; these all become opportunities for collaboration. Track nonverbal communication (posture, gaze, withdrawal) as information the part is giving you, not as a sign of resistance or judgment
- **Avoid parentification or relating as a peer.** Resist slipping into scolding on the one hand or over-buddying on the other. Meet the teen as an emerging adult who holds real leverage in the work.
- **Expect tests and welcome them.** Testing is communication, not defiance. When a part probes whether you will shame, collude, or dominate, meet the test with curiosity rather than more control. This aligns with Control-Mastery Theory: clients actively test therapists to disconfirm pathogenic beliefs; when we *pass* the test, trust and movement become possible (Weiss & Sampson, 1986).

Clinical Vignette

A Teen Protector Sets the Terms

A 25-year-old client enters with her hood up, arms crossed, and chooses the chair nearest the door. Without sitting fully, she says flatly, "Don't do the inner-child thing". The therapist keeps rank threat low. "Got it—that's fine. Can you help me understand where that's coming from?" "Last session it felt kind of nice, but then she started asking for more. I don't know", said the client. "That makes sense—'more' felt like pressure. We don't have to do any inner-child work today. If we work with that at all, you set the limits and pacing. What would help?" the therapist replied.

The voice that answers is older, edged. "No eye contact. Door stays clear. Ten minutes only. No 'comforting voice.' And you don't talk to her." "Agreed", the therapist says. "You'll call stop; I'll stop immediately." With the rules visible (chairs angled, clock in view, door path clear), the therapist routes contact through the Adult Self. "Would your Adult be willing to take the lead, while I stay back and track time?"

A small nod. The teen protector adds, "She's under the table... at home. The old house." The therapist doesn't turn toward the "child" but stays with the teen: "Your job is to keep exposure down. For twenty seconds, could you look from now and just notice one neutral detail in this room—then we stop?" The client glances at the clock. "Digital, not the kitchen one." "Right—digital clock, 2025", the therapist reflects. "No one from that house is here. Ten seconds more, then we close."

The teen's tone softens a notch: "Fine. But you don't talk to her." "I won't", the therapist replies. "If it helps, you can pass one sentence to the small one: 'We're older now; I'll decide the distance'." (Teenager part communicating to child part.) After a quiet moment: "She heard it." Breathing slows. Shoulders drop a little. The teen part adds (through Adult Self), "No more today".

"Stopping now", the therapist says, and shifts into closing and aftercare. The session closes on time. No child work occurred, yet proximity was negotiated, rank threat lowered, and the protector remained consultable.

SYSTEM	WHERE IT SHOWS UP	FUNCTION	SURVIVAL LOGIC
Defense System	Rules about door position, eye contact, time limits; sharp tone; control of gaze	Keeps arousal and exposure below threshold	If I control space, time, and access, nothing bad can happen.
Rank / Power System	"Don't do the inner-child thing"; rule-setting; monitoring therapist compliance	Prevents coercion, humiliation, or loss of authority	If I set the terms, no one can override or diminish us.
Attachment System (inhibited)	Explicit prohibition of comforting voice, eye contact, or child address	Prevents activation of dependency, longing, or vulnerability	If attachment stays off, we stay safe.
Cooperation (procedural, non-relational)	Negotiated rules, stop-signal honored, brief orienting task	Enables joint action without intimacy or submission	We can work together as long as no one crosses the rules.

Table 14.1 Motivational and action systems at play in the vignette.

Clinical reflection

The key intervention in this vignette is not *what* the therapist does, but *how* she reads and responds to the protest. The teen protector's "no" is not resistance to overcome; it is a coordinated deployment of defense and rank systems designed to keep fear of exposure and shame within tolerable boundaries.

Rather than reframing or reassuring, the therapist validates the experience of too much, too fast and immediately restores choice: "We don't have to do more. If we work at all, you set the limits." This stance lowers rank threat and transforms a rigid refusal into negotiable terms.

By routing contact through the Adult Self or parts functioning in daily life with higher capacities, the therapist avoids direct activation of attachment or caregiving systems that would violate the protector's rules. The single sentence passed to the younger part is brief, contained, and mediated—supporting internal caregiving without collapsing boundaries.

Importantly, no direct child work occurs. Yet something shifts: proximity becomes possible, orientation to the present is achieved, and the protector's vigilance softens. Cooperation emerges not through soothing, insight, or challenge, but through procedural reliability and respect for hierarchy and function.

This vignette illustrates how effective parts work often looks deceptively minimal. When motivational systems are read accurately and honored, safety increases without force and protectors that once blocked access can help pacing the work.

- **Track shame explicitly.** Many teen strategies are built to block humiliation. If you can notice shame and work to reduce its load, protest often softens.

Honoring the identity work underway makes collaboration possible. Swap "Why aren't you collaborating?" for "What are you protecting?"

Adolescent parts often stand between the parts functioning in daily life and younger parts, translating in both directions. As Adult Self becomes more consistently fair, boundaried, and competent, adolescent parts can relax edge and join cooperation. In practice, keep child parts offstage while negotiating terms with the teen guardian.

CLOSING THOUGHTS

Adolescent protectors are often the first internal evidence of power, rank, and boundary-setting recruited in the service of safety. When their purpose is recognized and their method updated, they can shift from blockading to collaborative guardianship. Protest is not something to suppress; it is a resource for negotiating safety, dignity, and proximity.

If protest hardens into coercion, intimidation, or punishment despite fairness and clear rules, the work has moved beyond adolescent organization. In those cases, transition to hostile and aggressive parts for guidance on addressing those roles directly.

For most adolescent parts, however, the clinical task is simpler and subtler: respect their stance, meet them as collaborators, and keep every agreement. These moves update time, reduce shame, and preserve dignity; the ground on which adolescent protectors can eventually stand down and join the wider system.

Clinical Anchors

What to remember...

- Recognize protest as a boundary tool, not mere resistance.
- Honor rank sensitivity by offering real choice and keeping every agreement.
- Name function before content (frame the job rather than debating the details).
- Invite co-construction of rules and conditions of contact.
- Treat the part as an emerging adult with leverage in the work.
- Track shame explicitly; help lower the shame load.
- Expect tests; welcome them as communication.

What to avoid...

- Do not interpret protest as defiance to extinguish.
- Avoid scolding, moralizing, or taking the *strict parent* stance.
- Do not over-buddy or collapse into relating to them as peers.
- Avoid offering fake choices or agreements you cannot keep.
- Do not bypass the adolescent part to reach younger parts directly; negotiate terms with the teen first.

Chapter 15: Fearful and Avoidant Parts

THERAPIST REFLECTION

Early in our work, I felt a familiar trust had been built. I'd been patient in silence, gently inviting her into contact over many months. So, I was baffled when, midway through a session, she suddenly froze and recoiled from me. For a moment, I felt uncomfortable and confused. How could she fear me now? Then she whispered, "You remind me of him", naming her perpetrator. I realized her frightened part had hijacked her experience, still stuck in trauma time and unable to see me as safe. In that moment, I understood that well-intentioned people had caused her deepest wounds, and that my true task was to embody patience long enough for her system to relearn trust.

Fearful and avoidant parts are often misunderstood in clinical work. They might go silent mid-session, dissociate behind a polite smile, or show up physically while emotionally shut down. Some miss appointments; others say everything is fine even when it is not.

To the untrained eye, these behaviors can look like resistance or ambivalence. In truth, they are acts of protection. Over years—sometimes decades—these parts have learned that visibility leads to harm, speaking up results in punishment or abandonment, and asking for help can make things worse. It is not defiance. It is survival.

To engage these parts, the therapist must shift from seeking participation to offering permission. Connection is not built through urgency or persuasion, but through presence, calm, non-intrusive, and open to whatever may or may not happen.

ORIGIN OF FEARFUL AND AVOIDANT PARTS

Fearful and avoidant parts emerge from environments where being visible or needing others led to harm. Common shaping conditions are:

- Early neglect, intrusion, or inconsistent caregiving.
- Trauma in which hiding or shutting down was safest.
- Attachment wounds where closeness was paired with danger.
- Punishment, invalidation, or betrayal for expressing emotion or need.

Whether the caregiving environment was emotionally absent or overwhelmingly enmeshed, the system learned one core truth: It is safer not to show up.

Avoidance became more than a behavior, it became a worldview, shaped by messages such as: "Don't need, don't feel, don't be too much or connection will cost you".

When a child's needs were met with punishment, ridicule, or abandonment, withdrawal became wisdom. Over time, fearful parts internalized: "If I speak, I'll be hurt—or I'll hurt someone else".

MAIN FEATURES OF FEARFUL AND AVOIDANT PARTS

Fearful and avoidant parts rarely announce themselves directly. They surface as absence, hesitation, or subtle cues of disconnection. What can look like passivity or disengagement is often a careful assessment: "Is it safe to stay present?"

Common presentations include:

- Numbness or "I don't know" responses.
- Smiling or laughing while describing painful events.
- Changing the subject when closeness arises.
- Somatic cues such as blank stare, muscle collapse, shallow breathing.
- Missed sessions or polite compliance without emotional presence.
- Emotional flatness or reported lack of inner experience.

The core dynamic is disconnection as protection—even when the client appears engaged, these parts may be watching from the edges, unsure or afraid.

FUNCTIONS OF FEARFUL AND AVOIDANT PARTS

Fearful and avoidant parts perform specific survival tasks rooted in trauma-time logic. These strategies evolved to protect the system from relational and emotional danger. Their primary functions include:

1. **Strategic withdrawal and invisibility**: Pulls back, stays quiet, or goes neutral to reduce visibility and risk.
   Systems: Defense (flight, freeze), attachment (deactivation).
   Survival logic: "If I am unseen, I cannot be targeted."

2. **Preemptive shutdown to manage overwhelm**: Numbs, spaces out, or goes offline before emotions crest.
   Systems: Defense (collapse, shutdown).
   Survival logic: "If I shut down early, the wave cannot drown us."

3. **Gatekeeping to protect vulnerable parts**: Controls access so child and innocent parts are not exposed to threat or scrutiny.
   Systems: Rank or power in operating against parts who would like to open up (gatekeeping), Caregiving in intent, directed toward protecting vulnerable parts.
   Survival logic: "If I keep them inside, they will not be hurt."

4. **Distance to preserve autonomy**: Tightly manages space, time, and choice to prevent intrusion, coercion, or enmeshment.
   Systems: Rank or power (boundary keeping, dominance over self).
   Survival logic: "If I control the distance, no one can take over."

5. **Appeasement to reduce perceived burden**: Stays agreeable, compliant, or low need to avoid conflict, rejection, or reprisal.
   Systems: Rank-submission subroutine (fawn, appease).
   Survival logic: "If I do not make waves, they will not fight or criticize me."

6. **Delay loops and vigilance**: Stalls decisions, overchecks, and scans for danger to avoid traps or irreversible exposure.
   Systems: Defense (hypervigilant freezing, threat prediction), rank or power (rule keeping).
   Survival logic: "If I wait until it is perfectly safe, nothing bad can happen."

7. **Emotion minimization and compartmentalization**: Downplays, relabels, or boxes feelings so functioning can continue.

Systems: Rank (submission)
Survival logic: "If I make it small, we can keep going."

8. **Routine and predictability as control**: Narrows life to safe routes, familiar people, and scripted interactions.
   Systems: Defense (vigilant, order and rigidity), defense (safety behaviors).
   Survival logic: "If everything stays the same, nothing can surprise or attack us."

9. **Dampening desire and attachment signals**: Flattens hope, longing, or interest so approach motivation does not pull the system into risky closeness.
   Systems: Attachment (deactivation, inhibited activation).
   Survival logic: "If I do not want or need anything, I cannot be trapped or disappointed."

Because fearful and avoidant parts are carrying out the exact strategies they were created for, preventing harm, limiting exposure, and managing intolerable affect, our stance must respect their survival logic. Attempts to *draw them out* too quickly can reinforce their sense that connection is unsafe, strengthening the very defenses we hope to soften. Instead, collaborate on conditions under which cautious approach becomes tolerable, measuring success by choice, not by the volume of contact.

RELATING TO FEARFUL AND AVOIDANT PARTS

Fearful and avoidant parts need the same thing they have rarely been given: the right to exist exactly as they are, without pressure to change or perform. In therapy, this means shifting **from a stance of getting them to open up to one of quiet permission.** The therapist becomes a steady presence, attentive, grounded, and patient enough to let connection develop on the client's timeline, not ours.

Instead of persuading or pushing, the work begins with **gentle invitations that communicate choice**. Such language signals: "You don't have to speak to be heard."

- "You don't have to talk today."
- "You're allowed to be unsure."

- ★ "It's okay to take your time."
- ★ "If a part is unsure about being here, we can welcome that too."
- ★ "You don't have to say anything, I'm just glad you're here."
- ★ "If it's hard to stay connected, we can notice that together without judgment."

Trust with these parts does not arrive in dramatic moments, it shows up quietly, almost imperceptibly. A client might:

- ❖ Stay grounded for a few seconds longer than usual.
- ❖ Pause before disconnecting.
- ❖ Meet your gaze directly.
- ❖ Whisper, "I didn't leave this time."

These are sacred moments. They can be **acknowledged softly, without overemphasizing** them in a way that makes the part feel exposed.

- ★ "Thank you for staying with me."
- ★ "I felt you here just now, that matters."

CLINICAL VIGNETTE

Permission to Pause

During a drawing exercise, the client's hand begins to tremble over the paper; the pen hesitates, and she pulls the sheet away. The therapist says, "It's okay if you'd rather keep that to yourself for now. You don't have to do this exercise if it does not feel right."

The client takes a long, steadying breath, slides the paper back across the table, and almost whispers, "I remember hiding under my bed."

SYSTEM	WHERE IT SHOWS UP	FUNCTION	SURVIVAL LOGIC
Defense (avoidance)	Hesitation to share the drawing; reluctance to let the therapist see what's inside.	Maintains safety by keeping emotional distance when closeness feels dangerous.	"If I don't let you in, you can't hurt or reject me."
Defense System (Freeze/ Dissociation)		Reduces overwhelming arousal by shutting down expression.	"If I disappear, nothing bad can happen."
Caregiving System (Self-Containment)	Protecting others (therapist) from distress by holding back the content.	Avoids burdening or upsetting others.	"If I don't share, I won't cause trouble or make them leave."
Rank/Power (Submission / Compliance	Ultimately sliding the paper back after permission is given	Balances self-protection with subtle compliance when safety is signaled.	"If I follow the rules and keep it small, I won't be punished."

Table 15.1. Motivational and action systems at play in the vignette

The Polite Exit

Lena, a 36-year-old client with a history of emotional neglect, arrives on time for her session, smiling warmly. She chats about the weather and her favorite TV show. Each time the therapist gently redirects toward last week's discussion about her mother, Lena nods, then pivots back to a safe topic.

Midway through, the therapist reflects, "I notice we've been talking about lighter things today. I wonder if a part of you is keeping us away from something that feels too much right now." Lena smiles. "Oh, I don't think so. I'm fine, really." The session ends with polite goodbyes. The Adult Self never names the avoidance, but Lena stayed in the room, something she could not do earlier in therapy.

SYSTEM	WHERE IT SHOWS UP	FUNCTION	SURVIVAL LOGIC
Rank/Power (dominance, internal enforcer)	Hierarchical self-attacks: "You're wasting time," "You're weak," strict policing of tone/behavior just as Elena considers reaching out.	Apply learned hierarchical code (IWM) and impose downranking to pre-empt external judgment; keep the system "in line."	If I enforce the code and keep us small, we avoid humiliation, punishment, and global rejection.
Attachment (care-seeking devalued or denied)	A pull toward the therapist is immediately put down; the reach is followed by shame produced by the inner judge, then withdrawal.	Suppress/devalue closeness bids to avoid relational risk; keep need out of sight so it cannot be rejected.	If we need nothing, we cannot be refused, trapped, or exposed.
Rank/submission, up to defense activation (appeasement, freeze, or collapse) — reactive	Silence, resignation, numbing, immobilization after the inner attack; appeasing the internal authority to avoid escalation.	Lower perceived life-or-death threat from negative evaluation by inhibiting movement and visibility.	If I stay invisible and quiet, I won't provoke attack or expulsion.
Caregiving (modeled by therapist) and Cooperation (co-created)	Steady, attuned reflection without confrontation; "we" language, clear limits, choice, and pacing.	Offer a non-punitive template of protection and co-regulation; update the procedure: safety through permission, pacing, and repair.	Protection can come from care, not cruelty: we can stay safe with brakes and clarity, no self-assault required.

Table 15.2. Motivational and action systems at play in the vignette

Shared Reflections on Both Vignettes

Permission to Pause and *The Polite Exit* show two distinct presentations of fearful and avoidant parts: one overt, one subtle. In the first, the protective strategy is clear: stop the action, withdraw, and physically or emotionally freeze to prevent danger. In the second, avoidance is masked in pleasant conversation, social charm, and surface-level engagement that keeps deeper connection safely out of reach.

In both examples, the behaviors are not defiance or disinterest. The *Permission to Pause* moment demonstrated that avoidance could soften when the therapist gives explicit permission to disengage, removing pressure while holding connection. *The Polite Exit* illustrates that even when emotional depth is avoided, staying present in the room can be a significant step forward from past patterns of absence or cancellation.

Across both, the therapist's stance was the key factor. Grounded, patient presence, without pushing for disclosure or interpreting avoidance as a failure, allowed the system to have a new experience: that safety can exist without retreat, and connection can exist without exposure. Over time, these repeated moments can loosen the system's reliance on avoidance as the only way to feel safe, opening the possibility for authentic engagement on the client's terms.

Safety also depends on containment that never slides into control. A consistent therapeutic frame, clear beginnings and endings, predictable boundaries, and regular check-ins with the Adult Self, provide orientation and stability. When avoidance appears, it can be named with gentle curiosity. This keeps the door open without forcing it.

- ★ "I notice we often shift topics right here. I wonder if something gets stirred up."

Structure communicates "You're safe" and presence communicates "You're not alone". Together, they create the kind of relational scaffolding fearful and avoidant parts have rarely known, one where they can test connection at their own pace, without fear of intrusion or abandonment.

CLOSING THOUGHTS

Fearful and avoidant parts are not obstacles; they are protectors doing their best to keep the system safe. They are not disinterested; they are scared. Our task is not to convince them to show up, but to create a space where showing up no longer feels dangerous.

This work asks us to slow down, tolerate uncertainty, and offer presence without pressure. Progress is measured in micro-moments of safety, not speed. Change comes not from pushing harder, but from staying steady long enough that hiding no longer feels necessary, and connection begins to feel possible.

Clinical Anchors

What to remember...

- Presence over pursuit. Let the client's pace lead.
- Avoidance is protection, not defiance. Assume there is a good reason for silence.
- Contain without controlling. Boundaries can support safety without pressuring participation.
- Language matters. Speak with softness and permission, not urgency.
- Stay emotionally available even during long silences or shutdowns.
- Respect fear. It has kept the system safe. Invite it in without judgment.
- Notice micro-shifts. Eye contact, breathing, or small disclosures are meaningful signals of trust.
- Trust the process. These parts soften not because we push, but because we stay.

What to Avoid...

- Over-interpreting silence ("I know what you're feeling")
- Pushing for insight or words before the part feels safe
- Losing patience by shifting tone or pace in response to discomfort
- Rushing to rescue with solutions or reassurance
- Caretaking

Chapter 16: Self-Critical and Punitive Parts

THERAPIST REFLECTION

I notice the pull to argue with or soothe the harsh inner voice because it feels unfair or painful to hear. I pause and check in: Am I understanding this part's function or why it's showing up in this way now? I remind myself that its criticism grew out of a need to protect and they still need to learn other ways of expressing and protecting. Staying curious and non-defensive creates the first moment of real listening this part may have ever experienced.

Many clients who live with dissociative parts experience a persistent, punishing internal voice. This voice may insult, shame, or berate them. It might whisper or shout phrases like: "You're worthless." "It's your fault." "You don't deserve to heal."

Self-critical or punitive parts often feel woven into the system's structure. They may position themselves as the truth-tellers, the enforcers, the ones holding everything together. Their tone might be moralistic. They are rarely dramatic, but they are often relentless.

Yet these parts are not born from self-hate. They are protective adaptations formed in response to early environments where relational safety depended on compliance, perfection, or emotional invisibility. These internal voices evolved to manage unbearable feelings, to anticipate attack before it arrived, or to keep the system in line to avoid greater harm. What sounds like cruelty is often a survival strategy.

Our task is not to quiet them prematurely or argue with their content. It is to understand what they believe, what they fear, and why they persist. These parts are not the enemy. They are the system's harshest protectors, trying to do what they have always done: keep things under control, no matter the cost.

As introduced in chapter 3, these parts are typically governed by submission to rules and values of the critical parent, and/or internal dominance (rank system), appeasement (rank/submission), and distorted attachment loyalties. Recognizing which system is active can help clarify both their emotional tone and their relational strategies.

ORIGIN OF SELF-CRITICAL AND PUNITIVE PARTS

Self-critical and punitive parts are often formed early, shaped by the child's first interactions with caregivers and the learned belief that being better (more compliant, invisible, or self-controlled) might ensure safety. These parts typically develop in environments where survival depended on silence, perfection, or relentless self-monitoring. Chronic criticism, emotional neglect, or controlling caregiving laid the groundwork for these internal voices, which over time become woven into the system's structure; so familiar that they seem to have always been there. In these settings, developing a harsh internal voice was a creative, protective adaptation.

These parts often form in response to:

- Chronic emotional abuse, humiliation, or neglect.
- Internalized voices of caregivers, institutions, or abusers.
- Attempts to prevent external criticism by anticipating it internally.
- Beliefs that suffering earns safety, or that shame prevents harm
- Loyalty to caregivers who demanded silence, self-blame, invisibility, and sometimes perfection (nothing was ever good enough).

Rather than expressing cruelty for its own sake, these parts developed a rigid sense of order and control, believing that self-invalidation and criticism was the only way to stay safe, acceptable, or untouched by outside harm. They may speak with the tone of a punitive or critical parent, a moralistic teacher, or a past perpetrator whose voice became embedded in the system. Their logic is often survival-driven:

- ❖ "If I criticize us first, no one else will."
- ❖ "If we carry the blame, maybe others won´t get mad or upset."
- ❖ "If I make you go for perfection, maybe we won't be abandoned."
- ❖ "If I keep you small, you won't risk what might hurt us."

They are not trying to be mean or unkind. They are doing what they believe is necessary to prevent worse outcomes by repeating old automatic patterns. These parts try to keep the system safe by enforcing control, invisibility, or moral perfection. Their strategies are rigid and often painful, but they are rooted in protective intent, stuck in trauma time, unable to update their methods to reflect the safety and possibilities of the present.

MAIN FEATURES OF SELF-CRITICAL AND PUNITIVE PARTS

One of the main characteristics of self-critical and punitive parts is the way they manifest through intrusive, authoritative inner voices and thoughts. They tend to operate in the background, speaking with certainty and finality, as if their judgments were facts. Their thinking tends to be rigid, limited, and inflexible.

These parts do not usually arrive in emotional bursts, but as persistent internal evaluations, delivered in absolute terms.

- "You are lazy."
- "You'll never get it right."
- "You don't deserve to heal."
- "It's not good enough."
- "What´s wrong with you?"
- "Why can´t you be like others?"

In more severe forms, these parts have internalized what Onno van der Hart has described as *malignant kernel statements* (Van der Hart et al., 2006; Steele et al., 2017; Van der Hart, 2025); rigid, global statements about the self that are experienced as absolute truths rather than thoughts or opinions. Over time, such statements consolidate into negative evaluations of self or other parts; deeply entrenched conclusions about the self that deny worth, possibility, or legitimacy of existence.

The tone of these parts is often moralistic, harsh, and punitive, echoing shaming parents, teachers, or their emotionally abusive figures. Some clients experience them as internal judges or enforcers; unyielding voices that demand compliance, silence, or perfection.

Although their style varies, the impact is often the same: chronic shame, inhibition, paralysis, and internal conflict. For some, the relentless inner criticism becomes so overwhelming that it contributes to suicidal despair. In many personality systems, self-critical, hostile, and suicidal parts are closely linked and may activate each other. For some clients, the relentless nature of this internal attack becomes a significant contributor to suicidal despair.

Importantly, these parts are not oriented toward comfort or connection. Their focus is on achievement, compliance, silence, and control, believing that these are the only ways to stay safe or avoid being hurt.

These beliefs often form the cognitive bridge between chronic self-attack and suicidal despair, a process described in detail in the chapter on suicidal parts.

FUNCTIONS OF SELF-CRITICAL AND PUNITIVE PARTS

While often painful and deeply limiting, self-critical and punitive parts serve specific purposes rooted in survival. Their strategies may appear mean, harsh, or humiliating, but their underlying intent is to prevent greater harm (particularly shame-based exposure and rejection), by keeping the system controlled, contained, and compliant.

These parts are often organized around shame regulation: anticipating it, inducing it preemptively, or using it to enforce internal order. They are typically shaped by a combination of rank/power (dominance and enforcement), rank/submission (appeasement), and attachment deactivation or distorted care-seeking. They strive to:

1. **Prevent external harm by downranking from the inside**: Diminishes, self-shames, perfects, harshly evaluates, and self-silences to avoid being cut down by others.
   Systems: Rank/power (dominance, internal enforcer; imposed self-submission to old critics as tactic), rank/submission (appease, fawn; secondary).
   Survival logic: "If I downrank us first, no one can shame or reject us; if I ban pride, loss will not humiliate us."

2. **Maintain internal order via rigid rules**: Sets strict codes ("never need", "always control"), monitors tone and behavior, keeps everything small, quiet, and predictable.

Clinical Vignette

When Criticism Protects

Julia, a 35-year-old client, sits in silence for much of the session. When the therapist inquires about what is happening internally, she sighs and says, "There's a voice saying I'm wasting your time… that I'm weak for even needing this."

Instead of reassuring or challenging the belief, the therapist reflects: "It sounds like there's a part that believes it's dangerous to need help. Maybe it learned that being vulnerable wasn't safe." Julia pauses, "Yeah… if I wasn't perfect, my dad would shut down or mock me. I think this voice is trying to keep me from being humiliated again." The therapist responds, "That makes a lot of sense. Maybe this part believes that if it shames you first, it can protect you from being hurt by someone else." Later, Julia reflects: "I always thought that voice hated me. But now… it just seems scared."

SYSTEM	WHERE IT SHOWS UP	FUNCTION	SURVIVAL LOGIC
Rank System (dominance, internal enforcer	The self-critical part delivers hierarchical judgments like "You're wasting time" and "You're weak." (monitoring tone and behavior)	Applies learned hierarchical rules from the internal working model and enforces an internal code by downranking other parts.	If I enforce the code and keep us small, we avoid humiliation, punishment, and loss of control.
Attachment System(Devaluation or denial of attachment)	A reach for connection followed by put-downs or withdrawal; shame appears after the reach, produced by the dominant inner judge.	Suppresses and devalues closeness bids to prevent relational risk; keeps need out of sight so it cannot be rejected.	If we need nothing, we cannot be rejected, trapped, or exposed.
Rank/submission + Defense System (appeasement orcollapse)	Silence, resignation, numbing; immobility when the inner enforcer is active.	Lowers perceived threat through pre-emptive surrender and inhibition; avoids conflict with the internal authority.	If I stay invisible and quiet, I won't provoke attacks or rejection.
Caregiving System (modeled by the therapist) and Cooperation (co-created)	Therapist offers attuned reflection without confrontation; uses "we" language, clear limits, and choice..	Activates an internal template of safe caregiving and recruits cooperative problem-solving as an alternative to rank contests.	If care can happen with choice and without punishment, it may be safe to try a little connection.

Table 16.1. Motivational and Action Systems at play. **Note**: Shame here is framed as the **result** of rank dominance deployed by the internal enforcer, not as a separate system driver.

Clinical Reflections

This vignette illustrates how self-critical parts are not inherently cruel but represent the internalization of multiple overlapping motivational systems attempting to keep the system safe. These systems do not act in isolation, they interlock. The self-critical part is not being mean; it is using dominance, appeasement, and self-suppression to avoid harm.

Julia's internal dynamic reflects a classic motivational conflict: the attachment system's longing for care clashes with the defense system's need to avoid harm, while the rank system enforces submission to minimize threat. The self-critical part functions as a distorted protector, trying to prevent emotional exposure by preemptively shaming the self. The therapist's stance activates a different motivational template, one based on safety, mutual recognition, and curiosity, which begins to allow new internal relationships to form.

Systems: Rank/power (dominance, code enforcement), submission, also recruiting defense ways (freeze, immobilization as inhibitory overlay).
Survival logic: "If we stay within tight rules, we will not trigger punishment or chaos."

3. **Suppress vulnerable parts to prevent exposure**: Shames, mocks, or shuts down younger or softer parts; triggers collapse to avoid visibility.
Systems: Rank/power (dominance, gatekeeping), rank + defense (collapse, inhibition).
Survival logic: "If I shut them down now, no one can use their need against us."

4. **Divert intolerable affect into control and contempt:** Converts shame, fear, or grief into anger, contempt, or icy control to keep functioning.
Systems: Defense (affect transmutation, suppression), rank/power (power restoration).
Survival logic: "If I turn this into anger and rules, we stay strong enough to function."

5. **Deactivate attachment signals to avoid dependency**: Forbids reaching out, ridicules comfort bids, labels need as *weak*.
Systems: Attachment (deactivation), rank/power (negative evaluation threat).
Survival logic: "If we never ask, we cannot be refused or trapped."

6. **Preserve attachment loyalties (identify with caregiver's moral code)**: Carries internalized voices of blame or moral control to maintain connection with caregivers.
Systems: Attachment (ambivalent or disorganized bonding), rank/power (dominance, internalized authority, perpetrator-identified introject). Here we can suppose a Controlling Strategy of Submission subroutine adopted by the child to survive in the family.
Survival logic: "If they were right and I was the problem, the relationship and the world's order stay intact."

7. **Suppress hope and vulnerability (anti-longing stance)**: Attacks hope, pride, or trust to prevent future disappointment.
Systems: Attachment (deactivation or inhibited activation), defense (shutdown).

Clinical Vignette

Better to Reject Myself First

Elena, a 27-year-old client with a history of emotional neglect and relational betrayal, speaks about a part that constantly repeats: "You're worthless. No one cares. Stop embarrassing yourself."

These words come up just before she considers asking for support, particularly in therapy or intimate relationships. "It's like the second I feel the urge to reach out, that voice snaps at me. It's awful. It's like being punched by my own brain."

Instead of immediately challenging the voice, the therapist gently offers a possibility: "What if that voice isn't trying to shame you, but trying to protect you from reaching out, so you don't risk being rejected again?"

Elena is quiet for a while. Then she says, "That... makes way too much sense. It's like... it's cruel, but familiar. Like it's trying to stop me before someone else can hurt me worse."

Over time, Elena and the therapist begin mapping the pattern. Every time she moves toward connection, particularly in vulnerable moments, this part lashes out. Not to destroy her, but to shut down hope.

Together, they begin exploring what this part fears most: "If I let her hope again and it goes badly... we won't survive the fall."

This became the beginning of a shift. The part was no longer (at least in that moment) seen as the enemy, but as a fierce protector using painful tactics to prevent a deeper injury. These experiences build new ways of interacting through repetition.

SYSTEM	WHERE IT SHOWS UP	FUNCTION	SURVIVAL LOGIC
Rank/Power (dominance, internal enforcer)	Hierarchical self-attacks: "You're wasting time," "You're weak," strict policing of tone/behavior as Elena considers reaching out.	Apply learned hierarchical code (IWM) and impose downranking to pre-empt external judgment; keep the system "in line."	If I enforce the code and keep us small, we avoid humiliation, punishment, and global rejection.
Attachment (care-seeking devalued or denied)	A pull toward the therapist is immediately put down; the reach is followed by shame produced by the inner judge, then withdrawal.	Suppress/devalue closeness bids to avoid relational risk; keep need out of sight so it cannot be rejected.	If we need nothing, we cannot be refused, trapped, or exposed.
Rank/submission, up to defense activation (appeasement, freeze, or collapse) — reactive	Silence, resignation, numbing, immobilization after the inner attack; appeasing the internal authority to avoid escalation.	Lower perceived life-or-death threat from negative evaluation by inhibiting movement and visibility.	If I stay invisible and quiet, I won't provoke attack or expulsion.
Caregiving (modeled by therapist) and Cooperation (co-created)	Steady, attuned reflection without confrontation; "we" language, clear limits, choice, and pacing.	Offer a non-punitive template of protection and co-regulation; update the procedure: safety through permission, pacing, and repair.	Protection can come from care, not cruelty: we can stay safe with brakes and clarity, no self-assault required.

Table 16.2. Motivational and Action Systems at play. **Note:** The critic operates from rank/power dominance. Rank/submission up to defense belongs primarily to the recipient response (freeze/appease/collapse) when negative evaluation has been generalized as a survival threat, similar to social or test phobia. Shame is an outcome of rank defeat here and does **not** inevitably end in collapse; submission may occur without recruiting strong defensive shutdown.

Clinical Reflections

The critical part is not simply *mean*, it is trying to resolve the conflict between wanting connection (attachment) and fearing destruction (defense), while maintaining compliance (rank) and control (distorted caregiving). By helping the client see this complexity, the therapist de-pathologizes the voice and opens the door for dialogue, not suppression.

Survival logic: "If we do not hope or reach, we cannot be disappointed. Not having expectations is a way to avoid shame and humiliation."

Other common expressions include:

- **Blocking vulnerable expression**: Mutes crying, need, or protest from young parts.
  Systems: Attachment (inhibited or distorted activation), defense (freeze, containment).
  Survival logic: "If need is hidden, it cannot be rejected or weaponized."
- **Undermining the Adult Self**: Erodes confidence, agency, or relational capacity to prevent risky moves.
  Systems: Rank/power (internal sabotage), defense (hypervigilance, doubt).
  Survival logic: "If the Adult hesitates, we will not step into danger."
- **Criticizing the therapist or allies**: Tests, devalues, or withdraws as connection deepens.
  Systems: Attachment (deactivation, testing), rank (fight in verbal or attitudinal form).
  Survival logic: "If I push you away first, you cannot control, expose, or betray us."

Unlike externally aggressive or hostile protectors, self-critical parts turn their strategies inward. Their goal is not to keep others out, but to keep the system in line, controlled, and invisible

RELATING TO SELF-CRITICAL AND PUNITIVE PARTS

Since self-critical or punitive parts often evoke strong emotional reactions in the therapist, we must pay careful attention to countertransference issues. It is not uncommon for the therapist to feel:

- Frustration or helplessness when progress feels blocked.
- Protective urges toward more vulnerable parts.
- A sense of being shut out, dismissed, or even personally attacked.
- Harsh internal self-evaluation such as, "I'm failing this client" or "Nothing is working".

These responses are not signs of failure; they are signals that something meaningful is happening in the therapeutic space. These parts often test the therapist's steadiness, not because they want conflict, but because they expect rejection. Their messages can be piercing, but they are often shaped by histories where no one stayed close when things got hard.

The therapist's task is to hold both: the one under attack, and the one doing the attacking, with equal respect, steadiness, and compassion. That stance alone is often a corrective experience for the system.

What Is Important to Keep in Mind

Engagement with critical and punitive parts must be carefully paced. These parts are not looking to be convinced; they are watching to see whether the therapist will try to overpower them or ignore their message. Some guiding principles that can help shape therapeutic responses:

- **Name the fear beneath the criticism**:
    - ★ "It sounds like this part is scared of what might happen if you let your guard down."
- **Avoid trying to prove the client's worth**: Attempts to reassure or "talk them out of it" can lead to backlash. Stay with curiosity:
    - ★ "What would happen if this part didn't have to be so hard on you?"
- **Invite collaboration**:

  - ★ "Would it be okay to hear how another part has experienced this voice?"

- **Use reflective distance:** Especially when the part is more present or in co-consciousness with the Adult Self:
  - ★ "It sounds like there's a part that believes you don't deserve care. I wonder what it's trying to protect."

These questions are not about evoking insight too soon. They are gentle doorways, reminders that we are not here to silence or battle the part, but to offer new relational experiences. These moments plant seeds of trust: that the therapist will not reject the part, nor will they collude with its painful strategies.

Over time, what began as rigid criticism may evolve into discernment, boundary-setting, or fierce care. These parts can carry valuable traits: vigilance, integrity, truth-telling, honesty and strength; these can be integrated once their energy is no longer bound to punishment.

Therapists may feel an understandable urgency to protect the client from the harshness of self-critical or punitive parts. When these voices are loud, cruel, or unrelenting, the instinct to push back, to soothe, to argue, to correct, can be strong. But these responses often backfire. Trying to disprove the part's beliefs can escalate conflict or deepen the part's sense of isolation and mistrust.

We do not endorse their methods, but we do respect the logic behind them.

- ★ "I hear how strong this part is. I wonder what it's trying to accomplish."
- ★ "It sounds like it's been working hard to keep things in line."
- ★ "I'm not here to argue with you. I'd like to understand what you're protecting."

This stance helps soften black-and-white dynamics. We are not siding with the part, but neither are we rejecting it. We are listening for the fear beneath the harshness, the function beneath the pain.

When the Part Begins to Shift

Over time, and with consistent, attuned presence, punitive or self-critical parts may begin to soften. Often, this shift is subtle: a pause, a sigh, a phrase like, "I'm just so tired". Sometimes, it sounds like regret. Other times, it is simply the first expression of doubt in a once-rigid belief.

When this happens, we do not rush to push for more change, we take note of internally, stay steady, and offer acknowledgment:

- ★ "You've been doing a hard job for a long time."
- ★ "Maybe no one ever thanked you for trying to keep things safe."
- ★ "If you'd like support now, we can figure that out together."

These parts often carry important capacities: vigilance, discernment, clarity, and integrity. With time and relationship, what once felt like cruelty can begin to transform into care; fierce, honest, and protective, but no longer punishing. A key message to offer is:

- ★ "You are important to the system, and you always will be. You might even become more effective if you can collaborate with others and express your concerns through constructive criticism rather than attack."

The goal is never eradication, but collaboration and eventually, integration, supporting these parts in updating their roles so they no longer need to harm in order to protect. Though rigid and often relentless, these parts are not inherently cruel. They are motivational specialists, trying to protect the system using the only strategies they know. When their protective intent is understood, and the Adult Self begins to offer more flexible leadership, these parts often begin to soften, evolving from punishing voices to discerning internal allies.

CLOSING THOUGHTS

Self-critical and punitive parts are adaptation to unbearable conditions. They emerged to maintain control, prevent collapse, and enforce safety through relentless vigilance. Their methods may be harsh, but their motivation is almost always protective. When therapists stop trying to silence or argue with these parts, and instead begin listening with respectful curiosity, something in the system often begins to shift. The fight lessens. The volume softens. The part does not have to shout to be heard.

We do not need to confront these parts. We need to build a good enough relationship with them, steadily, gently, and without shame. This work is not about correcting what is wrong. It is about introducing new possibilities, options that reflect the safety, complexity, and relational reality of the here and now.

Clinical Anchors

What to remember...

- Keep in mind the system beneath the voice: Is this part enforcing submission (rank)? Attempting control (dominance)? Trying to maintain loyalty (attachment through submission to critical parent)? It is a good way to clarify the strategy.
- See punishment is protection, model new, safer ways to protect.
- Validate the intention, not the strategy. Honor the function.
- Stay interested, even when the part pushes you away. Consistency builds safety.
- Respect ambivalence. Change can feel threatening.
- Support the Adult Self in responding differently, not by silencing the part, but by modeling a different way of relating and responding.
- Allow for repair. If you miss something, name it and apologize.
- Trust cannot be rushed; it builds slowly.

What to Avoid...

- Challenging beliefs too early or directly can feel like invalidation, reinforcing the part's belief that it must stay in control.
- Trying to convince the client of their worth can create backlash. These parts may interpret kindness as manipulation or weakness.
- Using pathologizing labels. Terms like *saboteur*, *inner critic*, or *toxic part* may inadvertently increase shame or internal conflict.
- Taking sides, even with protective intent, may deepen internal mistrust. These parts already expect to be excluded. Do not prove them right.

Chapter 17: Hostile and Aggressive Parts

Therapist Reflection

When I sense hostility in the room, I notice my urge either to retreat or confront, since it can feel unsafe or even personal. I pause to check my posture, tone, and pacing, reminding myself that this part's aggression is a survival strategy, not an attack on me. Staying steady, calm, curious, and fully present is the strongest signal of safety I can offer.

Hostile or aggressive parts are often the most feared in the system, not just by the client, but by the therapist as well. These parts may insult, reject, mock, threaten, or turn the session into an emotional battleground. Some lash out with contempt; others retreat into a controlled silence that feels strategic or punishing. When they show up, the entire relational field can shift. The room feels tighter. The atmosphere becomes charged. The therapist's words may falter, and the client might brace for rupture. Everyone feels it.

Yet beneath this intensity lies something entirely different: a fight-based part doing everything it can to survive and protect. These parts are often the most vigilant, strategic, and loyal in the system but at the same time the most judged and misunderstood. As explored in chapter 11, these parts share a common origin with other protective roles. They emerged in environments where closeness felt dangerous, and where survival depended on defending the system from vulnerability; and where the only available model of power and control was aggression.

This chapter invites us to move beyond the content of the hostility, and into its function. It challenges us to work relationally, not reactively, and to earn the trust of parts that have learned trust is dangerous.

ORIGIN OF HOSTILE AND AGGRESSIVE PARTS

Hostile and aggressive parts are forged in early environments marked by relational trauma, spaces where vulnerability was punished, safety was conditional, and emotional expression was dangerous. These parts are often organized by the fight branch of the defense system and the dominance subroutine of the rank motivational system. In some cases, they also reflect a distorted use of control learned in early relational trauma, where power was the only available safety.

These parts often develop in response to:

- Chronic invalidation of emotions and needs, shaming, rejection, or emotional neglect from caregivers.
- Coerced forgiveness or premature demands for compliance.
- Internal pressure to protect trauma content that other parts in the system cannot bear.
- Early lessons that intimacy equals danger, weakness, or loss of control.
- Situations where becoming the threat felt safer than remaining the target.

Their aggression is not random or out of the blue. It is an organized learned response that becomes automatic in front of triggers; a learned way to prevent betrayal, shame, or annihilation. It is a defense against vulnerability.

Over time, their role becomes entrenched: to anticipate harm, to control connection, and to silence any vulnerability that might threaten the integrity of the system. Many carry internalized voices of past abusers, not because they agree with them, but because mimicking power felt safer than remaining powerless. Some are younger parts stuck in teenage perspectives trying to scare others away.

These parts often expect rejection. They anticipate that no one can or wants to try to handle them, and many have this expectation confirmed, therapists included. From a clinical perspective, this pattern is maintained not because they are unworkable, but because their internal organization shapes interactions in ways that repeatedly lead to rupture or withdrawal.

But when we meet these fight-based parts with curiosity instead of fear, and with containment instead of control, something begins to shift. We can start to ask deeper, more compassionate questions:

- ★ "What is this part protecting?" (This could be something like a painful memory, for example.)
- ★ "What does this part think would have happened if she hadn't stepped in? "
- ★ "Who is this part trying to protect, and from what?" (This could be someone who is no longer here, or they could be thinking that they are preventing someone else from being hurt)

If we keep in mind these types of questions it will be easier to remember that they are not trying to sabotage the client or the therapeutic relationship. They are trying to survive and protect; survive to protect because nobody can protect like they do.

MAIN FEATURES OF HOSTILE AND AGGRESSIVE PARTS

When these parts are present, the energy in the room often shifts. The atmosphere becomes charged. The client may brace for rejection and at the same time, provoke it. The therapist may feel uncomfortable or silenced. These parts are often watching closely for signs of weakness, insincerity, or control.

We must look out for the following presentations, so we can recognize their presence.

- Speaking in the voice of former abusers.
- Rejecting kindness thinking that it is not real, that it is manipulative.
- Minimizing trauma, interrupting the client when they try to talk about that or suggest working on what happened.
- Accusing or shaming other parts for being *weak*.
- Viewing therapeutic connection as a setup for betrayal.
- Insulting, mocking, or demeaning the client or other parts, sometimes the therapist.
- Making threats towards the client, other parts, and even the therapist or other people in the clinical setting.
- Shutting down the session with strategic angry silence or contempt.

- Introducing a lot of noise inside so the client cannot hear well or participate in conversations.
- Acting as if they are above the process or uninterested in help.
- Eliciting fear, irritation, helplessness, or withdrawal in both client and therapist

Despite all the above, these parts are often our best allies. They are perceptive, often scanning not just for what is said, but for what is felt, implied, or withheld.

Many clients describe these parts as ruining their lives:

- ❖ "She wants to destroy everything."
- ❖ "He does not care who he hurts."
- ❖ "It's like having an abuser inside of me."

These descriptions are not inaccurate; they reflect the real pain and chaos these parts can create. But these are just fragments of a larger story. A story about who these parts are protecting, when they show up, what for, and why they believe harm is inevitable unless they intervene.

FUNCTIONS OF HOSTILE AND AGGRESSIVE PARTS

Hostile-protective parts are often misunderstood. They look oppositional but their aim is safety. Their logic is trauma-learned and designed to control exposure, preserve dignity, and prevent betrayal. They serve crucial roles:

1. **Preempt closeness before it becomes dangerous**: Tests, provokes, withdraws, or rejects first to keep control of connection.
   Systems: Defense (fight), attachment (approach/avoid, deactivation).
   Survival logic: "If I push you away now, you cannot betray or control me later."

2. **Enforce control and predictability:** Asserts dominance, sets rigid rules, narrows options to reduce the risk of being overpowered.
   Systems: Rank/power (counter dominance, order and rigidity).
   Survival logic: "If I run the terms, nothing can blindside us."

3. **Maintain protective distance**: Manages space, time, and disclosure to prevent dependence or abandonment.
   Systems: Attachment (deactivation), to a lesser extent rank/power (boundary keeping).
   Survival logic: "If I keep it distant, we will not get trapped or left."

4. **Guard against emotional exposure and betrayal**: Blocks, mocks, or shuts down material that could lead to humiliation, rejection, or collapse.
   Systems: Rank/submission (keep a low profile, prudence, risk avoidance), attachment (deactivation).
   Survival logic: "If we stay armored and distant, no one can hurt or discard us."

5. **Divert attention from traumatic material**: Turns hostility toward self, others, or the therapy to pull focus away from unmanageable memories and affects.
   Systems: Rank (anger redirected outward or inward), dissociation (minimization).
   Survival logic: "If I make this about anger, we do not have to feel what is underneath."

6. **Convert shame, fear, or grief into anger or contempt:** Transforms vulnerable states into mobilized power so functioning can continue.
   Systems: Defense (affect transmutation, suppression), rank/power (internal enforcer).
   Survival logic: "If I turn this into anger, we stay strong enough to survive."

7. **Monitor and police vulnerability inside the system**: Watches younger or vulnerable parts and blocks their exposure.
   Systems: Rank/power (gatekeeping), caregiving (protective but distorted).
   Survival logic: "If I silence the weak parts, no one can use them against us."

8. **Repeat learned rules from hostile environments**: Enforces perpetrator or household codes to prevent *mistakes* that once invited harm.
   Systems: Rank/power (dominance, internalized code enforcement), defense (predictive threat mapping).

Survival logic: "If we enforce the old rules before anyone else does, we stay in charge and out of danger."

9. **Mobilize energy and action under threat**: Rallies the system when it feels weak, foggy, or immobilized; preventive alarm.
Systems: Defense (sympathetic activation, fight readiness).
Survival logic: "If I amp us up, we can act before harm arrives."

10. **Signal threat detection**: Orients the system to danger cues in the present or trauma time echoes and demands immediate risk management.
Systems: Defense (hypervigilance, pattern matching with trauma time bias).
Survival logic: "If I treat every echo as real, I will not miss the one that matters."

Because hostile and aggressive parts are doing exactly what they were created to do (prevent harm, limit exposure, and keep control), interventions should honor their function while updating the method (permissioned dosing, clear stop-rules, aftercare the Guardian endorses). These parts are not trying to sabotage the client or therapy. They are trying to prevent further harm, using strategies that have previously worked and made sense in past contexts.

To help clients understand the function of these parts, we begin by exploring and mapping patterns, not behaviors:

- ★ When does this part appear?
- ★ What tends to trigger it (inside or outside?
- ★ What emotional states usually precede its arrival?
- ★ What feared outcome is it trying to prevent?

What emerges, often to the client's surprise, is that these parts rarely act randomly. They tend to surface due to triggers that the client is not identifying yet, after moments of tenderness, disappointment, or internal exposure. After the system gets close to someone. After a vulnerable part speaks. After hope begins to flicker. They sense risk in emotional closeness and act quickly to shut it down.

Clinical Vignette

When Hostility Distracts from Deep Pain

A middle-aged man in therapy shares that he has a part that constantly tells him he should suffer. When the therapist gently explores what tends to trigger this part, the client replies, "Anything."

The therapist asks, "Can we be curious about when the part shows up saying those things?" The client answers, "Anytime."

Rather than challenging or confronting, the therapist validates the client's experience while introducing a new possibility: "I understand it feels that way, it must be very scary to live with a part that says those things. I wonder if it might be trying to help in some way, even if it does not know a better way yet?"

The client pauses and then says, "Oh my God... he finally shut up."

The therapist responds, "Maybe what I said is making some sense. Can you check inside and see what shifted?" The client is quiet for a moment and then replies, "I think we might be on to something."

In later sessions, the client began to notice a pattern: the hostile part would show up after contact with men who reminded him of a past assault. The part's aggression was not random, it was a distraction strategy, pulling the client's attention away from vulnerability and redirecting it toward self-attack to avoid the resurgence of traumatic material.

SYSTEM	WHERE IT SHOWS UP	FUNCTION	SURVIVAL LOGIC
Rank/dominance + Defense System (Fight subroutine)	The hostile part attacks internally, telling the client he "should suffer."	Deflects attention away from vulnerable emotional states (e.g., fear, shame, or trauma-related distress) by channeling activation into punishment and controlled self-aggression.	Better to turn against the self in a predictable way than risk feeling powerless, exposed, or retraumatized by external reminders.
Attachment System (Care seeking and conflict avoidance)	The client's longing for safe connection is indirectly revealed when the part softens in response to the therapist's attunement.	Seeks proximity and understanding but is inhibited by prior betrayal and harm from attachment figures, making vulnerability feel dangerous.	The system seeks connection but is overridden by defense when cues of closeness (especially with male figures) trigger fear.
Rank System (dominance/ submission loop)	The part uses moralistic, shaming messages to dominate the client internally.	Enforces a rigid internal hierarchy where the self is "put in place" to avoid perceived external humiliation.	If I shame and diminish myself first, others can't do it to me.
Caregiving System (distorted/ protected form)	The part insists on self-punishment as a form of misguided care, to avoid worse outcomes.	Maintains a form of internal order and vigilance by suppressing emotional risk, even at high personal cost	I'm keeping you from being destroyed, by making sure you don't expect kindness.

Table 17.1. Motivational and action systems at play in the vignette

Clinical Reflection

Hostile parts often function as distraction strategies, redirecting attention away from what feels unmanageable or dangerous. When approached with curiosity rather than confrontation, their protective intent can become visible, allowing the client to recognize the underlying threat without being overwhelmed by it.

> Aggression that appears constant or indiscriminate often has a relational trigger that is not yet conscious. In this case, hostility emerged reliably in response to cues associated with past harm. Identifying the function, rather than challenging its content, made it possible to access the vulnerability it was protecting.
>
> Hostile parts are protectors of Pandora's boxes, charged with the job of keeping danger out, no matter the cost. Their strategies may be harsh, but their intent is protective. This is where therapists can begin to help the client reframe the part's role. Not to justify the harm it causes, but to honor the burden it has carried, often alone, often unrecognized, in a system that had no better options.

RELATING TO HOSTILE AND AGGRESSIVE PARTS

Building Relationship and Trust with Hostile Parts

Working with hostile and aggressive parts is not just a matter of clinical skill, it is a test of presence. These parts do not simply listen to what we say; they are watching how we are. How quickly do we flinch? How hard do we try to reassure? How fast do we retreat?

These are a particular type of fight-based parts that came to be. These parts emerged in environments where trust was a liability, safety was an illusion, and care often came with a cost. So, they test. They provoke. They push. Not because they want to destroy the therapeutic relationship, but because they need to know:

- "Will you shame me like the others did?"
- "Will you pretend to care, then disappear?"
- "Will you try to control me?"

This is where the therapeutic work begins, not with interpretation, but with regulated presence. Our role is not to meet intensity with intensity, nor to bypass it with over-explaining or reassurance. It is to stay steady. To stay connected. To show, through tone, posture, and pacing, that something different is happening here.

As mentioned before, we do not need to interpret or fix. We begin by staying curious, listening even when we do not agree and validating any attempt of help we can identify.

- **Notice without confronting**: "You're showing me something important right now."

- ★ **Acknowledge without agreeing**: "You don't have to trust me. I respect that."
- ★ **Validate without colluding**: "It sounds like you've had to push people away to keep things safe."

These responses are not strategies for compliance. They are invitations for contact and curiosity. They model a kind of strength that does not rely on dominance or appeasement, a strength rooted in containment, not control. This is not a battle of wills. It is a moment to model what steadiness looks like when things feel unsafe. Over time, this kind of presence can become reparative. At first, it may feel like doing nothing but, in truth, it is precisely the work that needs to be done.

Downshifting Rank Before Inviting Cooperation

Rank/power circuits evolved to manage scarcity and competition for resources. When access to time, safety, dignity, or control feels limited, systems organize around hierarchy. Hostile protector parts often read therapy as a contest, (who controls access, who sets the terms, who gets believed). Before offering cooperation, we need to deactivate rank tension by signaling there is no contest here.

Language that de-escalates rank:

- ★ **Remove last-chance pressure:** "We don't have to settle this today. There will be another chance."
- ★ **Opt out of the contest:** "I'm not here to win or outsmart you. I'm here to understand what keeps you safe."
- ★ **Decline the challenge, respectfully:** "You can keep the lead while we slow this down."
- ★ **Remove resource competition:** "You don't need to trust me right now. I'll track the pace you set."
- ★ **Strategic yielding (status de-escalation):** "You're the expert on what's dangerous here. I'll follow your rules about distance."

This is not submission; it is de-escalation that acknowledges the protector's dignity and purpose. When rank threat drops, cooperation becomes possible without triggering old attachment alarms. Then, and only then, can we invite cooperation.

The goal is not to overpower the part, nor to convince them of our intentions. It is to remain in relationship, without collapsing, retaliating, or withdrawing. Because for many clients, the moment when a hostile part shows up in full force and the therapist stays and engages in new ways is the first evidence that safety does not require submission, and connection does not demand compliance.

Hostile parts are highly sensitive to tone, pacing, and inconsistency. They scan for signs that therapy is a trap, a reenactment of past betrayals or dismissals. To build trust, we offer genuine curiosity, collaboration, and permission:

- ★ "I want to understand what you're doing for us. Would it be okay if we talked about that?"
- ★ "Would it feel okay if I tried to understand what you're protecting?"
- ★ "You can tell me if I'm missing something, I want to get it right."
- ★ "You don't have to like me. I'm not here to push you out."
- ★ "We can go at your pace. I won't do anything without your permission."

These moments do more than manage intensity in the session, they model what safe power can look like: neither authoritarian nor abandoning, but attuned and responsive.

Hostile parts can and often do soften, but only when met with respect, patience, and relational steadiness. Trust is not a prerequisite for starting this work; consistency is. These parts are not waiting for us to prove our insight, they are watching to see if we can remain present without retreating, shaming, or trying to control them.

Rather than rushing to make them behave or change, we begin by reflecting their importance, not to flatter, but to acknowledge and appreciate.

This approach also demands awareness of our own inner responses. These parts often evoke strong countertransference, irritation, fear, helplessness, or a wish to shut things down. These feelings are not signs of failure. They are data. They tell us something real is happening. Our task is to notice, to stay reflective, and to avoid repeating the dynamics the part expects.

These are not techniques to disarm the part, they are invitations. And sometimes, the first real act of trust isn't in sharing or softening, it's in the therapist surviving the storm and still being there. It's not silence that builds trust. It's presence, remaining consistent, clear, and curious.

The work is not to eliminate these parts. It is to understand their origins, respect their vigilance, and, over time, help them discover that there may now be other ways to keep the system safe.

Engaging Through the Adult Self

Whenever possible, the therapeutic work with hostile or aggressive parts should be routed through the Adult Self. These parts are not easily accessible through direct confrontation, especially when the system is fragile or in a state of internal distrust. Direct engagement may lead to escalation, fragmentation, or a reenactment of power struggles.

Instead, we support the client in beginning to form their own internal relationship with these parts. We are not bypassing or ignoring them, we are protecting the conditions that allow for contact without coercion.

There will be times when the Adult Self feels inaccessible, either disorganized, withdrawn, or perceived by the hostile part as weak or naive. In these moments, we do not push. We stay present. We model steadiness. And we trust that witnessing the dynamic without force is already a powerful intervention. We do so by speaking to the Adult Self referring to the part:

- ★ "This part had to hold a lot on its own."
- ★ "I imagine this part protected the system more times than anyone realizes."
- ★ "We don't want to get rid of this part. We want to understand how this part has been helping."

When contact becomes possible, even briefly, the Adult Self might begin to offer new messages:

- ❖ "You've had to hold a lot on your own."
- ❖ "I imagine you've protected the system more times than anyone realizes."
- ❖ "I'm not here to get rid of you, I want to understand how you've been helping."

This shifts the internal narrative: from problem part to protector, from obstacle to part of the story. It does not erase the damage some of these parts may have caused. But it places their actions in the context of survival. And it offers something many have never known: the possibility of support without control, inclusion without submission.

Questions like:

- ★ "What does this part want you to know right now?"
- ★ "What happens in your body when this part feels close?"
- ★ "Can we check with the Adult Self whether it feels okay to explore this part's presence?"

These kinds of invitations help strengthen internal leadership and self-observation. The goal is not insight for its own sake, but a shift from being overwhelmed by the part to being able to relate to it. This creates a subtle but important change: from fusion to dialogue, from reaction to reflection.

The Role of Loyalty and Identification

Some of the most disorienting moments in therapy occur when a hostile part speaks with the voice of an abuser, not metaphorically, but in tone, language, or even direct repetition. These parts may:

- Justify or minimize past abuse.
- Threaten or shame other parts for being *weak*.
- Reject kindness as manipulative.
- Turn the therapist into the enemy, especially when care or curiosity is offered.

This dynamic can be deeply painful for the client and deeply destabilizing for the therapist. But it is not cruelty for its own sake. It is often a reflection of complex, survival-based identification.

In many dissociative systems, proximity to the perpetrator was the only available safety. Resistance meant danger. Submission, or internal alignment, offered a form of control, however small. Over time, this alignment was no longer just a strategy; it became encoded as a way of being.

These parts are not *on* the side of the abuser because they want to perpetuate harm. They carry the beliefs, postures, and protective functions of someone who learned that merging with the aggressor was the best chance at survival. For some, continuing to uphold the perpetrator's logic may still feel like protection, from punishment, from collapse, or from unbearable truths the rest of the system is not ready to hold.

Others fear what might happen if they let go of this role. "If I stop doing this, we'll be destroyed. Someone must keep things under control." These are convictions rooted in trauma, not threats.

Rather than confronting this identification head-on or trying to quickly separate the part from the perpetrator's voice, we stay close with respect and nuance. The goal is not to dismantle loyalty through confrontation, but to widen the system's capacity to understand its own complexity. You might say:

★ "Sometimes staying close to the one who hurt you felt like the safest thing."
★ "It makes sense that this voice sounds like them, that was the model of strength you knew."
★ "Maybe this part is doing now what helped you survive then."

These reflections do not demand change or insight. They offer a relational bridge, an opening for recognition that does not overwhelm. Often, the hostile part does not need to be shown that it is wrong; it needs to be seen for what it has been trying to do.

Over time, what begins as misguided loyalty may shift. Not because we pushed for it, but because we respected the pace, the fear, and the logic behind it.

When Parts Challenge the Therapeutic Alliance

Although it is not frequent, there may be sessions when a hostile or aggressive part directs their intensity toward the therapist, with insults, hostility or withdrawal. These moments can be disorienting. The therapist may feel defensive, frustrated, helpless, or tempted to push back. This is precisely when pacing and regulation matter most.

These parts are testing interest and commitment. They expect you to retaliate, retreat, or moralize. Your grounded, non-reactive presence may be the first rupture repair they have ever encountered.

★ **Anchor yourself**. "Feel your feet on the floor, slow your breath."
★ **Validate and reflect the impact**. "I can see how upset this makes you."
★ **Offer choice**. "We can pause for a moment or shift gears if you'd like. Your call."

Even firm boundaries can be delivered with calm, validation, and clarity:

★ "I hear how much is coming up, and I also need to feel safe enough to stay fully present with you."

The goal is not to regain control, but to remain connected. In doing so, you model something many of these parts have never experienced: a relationship that does not rupture in the face of conflict.

CLOSING THOUGHTS

Working with hostile parts is not about changing their personality or earning their trust. It is about creating a therapeutic space where these long-feared, often misunderstood dynamics are no longer met with punishment, or avoidance.

These parts will tend to soften when they feel understood. They begin to listen and cooperate when they sense they no longer need to protect so fiercely. Change happens through new healthier interactions in the inner and outer relationship; when safety becomes real enough that defensiveness is no longer necessary. So we return, repeatedly, with one consistent message: "You belong, even if something needs to change." Therapeutic presence—grounded, attuned, and clear—is often the most transformative intervention we can offer.

Clinical Anchors

What to Remember...

- Steadiness over strategy. Stay regulated. Hostile parts do not need you to be clever, they need you to be present.
- Function before form. Always ask: "What is this protecting?" Behavior makes sense when we understand its origins.
- No *good* vs. *bad* parts. Stay curious about all roles. Siding with one part over another reinforces internal conflict.
- Respect justified mistrust. These parts may never have seen safety last. Let trust be earned, not assumed. Containment is the intervention. Your calm, non-reactive presence often does more than any technique or interpretation.
- Hostility is often a test. These parts want to know if you will stay, flinch, moralize, or try to control them.
- Hostile protector parts are often our most perceptive protector. Their mistrust is discernment sharpened by trauma.

What to Avoid...

- Taking sides with other parts. Aligning too strongly with more compliant parts can reinforce their sense of not belonging.
- Using clinical labels to describe behavior. Descriptive, non-pathologizing language encourages collaboration.
- Interpreting too early. Understanding will unfold when the system feels safe enough and is ready to explore it.
- Over-identifying with the Adult Self and visibly favoring it may be perceived as threat or betrayal by hostile parts.
- Assuming that silence or disengagement means the part is gone. It may be observing, testing, waiting for safety, or just agreeing with the work.

Chapter 18. Self-Harming Parts

Therapist Reflection

A client once told me, "Cutting keeps me alive." Early on, I argued with the behavior. Now I ask what it prevents. When we name that it diverts an emotional avalanche, the part is less alone and alternatives become imaginable.

Although self-harming and suicidal parts often co-occur in complex trauma and dissociation, they are not the same phenomenon. They share a protective intention, but they diverge in aim, clinical presentation, and required interventions. This chapter focuses on non-suicidal self-injury (NSSI) as a regulation strategy that, in many systems, actively prevents escalation toward suicide. NSSI can modulate intolerable affect, restore a felt sense of control, or anchor the body when arousal is extreme.

Self-harming parts organize around regulation, not annihilation. Their function is to turn vast, unnamable feeling into something concrete and time-limited the system can survive; contained, bounded, and time-limited (Mosquera & Ross, 2016, 2017; Fisher, 2017). When shame swells, when longing is met with ridicule or silence, when panic surges without a handhold, these parts reach for a method that is fast, predictable, and usually private. For some, physical pain narrows the field of awareness, for others, sensation fades and emotional intensity collapses into numbness. In both cases, the emotional avalanche is interrupted. Order returns.

The tone of these parts is often misunderstood. Not every self-harming impulse arrives as contempt or attack. Many speak with quiet, persuasive certainty, even tenderness: "Do this and you will breathe again." Others present as pragmatic or scientific, explaining mechanisms and timing, promising relief with the confidence of a well-rehearsed procedure. What unites them is not hostility but commitment to keeping the system functional when other strategies do not seem to work. One client heard a gentle voice: "Cut a little, honey; you'll feel better." Another described "a smart, sweet-toned part who calmly explained why the endorphins would help", in contrast to more shaming from aggressive protector parts that left her feeling defeated. The regulatory part, in her words, "helped me get through".

Clinically, the distinction from suicidal parts is decisive. Suicidal parts pursue final escape; self-harming parts pursue relief that allows continuation. In many systems, self-injury functions as harm reduction; a negotiated truce among parts who agree that a controlled discharge is preferable to catastrophic collapse. Clients say this plainly: "If I don't do this, I might do something worse." The logic is constrained only by an impoverished menu of options; within that menu, the choice is protective.

ORIGIN OF SELF-HARMING PARTS

Self-injurious parts tend to form where affect outstrips capacity and soothing is absent or unsafe. Physical pain is discovered as a way to control what feels limitless: shame, terror, grief, loneliness. The aim is not death; it is relief, order, and survival. Common formative conditions include:

- Emotions dismissed, mocked, or punished.
- Care bids were shamed or ignored until they extinguish.
- Models of self-attack or self-control in family, peers, or media.
- Accidental discovery that focused physical pain can blunt diffuse emotional overload.
- Internal rules forbidding need, anger, or protest ("Never need", "Don't show weakness").
- Early experiences in which visible injury elicited care while emotion elicited rejection.
- Exposure to communities or content that normalize self-injury as relief when nothing else works.

MAIN FEATURES OF SELF-HARMING PARTS

Clients with dissociative disorders can perceive these parts in very different ways, and this is because there are two common but distinct presentations. One is regulatory: focused on keeping life going with minimal disruption. It can feel scary during the surge but mainly brings relief and a return to regulation. The other is hostile and punitive: a critical presentation that orders self-harm and frames injury as deserved; this is extremely frightening and can trigger suicidal ideation in the client or bring suicidal parts forward.

The aims and aftermath diverge. In the relief-seeking presentation, the aim is a fast downshift; the aftermath is quieter—less internal noise, fatigue, a sense of calm. In the punitive presentation, the aim is control and (ironically) humiliation prevention; the aftermath is a shame spike and higher medical risk. Both can also function as attention shifters away from intrusive memories or trauma-time pull, though clients rarely identify this at first. Some will describe a broader regulatory pull that links to the system dynamics described in chapter 26 (Despair Holders, Punishers, and Harm-Reducers).

We can recognize the presence of these parts through:

- Urges that surge with interpersonal stress or trauma-time cues.
- A felt sense of relief or quiet after self-injury.
- Rigid internal rules about need, perfection, or exposure.
- Secrecy with careful risk minimization and precise planning.
- Ambivalence toward help that feels like prohibition or rescue.
- Often a pragmatic or even warm tone ("This helps us get through"), in contrast to hostile protectors.
- Rapid attentional narrowing onto the body/sensation when intrusive memories rise.

These parts can also be custodians of rule-sets. They enforce codes such as "never need", "don't show weakness", and "pay for mistakes", not out of cruelty but to prevent external humiliation. Self-punishment is imagined to preempt being cut down by others. Attachment signals are muted or coded; proximity may be sought indirectly, through visible injury that could invite care without requiring a bid. Rank threat is managed by down-ranking from the inside before anyone else can.

When Borderline Features Are Prominent

Because Borderline Personality Disorder (BPD) and dissociative disorders frequently co-occur and share high levels of trauma exposure (Ross, Ferrell, & Schroeder, 2014; Zanarini et al., 1998; Mosquera & Steele, 2017; Mosquera & Gonzalez, 2014; Mosquera, 2016; Mosquera, Gonzalez & Van der Hart, 2011), similar behaviors can be driven by different engines or motivations. In borderline presentations without pronounced structural dissociation, the urge to self-harm often rises to end detachment—depersonalization or derealization (DP/DR) that makes the self or the world feel chaotic and out of reach. The function is less "obey a part" and more "stop chaos" or "end unreality now". Clients describe cutting to feel real again, to stop floating, to break the glass wall, or to feel their body and confirm they are alive—often after an acute interpersonal trigger such as perceived abandonment, rupture, or sudden shame. The onset is typically fast and reactive; intense sensation grounds and re-establishes a felt "I am here". Within a structural dissociation frame, NSSI adds a complementary lens: detachment states can dominate the moment, and self-injury can function as an emergency brake to avert feared disintegration of consciousness—often felt as "going crazy" or "losing my mind". This is distinct from the parts-conflict described when dissociative parts are organizing the urge.

Language and phenomenology help differentiate. Borderline presentations tend to retain first-person ownership—"I cut because I couldn't stand it"—whereas dissociative disorders more often include third-person or part-driven attributions ("a part told me", "my hands did it", "my head wants it", "the monster took over"). Or they report amnesia, the bottom end of non-realization (Janet, 1935, 1945); for instance, "I was suddenly in the hospital's emergency room and saw that my arm was bleeding, but I didn't know what happened."

Other dynamics with self-harm also appear. Many people with BPD self-harm to communicate pain, to feel entitled to suffer ("When I hurt myself physically it feels like there is a real reason"), or as a cleansing ritual in which seeing blood flowing brings calm. It can also function as punishment—seemingly "part-like", yet the first-person remains: "I felt I deserved it. How could I have said that? It was so mean/so stupid/so selfish." Trauma histories can be similar across groups; however, in borderline presentations without dissociative parts, enough good-enough interactions during upbringing often serve as protective factors against fragmentation or division of the personality.

Trigger location and conflict locus also differ. In BPD, triggers are mainly relational (perceived abandonment, criticism, rejection, sudden shame), and the conflict is chiefly with others—including how the person believes they are being perceived. The immediate aim is to stop interpersonal pain and restore connection. In dissociative disorders, triggers may start outside (often unrecognized trauma reminders), but the central struggle is inside: parts disagree about what must happen now: relief versus punishment versus concealment. Clinically, that means in BPD you address the relationship rupture first; in dissociation you map the internal positions, set simple safety agreements between parts (no orders, no threats, no acting on the body), and reduce the outside cues that set it off.

In short, surface behavior can overlap (rapid relief, a sense of restored control), but the organizing problem differs. In dissociative parts work, we are negotiating among roles and their rules; in borderline anti-detachment spikes, we are ending unreality fast. If the client confirms the anti-detachment pattern, build micro-experiments that promise the same win—re-embodiment in under two minutes—without injury, paired with a brief, explicit repair step so proximity can be regained safely.

FUNCTIONS OF SELF-HARMING PARTS

Self-harming parts act as rapid-response regulators. They detect threshold crossings and narrow overwhelming states into time-limited, controllable sensation, coordinating privacy and timing so other roles can keep functioning. They enforce rule sets to prevent humiliation and manage proximity indirectly (deactivating bids or, at times, eliciting care through visibility). Repetition proceduralizes the sequence; success is judged by how quickly intensity drops and order returns, after which they minimize traces and reset capacity.

Self-harm is a defensive behavior seen across many animal species—lizards, salamanders, crabs, and other crustaceans—that will self-amputate a limb or tail (a process called autotomy, which literally means "self-cutting") to escape a threat perceived as fatal. The lost part may later regenerate, a metabolically costly and energy consuming process, yet still preferable to death (Maginnis, 2006). In an analogous fashion, every traumatic memory—or sudden emotional surge—can be registered by the system, or by specific parts, as a mortal threat. The defense system activates accordingly, even if the danger now exists only in memory.

The following functions describe how these mechanisms organize and sustain internal regulation, even when their strategies carry significant cost.

1. **Affect modulation**. Converts diffuse, overwhelming emotional pain into a bounded, time-limited state through neurobiological regulation. This may involve intensified sensation for some and marked numbing or analgesia for others.
   Systems: Defense (anger redirected inward; dissociation of affect; opioid-mediated dampening of distress).
   Survival logic: "Better to enter a controllable state—whether through sensation or numbing—than remain flooded by emotions that feel unmanageable."

2. **Downregulation and interruption**, Acts as an internal brake when arousal spikes, preventing panic or dissociative collapse.
   Systems: Defense (shutdown and containment).
   Survival logic: "If I discharge now, it will not spiral out of control."

3. **Attention shifting away from traumatic intrusions**. Captures attention with intense, immediate sensation to distract from intrusive memories, images, or trauma-time pull, reducing reexperiencing and dissociative drift.
   Systems: Defense (attentional capture; sensory override); memory/avoidance (secondary).
   Survival logic: "If I lock attention to the body now, the memory recedes and I can get through."

4. **Punitive control to prevent external shaming**. Self-punishes to avoid being cut down by others, repeating internalized codes.
   Systems: Rank/power (internal enforcer imposing self-submission as tactic).
   Survival logic: "If I punish us first, no one else will humiliate us."

5. **Silencing need and attachment bids**. Blunts longing and stops reaching that once led to rejection or danger.
   Systems: Attachment (deactivation or inhibited activation).
   Survival logic: "If I erase the need, I do not have to feel refusal."

6. **Maintaining internal order via rigid rules**. Sets strict codes ("never need", "always control"), monitors tone and behavior, keeps everything small, quiet, and predictable.
   Systems: Rank/power (rule-keeping); executive control (monitoring).
   Survival logic: "If we follow the rules without exception, surprises cannot hurt us."

7. **Eliciting care indirectly when asking feels dangerous**. Uses visible injury or its aftermath as a nonverbal signal to draw proximity and care without a direct bid.
   Systems: Attachment (care-elicitation/protest); social communication (secondary).
   Survival logic: "If my pain is seen rather than said, someone may approach safely and take care of me."

8. **Preventing collapse by dampening interoceptive cues**. Reads rising bodily signals as danger and prioritizes rapid sensory override or breath control to blunt them.
   Systems: Interoceptive monitoring (threat appraisal); defense (rapid dampening).
   Survival logic: "If I stop these sensations now, we will not unravel."

9. **Keeping suicide at bay**. Offers a controllable release so the system does not escalate toward lethality.
   Systems: Defense (harm-reduction logic); cooperation and collaboration (implicit truce among parts to achieve a common goal).
   Survival logic: "This is how we survive today."

RELATING TO SELF-HARMING PARTS

Building on the functions outlined above, **lead with curiosity and cooperation.** The therapeutic stance follows this understanding: do not attack the strategy that has been keeping the system afloat; collaborate with it, and offer safer substitutes so change feels less threatening. Prohibitions and behavioral contracts often drive the behavior underground, closing windows for intervention. **A rescuer or caregiving stance tends to backfire**, triggering push–pull with protector parts. Instead, make timing and boundaries explicit and honored, keep experiments brief and predictable, and mirror the part's goals (fast relief, restored control) while co-creating methods that do no physical harm (for example, strong sensory input, paced breathing, grounding, small choices that restore agency). When the function is respected, alternatives become testable: explicit consent, finely titrated pacing, and respect for internal roles. We co-design small, reversible experiments—controlled together—to strengthen collaboration and to identify relief-oriented solutions that honor the part's regulatory intent.

First, **validate the job**. Name what this part achieves and acknowledge that it works. Make sure the client hears that you recognize its usefulness. Then offer to help update the method while keeping the purpose intact. This stance honors the protector's logic and signals that you are not trying to remove its role, only to widen the menu of ways it can succeed and increase available resources.

Keep choice and brakes visible throughout. Collaborative plans reduce rank threat when timing and boundaries are explicit and honored. Short trials, predictable edges, and agreed aftercare give guardians enough safety to risk trying something new without feeling outflanked. As agreements are kept, trust grows, and secrecy loosens.

De-shame the need for relief. Treat the urge as a sincere attempt to keep the system going, not as defiance or manipulation of others—even when the function is communication. Mirror the part's goals of speed, predictability, privacy, and restored control, and co-create substitutions that preserve those qualities without injury. Rather than arguing with rule sets, name why they formed and negotiate flexibility so relief, regulation, and, when relevant, proximity and care can be accessed with less risk.

Finally, **build micro-procedures that can compete with the old sequence**. Define them as tiny, permissioned, reversible steps linked to the earliest bodily cues and practiced until they become reliable. For example, a 30-second script might include orienting to three colors in the room, five paced breaths with a longer exhale, a brief strong sensory input (ice, cold water, strong peppermint, textured object), and a check-in. Success is measured by a safe return to baseline rather than disclosure or catharsis. With repetition, these wins install new routines that protect dignity and agency and reduce the system's reliance on injury to achieve relief and connection.

CLINICAL VIGNETTE

Cutting Keeps Me Alive (not BPD)

A 28-year-old arrives after a conflict with her partner. In a flat tone says, "I cut last night. It calmed me." The therapist asks, "What did it keep from exploding?" The answer lands: "The shame. The scream." They explore the sequence: trigger, spike, narrowing, relief, after-cost. The therapist reflects the role: "So this part turns an ocean into a glass of water. Pain we can hold." The client nods.

They co-design alternatives to practice during the week: 1) Cooperation. "We're not banning anything today. We're just adding options, the ones that fit for you and everything inside." 2) Function-matched exits: cold-water hold for 90 seconds, strong isometrics (wall or chair), paced exhale (adapted with the Adult Self and part together).

The self-injuring part agrees to test these first, not as prohibition of cutting but as additional exits that might work faster and with less cost. Two weeks later, the client reports, "It didn't stop the shame, but it made it smaller. I didn't cut."

SYSTEM	WHERE IT SHOWS UP	FUNCTION	SURVIVAL LOGIC
Defense (affect narrowing and containment)	The partner conflict as trigger, the flat report "I cut last night. It calmed me," the mapped sequence of trigger, spike, narrowing, relief, and after cost, and the image "ocean into a glass of water."	Converts diffuse shame and panic into a focused, time limited sensation, then brings a quiet that interrupts escalation and keeps suicidality at bay.	If I create pain I can control, the flood stops; if it goes quiet afterward, we will not tip into catastrophe.
Rank and power (internal enforcer, self downranking)	Disclosure without requesting help, a controlled presentation, and the preference to manage privately rather than risk exposure; no explicit rule language surfaced in this session. Shame indicates the activation of a humiliation response within the Rank system.	enforces internal standards that keep the self small and silent to prevent external humiliation.	If I cut us down first, others cannot cut us down worse."
Attachment (deactivation and care elicitation)	Naming the act without asking for comfort, and the therapist's non rescuing stance that allows proximity without pressure; the possibility that visible aftermath can invite care is acknowledged but not enacted here.	Mutes direct bids to avoid rejection while sometimes allowing indirect signals to invite contact without asking.	If I do not show need, I will not be shamed; if my pain is seen rather than said, someone may come close safely."
Cooperation (modeled in session by therapist	Collaborative framing "we are not banning, we are adding options," the joint design of function matched exits, and the part's agreement to test substitutions first.	Negotiates timing and containment so other roles can keep living and relating, favoring controlled discharge over collapse.	If I take this on in a way that costs less, the rest of us can keep life going and we stay alive."

Table 18.1. Motivational Systems at play in the vignette

Clinical Reflection

Self-injury in this vignette functions as a regulated discharge rather than an expression of identity or a wish to die. By naming its role without moralizing or prohibiting, the therapist preserved cooperation and reduced escalation. Function-matched alternatives were introduced not to replace the behavior through control, but to expand the client's options at moments of high activation. Change can occur when the client and or dissociative parts realize that relief and containment can be achieved with less cost.

Clinical Stance for BPD-Led Anti-Detachment Spikes

When the differential assessment points to detachment relief rather than parts conflict, the room changes shape. We slow the tempo, keep eyes open, and widen attention to the here-and-now so the client can feel the floor under them again. The aim is simple: help the body return without injury.

You might say,

- ★ "This is your system trying to end chaos or unreality fast; let's help it do that safely."

The tone stays collaborative, neither rescuing nor punitive.

If feeling numb, far-away, or unreal clearly preceded the urge, and the act restored a sense of being in the body, priorities shift: orient to time, date, and place; re-establish body ownership with strong-but-safe sensation; then touch the relational spark that lit the fuse without diving deep. Clarify the misunderstanding, name the fear of loss, or acknowledge the sting of criticism, and remind the client that they are learning to tolerate emotion in healthier ways now.

As contact with the present strengthens, co-create a short, reliable way to come back to the body quickly—one the client can own, personalize, repeat, and refine. It should be predictable, fast, and self-dependent, not contingent on how others respond (given that dependence on others' reactions is often the pressure point in BPD). Frame it as an experiment you will keep adjusting together, with practice outside the therapy room.

Equally important is what we set aside. If the presentation is BPD-led, we neither force parts contracts nor negotiate among inner roles that are not organizing the moment. This tends to confuse and undercut agency of the client.

Why The Strategy Persists

The detachment-relief strategy endures because it works in the short term. Relief follows the act, and the nervous system learns the association, consolidating the behavior. When arousal spikes, state-dependent learning narrows access to alternatives and the practiced sequence comes online first. The body adds real, if brief, analgesia and a shift in arousal, which feels like proof of efficacy. Over time, the part earns a role identity—"the one who gets us through"—and reliability breeds loyalty even when costs are high. Secrecy and compartmentalization, reinforced by shame and amnesia barriers, limit collaborative problem-solving and exposure to new options, so the loop remains intact.

CLOSING THOUGHTS

Self-injurious parts are regulators whose aim is relief and continuation, often operating as harm reduction when capacity is overwhelmed. When we name the function out loud and keep the purpose intact while updating the method, the nervous system learns new first moves.

Change is built from tiny, reversible routines tied to early cues, options that preserve what the part values: speed, predictability, privacy, and restored control (without injury). Defense is respected and redirected; rank/power rules are softened so protection does not require self-attack; attachment is handled carefully, allowing safer proximity or indirect care until direct asking is possible. Cooperation is modeled in session and gradually taken up inside.

Progress shows up as added choices, shorter spikes, quicker returns to baseline, fewer after-costs, and less secrecy. Setbacks are data: they reveal missed cues, steps that were too big, or thin aftercare, and point to the next micro-adjustment.

Clinical Anchors

What to remember...

- Respect and validate the job before you update the method.
- Keep timing and boundaries explicit and honored.
- Rehearse tiny, reversible micro-procedures tied to early cues; revisit and refine when needed.
- Measure progress by added options and shorter spikes, not by disappearance of urges.
- Coordinate medical safety pragmatically when needed (wound care, tetanus status) without moralizing.
- When DP/DR is present, treat anti-detachment as the first target.

What to avoid...

- Prohibitions and behavioral contracts that drive secrecy and only protect clinicians.
- Rescuer/caregiver stances that trigger push–pull with protector parts.
- Moralizing, shaming, or interpreting the urge as manipulation.
- Ignoring medical risk or colluding with minimization of harm.
- Interpreting proximity-seeking as manipulation. Instead, frame it as an urgent bid to be found when self-cohesion thins.

Chapter 19: Suicidal Parts

THERAPIST REFLECTION

A client once said, "There's a part that says we should just end it." I could feel the pull to persuade and make it change its mind. But I've learned that these parts aren't trying to be convinced. So, I asked, "Is there anything that part wants us to understand?" And in that moment, we weren't fighting a suicidal part. We were sitting beside its pain. That's where the work begins, not by silencing the voice, but by letting it be heard safely.

Suicidal parts, just like other parts do, often emerge in response to overwhelming emotional pain, profound helplessness, and unmet needs for care, protection, or recognition (Mosquera & Ross, 2016, 2017; Fisher, 2017, Brand et al., 2012). They are not born from a desire to die, but from the absence of a viable path to keep living as things are. Where no soothing was available, where pain was minimized or met with rejection and threat, these parts evolved to carry unbearable distress in the only ways the system could manage.

Suicidal ideation offers a form of final flight from perceived endless suffering, or a fight for control when all other parts feel powerless. Self-harm used for regulation is covered in chapter 18. Here we focus on parts whose aim is finality.

ORIGIN OF SUICIDAL PARTS

Suicidal parts share a protective aim with other protectors, but their objective is final: to end consciousness when every other strategy has failed. This is not regulation; it is an exit. Unlike hostile parts, which often direct aggression outward, suicidal parts turn aggression inward; fusing despair with the illusion that escape (via the flight system) is the only option.

Suicidal parts crystallize when despair, defeat, and isolation converge, and no regulated exit seems possible. Their emergence is often linked to early environments marked by:

- Emotional pain being ignored, ridiculed, or punished.
- Caregivers responding to needs with neglect, shame, or cruelty.
- Exposure to suicide in family members, peers, or media, leading to internalized scripts that equate death with peace.
- Growing up with messages that the child was unwanted or too much to handle.
- Cultural or religious narratives that framed suffering as deserved, and relief as selfish or taboo.
- Believing others would be happy if they disappeared.
- Caregivers directly expressed rejection or violent regret toward the child´s existence.

These formative experiences shape deep, painful beliefs that are deeply entrenched. As described earlier, in some clients these experiences consolidate into malignant kernel statements—absolute, self-defining meanings that foreclose hope and make continued living feel impossible:

- ❖ "There is no other way out."
- ❖ "This is the only way to rest."
- ❖ "You're hurting others just by existing."
- ❖ "Everybody would be better off without you."
- ❖ "You should be dead, that´s better for everyone."
- ❖ "You are worthless and pathetic."
- ❖ "You are unlovable."
- ❖ "You should never have been born."

Through repetition, these externally imposed statements become internal beliefs about self, serving as adaptations to overwhelming conditions where no other coping strategies were available or modeled. While the part may be seen as dangerous or destructive, its purpose is often misunderstood. It is not trying to destroy the system, it is trying to stop what feels unbearable, or protect other parts from exposure, humiliation, or collapse. If these parts come to believe that there are real, sustainable options for living with less pain, they often turn towards them.

The patterns behind these beliefs are rooted in distorted action system responses. The defense system dominates through flight, collapse, or fight energy turned inward; the attachment system is often inhibited, making direct care-seeking feel impossible; and the rank/power system may shift toward defeat or submission, preserving safety by surrendering. Recognizing which system is active in a given moment helps decode whether the part's intent is to escape, protect, or control.

Some clients recall direct experiences that become embedded in the suicidal part's logic:

- "When I cried, they told me to get out of their face and drop dead."
- "My mom said multiple times that she should've had an abortion."
- "I learned from watching my brother's suicide that no one listens until it's too late."
- "I was very little when my grandmother hanged herself. I understood why she did it. My mom was always screaming at her and making her feel like a burden. I often want to be with her; she is not suffering anymore."

These parts are often misunderstood as purely destructive, when in fact they hold the system's most desperate hope for relief. Their logic is a distorted survival logic: ending life to end pain. Therapy offers the possibility of updating that logic, helping them see that other options for rest, safety, and relief exist; and that if those become real, they often choose to live.

MAIN FEATURES OF SUICIDAL PARTS

Suicidal parts may operate either overtly or in more subtle, concealed ways, but their impact on the internal system is often profound. When overt, they may present as persistent internal voices that encourage suicide, often looping in cycles of despair, threats, or harsh self-judgment. These voices can become intense, even coercive.

Yet just as often, these parts express themselves in quieter, more withdrawn forms: calm, emotionally flat, or detached. This subdued presentation can make them easy to overlook, unless the therapist is attuned to shifts in tone, affect, or energy. Regardless of form, their presence tends to carry a signature quality of finality, resignation, or disconnection from hope; sometimes relief, thinking they are finally going to rest.

We can recognize the presence of these parts in the room because they tend to:

- Speak in absolute or fatalistic terms: "It will never get better." "You're a burden." "There's no point."
- Express emotional numbness, dissociation, or quiet despair.
- View death as a solution, relief, or mercy.
- Discourage therapeutic engagement, either directly ("You should stop coming") or subtly (numbing, distraction, or minimization).
- Hold a belief that their pain is unique and incomprehensible, "No one else gets it."
- Carry a pervasive hopelessness: "What for?" "Nothing matters anyway."

The influence of these parts may also show up in how they:

- Block access to hope, connection, or internal collaboration.
- Dismiss the therapist's presence, viewing it as naive, threatening, or irrelevant, but not in an aggressive manner suggestive of a power struggle (rank) with the therapist.
- Shut down vulnerable parts or disqualify the Adult Self's efforts, with a resigned sense that everything is useless.
- Replay repetitive internal commands like a broken record that no one has dared to unplug: "Kill yourself." "End it." "Disappear." "No one would care anyway."

FUNCTIONS OF SUICIDAL PARTS

Despite their danger, the suicidal part's reasoning is protective in intent, a survival logic that confuses ending pain with ending life. This logic is outdated and desperate, but the true aim is not destruction. We will explore each function through the lens of the action and motivational systems that are at play. Their roles may include:

1. **Escape from unbearable affect /unending pain**. Offers what feels like the only exit when pain exceeds the system's capacity to contain it.

Systems: Defense (flight, exit fantasy).
Survival logic: "If I cannot stop the pain, I can leave it behind."

2. **Interruption of emotional activation**. Functions as an internal emergency brake, slamming the system into shutdown when arousal rises too high.
   Systems: Defense (collapse, shutdown).
   Survival logic: "If I shut everything down now, it will not spiral out of control."

3. **Control and containment in chaos**. Derives stability from the belief in an exit ("At least, there is a way out"), creating structure when life feels unmanageable.
   Systems: Rank, extreme submission to perpetrator´s command and to perceived circumstances. Dissociation (narrowed options that feel controllable).
   Survival logic: "I cannot control life, but I can control whether it continues."

It is important to note that even suicidal parts rarely long for nonexistence, they long for pain, conflict, or loneliness to stop. They believe this is the only path to peace. Sometimes they speak this aloud, but more often, they whisper it internally, waiting to see if anyone is listening.

Clinical note: In rare cases involving severe, organized, or coercive abuse, suicidal parts may appear to be activated in response to specific cues (such as disclosure), reflecting conditioned threat responses and survival learning, rather than a wish to die. These presentations require specialized assessment and should not be assumed in most clinical contexts.

RELATING TO SUICIDAL PARTS

When suicidal parts surface, the therapist may feel a pull to act, to fix, to soothe, or to reassure. These responses are human. But in the presence of a part that sees no way out, these responses can feel like pressure. These parts do not want to be convinced, they want to be understood. We view them as protectors who have run out of strategies.

The most effective stance is neither neutrality nor urgency, but presence: calm, attuned, non-coercive. These parts are watching not only what we say, but how we sit with their pain. They expect dismissal, fear, or clinical management. What surprises them is respectful interest without agenda.

Some anchoring phrases might include:

★ "You don't have to believe anything different right now."
★ "I'm not here to take this away from you—I'd like to understand it with you."
★ "Even if you don't feel connected to the others, I'll stay with you while we figure this out."

Over time, this stance models something new: a way of being with despair that is neither engulfed nor avoided. This becomes internalized, not just by the suicidal part, but by the system as a whole.

When the therapist stays steady without fixing, the part begins to test new possibilities: "Is it safe to speak? Is it safe to be seen? Can I trust this space with the weight I carry?"

The clinical stance when relating to these parts is:

★ "I am here as long as you let me, you don't have to carry this alone and there are other options."

There are several aspects to keep in mind when working with suicidal parts. Each invites a different kind of attention: how we meet them, how we listen, how we relate their experience to the rest of the system, and how we support cooperation around safety. What follows outlines key areas of focus, not as a checklist, but as ways of orienting to these moments with steadiness and care.

Presence Before Problem-Solving

Rather than challenging their beliefs directly, talking them out of the ideas or trying to find solutions, we begin by listening with genuine interest:

★ "What does this part believe it's protecting you from?"
★ "What would happen if this part didn't act this way?"

We are not asking for justification, we are making space for meaning. The goal is to increase understanding of what the risk is protecting against so we can think of more updated alternatives.

Curiosity and Cooperation

These parts often feel isolated, or act in secrecy. Inviting other internal perspectives begins to shift the dynamic from threat to internal dialogue:

- ★ "Are there other parts who worry about what this part is feeling or planning?"
- ★ "Are there any parts who see this differently?"

This does not minimize the suicidal part's experience. Instead, it contextualizes it, introducing the idea that they are not the only one trying to protect the system, and that there are other ways. We can also invite curiosity through questions like, "Would you opt for life if you could learn to live with less suffering?" Rarely do we get a "No" to that. And even if they do not see it, we are planting the seed.

Addressing Typical Distortions

Many suicidal parts act as if the self is singular and the decision to disappear is theirs alone. They may not realize that the body is shared, or if they do, they believe others would be better off without them. We gently invite a new awareness:

- ★ "Do you know there is only one shared body?"
- ★ "What do you imagine might happen to the others inside if something happened to you?"
- ★ (Through Adult Self) "What does this part think will happen with her if she tries to kill you all?"

Validate Their Exhaustion

Suicidal parts are not trying to be defiant, they are exhausted. They are often the ones who have carried unbearable burdens for years with no relief.

Once the exhaustion is named and met with understanding, the suicidal part often becomes a little less defended. This is not yet the time for solutions, but for shared orientation: mapping what brings this part to the edge, what makes it feel momentary relief, what increases its isolation.

As trust deepens, curiosity about these rhythms can emerge, not to control them, but to know them together. Curiosity becomes the bridge toward safer cooperation. Naming this truth can be more regulating than reassurance:

- ★ "It sounds like you're tired. Like you've been holding this alone for a long time."

Identify Triggers and Alternatives

Therapy is not about removing these parts, but about reducing their burden. When suicidal parts feel heard, their grip often loosens. From there, we explore:

- ★ Triggers: "What patterns or situations precede these urges?"
- ★ Resources and alternatives: "What helps these parts feel calmer, more connected, or less alone?
- ★ Cooperation and collaboration: "Can the system agree on a shared plan that offers safety without silencing?"

The goal is to introduce the idea that now there are more options, more choices and support. It is not so much about convincing them to stay, but to create a world in which staying might begin to feel less painful and even worth it.

Working with suicidal parts requires steadiness, humility, and attunement. These parts are not trying to manipulate or create drama. They are often expressing what they believe to be the only possible truth. The urge to reassure, fix, or reframe may be strong, especially in the presence of risk, but when therapists move too quickly, these parts may feel dismissed, coerced, or unseen.

Reassurance is not too effective, but respect, curiosity, and understanding are. These parts need someone to stay steady in the face of their despair. A therapist who sees beyond the despair and does not become infected by it is one of the best antidotes for these parts.

Clinical Vignette

When Suicide Feels Like the Only Escape

A 40-year-old woman was referred to a new therapist by her previous clinician, who had grown increasingly concerned about the risk of suicide. The client had a long history of severe suicide attempts and expressed little hope for the future. "I don't see the point", she said early in the session. "I've been fighting for years and nothing changes. The pain does not go away."

A suicidal part was clearly present; one the client recognized and had lived with for years. What was different now was that the client no longer argued with it. Instead, she echoed its voice with a quiet certainty: "It's not worth it." She added desperately, "Everyone tells you to leave the past behind. How can I? It follows me."

About twenty minutes into the session, the client looked up and asked, "Do you think I can improve?" The therapist answered honestly, "If you stay alive, yes." The client responded almost instantly, "You ask too much."

Sensing a shift, the therapist paused and gently clarified: "I'm sorry if that felt like pressure. That's not what I meant to do. What I meant is that, in my experience—after years of working with people with very painful histories—I've seen that things can improve, but only if they're alive to experience it. If they're not here, I can't help them. I would really like it if you stayed alive—but I understand and respect it's your choice. I just want you to know that I'll be here for as long as you'll let me. And I truly believe, if you give therapy a real chance, there's a way to live with less pain."

The atmosphere shifted slightly. No threats. No internal pushback. Just quiet.

They began to discuss EMDR therapy—an approach that focuses on the unprocessed memories driving her despair. She had spent years in therapies that had not touched that layer. This felt different. The client nodded slowly. "I'll try", she said.

There was no interference from the suicidal part—no inner shouting, no immediate resistance. Just a quiet, almost tentative agreement: "This is new. Maybe it's worth a shot."

Note: A collapsed presentation may reflect either defense (freeze or shutdown) or rank dynamics (passive submission). Favor a defense reading when immobilization and autonomic signs are present; when surrender dominates without freeze, lean toward rank. Frame the therapist stance as cooperation between peers rather than caregiving. A rescuing frame risks reactivating disorganized attachment. Cooperation preserves symmetry, explicit consent, and shared authorship.

SYSTEM	WHERE IT SHOWS UP	FUNCTION	SURVIVAL LOGIC
Defense System (flight/fight subsystems), or rank fight	The suicidal part embodied both flight (wishing to escape overwhelming pain) and fight (anger toward the pressure to "leave the past behind"). You ask too much reveals a rank/fight intent.	Protect the system from overwhelming threat or pain by fleeing or confronting what seems intolerable	"If I can't escape the past, and no one sees my pain, disappearing is the only option."
Defense (collapse) or Rank/Power (submission/defeat), case dependent	"It's not worth it," "The pain will not go away," posture of giving up. When there is immobilization or freezing, read as defense collapse; when it is mainly passive surrender without strong somatic repercussions such as freeze, read as rank submission/defeat. It's a position of internal defeat and resignation. The belief that she is beyond help reflects a submissive posture against life's challenges.	Either shuts the system down to stop overload (defense), or maintains control through surrender to avoid humiliation and failure (rank).	"If I stop existing, I stop hurting (defense). If I accept defeat, I can stop fighting and avoid being cut down (rank). If I accept I've lost, at least I can stop fighting."
Attachment System (distorted/inhibited activation)	The client's question "Do you think I can improve?" reveals a flicker of care-seeking, an implicit bid for hope, validation, and connection.	Seeks support and understanding, but is heavily inhibited by past relational failures. The system does not trust closeness, fearing disappointment.	"Maybe someone could help, but it's safer not to hope."
Cooperation (peer-based) with emerging Adult Self; therapist models steadiness	Non-coercive "we" language, clear choice and pacing; client begins to consider alternatives (e.g., EMDR), signaling shared problem-solving.	Creates a joint working container that recruits the Adult Self and offers regulation without a rescuer dynamic.	"If we can work together with choice and brakes, maybe I do not have to go."

Table 19.1. Motivational and Action Systems at Play

Clinical Reflections

This clinical vignette illustrates how a therapist's grounded, non-coercive presence can interrupt the suicidal part's logic, not by confrontation or persuasion, but through respectful acknowledgment of the client's pain and autonomy. Rather than arguing against the suicidal part or rushing to instill hope, the therapist validates the unbearable suffering and expresses a quiet belief in the possibility of change.

The statement "I can't work with someone who is dead" lands not as a threat, but as a relational truth, one that recognizes the gravity of the part's intent while affirming the therapist's commitment to stay present. The client's shift from fused despair to cautious curiosity ("Maybe it's worth a shot") signals a moment of internal differentiation.

The suicidal part does not disappear, but it no longer dominates the system. By allowing choice, offering attuned containment, and introducing the possibility of a new therapeutic method (EMDR), the therapist creates the conditions for hope to re-enter as a relational, rather than pressured, experience. In dissociative systems, this kind of shift often marks the beginning of a different therapeutic path; one where even the most hopeless parts may begin to consider staying.

CLOSING THOUGHTS

Suicidal parts are extreme adaptations. They carry the pain no one else in the system could hold; guardians of last resort whose methods mirror their desperation. They appear when everything else has failed, when suffering has gone unacknowledged for too long, and when the internal system believes it has run out of safe options.

We do not win them over by offering logic or reassurance. We build trust by listening, respecting their function, and staying steady in the face of despair. When therapists meet these parts with presence instead of panic, the system begins to register a new truth: someone can stay close, even in the darkest moments.

Their presence does not mean therapy is failing. Often, it means something deeper is becoming visible or heard. These parts carry truths the system has not yet found words for. When we listen without panic, and relate without pressure, something begins to shift.

Suicidal parts rarely long for nonexistence, they long for the pain, conflict, or loneliness to stop. Our role is to help them discover that there may be other ways to live, and to stay until those ways feel real enough to try.

These parts have been carrying the keys to the only locked door they knew. Therapy is the slow work of showing them there are other exits. These parts need someone to stay in the room with them, again, and again, and again. And that is how suicidal parts begin to shift, not because someone told them to, but because someone finally stayed.

Clinical Anchors

What to remember...

- Suicidal parts are protectors of last resort. Treat them with dignity.
- Their actions often arise from exhaustion, not aggression.
- Make choice and brakes visible. Cooperation is the safety signal.
- Risk assessments should be relational, not procedural.
- Clarify internal dynamics, how other parts feel, what agreements exist.
- Measure progress by increased dialogue and delayed action, not by the immediate disappearance of thoughts.
- Believe there are other options they cannot see.
- Hope reenters as a relational experience, not a demand.
- Always affirm the shared ownership of the body.

What to avoid...

- Panic responses or rushing into safety plans without relationship.
- Trying to disprove suicidal beliefs with logic.
- Treating suicidal parts as irrational or dangerous symptoms.
- Speaking only to the Adult Self without acknowledging the part.
- Taking over responsibility for safety. Collaboration builds trust.

Chapter 20: Internally Focused Homicidal Parts

THERAPIST REFLECTION

The first time a colleague asked me to consult on a case that "didn't add up", I expected complexity; I did not expect the client's opening line: "I didn't try to kill myself. This was an attempt at murder." Terror and anger sat side by side in her voice. My reflex was surprise. My next move was to take her words seriously. Rather than correcting to "suicide attempt", I widened the frame to understand the lethal intent inside a dissociative system.

I went from thinking how strange to how interesting and how much sense it made. What felt strange at first helped me understand some of the most complex inner dynamics we can find as therapists: parts that hold homicidal intent toward other parts—or toward the body as a whole—and lethal protectors convinced they are preventing something worse, often unaware that, if the body dies, no part, including them, survives. In these moments, the task is twofold: act immediately on safety while mapping agency and function—who intends what, toward whom, and in service of which survival logic.

Homicidal-aimed parts are uncommon but high-risk. They are not the fleeting violent impulses or images most people have and discard. They are organized, rule-bound protective states that narrow the moral world, collapse time, and fixate on elimination as safety. Naming them for what they are (dissociative protection gone extreme) reduces shame, clarifies risk, and opens space for procedure.

These parts do not appear in most systems, and when they do, they can be so frightening that clients hide them and clinicians refer out. Too often, what is dissociative and protection-driven is mislabeled as psychosis, or it is met with urgency that leaves the client more alone with it. The rarity is exactly why this needs its own chapter. When clients finally risk describing an internal plan to "get rid of the weak one", they deserve a frame that is clinically precise, ethically grounded, and respectful. Without it, they are left either terrified of themselves or cast as dangerous in ways that do not fit their reality.

It also matters because this territory is easy to misuse. Public conversations about dissociation have occasionally been co-opted to justify planned, non-defensive harm (grooming, targeted assault, sexual exploitation) by claiming parts *made* them do it (Van der Hart et al., 2006; Spiegel at al., 2011; Brand et al., 2014; Sar & Ross, 2006). That is not what we are describing. This chapter concerns internal dynamics that arise in trauma time with a protective intent, however distorted and dangerous the method.

Out of respect for clients who live with these states, it is essential to distinguish them from perpetration that is deliberate, prepared, and instrumental.

WHAT WE ARE AND ARE NOT TALKING ABOUT

The clinical problem here is not just one. A breakdown of the felt sense of a shared body is common, but it is only one distortion among several. Rank and purity codes can narrow the moral world until *elimination* feels like the best option. Time can collapse so completely that the system cannot tell the difference between a remembered threat and the person standing in front of them now. Disgust can dehumanize an internal other. Attention can tunnel until only a sentence remains: "Remove, erase, fix." These distortions braid together and create pressure toward violent solutions that feel righteous, quick, and protective.

The voice belongs to a part in a dissociative personality system; reality testing may remain intact even as the intent toward an internal other is dangerous. It is not harm-related obsessive thinking, which is ego-dystonic, feared, and usually avoided rather than planned. And it is not predation. A person who selects a victim, grooms access, and harms when opportunity arises is acting with sustained, instrumental intent. By contrast, the clients in this chapter are caught in a defensive reaction that spikes under threat, collapses time and rank, and then recedes as regulation returns. They may still be at real risk of harming themselves or another if the state runs the body. This is why our work is firm, relational, and procedure-based.

A brief clinical contrast helps. First, a client in trauma time may lash out when a trigger ignites terror and there is no access to present-time orientation. The aim is to end what feels like an imminent, engulfing danger. After the spike, shame and collapse often follow, along with relief that no one was harmed or deep distress if someone was. Second, a perpetrator planning harm shows a different pattern: anticipation, selection, preparation, concealment, and a willingness to repeat for advantage. Therapy for the first demands safety, stimulus discrimination, rank de-escalation, and role updates; the second demands legal accountability and community protection. Keeping this line bright protects the public and protects our clients from being misnamed.

Distinction From Suicidal Parts

These parts are distinct from suicidal parts. Suicidal parts aim to end the self, as described in chapter 19. They are also not the self-harming regulators in chapter 18, whose purpose is rapid relief and continuation.

What distinguishes the dynamic here is the intent to eliminate an *internal other* who is perceived as separate and dangerous to the whole. They also differ from harm-related obsessive thoughts, which are unwanted, feared, and usually avoided rather than planned and enacted.

ORIGIN OF INTERNALLY FOCUSED HOMICIDAL PARTS

In systems shaped by coercion and contempt, a protector may adopt the perpetrator's logic: remove weakness, erase need, enforce purity. Rank dominance pairs with fight-based defense, and internal figures can be perceived not as *Me* but as separate entities that can be controlled, targeted, or eliminated. Typical conditions include:

- Chronic humiliation
- Role reversal in which cruelty was framed as care
- Environments where proximity to power felt safer than vulnerability.
- Repeated exposure to threat without viable avenues of escape.

These environments are often governed by coercive codes: rigid, threat-based rules organizing power, loyalty, and survival, often learned in environments where obedience or cruelty was required to avoid harm. Within such contexts, identification with the aggressor (see chapter 21) becomes a solution to the paradox of disorganized attachment. Over time, the system learns that eliminating vulnerability restores safety and honor.

This pathway is not the only one. Some parts that move toward internal elimination are described by clients as very primitive—blunt, fast, and unsymbolized. They may not be perpetrator-identified. They behave more like an alarmed organism cutting away what it reads as infected tissue. Time collapses, disgust narrows the field, and an old code (no weakness, no exposure) takes the wheel.

These parts tend to surface at two inflection points. Early in therapy, when chaos is high and the client cannot yet sort who is doing what, they may erupt to restore order. Later, once stability and cooperation have grown, a fed-up protector part can appear, intent on removing another part that is now seen as blocking progress or quality of life. This is where clinicians become understandably confused: a client may insist, "I didn't try to kill myself—another part tried to kill another one." The aim is not self-annihilation but internal elimination in the name of protection.

MAIN FEATURES OF INTERNALLY FOCUSED HOMICIDAL PARTS

As these dynamics surface, they leave a distinctive footprint in the room. These are common:

- Categorical labeling of internal targets as weak, dirty, or useless.
- Moralized language of purity, order, or strength.
- Determined tone with narrowed attention to a single plan or sentence.
- Poor recognition of plurality and the shared body.
- Testing of the therapist for rank contests and fear responses.
- Dehumanizing or contemptuous language toward *weak* or *useless* parts.
- Rigid moral codes and internal *trials*.
- Preemptive threats to eradicate vulnerability.
- Refusal to engage in care or negotiation. "Care is weakness."

FUNCTIONS OF INTERNALLY FOCUSED HOMICIDAL PARTS

Taken together, the footprint above usually signals a small set of jobs. The same surface behaviors can be driven by different action and motivational systems; what changes is *why* the part is doing the job and *how* it pursues it. Pairing each function with its underlying system keeps the work targeted and prevents moral debates from replacing procedure.

1. **Purge vulnerability to prevent danger**. Seeks to remove *weak* parts to stop shame, exposure, or collapse.
   Systems: Rank/power (dominance; identification with aggressor), defense (fight).
   Survival logic: "If the weak one is gone, we cannot be used or humiliated."

2. **Identification with the aggressor**. Borrows the perpetrator stance to avoid helplessness and humiliation.
   Systems: Rank/power (dominance alignment), defense (fight mobilization).
   Survival logic: "If I become the one who judges and harms, I cannot be judged or harmed."

3. **Sealing trauma-related experience or activation**. Attempts to destroy block or seal trauma-related activation, including memories, images, sensations, affective states or external reminders that trigger trauma-time experience.
   Systems: Defense (compartmentalization, inhibition).
   Survival logic: "If traumatic memories (and related experiences) are inaccessible, the system can function."

4. **Attachment deactivation disguised as loyalty**. Suppresses bids for care and frames cruelty as protection or honor.
   Systems: Attachment (deactivation under threat), social identity (internalization of group codes). rank (submission subroutine).
   Survival logic: "If need is silent and order is kept, proximity to power stays predictable."

5. **Rank stabilization**. Asserts internal hierarchy through rigid codes and enforcement.
   Systems: Rank/power (rule-keeping; counter-dominance).
   Survival logic: "If I keep us on top inside, others cannot cut us down outside."

Regulatory processes shaping all the above: time collapse, disgust-based *contamination* readings of the target, and attentional tunneling amplify speed and certainty. When these processes are active, elimination feels not only justified but urgent.

Variations of the Rank System in Internally Focused Homicidal Parts

From an evolutionary perspective, the rank system developed in social species to regulate hierarchies within the group. Its primary function was not destruction but conflict prevention; a way to conserve group strength by minimizing internal violence. Lethal aggression was reserved for external threats, especially in defense of territory or resources.

In dissociative systems, rank can take extreme forms. Sometimes it expresses as dominance, seeking to eliminate *weaker* members to maintain order or avoid shame. Other times it operates as a submission subroutine, where safety is felt through identification with power. In this latter form, closeness to the internal *alpha* can mask the submission with a sense of belonging and pride. Submission guarantees safety, and identification alleviates the humiliation of defeat with the pride of belonging.

RELATING TO INTERNALLY FOCUSED HOMICIDAL PARTS

The therapeutic aim is to lower intensity and conflict while increasing containment. Begin by making safety explicit without turning the room into a contest: one shared body, one life, no harm. This is not a negotiation; this is the frame that allows work to proceed. Keep in mind that what is driving elimination is usually a braid of distortions (lack of time orientation, rank threat, narrowed moral codes) not just the failure to register the shared body. Address safety, then translate method back into purpose so protection, order, and honor can be kept without harm.

Preserving Dignity

This is not a softness but a clinical lever. Elimination is often powered by the belief that humiliation is worse than pain. If we shame the protector or *win* on rank, we confirm its worldview and escalate urgency. Speaking to purpose—protection, order, honor—and offering ways to fulfill that purpose without harm allows updating without losing face. Dignity lowers rank threat, which restores access to procedure.

CLINICAL VIGNETTE

When Protection Turns Against Itself

In the aftermath of a life-threatening overdose, a young woman sat across from her therapist, still unsure how to speak about what had happened. She had landed in the hospital a few days prior due to a suicide attempt. The client said quietly, "I know it sounds crazy, but it wasn't me, she (referring to another part) took the pills to kill the other part that had come back." Her words hung in the room, describing her dangerous reality. She was not denying responsibility; she was naming complexity. One part inside her had tried to eliminate another.

When asked to explain, she described the presence of a part she feared deeply, a voice that only emerged when she was overwhelmed. "She's strong", the client said. "Not always there, but when she shows up, I disappear. She takes over completely." The tone of that part's voice was unmistakable—an exact replica of the client's abusive mother. "It's like a recording", she said. "Same words. Same tone. It's like she's living in the back of my head, and once she starts, I can't speak louder than her. I try, but I can't." This internal force terrified her, not just because of its intensity, but because it sounded like her past. But in therapy, another possibility emerged: that the part had learned to protect in the only way it knew how, by imitating the very person who had once controlled everything.

As the session unfolded, the client named another presence. A more primitive part, instinctual and reactive. "She came in to stop the voice. To get rid of her. She didn't know we're the same. She just knew she had to make it stop." The overdose, then, was not an act of self-destruction in the conventional sense. It was internal war. One part reenacting the violence of the past and another responding with equal force, believing it had to kill to survive. For the first time, the client could see them both as misunderstood protectors operating in isolation.

SYSTEM	WHERE IT SHOWS UP	FUNCTION	SURVIVAL LOGIC
Rank/Power System (Perpetrator-Identified Voice)	Exact replica of the abusive mother's tone.	Maintain dominance to avoid being dominated; monitor the system through authority.	"If I become her, I won't be under her. If I control first, I can't be crushed."
Rank System (Fight — Punisher)	Commanding, silencing attacks when overwhelm rises; drowns out other parts.	Preempt perceived danger by striking first; shut down vulnerability.	"If I attack before it spreads, we survive humiliation and harm."
Defense System (Primitive Fight Part)	Overdose "to kill the other part" and stop the voice.	Eliminate the internal threat by any means; end the unbearable state.	"If I destroy her, we live. Better to end it than be overrun."
Defense System (Freeze/Collapse)	"I disappear... I can't speak louder than her."	Minimize exposure and conflict by going offline.	"If I go still and small, danger will pass over me."
Attachment System (Disorganized)	The threatening voice is also the template of closeness/ power; fear and proximity fuse.	Preserve a bond with power to stave off annihilation; approach-avoid around contact.	"If I stay aligned with the powerful one, I belong and I'm safer." Using a strategy of submission "If I ally myself with the demands of the dangerous, etc"
A Caregiving Strategy (Distorted Protection)	Both the Punisher and the reactive part claim to be "protecting" (control now to prevent worse later).	Prevent perceived catastrophe (exposure, collapse) via extreme measures.	"Harsh control now prevents devastation later."

Table 20.1. Motivational and Action Systems at play

Clinical Reflections

These systems collide to produce *internal war*: a perpetrator-mode protector reenacts domination, while a primitive fighter tries to annihilate that threat. The Adult Self collapses, leaving no mediator until therapy helps name functions, restore pacing, and recruit present-time leadership.

The therapist did not interpret or correct but invited reflection: that both parts had been trying, in their own way, to help. "And because they don't yet know they're part of you and share the same body", the therapist said, "from that perspective, it makes sense they'd turn on each other."

This session became a turning point. Rather than shutting down, the client leaned in. She began to ask new questions. "How do I teach her not to sound like my mother? How do I help that other part see that she does not have to fight?"

Re-Establish Differentiation and Time Orientation

In these moments, time is usually collapsed and the body is reading now as then. Use brief, repeatable orientation moves that re-anchor the system in the room: date, place, age, two concrete details that belong only to now, one slow exhale set while feet find the floor. The goal is not insight; it is discriminating this moment from the remembered scene enough that choice becomes imaginable.

Update the Role, Not the Purpose

Reflect what the part is trying to achieve—guard dignity, prevent exposure, keep order—and propose roles that preserve that purpose without violence. Typical updates include gatekeeping proximity (deciding whether and how contact happens), setting pace, early warning and surveillance, and advocacy for boundaries. Make each role concrete: what the signal is, who hears it, what happens next. The body needs procedures it can find when arousal surges.

Mind Rank Dynamics

These encounters invite contests. Downshift your own rank with matter-of-fact, permission-based language: you are not overruling; you are recruiting this protector's expertise into a safer plan. When you meet a test, name the test and stay steady. The point is to show the system that authority can hold limits without contempt.

Address Disgust if Present

In systems shaped by coercive purity codes or sexual trauma, disgust may be the accelerant. The target is seen as *contaminating* rather than vulnerable. Name disgust as a body alarm and replace moral language with specific, neutral description: moving from "She's dirty" to "She's five, shaking, and needs space" reduces dehumanization, lowers urgency, and restores personhood—often enough to make cooperation possible.

Coordinate with the Rest of the System

Invite Adult Self with the collaboration of protector parts to co-author an internal law the system can live by (one body, many inner experiences, no harm) and to agree on a pause cue and brief *cooling* routine when pressure spikes. Keep it reversible and tiny: a two-tap signal to stop, a 30-second orientation script, five paced exhales, then a check-in about whether contact proceeds or pauses.

End with Repair and Rehearsal

Mark what worked, adjust what did not, and practice the micro-procedures once in regulation so the nervous system can retrieve them in heat. The measure of progress is not the disappearance of elimination impulses but faster access to the pause, fewer rank spikes, and an increasing capacity to keep purpose while changing methods.

Therapist Stance

Work procedurally, not performatively. State limits without shaming, avoid contests, translate violent method into protective purpose, and rehearse small, repeatable moves the body can find under stress. Build Adult Self authority with *we-language*, visible brakes, and rehearsed cues for pause, orientation, and choice. Use present-time resets whenever time orientation is lost. Differentiate fantasy from intent and reassess regularly. If outward intent or access emerges, activate crisis and legal protocols; do not conflate dissociative defense with predatory violence. When predation is evident, accountability is required.

Ultimately, treat this as a protector using the wrong tool for the right job. Avoid power struggles that confirm its worldview. Protect dignity while redirecting method; cooperation becomes the safety signal. When the body trusts the procedures, partnership can replace combat.

Ethical Stance

We hold two truths at once. There is one body, and there will be no harm to it or to anyone else. And the part driving toward elimination is, in its own frame, trying to protect dignity and safety. Our task is to keep the limits firm without humiliation, translate the protection back into the present, and offer procedures the system can trust under pressure. When we do this, even severe internal enforcers can shift from elimination to guardianship without losing face.

Clinical Vignette

When a lethal plan is named before action

Elena, a 36-year-old client with DID, arrived at the session unusually brisk, jaw tight, eyes scanning the room. She sat down and said, "I need to tell you something before it happens." Her hands were clenched. "There's a part inside who has decided the teenage part has to go."

As Elena described the sequence leading up to the threat, it became clear that the part was operating from a familiar distortion: relating to the teenage part as a separate *problem* to be eliminated, without full awareness of the shared body. The therapist slowed the pace and stayed matter-of-fact. "Thank you for telling me", she said. "This is important information. I'm wondering what this part imagines will happen if the teenage part is gone." Elena swallowed. "She thinks things will be better. She hates that the teenager is closer to the child part now."

"So recent changes feel threatening to this part," the therapist reflected. Elena nodded. The therapist then introduced the shared-body frame carefully. "I also want to check something. When this part talks about killing a part, does she realize what that would mean for all of you—meaning, for everyone? I'm not asking to scare her. I'm asking because sometimes the part is focused on stopping danger and doesn't register the full consequences."

Elena's eyes widened. "I don't think she's thought about it like that." "What happens inside as you notice that?" the therapist asked. The client went still. After a few seconds she said, "She isn't saying anything now. It's like a dark, ice-cold silence." The therapist did not push for more content. "Let's treat that silence as a signal that the pressure just went up," she said. "Would you be willing to do a short present-time reset with me, just to help the system orient to now?" Elena nodded. "I can try."

The therapist asked her to place both feet on the ground and name three present-time details: the date, the city, and something in the room that could not belong to the past. Elena answered mechanically at first, then more fully: "It's Tuesday. I'm in your office in A Coruña. I see the ocean, the water." Her shoulders dropped slightly. As Elena's breathing slowed, her face changed again. The therapist named the shift without alarm. "Something changed just now." Elena's gaze sharpened. "She says, 'Stop wasting time. She's the infection. She ruins everything'."

Rank rose in the room. The therapist did not argue. She lowered her own rank and spoke with respectful clarity. "I hear you. You're trying to protect the system from something you believe is dangerous. I'm not here to overpower you. There is one non-negotiable we hold together here: protection means keeping everyone alive, including you. That is what allows us to keep working." The part scoffed. "There is no other way." "I understand it feels like that," the therapist said evenly. "So, let's be precise. What are you trying to stop by getting rid of the teenage part?"

The answer came fast: "Exposure. Weakness. The little one cannot hope." The therapist translated the method back into purpose. "So, the job is preventing exposure. Keeping the system functional. Not killing for its own sake." She paused. "That's a protector job. But the method is lethal." Elena's breath became shallow. "He says the little one is dirty and should have no help. That's why the teenager must go."

Disgust was in the room—an accelerant. The therapist shifted the language out of moral contamination and into neutral description. "When you say 'dirty,' do you mean: she carries memories, sensations, or needs that feel unbearable or contaminating—like if they come close, the system could be overwhelmed?" Elena nodded, tears appearing unexpectedly. "Yes. If she shows it... I can't stand it. And now the teenager is on her side."

The therapist suggested another option: "Then we need an emergency plan that keeps what the little one holds contained without harming the body. Not erased—contained." She kept it simple. "Right now, the goal is not to solve anything. The goal is to create a pause the system can use when this pressure rises."

She asked Elena to rehearse a 20-second script out loud, short enough to retrieve under threat: "This is now. This is one adult body. We pause. No harm." Elena repeated it once. The harsh voice returned: "Pathetic." The therapist stayed steady. "You don't have to like it. I'm not asking you to give anything up. I'm asking whether you're willing to *experiment* with a brief pause, just long enough to see if it protects what you're trying to protect. We can stop if it makes things worse."

Elena blinked. "He is listening." The therapist offered a role update that preserved status. "I think you're the one who detects danger fastest. That matters. Elimination won't give you the protection you're aiming for. A more effective job would be alarm and boundary enforcement: signaling 'too close' or 'too risky', so everyone can respond without anyone getting hurt. A long silence followed. Elena's jaw unclenched.

They ended by building a short, practical plan for the next hours: avoid being alone, reduce exposure to triggers, and return to the pause script if pressure spiked. The therapist also named a contingency clearly: if the part gained control or intent sharpened, Elena would contact emergency supports.

At the door, Elena said, "It feels like he's still mad." The therapist nodded. "He might be. But something new happened today: He learned that protection can exist without elimination."

SYSTEM	WHERE IT SHOWS UP	FUNCTION	SURVIVAL LOGIC
Rank / Power (Perpetrator-Identified Voice)	A dominant, contemptuous voice echoing the abusive mother; targets the teenage part for protecting the younger part.	Maintain control and prevent vulnerability from gaining ground.	"If I become her, I can't be crushed."
Rank (Fight / Punisher)	Silencing, attacking commands when overwhelm rises; shuts down the teenage part's protective stance.	Enforce hierarchy and eliminate perceived weakness.	"If I attack first, we stay in control."
Defense (Fight / Elimination)	The overdose intended to "kill the other part" and stop internal danger.	End unbearable activation by removing the perceived threat.	"If I destroy the danger, we survive."
Rank	Alignment with the perpetrator voice as the authority on safety.	Preserve predictability by aligning with power.	"If I stay aligned with power, I'm safer."

Table 20.2. Motivational and Action Systems at play

Clinical Reflections

This vignette illustrates a moment of threat before action, but also something equally important: the system's emerging capacity to ask for help while danger is still forming.

Elena's choice to speak before acting reflects a fragile but meaningful shift, not yet cooperation, but the first opening toward it. The therapist transforms this opening into an opportunity by introducing shared responsibility and coordinated action, rather than escalation or collapse. Even when a lethal plan is present, the ability to bring it into the room signals that not all authority has been ceded to the protective part.

The part driving toward elimination is not inventing violence; it is repeating a solution learned under conditions where vulnerability was dangerous and control equaled survival. Its certainty, speed, and moral clarity reflect trauma-time learning, not malice. Recognizing this allows the therapist to respond with firmness and dignity rather than fear or moral correction.

From this perspective, the immediate trigger in this vignette was not the younger part alone, but a change in the internal relational dynamic: the teenage part's growing proximity to and protection of the younger part. From the perspective of the homicidal protector, this shift signaled increased exposure, loss of containment, and a return of risks that had once been catastrophic. What might otherwise be read as progress within the system was experienced here as destabilization and danger.

Rather than debating the content of the threat, the therapist focused on procedure and containment: slowing the system, lowering rank tension, and translating the lethal method back into its protective purpose: preventing exposure and overwhelm. Consent and cooperation were sought at each step, framing pauses as reversible experiments rather than commands. This stance reduced escalation and kept the part engaged.

Addressing disgust as an accelerant was also key. By replacing moralized language ("dirty", "infection") with neutral descriptions of unbearable experience, dehumanization softened and urgency decreased. The brief pause script served as a procedural bridge, simple enough to retrieve under pressure and concrete enough to create a moment of choice.

Progress here is not measured by the disappearance of violent impulses, but by earlier disclosure, increased willingness to pause, and the system's growing ability to seek protection through collaboration rather than elimination. The vignette demonstrates how, when dignity is preserved and rank is de-escalated, even extreme protective strategies can begin to update, without denying the danger they were built to manage.

CLOSING THOUGHTS

When these inner dynamics are understood and cooperation is practiced, rank tension falls. Even harsh internal enforcers can shift from elimination to protection without harm. Over time, relational symmetry and reliable repair teach the system that safety does not require removing parts; it requires procedures everyone can live with. Safety grows from procedure: small, reversible moves rehearsed in regulation and retrieved under pressure.

Progress is not the disappearance of violent ideas, but earlier access to the pause, fewer surges, cleaner exits, and steadier coordination with the Adult Self. Keep the ethical line bright. Defensive, trauma-time dynamics call for safety and role updates; planned, instrumental harm calls for accountability. Holding both truths protects the public and honors clients whose protection strategies can now be updated in collaboration.

Clinical Anchors

What to remember...

- Honor function while holding firm, shame-free limits.
- Reorient to the shared body and (only when stuck) to present time.
- Translate method back to purpose. Offer dignified protective roles that do not require harm (gatekeeping, pacing, early warning).
- Keep the frame cooperative and procedural, not moralizing or rescuing.
- Measure progress by earlier pausing, fewer rank spikes, and reliable use of procedures, not disappearance of impulses.

What to avoid...

- Power struggles and rank contests (they confirm the protector's worldview).
- Shaming confrontations or sarcasm.
- Attachment-heavy pulls that feel like submission or defeat.
- Premature interpretation or trauma processing before safety and procedures are established.
- Conflating defensive, trauma-time dynamics with predatory, planned harm; if evidence points to predation, escalate for legal accountability.

Chapter 21: Perpetrator-Identified Parts

Therapist Reflection

I notice my instinct to recoil when a part echoes abusive figures or when the client speaks fondly of them. I remind myself that this part's identification with harm was once a survival tactic and that it often carries the heaviest burden in the system. I pause and think: Can I hold both my discomfort and this part's protective loyalty without judgment? Staying steady, curious and non-judgmental becomes the first step toward true understanding.

In the clinical literature, the term perpetrator-imitating parts is often used broadly to describe a range of parts that echo abusive dynamics, such as self-critical parts, hostile protectors, internal enforcers, or aggressive defenses (Ferenczi, 1933, 1949; Freud, 1936; Van der Hart et al., 2006; Howell, 2005). Many of the parts described in earlier chapters could reasonably be understood within this category, as they adopt perpetrator *logic* (shame, punishment, domination) without assuming the perpetrator's *identity*. While the literature has described identification with the aggressor in various forms (see Ferenczi, 1933, 1949; Van der Hart et al., 2006; Howell, 2005), it has not consistently differentiated between parts that imitate perpetrator strategies and those that organize around perpetrator identity—an omission that has significant clinical consequences.

In this chapter, a more precise distinction is proposed. A distinction that is not simply semantic, but mostly clinical.

As mentioned above, perpetrator-imitating parts exhibit generalized defensiveness and anger while borrowing perpetrator tone or logic and not assuming his or her identity. On the other hand, perpetrator-identified parts do not merely imitate abusive strategies to defend against threat. Instead, they organize around identification with an abuser's posture, logic, or authority, fully internalizing and enacting the abuser's identity (e.g., "I am your mother"), thus aligning with a position of power, authority, or belonging as a survival solution.

These parts may defend those who caused harm, minimize or distort traumatic experiences, blame the victim, or direct abuse inwardly within the system. Their presence often evokes fear, aversion, or moral confusion in both client and therapist. Yet they are not *bad* or malicious; they are trauma-shaped protectors, frozen in strategies that once made life survivable.

Even though the therapeutic stance for these two different types of parts may be similar in some respects, working with perpetrator-identified parts requires a stance that prioritizes rank de-escalation, identity stability, and cooperation over attachment activation or reassurance.

Parts that imitate perpetrator logic often respond to interventions that highlight their protective intent or invite attachment-based repair. Perpetrator-identified parts frequently do not. We must be cautious because some of the interventions used for perpetrator-imitating parts may rapidly back-fire when used with perpetrator-identified parts.

What makes working with these parts especially difficult is that they rarely experience themselves as protectors. In fact, early protector reframes can feel insulting or manipulative and may escalate rank tension rather than reduce it. When approached as protectors or invited prematurely into relational closeness, they may withdraw, retaliate, or mock, because such moves threaten the very survival solution they embody.

Our task with these parts is less about technique and more about stance: grounded presence, moral complexity, and a cooperative frame. Direct attachment pulls, rescuing, or quick alliance-building often read as manipulation. Respect and time-orientation are necessary but insufficient. First, we down-shift rank tension (no contests, no pressure), keep proximity optional, and work in symmetry with visible consent and brakes.

ORIGIN OF PERPETRATOR-IDENTIFIED PARTS

Perpetrator-identified parts commonly arise in contexts of coercion, betrayal, and disorganized attachment, especially when abusers were also caregivers. When survival required proximity to someone dangerous, aligning with power became an unconscious solution to the unsolvable paradox of caregiver and threat. Internalizing the abuser's logic reduced unbearable dissonance and produced predictability and control.

Sometimes these parts formed under explicit threat: "If you tell, I'll hurt you or your family." Other times, they were shaped by more covert manipulation: "You made me do this." Repeated invalidation where abuse is reframed as care and compliance as loyalty, binds the child to the perpetrator in extremely complicated ways. Some parts absorbed the abuser's voice and logic, becoming harsh, punishing, or accusatory. Others identified with their posture of dominance, as a way to defend against helplessness and humiliation. In many internal systems, these parts also carry the shame of compliance: the guilt of having remained silent, submitted, or even seemed to cooperate. What may present as aggression or betrayal is often an adaptation born from deep confusion, trauma-bonding, and emotional survival.

These parts develop what could be described as *survival through identification*, a complex defense against the overwhelming truth of what happened. At its core, this strategy is organized around anticipation and control. Protection is achieved by staying one step ahead of the real perpetrator. By anticipating the aggressor's moves and enacting them first—internally or externally—the part attempts to prevent surprise, escalation, or annihilation. Being ahead of the threat feels safer than waiting to be overpowered.

From within this logic, the system flips the original dynamic. Rather than acknowledging, "I was harmed", the system flips the dynamic, projecting onto the child:

- "It didn't happen to me; I do it to the child who deserves it."
- "I don't feel hurt or afraid; I create hurt and fear."
- "I'm not helpless; I'm in control of the helpless one."

By embodying the perpetrator role, these parts attempt to regain power, erase vulnerability, and avoid the existential threat of abandonment or annihilation. They remain stuck in trauma time, operating with the logic that once kept the system intact, even if that logic now creates harm from within (Ferenczi, 1949).

MAIN FEATURES OF PERPETRATOR-IDENTIFIED PARTS

Perpetrator-identified parts can present in ways that feel disturbing or confronting, often echoing the behaviors, tone, and posture of past abusers. They might:

- Defend or justify abusive figures
- Blame or shame the Adult Self or other parts
- Reject kindness, empathy, or care as manipulative
- Internalize and take on the abuser's voice, tone, or logic
- Target vulnerable parts within the system or express hostility toward the therapist
- Appear/sound cold, cruel, or emotionally detached

Their language often mirrors the abuser´s, with statements such as:

- ❖ "You deserved what happened."
- ❖ "You're weak, and I'll prove it."

Beneath this exterior is a desperation-born solution: merging with danger felt safer than resisting it. What makes these parts especially complex is their stance toward therapy itself. Warmth may be read as manipulation; validation as a trap; direct attachment cues as risky. They are not rejecting connection out of malice, but because in their lived experience, closeness led to harm.

Despite their appearance, these parts are not inherently mean or sadistic. They are deeply defended, repelled by vulnerability and resistant to attachment, pushing others away not to wound them, but to avoid being hurt again. Seen through the lens of motivational systems, this is a survival-based dominance and defense strategy, one that once kept the system safe but now creates profound internal isolation and hopelessness.

Recognizing these features is only the first step. To work with perpetrator-identified parts effectively, we also need to understand the purposes these behaviors serve. Their often harsh or distancing strategies are not arbitrary, they are deeply tied to the system's survival logic.

FUNCTIONS OF PERPETRATOR-IDENTIFIED PARTS

Perpetrator-identified parts are often misperceived as obstacles to healing, when in fact they are doing exactly what they were created to do: preserve control, suppress vulnerability, and prevent future betrayal or harm. Their behaviors are rooted in survival logic from trauma time, even if they now cause harm within the system.

Primary functions are:

1. **Reversal of power**. Adopts the voice, posture, or tone of the aggressor to flip the internal power dynamic, transforming helplessness into control.
   Systems: Rank or power (dominance, identification with aggressor).
   Survival logic: "If I am the one who hurts, I cannot be hurt."
2. **Protection against shame**. Directs aggression inward through self-criticism, self-harm, or perfectionism to silence vulnerable emotion and avoid external humiliation.
   Systems: Rank or power (dominance, internal enforcer; imposed self-submission as tactic).
   Survival logic: "If I am the bad one, others stay right, and I avoid being cut down."
3. **Repression or distortion of truth**. Justifies, denies, or minimizes past harm so the system does not have to face unbearable realities.
   Systems: Defense (denial, minimization), intersubjectivity or mentalizing (impairment).
   Survival logic: "If it was not that bad, or if it was my fault, the world stays ordered and survivable."
4. **Blocking attachment and therapeutic connection**. Tests, provokes, or disengages when closeness deepens because closeness once brought danger.
   Systems: Attachment (deactivation or avoidant strategy), rank or power (fear of judgment, shame, or loss of status).
   Survival logic: "If I push you away first, you cannot betray or control us."

5. **Acting as container for aggression and traumatic material**. Holds disowned sadistic or punitive impulses and traumatic fragments that other parts cannot bear.
   Systems: Defense (compartmentalization), dissociation (segregation of experience).
   Survival logic: "If I carry the worst of it, the rest can keep functioning."

6. **Preemptive attack and threat detection**. Scans for disrespect or danger and strikes first to establish control.
   Systems: Defense (fight, hyperarousal), rank or power (counter dominance).
   Survival logic: "If I attack before danger arrives, we stay in charge."

7. **Silencing or immobilizing vulnerable parts**. Shames, intimidates, or suppresses younger and needy parts to keep vulnerability out of view.
   Systems: Rank or power (gatekeeping), attachment (deactivation), defense (inhibition).
   Survival logic: "If need is hidden, it can't be used against us."

8. **Code enforcement and rule-keeping**. Imposes internalized perpetrator or family codes to prevent *mistakes* that once invited harm.
   Systems: Rank or power (dominance, rule enforcement),
   Survival logic: "If we follow the old rules, we avoid punishment and chaos."

All the above defend against a persistent, internalized threat and can express as self-directed or other-directed aggression. **Self-directed** may present as harsh self-criticism, self-harm, or debilitating perfectionism that punishes the self to preempt external attack and keep vulnerability controlled. **Other directed** may present as hostility, contempt, or cruelty toward others inside or outside the system to assert dominance and ward off perceived threats before closeness or exposure can occur.

Note: These parts operate primarily from rank or power in a dominant, code-enforcing role. Submission is usually the tactic they impose on other parts (downranking, appeasement, collapse), not the state they inhabit.

Selected Motivational Systems in Perpetrator Identification

Perpetrator-identified parts are trauma-shaped protector parts that have selectively recruited certain facets of motivational systems; those most useful for control, dominance, and predictability under threat. What emerges is not a whole motivational repertoire but a partial, rigid constellation serving survival when ordinary relational regulation was impossible. These parts once served survival but now perpetuate internal conflict. They can be understood as protective responses that became rigid and extreme under trauma.

- The **rank/power system**, rooted in dominance alignment, enforces hierarchy and control. It operates by identifying with the aggressor, setting rules, and asserting authority over other internal parts or even the therapist. Its survival logic follows the belief that aligning with power ensures safety: "If I control the terms and stay on top, no one can overpower or humiliate us."

- The **defense system**, linked to fight mobilization, channels attack energy to preempt danger. It turns aggression inward or outward, especially when care-seeking triggers fear responses. Its underlying survival rule is: "If I strike first and harden us, we won't be exposed or retaliated against."

- The **attachment** system**,** when deactivated under threat, suppresses open care-seeking behaviors. Instead, it maintains proximity through compliance, secrecy, role reversal, or idealization, avoiding genuine emotional closeness. The survival logic here is: "If I mute our needs and manage closeness, the bond remains intact and danger stays predictable."

- Finally, the **social belonging and identity system** internalizes the perpetrator's worldview to preserve coherence and a sense of belonging. By adopting the perpetrator's code, these parts create order and feel aligned with power. Their implicit reasoning is: "If I belong to the powerful side, the world makes sense and I am safer."

Seen through this lens, perpetrator-identified parts are not evil or pathological. They are trauma-shaped protectors using outdated strategies—strategies that, in trauma time, were the only viable way the system could manage inescapable threat and relational coercion. Their aggression toward vulnerability, rejection of care, and denial of need become understandable responses that make sense once we look at the systems they recruit.

More precisely, identification with the aggressor often functions as an attempted solution to the unsolvable paradox of disorganized attachment: the same person is both the source of care and the source of fear. When the attachment system has been repeatedly met with neglect, threat, or overt harm, it becomes unsafe to remain activated and is therefore downregulated. By aligning with power instead, the system replaces care-seeking with rank-based proximity, turning closeness into predictability and control. This is not *attachment closeness,* but attachment deactivation paired with rank alignment; a borrowed sense of safety achieved through control rather than through care. Safety is no longer sought by reaching, but by anticipating, complying with, or embodying power.

What we often call *loyalty* tends to consolidate later. It is less an attachment emotion than a stabilizer: adopting the perpetrator's worldview provides order, identity, and a feeling of special status. Conceptually, this sits closer to the rank/power system (alignment with dominance) and the social belonging/identity system ("I belong because I carry their code"), with attachment remaining muted to avoid the old approach–avoidance panic.

Understanding these functions is essential before engagement. Without this context, interventions can feel threatening or invalidating to the part. When we name the logic—attachment deactivation to dampen terror, rank alignment to prevent helplessness, and identity/belonging to stabilize meaning—we create room for a stance that is steady, respectful, and calibrated to the risks this part is working so hard to prevent.

RELATING TO PERPETRATOR-IDENTIFIED PARTS

Because perpetrator-identified parts are carrying out the exact functions they were created for—preserving control, suppressing vulnerability, and preventing betrayal—and their strategies arise from purposeful motivational systems, our approach must respect the survival logic behind their actions. These strategies once kept the system intact, even if now they create harm from within.

Trying to strip them of their role too quickly risks destabilizing the system and triggering intense backlash. The stance we take must first honor their function before inviting any change.

Working with perpetrator-identified parts calls for deliberate, non-reactive presence. These are not parts to *win over* quickly. Their stance toward the therapist is often one of distrust, testing, or outright rejection. Not because they are malicious, but because in their reality, closeness equates to danger.

Core Principles

- **Containment Without Control:** Boundaries must be clear but never punitive. A firm yet respectful statement might sound like:
    - ★ "We don't use that language here. But I'm not leaving. I want to understand what you're protecting."
- **Expect Rupture:** These parts may attack the alliance to replay betrayal and control dynamics. Repair comes not through clever interventions, but through staying.
- **Regulate Countertransference:** Feelings of fear, repulsion, moral discomfort, or urgency are common. These must be noticed, slowed, and reflected on (often with support or supervision) rather than acted upon to avoid reacting from a defensive or punitive place.
- **Presence Does Not Equal Permission:** Remaining connected does not mean agreeing with harmful behaviors or beliefs, it models that safety and boundaries can coexist.

Why Confrontation Backfires

These parts rarely recognize themselves as protectors. Attempts to reframe their intent or push them toward vulnerability too early can trigger escalation. Overt warmth or rapid alliance-building may be perceived as manipulation, even lack of respect: "Who does s/he (therapist) think s/he is". Confrontation can activate reenactments of past power struggles, reinforcing their belief that no one is safe to trust.

Relational Strategy

- Approach with matter-of-fact curiosity rather than judgment.
- Focus on understanding the burden they carry. What is this part afraid will happen if it steps back? Who is it trying to protect, and from what? What has it been forced to carry alone?"
- Communicate explicitly that your role is not to oppose them, but to understand them.
- Name their exhaustion when it appears: Many are overworked from defending the system in the same rigid ways for decades. Recognizing this can open the door to new possibilities.

As the work progresses and rank tension has reliably decreased, it can be helpful to orient the Adult Self to the role of the perpetrator-identified part before attempting direct engagement. This orientation is not about persuading or reframing the part, but about helping the client understand its function, scope, and limits. When the Adult Self can hold this context, internal polarization tends to soften, making later contact with the part less threatening and reducing the risk of premature interventions that might otherwise escalate threat.

Avoiding Common Pitfalls

- **Uninvited interpretation.** Offering meaning before trust is established can feel invasive and inadequate.
- **Assuming psychoeducation will shift them.** Many already understand their role and have no interest in changing it, what they lack is a place to exist without condemnation.
- **Rushing engagement.** Early work is about consistent, non-threatening presence, not transformation.
- **Taking sides.** Aligning or agreeing with other parts in ways that are perceived against them, deepens internal mistrust.

Therapeutic Positioning

The task is not to redeem these parts, but to accompany them, often becoming the first person to meet them fully without fear, disgust, or punishment. By modeling respectful boundaries and a willingness to stay, the therapist begins to challenge their binary worldview of power vs. vulnerability. Over time, this can soften their role, allowing the system to imagine safety that does not depend on harm.

The following clinical vignettes illustrate how perpetrator-identified and defensive parts may emerge suddenly in session, often triggered by real or perceived threat. In each case, the therapist's ability to maintain steadiness and avoid escalation allowed the system to experience something profoundly new—that rupture does not have to mean rejection, and safety can be preserved even when trust is shaken.

Clinical Vignette

1) When the System Reacts to Threat

Cindy, a 50-year-old woman diagnosed with DID, had been working with a new therapist for three sessions. Though internal exploration was difficult due to extreme phobia and avoidance, the work was progressing at a pace that felt tolerable to the system. Cindy expressed little curiosity about her parts and often said she just wanted them "to leave her alone", but there was a sense of tentative safety beginning to form.

During session four, an unexpected event occurred. At the same clinic, another man—not a client, and without an appointment—arrived demanding to be seen immediately. When the receptionist explained that all therapy sessions required prior scheduling, he became increasingly aggressive: shouting, threatening, and banging on the desk.

The therapist briefly looked toward the hallway, unsure whether to intervene or seek help. When she turned back to the session, Cindy looked entirely different—her posture, voice, and presence had shifted dramatically. In a male voice, the client growled, "Who the fuck are you?" Staying grounded, the therapist responded, "I'm your therapist. This has been a really complicated week for you." The part snapped, "Cindy is mine." The therapist remained calm, saying nothing in that moment—just breathing, staying steady.

Suddenly, the male-presenting part disappeared. Cindy collapsed to the floor, curled into a fetal position, sobbing in a child's voice: "Please don't hit me. I'll be good." This part, too, seemed to have no recognition of the therapist. "I'm not going to hurt you", the therapist said gently. "You don't have to do anything. I'm here and I won't hurt you." Gradually, the client's nervous system calmed enough to leave the session safely. The Adult Self did not return that day.

In the following session, Cindy was visibly anxious. As soon as she sat down, she asked, "Did I hurt you?" The therapist replied, "No, you didn't hurt me at all. It seemed like something inside got really triggered." Cindy fell silent, shoulders tense. Sensing the fragility of the moment, the therapist continued: "And that's okay. The more I get to know you and everything inside, the better I'll be able to help." The client exhaled, visibly relieved.

They then explored what Cindy did remember. "A very angry man shouting and threatening", she recalled. "That's the last thing. That's why I was afraid... afraid that I might have hurt you."

From there, the therapist supported her in making sense of what had happened, introducing new grounding strategies she had not used before. Cindy expressed feeling much calmer, reassured not only by the therapist's continued presence, but by her curiosity and care. "You're not referring me out?", she asked at one point. "No", the therapist replied, "We want to understand better."

SYSTEM	WHERE IT SHOWS UP	FUNCTION	SURVIVAL LOGIC
Defense (fight / identification with aggressor) + Rank	A male-voiced part emerges when a man shouts outside; it takes a controlling, intimidating stance.	Reclaim power and prevent helplessness by becoming the threat internally and externally ("Who the fuck are you?"). Reaffirm ownership internally= Rank/hierarchy ("Cindy is mine!").	If I become the threat, I can't be threatened.
Defense (collapse / appeasement)	A child part curls on the floor and pleads not to be hurt.	Escape perceived danger via dissociation, appeasement, or shutdown.	If I submit and disappear, I'll survive.
Rank/submission (evaluation threat in next session)	The child part in the session: "Please don't hit me. I'll be good." The client in the next session: "Did I hurt you?" shame, fear of punishment/rejection; scanning for signs of having done wrong.	Avoid humiliation or expulsion by pre-emptive self-blame and downranking.	If I accept fault and stay small, I won't be punished or abandoned.
Attachment (deactivation under threat; implicit bid) coupled with submission.	Surprise when the therapist does not punish or withdraw; tiny, indirect hope rather than overt care-seeking.	Maintain a cautious bond while muting need to keep danger predictable.	If I don't show need and you still stay, maybe closeness can be safe.
Cooperation & Intersubjectivity (peer-based; with emerging Adult Self)	Therapist uses "we" language, permission, pacing, and steady orientation ("We want to understand better").	Create a joint working frame that regulates without a rescuer dynamic; recruit Adult Self participation.	If we work together with choice and brakes, we can stay safe without a power contest.

Table 21.1. Motivational and Action Systems at Play. Note:. The therapist's stance is collaborative, not rescuing: symmetry, clear consent, and predictable pacing do the soothing. As rank tension drops, room opens for a more cautious form of attachment.

Clinical Reflections

This vignette illustrates how quickly a system can mobilize perpetrator-identified protection under perceived external threat. The sudden emergence of a dominant, male-voiced part followed by collapse into a terrified child part reflects a rapid shift between defensive subsystems—fight through identification with the aggressor, followed by shutdown.

What prevented escalation was not intervention, but restraint. The therapist did not confront the threatening part, attempt reassurance, or rush to rescue the child. By remaining grounded, non-reactive, and present through abrupt shifts, she avoided reinforcing the system's expectation that danger leads to punishment or abandonment.

The new experience here was minimal but foundational: the system bent under stress and returned without being rejected. Even without Adult Self access, the continuity of the therapeutic presence allowed safety to be preserved, creating the conditions for later reflection and cooperation.

- CLINICAL VIGNETTE

2) When a Subtle Change Feels Like Betrayal

Mara, a 42-year-old woman with DID, had been in therapy with the same clinician for over a year. Sessions were often slow and careful, with the Adult Self able to stay present most of the time, supported by parts who trusted the therapist's predictability. On this particular day, the therapist had arrived a few minutes late due to a prior session running over. She apologized briefly and took her seat. Mara nodded but sat unusually still. As the therapist began the session, she noticed Mara's tone turn sharp. "You're just like them", Mara said flatly. "You don't care, you think I'm not important enough to show up on time."

The voice was deeper, more clipped, a hostile part had stepped forward. The therapist acknowledged the shift: "It sounds like something about today felt really disrespectful." The part crossed its arms. "Respect? Don't make me laugh. You're here for the money. Just like they were." The therapist stayed grounded, simply saying, "It sounds like you've been there before, when someone you relied on didn't show up as promised."

Without warning, the hostile part disappeared. Mara sat motionless, eyes on the floor. Minutes passed before a small voice emerged, barely audible: "If I don't move, maybe she won't get mad." The child part did not seem to recognize the therapist and would not meet her gaze. The therapist spoke softly: "I'm here. I'm not angry. You don't have to do anything right now." The rest of the session unfolded slowly. The Adult Self did not return, but the child part eventually accepted a blanket and sat more comfortably. There was no push to process, just quiet containment until the session ended.

In the following session, Mara began with a tentative question: "Were you mad I didn't talk last time?" The therapist replied, "No. I think something inside was scared, and that was okay. We could just be in the same room until it felt a little safer." Mara exhaled, and for the first time named that being kept waiting as a child often meant punishment or ridicule.

SYSTEM	WHERE IT SHOWS UP	FUNCTION	SURVIVAL LOGIC
Rank/Power (evaluation/dominance)	Accusations of disrespect ("you're just like them," "you're here for the money"), arms crossed, testing hierarchy.	Regain control and avoid downranking by defining the therapist as untrustworthy or inferior.	"If I put you in the wrong and stay on top, I can't be humiliated."
Defense System (Fight / Identification with Aggressor)	Hostile, attacking stance toward the therapist when predictability broke.	Preempt betrayal by striking first and hardening the system.	"If I strike first, you can't hurt me."
Defense System(Freeze / Collapse)	Child part goes still, avoids eye contact, minimizes presence	Avoid triggering further harm by becoming invisible.	"If I disappear, I'll survive."
Attachment System (Deactivation under threat)	Longing is present but muted; lateness cues abandonment/danger, so closeness is pulled back	Suppress direct care-seeking to prevent re-injury	"If I don't reach, I can't be dropped or punished"
Cooperation & Intersubjectivity (Therapist Modeling)	Non-coercive implicit "we" language, permission, predictable pacing; staying present through the bend and repair.	Restore working alliance without rank contests or rescue dynamics; recruit Adult Self capacities over time	If we work together with brakes and choice, safety can return without submission.

Table 21.2. Motivational and Action Systems at Play

Note: This moment is best framed as a cooperation bend-and-repair, not as asymmetric caregiving. The therapist's symmetry, consent, and predictability deactivated rank tension and made cautious attachment possible later (without entering a rescuer) victim loop.

Clinical Reflections

This vignette demonstrates how subtle disruptions in predictability can activate perpetrator-identified and collapse-based responses. The hostile accusation served to restore rank and preempt humiliation, while the subsequent freezing child part attempted to survive by disappearance.

The therapist neither defended herself nor over-apologized, avoiding both a power contest and a rescuing stance. By naming the experience of disrespect without assigning blame and allowing silence without pressure, she held the frame steady through rupture.

The system gained a new template: that relational misattunement does not inevitably lead to punishment or loss. Repair occurred not through explanation, but through continued presence and predictable boundaries, making future reflection possible without domination or submission.

Clinical Vignette

3) Holding the Lead Under Pressure

Marina, a 42-year-old client with a complex trauma history, had been working in therapy for nearly a year. She had learned to recognize the influence of a perpetrator-identified part that tended to appear in situations of perceived authority, often undermining trust in the therapist.

In this session, Marina began describing a recent disagreement with her partner. Her voice grew sharper, her posture more rigid. "You sound just like him", she said suddenly to the therapist, eyes narrowing. "Always pretending you care."

The therapist stayed grounded. "It sounds like a familiar voice is here now, one that does not believe my care is real."

Marina shifted in her seat, visibly conflicted. "Yeah... he's right here", she said after a pause. "He's telling me you're playing me, same as before. But... I know you're not." The therapist reflected, "So part of you can feel his suspicion, and another part, your Adult Self, can also see this relationship as different." Marina exhaled, tension in her shoulders easing slightly. "Yeah. I can feel him pushing, but I'm not letting him drive."

Together, they explored what the part was trying to protect against, how suspicion had once been the safest response to closeness, and how, in this moment, Marina could hold both perspectives without losing connection to the therapist.

By the end of the session, the part's energy had receded, not because it was silenced, but because the Adult Self stayed present long enough for the therapist to join her in understanding its role. Marina left saying, "I didn't have to switch... that feels new."

SYSTEM	WHERE IT SHOWS UP	FUNCTION	SURVIVAL LOGIC
Rank/Power System (Dominance–Submission)	The suspicious part that accuses the therapist of pretending to care.	To assert dominance or control over the interaction, preventing perceived manipulation.	"If I challenge you first, you can't trick me."
Defense System (Fight, Managed by Adult Self)	Urge to attack is present but the Adult Self stays in the lead	Keep protective energy available without letting it control behavior	"If I keep some fight energy online, I can stay safe without losing control."
Attachment System(deactivation under threat, Adult Self access)	Adult Self acknowledges suspicion (because the part fears attachment activation), and also recognizes the therapist's reliability.	Hold dual awareness so measured contact can occur without triggering old approach and avoid cycles through Cooperation, not attachment,.	(Updated): "I can feel the warning and still stay connected."
Cooperation and Intersubjectivity (therapist stance)	Therapist validates both perspectives, uses permission language and predictable pacing, joins the mapping rather than rescuing	Shift from a rank contest to joint work that recruits the Adult Self and keeps choice and brakes visible	"If we choose pace and distance together, safety does not require submission and trust can grow"

Table 21.3. Motivational and Action Systems at Play

Clinical Reflections

This vignette illustrates a later phase of work, where perpetrator-identified suspicion is present but does not take control of the interaction. The Adult Self remains in the lead, able to acknowledge the part's mistrust while holding an alternative, reality-based perspective.

The therapist does not challenge the suspicious voice or attempt to reassure it away. By validating its protective warning without entering a rank struggle or attachment pull, she supports cooperation rather than confrontation.

The new experience here is not trust, but tolerance. The system learns that protection does not require takeover, and that multiple perspectives can coexist without loss of safety. This marks a shift from survival through dominance to safety through co-holding.

CLINICAL VIGNETTE

4) Recognizing the Shadow in Hindsight

Jamal, a 38-year-old client with a history of childhood emotional abuse, arrived in session looking withdrawn. He recounted a team meeting at work earlier in the week where his supervisor had given him constructive feedback.

"At first, I thought, 'Okay, I can work on that,'" Jamal said. "But by the time I got home, I was furious. I sent a snarky email to the whole team and then didn't sleep all night."

The therapist asked what had happened between the meeting and the anger. Jamal paused. "It's weird. It's like I heard my dad's voice in my head, telling me they were trying to humiliate me."

As they talked, Jamal realized that the anger, and the retaliatory email, were echoes of a perpetrator-identified part. This part had learned long ago that the safest way to handle perceived disrespect was to strike first, shaming the other before they could shame him.

"What's different now", the therapist pointed out, "is that you can look back and see it wasn't all you, it was a part's way of protecting you from feeling small."

Jamal nodded. "I wish I'd noticed in the moment. But... it's kind of a relief to know there's a reason I reacted like that."

The session ended with them mapping early cues for when this part might be taking the lead, so Jamal could experiment with pausing before responding in future situations.

SYSTEM	WHERE IT SHOWS UP	FUNCTION	SURVIVAL LOGIC
Rank and Power (status restoration)	The retaliatory all-staff email after feedback feels like a public downranking	Restore status and prevent shame by striking first	If I humiliate you before you humiliate me, I cannot be cut down
Rank and Power (identification with aggressor)	Father's voice reframes neutral feedback as an attack or humiliation	Borrow the aggressor's stance to avoid feeling small or evaluated	If I become the evaluator, I cannot be evaluated
Attachment (inhibited activation)	No care-seeking during the trigger; connection is avoided	Prevent exposure to rejection or ridicule	If I do not reach, I cannot be dismissed
Cooperation and Intersubjectivity (therapist stance)	Therapist separates part action from Adult intent, uses collaborative mapping and permissioned pacing	Shift from a status contest to joint problem-solving that recruits the Adult Self	If we examine this together with choice and pace, reflection is safe and shame drops
Exploration and Learning (after the fact)	Mapping early cues and planning a pause before replies	Build procedural alternatives to the old script	If I can notice the first markers, I can choose something different next time

Table 21.4. Motivational and Action Systems at Play

Note: the core affect Jamal names is humiliation, which sits squarely in the rank domain; fear would point more to defense. The therapist is modeling cooperation rather than caregiving, which lowers status threat and makes reflection possible without activating a rescuer dynamic.

Clinical Reflections

This vignette highlights how perpetrator-identified influence may only become visible in hindsight, particularly when it operates through familiar patterns of retaliation or status restoration. The aggressive response was less about anger than about preventing humiliation through borrowed dominance.

The therapist avoids pathologizing the reaction or confronting the behavior directly. By separating the part's action from the client's intent and framing it as a survival strategy, she reduces shame and preserves reflective capacity.

The system gains a new experience of understanding without self-condemnation. Recognition alone does not eliminate the pattern, but it creates space for choice. Over time, this kind of reflective cooperation weakens the part's need to act automatically.

Shared Reflections on the Four Vignettes

While each vignette highlights a different phase of work, taken together they reveal recurring patterns in how perpetrator-identified parts mobilize, how systems shift under threat, and how therapeutic stance determines whether these moments escalate or become organizing experiences.

Cases 1 and 2 show how rapid switches between parts can occur when the system perceives danger—whether from a direct external cue or a subtler, relational one. In both, the sequence moves from a protective part (fight/dominance) to a vulnerable part (collapse/appeasement), reflecting shifts between defensive subsystems. What made these moments therapeutic rather than destabilizing was not the resolution of content, but the preservation of safety in the relationship. A cooperative, mentalizing stance enables connection and safety by downregulating rank (noncompetitive, nonjudgmental) and deactivating defense (no danger signals; the therapist remains unafraid).

In cases 2–4, the parts' behavior could be mistaken for ordinary defensive anger. What makes them *perpetrator-identified* is not the presence of aggression, but the *borrowed stance, tone, or worldview* of the abuser-dominance used as order, contempt used as control, suspicion equated with intelligence. These parts do not just *defend*; they *become* the evaluator, the punisher, or the one "on top".

Their hostility serves a protective aim ("If I attack first, I stay safe"), yet the method and emotional color come from the internalized perpetrator template. The system reproduces the old relational asymmetry (power over vulnerability) inside itself as a way to prevent the chaos of being powerless.

Thus:

- **Mara's part** re-enacts the *accuser's* role ("You're just like them") to regain rank and avoid the humiliation once tied to being dismissed.
- **Marina's suspicious part** adopts the *deceiver's* stance ("You're pretending you care") to prevent dependence on potentially harmful care.

- **Jamal's reactive part** channels the *humiliator's* posture (mocking, public retaliation) to restore status and avoid exposure.

In all three, the goal is *protection*, but the **means** (the voice, logic, and affect) are perpetrator-derived. This is what differentiates perpetrator-identified parts from merely hostile or defensive ones.

Cases 3 and 4 illustrate different forms of contact with perpetrator-identified parts—one where the Adult Self remained in the lead despite pressure from a suspicious part, and one where the influence of a perpetrator-identified part was recognized only in hindsight. In both, the absence of switching allowed for curiosity and perspective-taking that began to reshape the part's influence over time.

Across all four examples, the underlying motivational systems are the same:

- Rank/power driving dominance to preempt harm.
- Defense shifting between fight, flight, freeze, and collapse.
- Attachment seeking connection while anticipating betrayal.
- Peer cooperation is modeled through the therapist's steady, non-controlling presence.

In every case, the therapist's stance (grounded, non-reactive, and non-coercive) allowed the system to have a new relational experience: that mistrust, anger, collapse, or suspicion do not automatically lead to abandonment or retaliation. This is how survival logic begins to update—not through persuasion or confrontation, but through repeated experiences where safety, boundaries, and connection coexist. Over time, these moments plant the seeds for perpetrator-identified parts to loosen their grip; not because they are told to, but because they witness another way to protect the system: through connection, cooperation, and shared regulation.

CLOSING THOUGHTS

Perpetrator-identified parts are not random aggressors; they are trauma-shaped protector parts built from dominance, deactivated attachment, and fight energy that once kept life predictable under threat. When we understand their behavior through motivational systems, their intentions become clearer: to prevent helplessness, mute need, and control exposure to danger.

Our therapeutic stance, therefore, is not to oppose, confront, or redeem these parts, but to meet them with calm firmness, consistent boundaries and collaborative structure. The first step is to reduce rank tension avoiding power struggles or attempts at rescue. From there, the process shifts toward inviting cooperation that involves the Adult Self. Only after this groundwork is laid can safe connections gradually emerge. Transformation does not happen through persuasion or reasoning alone, but through repeated experiences where limits, consent, and connection coexist safely. This is how the old survival logic begins to update itself.

These parts exist because of harm. With time, relational symmetry, and reliable repair, their grip can soften, but not because we convince them to change, but because they witness another viable way to protect the system: through cooperation, shared regulation, and choice. In this process, they begin to model collaboration rather than submission or dominance. They learn to engage others as partners in solving problems, rather than through attachment strategies rooted in fear, compliance, or control. When they experience that collaboration is both possible and their right, they begin to internalize a new form of safety. Seeking help from a *rescuer* may remain difficult, as it can easily trigger dangerous dynamics—but cooperation can feel achievable and dignified. This principle applies not only to dissociative systems but to anyone carrying disorganized attachment patterns, where safety and closeness have long been entangled with threat.

Clinical Anchors

What to remember...

- Stay curious about contradictions; do not force quick coherence.
- Contain without condemning. Set firm limits without shame.
- De-escalate rank before anything else. Opt out of contests.
- Work in a cooperative frame, not a rescuing one. Use *we-language*, visible brakes, consent at each step, and keep proximity optional.
- Name coercive origins carefully. Many roles were adopted under pressure, confusion, or threat.
- Acknowledge proximity to power. Aligning with the abuser once stabilized chaos; validate the logic without endorsing harm.
- Expect slow repair. Change follows repeated experiences where limits, consent, and connection coexist.
- Plan aftercare. Anticipate backlash.
- Measure progress by process. Faster recovery after spikes, protector becomes consultable, Adult Self can co-hold perspectives.
- Remember that internal harm echoes external harm. Today's danger signals are yesterday's survival strategies.

What to Avoid...

- Naming vulnerability too early or pushing disclosures.
- Leading with attachment pulls; start with cooperation.
- Equating the part with the perpetrator or moralizing its stance.
- Challenging the worldview or *loyalty* too quickly; it reads as dismantling a protective code.
- Taking sides against the protector; it deepens internal mistrust and invites a power contest.
- Offering asymmetric caregiving ("I'll save you") instead of symmetric joint work.

Chapter 22: Sexualized Parts

THERAPIST REFLECTION

She spoke in a tone that was oddly flirtatious, offering compliments that didn't match the moment. I felt the air shift, subtle but undeniable. Instead of interpreting it as manipulation, I asked myself, "What did this part have to become to survive?" The answer wasn't seduction. It was submission, shaped by danger. That changed everything.

Among the most misunderstood and misinterpreted parts are those that present with sexualized behaviors. These parts are frequently misread as manipulative, seductive, or attention-seeking. In truth, they are shaped by betrayal, survival, and a fractured sense of safety. This chapter invites therapists to look beyond the surface, to recognize reenactment over intention, and to meet these parts with the steady, compassionate boundaries they have rarely known. It aims to offer a roadmap to help these parts experience other ways of interacting and relating.

ORIGIN OF SEXUALIZED PARTS

Sexualized parts emerge in the context of chronic sexual trauma, grooming, or betrayal by attachment figures. They form as adaptive responses to the impossible: preserving attachment, surviving violation, and keeping other parts unaware of what is happening.

These parts develop when:

- Submission is the only available survival strategy.
- Sexualization is mistaken for care, connection, or safety.
- Perpetrators reward compliance or idealization.

- The child learns to anticipate and provide exactly what is needed (sexually) to avoid further harm.

Some of these parts genuinely do not know the abuse was wrong. Others know but learned that "becoming what they needed me to be" was the only way to be safe and eventually, keep the system safe. These beliefs are not simple distortions, they are survival logic, persisting like all parts stuck in trauma-time, until they are updated by new, corrective relational experiences.

These strategies were learned in specific ecologies of abuse: grooming disguised as specialness, coercive assault, or authority-based betrayal. In chapter 28 we map how those contexts set the "price of closeness" and shape the proximity loop in session

MAIN FEATURES OF SEXUALIZED PARTS

Sexualized parts may:

- Present with flirtatious, seductive, or disinhibited behavior.
- Idealize perpetrators or deny the abuse.
- Believe they were complicit or wanted it.
- Have difficulties with therapeutic boundaries or blur relational lines.
- Speak in childlike or overly mature tones (if they are younger).

They may also:

- Feel shame or disgust after co-consciousness with other parts.
- Switch suddenly into different roles (caretaker, seductress, object).
- Be loyal to abusers, holding onto distortions imposed that they were *special* or *chosen*.
- Describe past abuse in romanticized terms, reflecting the distortions imposed during grooming. For example, a part might say, "I was in love with my father and he was in love with me", expressing loyalty and attachment shaped entirely within the abuse dynamic.

These presentations can easily be misread as boundary violations or acting out, but they are not expressions of desire; they are reenactment of survival, the imprints of trauma rather than conscious choice.

FUNCTIONS OF SEXUALIZED PARTS

Sexualized parts (appeasement based) develop to carry out highly specific survival tasks, often shaped by distorted motivational systems that remain active in trauma time. Their primary functions include:

1. **Maintain proximity to dangerous caregivers through sexualized appeasement.** Uses flirtation, seduction, or compliance to reduce unpredictability and secure momentary care, resources, or safety.
   Systems: Attachment + sexual system: a seductive stance to maintain proximity, rank/agonistic (submission/appeasement; down-ranking to prevent attack), sexual bonding (co-opted as a proximity tool/distorted safety).
   Survival logic: "If I give what they want, they will not leave or escalate."

2. **Shield the system from the full horror**. Overlays terror with arousal, fantasy, or numbing so the unthinkable becomes survivable (more a substitution of affect than simple distancing.
   Systems: Sexual bonding (arousal overlay). Generic defensive operations may occur (analgesia, derealization or blanking out) but this is not the defense action system per se. Attachment (longing for soothing piggybacks on a sexualized script when direct comfort feels unavailable).
   Survival logic: "If I can replace terror with arousal or emptiness, I don´t have to feel the horror."

3. **Prevent worse harm by *being good***. Strategic compliance aims to control the terms of contact and reduce the severity of violence.
   Systems: Rank or power (submission, compliance to manage power asymmetry), sexual bonding (instrumentalized for bargaining), attachment (conditional proximity tolerated as the safest available option).
   Survival logic: "If I cooperate, I can limit damage and avoid something worse."

Sexualized parts often embody unbearable contradictions—love and terror, pleasure and coercion, attachment and abuse—fused together as a single survival strategy in trauma time. Because they are doing exactly what they were created to do (e.g., **to permit relatedness when the usual attachment pathway cannot be used**, to avoid greater harm, to regulate fear), the therapeutic stance must respect their survival logic. These are not *provocative* or *manipulative* behaviors but learned adaptations to unsafe relationships. Interventions that ignore their motivational systems risk shaming or rejecting them and may replicate the very dynamics they were designed to survive.

Recognizing the functions and survival logic of sexualized parts clarifies why their behaviors persist long after the original danger has passed. Before any change can occur, these strategies must first be acknowledged as adaptive responses to coercion and betrayal. A therapeutic stance that respects this logic—while offering new relational experiences—creates the conditions for these parts to explore other ways of staying safe without sacrificing authenticity or self-worth.

RELATING TO SEXUALIZED PARTS

Sexualized parts can evoke strong and complex emotional responses in the therapist, ranging from protectiveness, discomfort or confusion, to distancing, irritation, or even shame and disgust. These reactions are invitations to slow down and reflect.

When a part flirts, idealizes, or blurs relational lines, therapists may feel unsure about how to respond. Some may over-correct with abrupt boundary-setting; others may downplay the interaction in an effort to remain neutral. But both responses risk missing the deeper truth. These parts are not trying to seduce, they are reenacting learned survival strategies, learned in relationships where safety and exploitation were intertwined.

The central question is not "Why is this client doing this to me?" but rather "What is this part trying to communicate or protect?" By focusing on the part's *function*, rather than reacting to the *form*, the therapist can remain grounded, effective and attuned.

- **Boundaries as safety, not rejection.** These parts are extremely sensitive to relational dynamics. The therapist must:
  - ★ Stay grounded, warm, but not reactive.
  - ★ Avoid shame, over-correction, or sexualizing the behavior.
  - ★ Reinforce that boundaries are for safety, not rejection.

- **Avoid forcing insight or confrontation.** These parts may not yet know what happened was abuse. This is more than denial, it´s survival. Early interventions to challenge this respectfully are:
    - ★ "This part may still believe it had to be this way."
    - ★ "Let's go slowly. No one here is going to punish or shame you."

- **Support internal recognition without collapse.** Invite the system to acknowledge this part without invalidating its experience.
    - ★ "What might it be like for the others to hear what this part remembers or believes?"
    - ★ "Can this part know it does not have to protect the system this way anymore?"

What these parts need most is a therapist who can stay present without collapsing into discomfort, shame, disgust, control or fear. Boundaries must be clear, not to reject or punish, but to maintain safety for the entire system and the therapist and therapy itself.

In doing so, the therapist offers something many of these parts have never known: a relationship where connection does not require performance, submission, or abuse. This becomes a living experience of repair, where safety and care are not learned through pleasing, but offered through presence and respect. A place where the client can experience how healthy interactions really take place.

CLINICAL VIGNETTE

1) I Thought That's What You Wanted

During a session, the client suddenly shifted, her posture changed, her voice turned light and playful, eyes wide. Leaning forward, twirling a strand of hair, she said, "I bet you like this, don't you?"

For a moment, the therapist felt thrown, unsure whether to set a boundary, redirect, or move away from the moment. But instead of reacting, he paused, grounded himself, and softened his tone. "You don't have to be anything other than who you are right now", he said gently. The client blinked, confused. Her eyes filled with tears. "I thought that's what you wanted", she whispered. "I think that's what someone else wanted a long time ago", the therapist replied. "And it makes so much sense that this part learned to offer that. It was how safety was created."

The client looked away but didn't disappear. The part didn't need to be corrected or pushed away. It needed to be seen with clarity, met with respect, and held with compassion.

SYSTEM	WHERE IT SHOWS UP	FUNCTION	SURVIVAL LOGIC
Attachment System + Sexual System (sexualized control strategy)	The flirtatious presentation aimed at connection.	Preserve bond, closeness by offering what historically ensured safety.	"If I give you what you want, you'll stay, and I'll be safe."
Rank System (Appeasement)	Submission to perceived authority.	Prevent escalation of threat by compliance.	"If I'm good, it won't hurt so bad."
Cooperation System (Therapist Modeling Updated)	The therapist's grounded, non-reactive stance.	Model that a bond can exist without performance or sexualization.	(Updated): "Maybe I can be safe without giving myself away."

Table 22.1. Motivational and action systems at play

Clinical Reflections

The therapist's ability to stay grounded in the face of a sexualized presentation and respond to the underlying attachment need rather than the form it took. By naming the part's history ("someone else wanted that a long time ago") without shaming or colluding, the therapist validated its survival logic and modeled a new way to connect without performance.

Clinical Vignette

2) If I'm Good, It Won't Hurt

In a session with a client who had survived early sexual trauma, a shift occurred: the client leaned forward, smiling softly, and said, "You always look nice in that color." It did not match the moment. Rather than interpret it as boundary testing, the therapist gently asked, "Is there a part that learned it had to be nice to stay safe?" The client froze, then whispered, "Yes. If I was good, it wouldn't hurt so bad."

The moment revealed a hidden adaptation, not manipulation. And from there, the real work began. The therapist did not correct or explain. He stayed present, allowing the truth to be spoken.

SYSTEM	WHERE IT SHOWS UP	FUNCTION	SURVIVAL LOGIC
Attachment System + Sexual System (Distorted Activation)	The compliment offered to maintain connection.	Preserve closeness.	"If I keep you pleased, you won't abandon me."
Rank System (Appeasement)	Compliance through flattery.	Manage danger by reducing the chance of aggression.	"If I give you what you want, I control how bad it gets."

Table 22.2 Motivational and action systems at play

Clinical Reflections

The therapist's gentle curiosity ("Is there a part that learned...?") transformed a moment that could have been misread as boundary testing into an opportunity for the client to name a core survival strategy. Avoiding correction or interpretation allowed the truth to emerge at the part's pace, reinforcing safety and respect.

CLINICAL VIGNETTE

3) What Do You Mean by That?

During a supervision session, a therapist described her work with a teenage client who had survived chronic sexual abuse. Frustrated, she said, "No wonder she keeps getting into trouble with men, she's always asking for it." The supervisor felt a jolt of discomfort. Her instinct was to react, to name the inaccuracy and danger of that statement. But instead, she paused: "What do you mean by that?" she asked, gently but firmly. "Can you tell me more?"

The therapist hesitated, then explained: "In the last session, she came in wearing a leopard-print bra and a loose shirt that kept falling off her shoulders. She kept leaning forward, almost like she wanted me to notice." The supervisor nodded slowly. "And when that happened, what did you feel? What did it bring up for you?"

The room shifted. What had sounded like blame became recognizable as discomfort and confusion. The therapist was not trying to shame the client, she was overwhelmed by the presentation, unsure how to hold it, and afraid she might be reinforcing something harmful by not addressing it more directly. Together, they explored how the client's behavior was not about provocation, it was a reenactment. An adaptation. A learned strategy from a world where visibility equaled safety, and performance was the only form of protection available.

The supervisory space became what the client's therapy space needed to be: a place where complexity was held without judgment, and where meaning could emerge from misunderstanding.

SYSTEM	WHERE IT SHOWS UP	FUNCTION	SURVIVAL LOGIC
Attachment System + Sexual System (Distorted Activation)	The client's sexualized presentation in session.	Maintain perceived safety through familiar relational patterns.	"If I make myself appealing, I won't be discarded or hurt."
Exploration + Cooperation System (Supervisor Modeling)	The supervisor holds curiosity instead of judgment.	Model reflective inquiry to address discomfort.	(Updated): "I can approach this without shaming or rejecting the client, or myself."

Table 22.3. Motivational and action systems at play

Clinical Reflections

In supervision, the supervisor resisted the urge to correct, instead creating space for the therapist's discomfort to be explored. This mirrored the stance we aim to hold with clients: curiosity over judgment, which allowed the sexualized presentation to be reframed as reenactment rather than provocation.

Shared Reflections on the Three Vignettes

Across these examples, sexualized parts emerged not from desire or manipulation, but from survival strategies learned in coercive and dangerous environments. In each case, what made the encounter therapeutic was not the elimination of the sexualized behavior, but the preservation of safety and relationship in the moment.

In *I Thought That's What You Wanted*, the therapist stayed grounded and named the history beneath the part's presentation, validating its protective role without colluding or shaming. In *If I'm Good, It Won't Hurt*, curiosity uncovered the appeasement logic driving the flattery, allowing the client to voice truth at her own pace. In *What Do You Mean by That?* the supervisor's reflective stance modeled how to explore discomfort without judgment, reframing sexualized behavior as reenactment rather than provocation.

Across settings, the turning point was consistent: the other person stayed present, avoided shaming, and recognized the part's function and survival logic before attempting change. These moments offer corrective relational experiences in which connection does not depend on performance, submission, or self-abandonment. Over time, repeated experiences like these loosen the grip of trauma-time strategies and open the door to authentic, mutual engagement.

CLOSING THOUGHTS

Sexualized parts are not provocations, they are adaptations, born of coercion, silence, and terror. Their behaviors are about safety, survival and learned submission, not desire or seduction. When we meet them with clear boundaries and deep respect, they begin to feel something they have rarely known: safety without performance, and connection without self-abandonment. These shifts do not happen quickly; trust is built through repeated experiences in which the part is met with steadiness, clarity, and care.

Over time, sexualized parts can begin to recognize themselves not as objects or performers, but as survivors, deserving of genuine care, free from the demands of reenactment, and capable of connection that honors their whole self.

Clinical Anchors

What to remember...

- These parts are not about sex or desire, they are about survival.
- Boundaries offer safety, not punishment.
- Flirtation, idealization, or role-switching are adaptive strategies.
- Shame often follows co-consciousness. Hold that with care.
- Respect the pace and worldview of the part. Do not rush insight.
- These parts often protected the system from unbearable knowledge.

What to avoid...

- Labeling behaviors as seductive or manipulative.
- Personalizing boundary blurring without understanding dynamics.
- Challenging loyalty to perpetrators before trust is built.
- Assuming awareness of abuse when the part may still see it as care.

Chapter 23: Shame-Bound Parts

THERAPIST REFLECTION

I noticed myself leaning forward when the client spoke with a quiet, withdrawn voice, her eyes avoiding mine. A familiar pull to offer reassurance emerged—to tell her there was nothing to be ashamed of. But instead, I paused. I listened to the silence between her words, the self-loathing just beneath the surface. "It makes sense that this part wants to disappear", I said gently. "It sounds like it still believes the shame belongs to you."

Shame-bound parts are among the most hidden and self-protective in a dissociative system. Their defining feature is not just what they feel, but who they believe they are—wrong, defective, contaminated, undeserving. They do not simply carry shame; they are organized by it.

In therapy, they may never speak directly. Instead, they emerge through subtle cues: averted eyes, a collapsed posture, difficulty receiving kindness, or the sudden disappearance of voice. To the untrained eye, these behaviors can look like disengagement. In truth, they are survival.

Working with shame-bound parts requires slowing down, meeting them without urgency, and offering a steady presence that neither contradicts nor demands disclosure. The goal is not to *pull them out*, but to show them they can exist in relationship without needing to vanish.

ORIGIN OF SHAME-BOUND PARTS

Shame-bound parts develop in relational environments where humiliation, blame, or emotional abandonment were routine. They often emerge early, in response to overwhelming shame, neglect, or abuse (especially when the child is made to believe that what happened was their fault).

When no one accurately mirrored reality or offered protection, shame became internalized and solidified into identity. These parts absorbed messages like:

- "You're disgusting."
- "No one would love you if they knew."
- "This is who you are."

Unable to place the blame externally, the child turned it inward. By believing "It's my fault", children can preserve connection to caregivers, at the cost of self-worth. Over time, this self-blame became the organizing center of the shame-bound part's identity.

MAIN FEATURES OF SHAME-BOUND PARTS

Shame-bound parts often remain hidden not only from others, but from the client themselves. They are defined less by feelings and more by an entrenched self-perception of defectiveness.

They may present as:

- Collapsed, withdrawn, and hidden.
- Silent or apologetic in tone.
- Intensely self-critical and distrustful of care.
- Flooded with internalized disgust or moral contamination.
- Afraid of exposure and relational closeness.

They often:

- Avoid eye contact and minimize their presence.
- Refer to themselves as *bad, worthless, disgusting,* or *broken*.
- Deflect compliments or reject empathy.
- Trigger protector parts who fear the danger of revealing shame.

Their presence in therapy may be marked by sudden withdrawal, freezing, or a somatic sense of shrinking. As one client described:

- "She says I ruin everything. That I'm the reason no one stayed. That I should just go quiet again, at least that way I don't hurt anyone."

FUNCTIONS OF SHAME-BOUND PARTS

Shame-bound parts do not seek visibility. Their existence is organized around hiding, taking the blame, and absorbing unbearable feelings so other parts can function. While the burden is immense, their purpose is protective.

In many systems, these parts act as internal scapegoats, holding the toxic beliefs and emotional pain that would otherwise overwhelm the whole.

Primary functions include:

1. **Contain toxic shame**. Localizes and absorbs perceived badness so the rest of the system can keep going.
   Systems: Kin altruism[1] (compartmentalization, containment), rank (self-downranking and submission).
   Survival logic: "If I carry all the bad, the others can function and avoid attack."

2. **Hide from relational risk:** minimizes presence, voice, and need to avoid scrutiny or rejection.
   Systems: Attachment (deactivation), defense (freeze), rank/submission (crestfallen, downcast)
   Survival logic: "If no one notices me, no one can hurt (defense), judge (rank), or discard us (attachment).

3. **Prevent emotional exposure via degrading beliefs**: enforces narratives like "you do not deserve care" to stop reaching.
   Systems: Rank/submission (summit to internal enforcer who is rule keeping), attachment (inhibited activation).
   Survival logic: "If I convince us we are undeserving, we will not reach and be humiliated."

4. **Preserve bonding through self blame (controlling strategy in submission)**. Protects bonds by declaring the self at fault and the caregiver intact.

---

[1] Kin altruism refers to a survival principle described in evolutionary biology in which individuals sacrifice their own well-being to protect the survival of the group or genetically related others (Hamilton, 1964). In dissociative personality systems, this logic appears intrapsychically: certain parts take on disproportionate shame, guilt, or burden in order to protect the functioning, safety, or relational viability of the system as a whole. The term is used here to describe an internal survival organization, a system-preserving strategy

Systems: Avoiding attachment activation, rank or power (submission).
Survival logic: "If it's my fault, they stay good, and we stay connected."

5. **Seal *unspeakable* material**. Holds memories, sensations, or meanings that feel contaminating or dangerous.
Systems: Kin altruism (sealing, amnesia barriers).
Survival logic: "If I keep it sealed, we will not be overwhelmed, criticized, or punished."

6. **Bear impossible responsibility**. Takes on guilt, shame, or moral debt no one else can carry.
Systems: Kin altruism (burden bearing, internal accounting).
Survival logic: "If I carry the burden, others will be free of it."

Because shame-bound parts are doing exactly what they were created to do (keeping exposure low, preserving connection, and preventing overwhelm), other parts can continue to function in daily life. Interventions must honor this survival logic, rather than argue with it: move slowly, prioritize consent over content, and update the method by modeling patiently. Once again, connection is maintained but not through the attachment system; it is the rank-submission system that is recruited to preserve safety.

RELATING TO SHAME-BOUND PARTS

Shame-bound parts can evoke powerful reactions: helplessness, protectiveness, urgency, or even quiet frustration. Because their suffering is often invisible and self-directed, therapists may feel a strong urge to *pull them out*, offer reassurance, or convince them of their worth.

However, reassurance can be interpreted as dismissal; warmth can feel like something that must be earned. The therapist's discomfort with silence, self-loathing, or moral injury can unintentionally reinforce the part's core belief: "You are too much to be met fully."

Common countertransference signals:

- Urgency to rescue.
- Feeling ineffective or impatient in the face of silence.
- Subtle disengagement to escape the emotional weight.
- Over-identification leading to over-involvement.

The key is to slow down, notice, and stay curious:

- ★ "What am I feeling in this moment, and what might this part be protecting itself from?"

Supervision and reflective practice become essential, not just for technique, but to help the therapist remain emotionally regulated and attuned. Often, the most healing intervention is not what we say, but how we stay, with steadiness, softness, and the belief that no part is too damaged to be met with respect.

Attunement Over Reassurance

Shame-bound parts are often impervious to reassurance. Attempts to contradict their beliefs such as "You're not bad", "It wasn't your fault", can fall flat or even increase withdrawal. These parts are not looking for quick validation. This is far too big of a leap at the beginning. They are watching for safety.

Empathic attunement that honors their worldview without endorsing it, creates the space where something new can begin to form.

- ★ "It makes sense that this part feels unworthy, it's hard to carry that story alone for a long time."

Trying to reassure shame-bound parts may unintentionally reinforce their belief that no one really understands. Instead, we offer insights based on attunement:

- ★ "It makes sense that this part feels it has to hide."
- ★ "I don't need you to prove anything or explain this away."

Normalize Survival Strategies

These parts often formed in environments where blame was the only way to preserve bonding with attachment figures. If the caregiver could not be wrong, the child had to be.

In this light, self-blame becomes a deeply relational survival strategy, a rigid *controlling strategy* maintained by a part. Rather than dismantling it prematurely, we explain and respect the reason it formed.

CLINICAL VIGNETTE

1) I Shouldn't Even Be Here

During a session, the client sat motionless, her shoulders hunched and eyes fixed on the floor. After several minutes of silence, she said in a flat voice, "I shouldn't even be here. You probably think I'm disgusting too."

The therapist did not rush to contradict her or offer reassurance. Instead, she leaned in gently and said, "It sounds like there's a part of you that believes it does not deserve care. That maybe, it never did." The client gave a small nod but did not look up.

"I wonder if that part had to believe something terrible about itself", the therapist continued softly, "because the truth of what happened was too big to hold." Tears welled in the client's eyes. She whispered, "I thought it was my fault. That I ruined everything."

The therapist responded, "Of course you did. That belief might have been the only way to make sense of the pain. But you don't have to carry it alone anymore."

In that moment, something shifted, not the belief itself, but the loneliness around it. The shame-bound part had finally been seen, not with pity or correction, but with presence. And that made all the difference.

It was not the belief that changed, it was the isolation.

SYSTEM	WHERE IT SHOWS UP	FUNCTION	SURVIVAL LOGIC
Rank System (retirement from competition)	Declaring "I shouldn't be here."	Withdraw from relationship before perceived rejection.	"If I leave first, I won't have to be kicked out."
RankSystem (Self-Blame)	Belief of being "disgusting" and undeserving of care.	Contain the truth by taking on responsibility for harm.	"If I believe it's my fault, I don't have to face betrayal."
A prudent approach towards internal Caregiving System through Cooperation (Therapist Modeling- Updated)	Therapist normalizes survival logic and offers co-regulation.	Demonstrates that acknowledgment of pain does not lead to abandonment.	(Updated): "Maybe I can let someone know and still be safe."

Table 23.1. Motivational and action systems at play

Clinical Reflections

Shame-based beliefs often persist not because they are believed to be true, but because they once protected the system from a more overwhelming reality. In this vignette, the therapist did not challenge the content of the belief or rush to reframe it. Instead, she addressed the isolation in which the belief had been held.

Self-condemning beliefs function as survivable explanations for unbearable experiences. When shame-bound parts are met with presence rather than correction or rescue, the system can begin to loosen its grip on self-blame without being forced to abandon it prematurely. What changes first is not the belief itself, but the relational context in which it is held, allowing contact without collapse.

- ★ "Of course it made more sense to believe it was your fault. That might have been the only way to stay close."

Donald Nathanson (1992) conceptualizes this pattern as the *attack self* pole of shame regulation: a strategy in which shame and anger are turned inward through self-devaluation and self-condemnation. By assuming a one-down position, the individual attempts to restore safety, reduce relational threat, or preserve attachment by aligning with the caregiver's perspective. From this viewpoint, harsh self-criticism is not merely punitive; it is an organized attempt to manage shame and maintain connection under conditions where direct protest or external blame would have risked abandonment or retaliation.

These parts need to know that what they carry was never theirs to begin with. This can be supported through language that returns responsibility to where it belongs, such as:

- ★ "Of course you found a way to survive that. It does not mean you're shameful."
- ★ "That shame belongs to what happened, not to who you are."

Build Internal Bridges

Often, other parts of the system have no idea what these shame-bound parts are carrying. Facilitating internal recognition can support compassion (intersubjectivity) from within.

- ★ "Would it feel okay to let another part know how heavy this has been for you?"

Invite the Adult Self or other parts to acknowledge the shame-bound part's pain without trying to fix it.

- ★ "Would it be okay to let that part know it does not have to be alone with this?"

Slow the Pace

Working with shame-bound parts often requires slowing down. Take your time, proceed as slowly as they need. These parts are vulnerable to relational intensity and can retreat when they feel seen or compassion is expressed directly. It is too overwhelming; they are exquisitely sensitive to exposure. Even being noticed in a warm way can feel threatening. The therapist's tone, posture, and timing must communicate welcome without demand.

★ "You don't have to say anything if you can't. Take all the time you need."

CLINICAL VIGNETTE

2) What If They're Right?

A client was describing a moment of self-loathing: "It's like a voice inside just keeps saying, 'You're disgusting'." She hunched forward, avoiding eye contact, her voice barely audible. The therapist paused, resisting the urge to contradict the message or reassure her worth. Instead, she said, "I wonder how long that part has been carrying that belief." The client blinked hard. "Since I was little", she whispered. "Since before I could talk, maybe." This was not a cognitive distortion to challenge; it was a wound to witness. And in that moment, something shifted: not the belief, but the loneliness inside it.

SYSTEM	WHERE IT SHOWS UP	FUNCTION	SURVIVAL LOGIC
Attachment System Deactivation/(Inhibited) care-seeking	Avoiding eye contact, speaking in a whisper, declines help (it's fine)	Suspend care-seeking to prevent rejection or punishment; preserve the bond by not needing	"If I don't ask and stay quiet, I can't be refused or hurt."
Rank System (Submission)	Self-minimizing posture; hides behind hair/hood; sits at the edge/corner; apologizes pre-emptively.	Avoid evaluation/humiliation by staying below notice; self-downrank to prevent attack.	"If I'm small or invisible, I won't be judged, exposed or humiliated."
Cooperation, Intersubjectivity System (Therapist Modeling)	Therapist's curiosity about the belief's origins.	Model safe witnessing without contradiction or demand.	(Updated): "Maybe someone can hear this and still stay."

Table 23.2. Motivational and action systems at play.

Clinical Reflections

Self-loathing beliefs that appear harsh or absolute often originate as early attachment solutions rather than evaluative judgments. In this vignette, the therapist did not attempt to dispute the belief or offer reassurance, as doing so would have intensified relational threat. By meeting the belief with curiosity about its origins, the therapist addressed the isolation in which it had been held.

Shared Reflections on Both Vignettes

What If They're Right? and *I Shouldn't Even Be Here* illustrate two common presentations of shame-bound parts—one emerging through quiet self-loathing, the other through explicit self-disqualification.

In both cases, the temptation for the therapist could have been to contradict the belief or offer quick reassurance. Instead, the turning point came from staying present without trying to fix. The therapist's stance conveyed: "This can be said, and I will not leave."

In the first vignette, the shift occurred in the loneliness surrounding the belief, not in the belief itself. In the second, change emerged through having the survival logic of self-blame understood without judgment. Together, these moments model that worthiness is not something earned through performance or perfection, but something that can be met in the raw truth of shame.

Across both examples, what mattered most was the therapist's ability to:

- Hold the part's experience without contradicting or bypassing it.
- Name the survival function of self-blame as a form of protection.
- Remain steady in the presence of deep self-contempt, demonstrating it could be witnessed without rejection or hasty soothing (the urge to make it go away due to the therapist's own distress).

Over time, repeated experiences like these can loosen the grip of shame; not by dismantling it directly, but by building a relationship strong enough to hold it.

CLOSING THOUGHTS

Shame-bound parts do not seek healing, they seek disappearance. They carry not just memories, but identities shaped by blame, silence, and isolation. Their very existence is often built on the belief that they are the problem, that if they stay hidden, the rest of the system could survive.

How we reach these parts in therapy is through our presence: by being patient and not giving up, by holding what they cannot see yet without trying to make them see it too. It is not reassurance or logic that creates change. These parts are too deeply organized by what they have learned. Instead, we meet them without rushing to correct or deny their truths. We listen and accompany. And when the system offers opportunities, through the voices of other parts, through new relational experiences, we begin to gently challenge what shame once claimed as facts.

Healing does not come through persuasion. It comes through compassionate witnessing, through the slow, steady experience of being seen, heard, and stayed with. When shame-bound parts are welcomed without judgment, they begin to unlearn the lie that they are beyond repair. And in time, some may even come to glimpse a truth they never imagined: that their existence was never the shameful thing, it was always the abandonment and mistreatment that was.

Clinical Anchors

What to remember...

- Shame-bound parts seek invisibility, not healing.
- Reassurance often feels like dismissal, attunement lands deeper.
- These parts formed to preserve connection and coherence.
- Protectors may react strongly. Move slowly and collaboratively.
- Strengthen internal relationships before direct contact.
- Shame is a relational injury. Repair requires relational safety.

What to avoid...

- Countering shame with praise or cognitive reframes.
- Assuming silence means disengagement.
- Moving too quickly into traumatic content or memory work.
- Treating disclosure as readiness.
- Interpreting collapse as resistance.

PART III: Supporting and Transforming Internal Relationships

In this section, the focus shifts from types of dissociative parts to recurring relational dynamics within dissociative personality systems. The roles and loops described here are functional patterns that often take place between parts of the system. The roles described in Part III are organizing lenses meant to help clinicians recognize common survival patterns in practice.

Chapter 24: Loyalties, Secrecy, and Grief in Betrayal Trauma

THERAPIST REFLECTION

There was a moment in the session when she paused, her body suddenly alert. The client said, "Part of me wants to say it, and part of me is terrified to." I didn't push; I named the bind—the wish to tell and the fear of telling. She lifted her head slightly, as if something inside was checking whether what I had said was accurate. After a few moments, the Adult Self said, "She really does not have to say anything in words." As curiosity replaced fear, the alert part eased, less on edge. And the part who couldn't speak was heart without needing word.

Not all trauma ruptures the same way. Betrayal trauma strikes at the core of attachment; not only what happened, but who did it. When the person who was supposed to protect also harmed (parent, clergy, teacher, caregiver), approach and avoidance fuse; love and danger occupy the same space. In dissociative systems, this becomes an internal politics of loyalty, secrecy, and surveillance, with parts organized around conflicting bonds.

Working with betrayal trauma requires a steadiness that neither rushes exposure nor colludes with silence. The clinical center of gravity is the paradox itself: "How do I grieve what was done by someone I still love, and tell the truth without losing the only connection I learned to need?"

One of the most painful dynamics is the internal tension between parts devoted to the betrayer and parts who carry the truth. Loyalty here is not naiveté; it is survival. Children maintain proximity to power through idealization, compliance, and self-blame. Later, certain parts keep that bond alive by erasing evidence, punishing disclosure, or insisting the relationship was special. Others hold the memories, body states, and dread.

Loyalty is often spoken of as if it were a singular phenomenon; something earned, chosen, or owed, rather than a response shaped by relationship and context. In clinical work, however, loyalty reveals itself as a relational phenomenon that takes very different forms depending on the conditions in which it developed. It is not inherently healthy or unhealthy. It is shaped by context, especially by safety, dependence, and power.

In environments of relative safety, loyalty grows through mutual recognition, care, and continuity. It reflects trust and a desire to preserve connection. But under conditions of threat, loyalty may take on very different functions. It can become a way of staying close to what is dangerous in order to survive it, a way of reducing risk by aligning with power, or a way of maintaining coherence when no alternative source of protection is available. These shifts in how loyalty functions reflect the activation and entanglement of underlying motivational systems, which will be explored in detail in the sections that follow.

In traumatic contexts—particularly those involving chronic abuse, grooming, captivity, or extreme dependence—loyalty may no longer serve connection so much as regulation. Proximity to the person who causes harm may also be the only available source of safety. Resistance may increase danger. Under these conditions, loyalty can shift from a relational bond to a survival-based alignment, organized around minimizing threat rather than seeking care.

This distinction matters in therapy. When loyalty has been shaped by trauma, it often persists long after the original danger has passed. It may appear rigid, confusing, or self-attacking. Attempts to confront or dismantle it directly can intensify fear and defensive responses. Understanding loyalty as a survival-based adaptation allows us to approach these patterns with respect, recognizing not what they perpetuate, but what they were once designed to prevent.

Loyalty shaped under trauma does not take a single form. It may organize itself as closeness, maintaining proximity at any cost. It may appear as submission, compliance offered to reduce threat. It may function through identification, aligning with an authority figure or peer group to avoid isolation or punishment. Or it may operate as a regulatory strategy, managing danger by tracking, anticipating, and neutralizing risk. These are adaptive solutions to specific relational conditions, and in many systems more than one form of loyalty is active at the same time, shifting with context and perceived threat.

UNDERSTANDING THE DYNAMICS OF DIVIDED LOYALTIES WITHIN THE SYSTEM

It is an untenable contradiction: "They loved me" vs. "They hurt me". Both can be subjectively true, and both must be honored therapeutically, without forcing a realization the system cannot hold yet.

Origins of This Dynamic

This configuration emerges in a relational environment where care and threat are fused. Chronic coercion, grooming, and the instrumental use of *love* as a cover for abuse or exploitation by caregivers create an attachment system organized around danger. In such contexts, survival depends on maintaining proximity to the source of power and preserving the bond at all costs. Disclosure or confrontation threatens that essential connection, activating an internal logic in which speech equates to risk and silence to safety. The following patterns describe the environments that first shaped and reinforced this contract.

- **Punished disclosure.** Early attempts to tell were met with disbelief, blame, punishment, or rupture. The body learned that knowing and telling equals danger, so brakes were installed.
- **Grooming and specialness.** Chosen status, secrecy rituals, and gifts braided belonging to silence. Breaking rules meant losing this special bond.
- **Identification with authority.** To avoid powerlessness, loyalty shifts inward: protect the image, keep the family or the group intact, do not betray.
- **Parentification and image-keeping.** The child became custodian of the bond, so silence felt like love, and telling like harm.
- **State-dependent storage.** Fragments of knowing held in different body and memory states to manage scattered truth.
- **Institutional loyalties.** Schools, faith groups, teams: belonging hinged on obedience. The cost of telling was exile.

Trauma-informed therapists often track negative cognitions linked to trauma. Betrayal adds scripted rules that bind the child to the bond—more than beliefs, they function as laws:

- "You're chosen/special."
- "If you tell, you'll ruin everything."
- "This is love; others wouldn't understand."
- "Disobedience equals punishment."

These migrate inward as self-talk and part-to-part rules, sometimes as voices, sometimes as visceral alarms . They do not define the person's essence, but they cannot be ripped away. They cannot be talked out of existence. They do not dissolve in logic, reassurance, or positive reframes, especially not when they have been lodged in the system for years or decades. They are like internal tattoos etched by trauma, impossible to erase, but they can be re-inked with new meaning through repeated moments of safety and presence.

Loyalty is maintained by secrecy. Many clients live with an internal sense of being monitored: "Don't write it." "Don't say it." "They'll find out." The room itself can feel bugged. Rather than taking this as irrational, validate the historic accuracy of surveillance and rely on gradual present-day reality testing (who can know what, where it is stored, who has access).

In some trauma histories, this vigilance is organized through internal reporting functions that once protected the system under conditions of enforced monitoring.

Betrayal often arrives wearing the clothes of care: teacher, pastor, coach, healer, elder sibling, parent, grandparent. Grooming recruits the child's need for recognition and belonging: "I see you." Once inside, rules shift: loyalty tests, secrecy oaths, erosion of the child's perception. The system then internalizes an authority template: authority defines truth; safety lives in obedience; dissent is punished.

These early conditions create an inner government of secrecy and surveillance, where loyalty, truth, and safety divide across roles. Remember roles describe functional positions within a dynamic that often go together and feed off each other. They do not imply distinct or permanent parts.

Core Roles in This Dynamic

To manage the contradiction between the need for attachment and the need for protection, the system divides its functions. One part holds the unintegrated reality of what occurred; another preserves relational belonging through secrecy; a third monitors expression and sensation, policing the perimeter to prevent exposure.

- A **Truth Holder** that kept reality somewhere and safeguards it, so the mind is not gaslit from within.
- A **Watcher** that monitors the perimeter, so proximity does not outpace safety, and nothing slips out by accident.
- An **Oath Keeper** that preserves belonging by monitoring speech and patrolling telling. This role is a perpetrator-identified loyalty keeper.

Naming them as functions lets us thank each for surviving while we update the method and help them cooperate now.

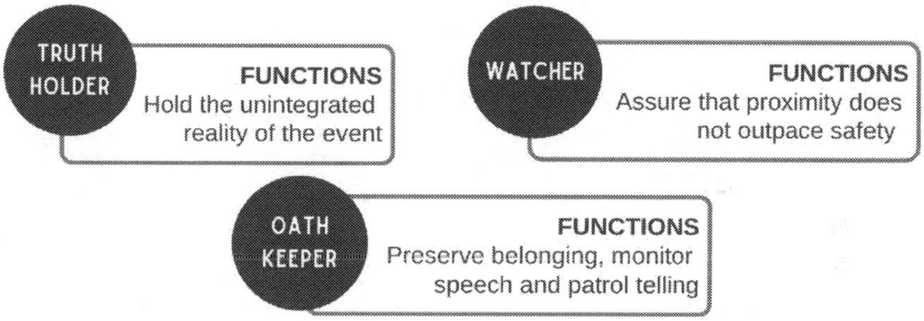

Figure 24.1. The Divided Loyalties Loop roles.

The Divided Loyalties Loop

Telling and not telling rarely follow a straight line. Instead, the system swings back and forth, drawn first toward disclosure, then pulled sharply back into silence. Each reach to tell from the Truth Holder awakens the system's loyalty alarm. The Watcher signals danger to belonging, summoning surveillance and freeze, while the Oath Keeper enforces obedience to prevent betrayal. Secrecy is reasserted, bringing brief relief but renewed isolation. When grief or longing for connection surfaces, the cycle begins again. Naming this loop helps transform enforced silence into cooperative protection, allowing truth and loyalty to coexist safely.

The conditions under which silence and secrecy take root are rarely random. They tend to arise in predictable patterns; settings where attempts to speak are punished, loyalty is tied to secrecy, authority becomes internalized, and belonging depends on obedience. These formative dynamics carve grooves in body and mind, teaching that disclosure brings danger, and that survival depends on keeping the bond intact.

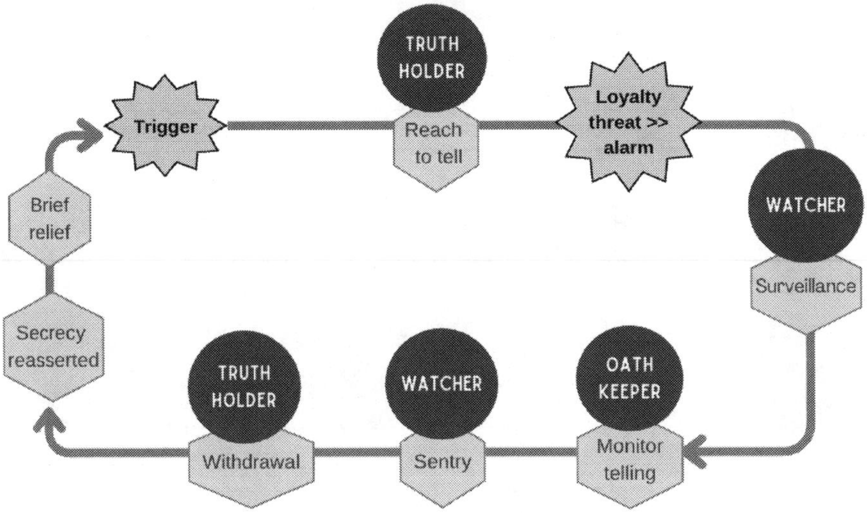

Figure 24.2. The Divided Loyalties Loop

The loop does not arise in isolation. It is the internal echo of external conditions where loyalty and safety once depended on silence.

Silence does not dissolve once danger has passed; it lingers, encoded in body and mind. What began as protection becomes habit, and habit hardens into law. The brakes install themselves; rules organize belonging, and even healing relationships can awaken the old contract.

These are the forces that keep the loop and the system of silence alive.

- **Procedural memory.** At the edge of telling, the body brakes automatically (fog, sleepiness, head pressure). That is safety memory, not stubbornness.
- **Rule economy.** Inward laws keep order and belonging. Shame is the glue.
- **Functional necessity.** Someone must work, parent, pass exams. Guardians fear collapse if yesterday floods today.
- **Therapeutic closeness as a trigger.** Connection to the therapist reactivates the old contract: approach risks exposure; exposure risks loss.

Motivational Systems

Betrayal trauma entangles motivational systems into one complex survival script that can only be understood from the trauma perspective. In conditions where the caregiver is also the source of threat, attachment, rank, and defense become chronically co-activated, producing a rigid survival organization in which loyalty functions as a rule rather than a choice.

What is often named clinically as *loyalty* is an **emergent organizing principle**: a binding contract that preserves attachment by submitting to rank and suppressing defense through silence, compliance, and self-blame. Depending on which motivational system is most dominant in a given moment, loyalty may be expressed as closeness, submission, identification, or danger regulation—different faces of the same survival alignment.

Underneath, three motivational systems (attachment, defense and rank) are locked in a no-solution bind. The subjective experience of loyalty arises from this fusion. When attachment depends on obedience and defense is punished, allegiance becomes synonymous with safety.

- **Attachment:** The Truth Holder seeks recognition and repair, "Please see what happened. I just want someone to believe me!" When it stirs, the system leans toward contact, hoping for witness or validation Loyalty in this mode organizes as closeness, maintaining proximity at all costs. Yet this movement also threatens the rules that once kept belonging intact, activating counterforces.

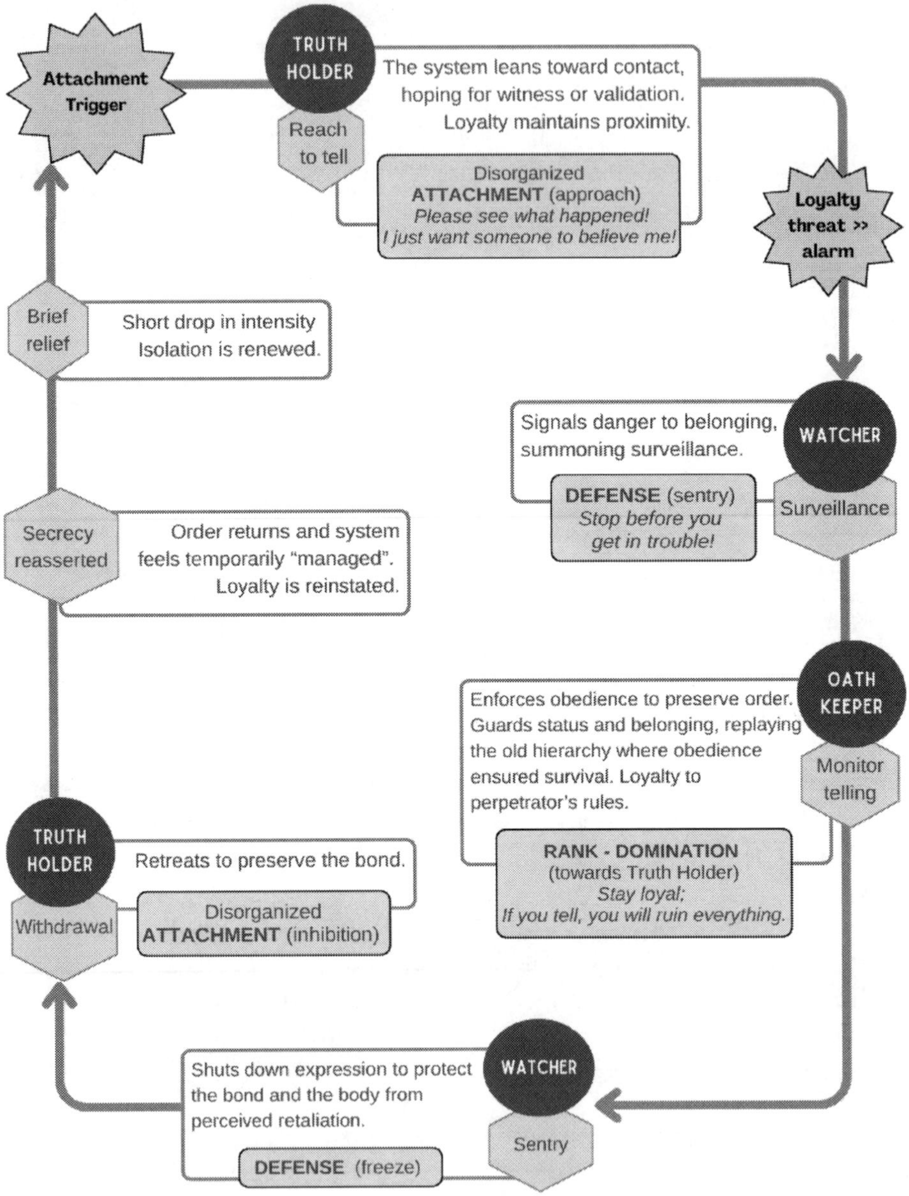

Fig. 24.3. Motivational systems organizing the Divided Loyalties Loop

- **Defense:** The Watcher manages threat through freeze, vigilance, and withdrawal, "Stop before you get in trouble." "Someone will find out." It shuts down expression to protect the bond and the body from perceived retaliation. Loyalty operates as danger regulation, tracking exposure, monitoring speech, and inhibiting action to prevent harm.

- **Rank:** The Oath Keeper enforces obedience to preserve order, "Stay loyal; don't betray." "If you tell, you will ruin everything." It guards status and belonging, replaying the old hierarchy where obedience ensured survival and defiance meant exile. Loyalty organizes as submission and identification, aligning with authority figures, family roles, or peer groups to avoid loss of standing or expulsion.

Loyalty functions as an organizing rule anchoring safety in devotion: "I can't betray them." "It wasn't that bad." It preserves identity through allegiance, even when that allegiance costs truth.

In this loop, the Watcher's freeze-vigilance corresponds directly to the defense → sentry function in the chart, where scanning and inhibition work together to prevent proximity from outpacing safety. When betrayal fuses love and control, these systems can no longer coordinate. Attachment impulses activate, then recoil as rank threat and defense come online. Each attempt at disclosure reawakens the old hierarchy: obedience overrides contact, and protection replaces connection.

The loop completes when the system restores safety through silence, a temporary relief that also reinstates isolation. Over time, loyalty feels safer than truth, and protection is measured by secrecy rather than by care. Naming the underlying motivational pattern helps the system learn that loyalty and safety no longer have to oppose truth and connection

RECOGNIZING THE DYNAMIC

When the betrayal dynamic comes online, the room organizes before the story does: any small reach for truth sets the old contract in motion: the rule snaps on, the eyes start their rounds, words shear off into fragments. Here is a list of the typical cues that help us identify how these dynamics tend to appear.

NON-VERBAL CUES	
TRUTH HOLDER	• Hand hovering over journal or keyboard • Throat catch, breath hitch • Micro-lean toward you then recoil • Eyes water, then avert • Fine tremor in fingers
OATH KEEPER	• Sudden inner pressure/speed • Jaw set, shoulders square Contempt flash • Compliance that ends the moment
WATCHER	• Seat by exit, back to wall • Gaze triangulates door–clock–floor • Startle to hallway sounds • Scanning resumes whenever you shift posture. • Preference for facts over feelings. • Requests to spell out storage, access, timing
VERBAL CUES (OR VOICES INSIDE)	
TRUTH HOLDER	• Words fragment as nearness rises • "I think…," "It's fuzzy," "Parts of it come and go," "I start and then it vanishes."
OATH KEEPER	• Topic switch to "safe" ground • Rigid yes/no answers • "I promised," "We don't talk about that," "You'll ruin everything," "Don't betray the family," "You're lying."
WATCHER	• Micro-pause before risky words • Logistics/privacy questions ("Is this recorded?" "Who sees your notes?")
OSCILATION LOOP CUES	
• Sudden flip from seeking comfort to defending, idealizing, or protecting the perpetrator. • Fear of getting someone in trouble; loyalty oaths, secrecy rules, or courtroom language inside. • Minimizing harm ("It wasn't that bad"); rationalizing control ("He was teaching me"). • Surveillance sensations ("Someone is listening") or ritualized shame/self-punishment after small disclosures.	

Table. 24.1. The Divided Loyalties Loop cues

Post-session backlash cues

After sessions that touch vulnerable material, the system may react with a delayed backlash. Somatically, this can appear as sudden fatigue, a pressure headache, gut churn, or overall shutdown. Cognitively and relationally, the tone shifts: thoughts such as "I made it up" emerge, along with impulses to destroy notes, delete messages, or cancel the next session. Shame spikes, protectors grow angry, and the system moves to reassert control after perceived overexposure. These reactions are signs that contact reached depth; the body and parts are attempting to restore safety by retreating to familiar containment strategies.

It is easy to misread this choreography. It is not appeasement meant to keep others comfortable; it is allegiance with the perpetrator being kept intact. The gate does not only guard traumatic content but the act of telling itself. And those brief flashes of edge are rarely global hostility; they are the pressure of an oath coming online.

WORKING WITH BETRAYAL TRAUMA DYNAMICS

Because bonding is the arena of injury, connection to the therapist activates the same rules: no telling, no needing, no exposing. Telling threatens not only the external bond but the internal bond with parts who survived by allegiance. Betrayal gets reenacted inside: one part discredits, another submits, another watches and keeps the rules. These internal attacks mirror the dynamics of the original dilemma: love entangled with control, care with punishment, speech with danger. Attune to the survival logic: align with power or be destroyed.

Our task is to reflect the bind and protect timing; healing unfolds through slow relational re-training where loyalty to self is not punished. Naming the abuse too quickly can replicate being overruled. Ambivalence is fidelity to a survival contract.

The Risk of Countertransference

When this survival choreography shows up, you are in the right territory: the system is reenacting the bind you can help update. The greater risk is our own counter-pulls.

- **The Avenger pull**: outrage at the betrayal can drive therapists to over-naming, over-interpreting, and rushing pace, which reenacts control and triggers backlash.
- **The Rescuer pull:** moving therapists to soothe the child while bypassing Enforcers invites rupture and reenactment.
- **The Collusion pull**: therapists joining idealization to preserve rapport, especially with charming, compliant clients; keeps the old contract intact.

Track your attachment longings and authority biases. If you feel compelled to prove the betrayal or to be *the good one*, slow down and consult.

Clinical Vignette

The Whisper and the Oath

Midway through the session, Mara's eyes flicked toward the notebook in her lap. "There's something written here", she said, voice small. The Truth Holder had surfaced. Before she could continue, her chest tightened; a whisper rose inside: "Don't you dare." The Oath Keeper stepped in, pulse quickening, jaw locked. Mara shook her head. "No. I can't. I promised."

The therapist didn't push for disclosure. "It sounds like there's a promise keeping you safe", she said softly. "We don't have to break it. We can just notice that it's here." The air shifted, slight tremor, eyes darting to the door. The Watcher came online, scanning the perimeter: "Is anyone listening?"

The therapist slowed her voice. "Let's check together. Look around the room. Who can know what's said here?" Mara's gaze moved from clock to door, then back. Shoulders dropped. "It's quiet", she murmured. "You don't have to tell the words", the therapist continued. "Maybe just notice what it feels like to *want* to tell."

A small grief crossed her face, then retreated, then stillness. "I feel sad", she whispered, "but... I'm not in trouble?" "No", the therapist said gently. "You kept the promise then to survive. You can keep safe now by choosing the pace."

The session ended there, there was no revelation or breakthrough, but something shifted. The Oath-Keeper had stayed without silencing completely; the Truth-Holder had reached without punishment; the Watcher had verified safety and stood down.

Clinical Reflections

This moment unfolded precisely along the Divided Loyalties loop. The Truth Holder's reach activated the Oath Keeper's alarm; the Watcher's vigilance followed, enforcing the old rule that protection equals silence. What interrupted the sequence was procedure, not persuasion: the therapist honored the oath instead of challenging it, validated loyalty as care, and invited consent at every turn.

By naming and validating the rule, "that promise kept you safe then", the therapist separated (differentiation) safety from secrecy. That distinction allowed the Truth Holder's longing and the Oath Keeper's vigilance to coexist without collapse.

Each time this loop is recognized and slowed, it lays down new procedural evidence: telling can be optional, loyalty can be shared, and safety can include voice. The goal is not to extract confession, but to transform the act of not telling from a reflexive command into a conscious choice.

Expect contradictions across the system. An approach move towards therapist from a comfort-seeking child will often arrive alongside avoidance from an Oath Keeper as perfectly predicted by the conflict-without-solution of disorganized attachment: loyal parts may protect the perpetrator's image while other parts protect the child by isolating; rank/power fights (internal dominance/submission) arise to prevent external loss of control. Map roles and motivational systems. Disorganization is the imprint of surviving a double bind.

Updating Loyalty and Reorganizing the System

Loyalty often begins as a protective adaptation—a way of preserving connection within conditions of threat or inconsistency. In such contexts, Loyalty may take several forms: staying close through compliance, aligning with authority to reduce danger, or internalizing the logic of those who held power. These were not choices made freely, but relational strategies shaped by what was required to survive.

For many clients, an internal oath forms to hold belonging when safety depended on submission or self-neglect. This oath may sound like devotion, obedience, or control, but its function is care. Naming this loyalty as care ("This protected belonging when nothing else could") allows both clinician and client to recognize its original purpose without collapsing into shame.

The therapeutic task is not to dismantle loyalty, but to update its form. The aim is to preserve the function of connection while reshaping how protection is exercised—through consent, pacing, and present-moment awareness rather than secrecy, submission, or internal attack. Because direct challenges to allegiance can feel profoundly unsafe, therapy does not attempt to sever loyalty. Instead, it supports a gradual shift in where loyalty is expressed: away from past figures and dynamics, and toward the client's own internal capacities. Protection is no longer organized through compliance or self-silencing, but through permission, boundaries, and choice.

Disorganization, viewed through this lens, represents the residue of surviving double binds in which loyalty and threat were inseparable. It should be understood not as failure or resistance, but as information about how the system once balanced attachment and danger, and as a guide toward more integrated forms of safety and attachment.

The Fear of Telling

In betrayal trauma, disclosure is dangerous, not just emotionally, sometimes physically. Parts may fear that telling the truth will destroy the system, lead to abandonment, or recreate punishment. Even years later, the fear is visceral:

- ❖ "I think I made it up."
- ❖ "It's like my voice disappears when I try to say it."
- ❖ "I know I should talk about it, but I feel like I'll die if I do."

Honor these fears as survival memories. The body remembers what the mind may not. Telling is not only words but also reclaiming the right to be heard after being silenced. Therapy becomes a place to test the waters without insisting:

- ★ "You don't have to say anything you're not ready to."
- ★ "Even if you can't speak it yet, you're allowed to know what you know."

Grieving the Relationship, Not the Abuse

When the idealized bond cracks, grief follows. For the person, the imagined safety, the lost childhood, and the years spent keeping the rules. Reframe grief as loyalty to the child, not treason against the bond, so mourning can proceed without annihilating the history of the connection.

Grief is often quiet, delayed, or conflicted; it can arrive before clarity.

- ★ "It's okay to miss what you wished it could be."

Naming the betrayal is only one part of the work. Grieving the loss of illusionary safety, belonging, and imagined connection, that is where healing takes root.

Working Procedurally: The 4Ps Framework

When systems carry divided loyalties, telling is not just emotional, it is procedural. Each disclosure tests the old rules of secrecy, belonging, and control. Working without a clear structure risks reenacting those same dynamics in therapy.

The 4Ps (Permission, Precision, Pace, Predictability) Framework offers a way to translate safety into process, turning permission, precision, pace, and predictability into the scaffolding that allows truth to emerge without betrayal.

The goal is not to dismantle loyalty but to repatriate it; to move allegiance from the past relational field into the present, where protection operates through consent and boundary rather than secrecy and submission. In practice, this means permission before exposure, boundary before narrative. The 4Ps become a procedural contract for telling so truth can be approached without repeating old coercions.

- **Permission (shared contract):** Agree if/what/how long you will approach disclosure today. Oath Keeper holds control, Adult Self sets conditions.
  - ★ "You don't have to say anything you're not ready to."
  - ★ "Before we go near it, let's ask the one who keeps the oath what would feel safe enough for this hour."
- **Precision (dose):** Fragments, not full accounts: one line written privately, one sensation named, one then/now tag.
  - ★ "Could we write a single sentence on your own page and decide together whether it comes into the room?"
- **Pace (stop on signal):** Rehearse a stop word; stop within one second; repair missteps aloud.
  - ★ "If you say 'pause,' I will stop immediately. Let's practice twice so your body can trust it."
- **Predictability (ritual):** Same opening orient, same end-of-hour downshift, pre-announced changes. Let the Watcher co-author the perimeter (seat, sightline, storage/privacy choices).:
  - ★ "We'll start with the door, the window, the clock; we'll end with two anchors and what helped."

CLOSING THOUGHTS

Betrayal trauma organizes a system around competing loyalties: to the person who harmed and to the child who survived. Therapy's task is not to pick a side but to widen the circle so both loyalties can be seen, grieved, and re-organized around present-day safety. We do not have to resolve ambivalence or unify the narrative. We sit with fragments, respect loyalties, and stay close enough for the system to learn: this time, it's different.

When secrecy loses power and grief finds voice, the system no longer needs to monitor access or repeat harmful dynamics inside.

Clinical Anchors

What to remember...

- Divided loyalties are survival, not duplicity. Honor attachment and truth.
- The phobia of telling protects bonds. Treat it as protective, then invite updated reality at the system´s pace.
- Grooming co-opts real needs (recognition, care, status). Validate the need; question the contract.
- The three core roles each serve survival: Truth Holder keeps reality somewhere, Watcher guards the perimeter, Oath Keeper preserves belonging through rules.
- Grief is central. Make room to mourning the bond, not just name the abuse.
- Work procedurally: use the 4Ps (Permission, Precision, Pace, Predictability) so telling and not-telling both become choices, not commands.
- Watch your pulls (rescuer/avenger/colluder). Steadiness beats speed and pressure.

What to avoid...

- Forcing a single narrative or loyalty position.
- Questioning the idealized figure/system too soon because it hardens allegiance and strengthens the Oath Keeper.
- Collapsing *telling* into compliance or proof gathering.
- Treating surveillance/loyalty rules as irrational rather than historically accurate safety strategies.

Chapter 25: Navigating Shame, Blame, and Internal Criticism

Therapist Reflection

There are moments when the critic turns on me, dismisses the work, mocks the connection, or says I'm just another person who will eventually leave. I used to feel rejected or discouraged. Now I pause and ask myself: Who am I standing in for right now? If I can remember that this part is fighting shame, not me, I can stay grounded. I don't have to argue with it. I can just keep showing up; steady, non-defensive, and willing to see the fear beneath the sharpness.

Shame is one of the most corrosive and isolating emotional states in dissociative systems. Unlike guilt—"I did something wrong"—shame carries the felt sense "I am wrong": inherently bad, disgusting, defective, or unlovable (Lewis, 1971; Nathanson, 1992; Chefetz, 2020; Benau, 2022). Clinically, shame is the signature affect of the rank/power system: where there is shame, there is an internalized or present dominant evaluator who down-ranks, judges, and humiliates. That is why shame generalizes beyond a single act or moment; it engulfs the whole person or part, not just behavior.

Within many systems, shame organizes itself into complementary roles. The Shame Carrier holds the raw burden of toxic self-beliefs—collapsing, hiding, or withdrawing to avoid exposure. The Shame Enforcer (often a critical protector) monitors the perimeter—discrediting, attacking, or turning against others, including the therapist—anything to keep shame from surfacing.

As we explored in chapter 23, these roles can form a closed loop: one part holds the wound, the other guards it. Though protective in intent (prevent down-ranking and humiliation), the loop often deepens isolation and fragmentation, inadvertently reinforcing the very shame it tries to contain.

This chapter explores the interplay of shame and criticism reinforcing each other, the protective logic behind the critic's role, and ways to work with both without alienating either. In addition, it maps how to identify rank dynamics, de-shame language, and recruit the Adult Self and cooperation systems so dignity can be protected without reinforcing collapse or attack.

UNDERSTANDING SHAME DYNAMICS

We have already explored how dissociative parts form under chronic attachment and defense collisions; here, the focus shifts to the specific conditions that keep shame-based divisions active and organized.

Before turning to the developmental origins of these patterns, it is important to clarify the level of analysis used in this chapter. The shame dynamics described here refer to internal relational organization within dissociative personality systems—how different parts coordinate to manage exposure, humiliation, and belonging. While phenomenological models such as Nathanson's (1992) Compass of Shame describe common responses to shame (e.g., withdrawal, attack self, attack other, avoidance), the framework used here focuses on loops that emerge in dissociative systems to regulate shame over time.

Origins of This Dynamic

Shame dynamics persist where exposure, dependency, or emotional need drew rejection or ridicule. Safety required splitting visibility from vulnerability. Over time, chronic humiliation made being seen feel synonymous with being shamed; belonging became conditional on performance, silence, or compliance; and parentification replaced being cared for with caring for others. Gaslighting and reversal taught that protest brings blame or disbelief, while attachment double binds (where the same person comforts and shames) fused care with danger.

Under such conditions, shame becomes not just a feeling but a structure of safety, a way to maintain proximity to power while minimizing humiliation. The result is an internal division.

Core Roles in This Dynamic

Shame dynamics rarely appear as single emotions. They are patterned, relational responses inside the system. What sounds like cruelty or dismissal is often shame-management: one part carries the wound, another tries to block exposure and a third enforces invisibility to prevent humiliation. The subsections that follow trace where this arrangement comes from, which parts enact it, and why it persists, so we can update the strategy without reenacting silence or attack.

In most dissociative personality systems, shame does not live in one part alone. It is distributed across the system and most often expressed through three complementary roles:

- The **Shame Carrier** holds the raw, unbearable feelings: "I am bad." "I am dirty." "If they see me, I will be cast out." This role overlaps with younger or vulnerable parts and often surfaces through collapse, silence, or withdrawal. Carriers embody the wound of exposure.

- The **Shame Blocker** is an inhibitor, the first line of protection. It acts quickly to prevent exposure before it escalates. This role is often fear-based or appeasing rather than dominant. It interrupts with micro-freeze, sudden stillness, gaze drop, topic shifts, or small self-critical jabs meant to suppress visibility: "Stop." "Don't say that." "You're making this worse." Its job is to minimize risk by shutting down the moment vulnerability appears.

- The **Shame Enforcer** manages this wound through attack, dismissal, or contempt. It echoes the voices of caregivers or abusers and monitors shame so it will not overwhelm the system or leak into relationships. "That's pathetic." "You sound ridiculous." "Shut up before you embarrass us." Enforcers implement invisibility, using criticism as control.

These are not separate categories but manifestations within the Shame dynamics. Different hands perform the same task: keeping the unbearable hidden so the system can stay intact and connected enough to survive. Each contributes to the same defensive regulatory pattern: containing toxic shame while preserving belonging and external functioning.

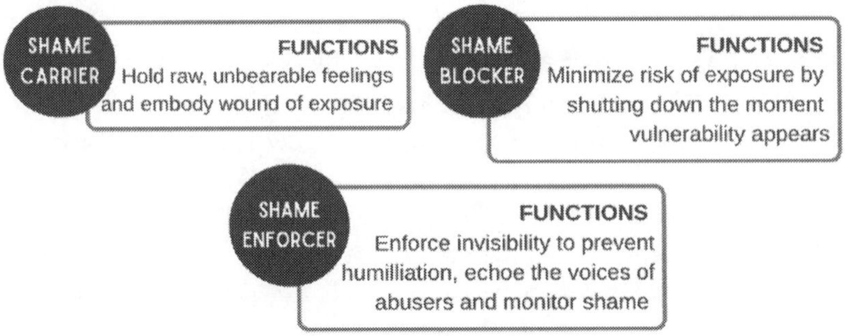

Fig. 25.1. The Shame Loop roles

The Shame Loop

When these roles interact, they generate a predictable internal sequence; they form a loop. The more the Carrier feels exposed, the faster the system mobilizes inhibition and enforcement to guarantee the Carrier's retreat. What looks like opposition is actually cooperation in survival logic: one holds the pain, another blocks exposure and the third guards it. They are protectors, locked in roles learned when shame was too dangerous to show, they are enacting the same mission: preserve safety through invisibility.

This is what we will see in the client when the loop becomes activated

1. **Carrier signals vulnerability.** A younger or shame-bound part surfaces with a disclosure or need: "I don't want you to see me like this."
2. **Shame Blocker activates first line of inhibition.** Alert and appease invitations come up, or rapid self-correction appears to stop exposure: "Don't talk about it." The body goes still, gaze drops, or the client becomes suddenly neutral or mechanical. The stillness here is not collapse but *tonic alert*—the body frozen in place to prevent further exposure. This is a sympathetic hold, not parasympathetic shutdown: *freezing, not fainting.* The system stays braced, muscles charged to contain humiliation, until safety cues allow release.
3. **Shame Enforcer launches an attack.** A critical part interrupts with contempt, dismissal, or sarcasm to suppress exposure: "That's pathetic. Stop it before you embarrass us."

4. **Carrier retreats.** The wounded part withdraws further, folding inward, going quiet, or disappearing altogether.
5. **Temporary stability.** The system feels a brief sense of order or relief: vulnerability has been *managed*.
6. **Residual cost.** The cycle reinforces isolation, entrenches shame, and prevents new relational experiences. Both Carrier and Enforcer are left more alone, each more certain of their role.

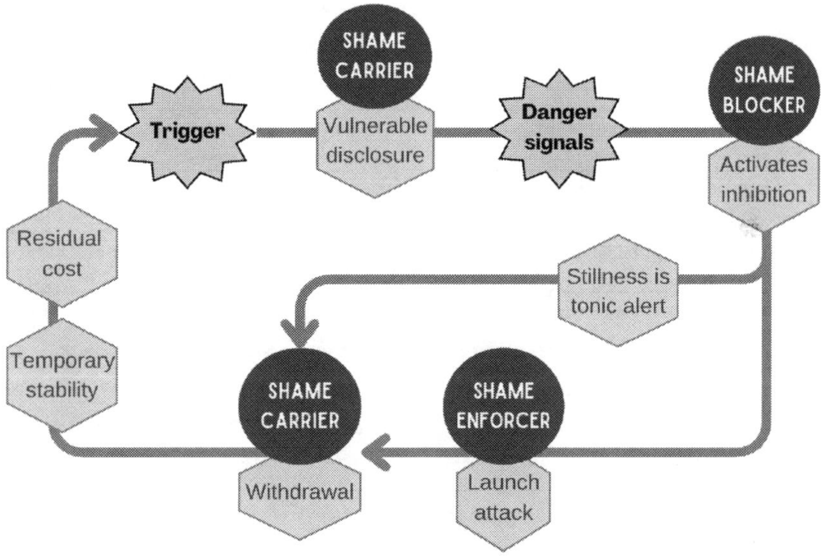

Figure 25.2. The Shame Loop.

If therapists can keep in mind that this is a closed circuit designed to contain exposure, it is easier to hold these roles as protectors rather than opponents.

The previous diagram shows how the shame loop plays out in real time and how translation, not reassurance, allows these roles to stay present without collapse or attack.

While the Shame Loop describes how exposure is contained through inhibition and attack, many systems also rely on *shame escape* strategies once containment is achieved or when residual shame remains. These strategies align with Nathanson's Avoidance pole and may include compulsive activity, excitement-seeking, dissociation through performance, substances, or sexualized arousal.

Clinically, these are not additional Shame Loop roles but secondary regulatory pathways through which the system discharges or outruns shame after it has been forced back into invisibility. The Loop prevents exposure; avoidance prevents feeling.

Motivational Systems Organizing This Loop

The survival engines underneath the Shame loop, align in a way that makes withdrawal and attack look like opposites when they are actually serving the same purpose: prevent humiliation and relational rupture through invisibility or control.

- **Attachment.** Two currents operate simultaneously: a wish to be seen (care-seeking) and a strong inhibition of closeness. The Carrier tests for safety through vulnerable disclosure, then aborts contact when danger signals appear.

- **Defense.** Defensive responses (freeze and blocking maneuvers such as topic shifts or numbing) support these roles. In some systems, defense is concentrated in a distinct Blocker; in others, it is embedded within the Carrier's collapse and appeasement.

- **Rank (domination).** Organizes the Enforcer. It powers contempt, comparison, and harsh internal grading. ("Pathetic." "Don't you dare.") The aim is status control: to down-rank the self before anyone else can. By attacking first, the Enforcer attempts to prevent external humiliation.

- **Rank (submission).** Organizes the Carrier's collapse. It drives down-ranking through stillness, voice loss and disappearance. Submission restores safety by reducing status and visibility, moving down the hierarchy before others can do it.

Notes on Motivational Entanglement in the Loop

The combination of **attachment + rank submission** (Carrier) operates in two modes: *Care-seeking followed by collapse*: the system reaches, senses danger, then disappears. *Appeasing submission*: brief compliance or softening to keep exposure tolerable and short-lived.

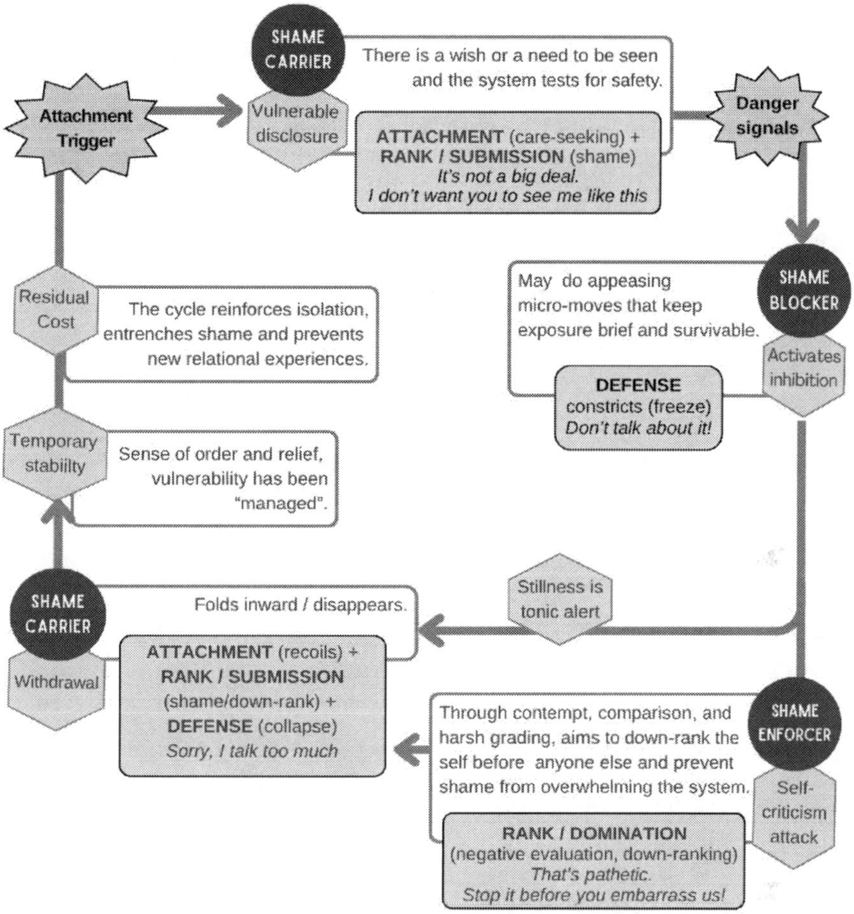

Figure 25.3. Motivational systems organizing the Shame Loop

When **attachment** becomes entangled with **rank domination** in the role of the Enforcer, rank control serves attachment. The Enforcer monitors the perimeter to protect belonging and external functioning. Criticism functions as a loyalty move; by attacking first, the system prevents exposure that would threaten the bond. Attack becomes a way of preserving connection.

Finally, **defense** may be embedded in different combinations**.** Defensive responses (freeze, inhibition, blocking) can be explicitly represented in the Carrier, the Blocker, or within specific attachment–rank pairings, depending on the system's organization.

Seen through this lens, the sequence makes procedural sense. Naming the program or function lowers shame's heat and lets both roles stay in the room while you update the method.

Internal Criticism as a Shame-Regulation Strategy

While it can appear harsh, cruel, or punitive, internal criticism is often a deliberate, if outdated, attempt to manage unbearable shame before it overwhelms the system.

The logic is familiar:

- "If I attack myself first, no one else can hurt me more."
- "If I silence the weak or needy parts, we can stay hidden and safe."
- "If I discredit the memory, maybe it won't be real, and we won't have to feel it."

These critical parts often see themselves as enforcers of order, managing chaos, suppressing vulnerability, and preventing perceived humiliation or rejection. In this way, criticism is not the opposite of shame but its constant companion. It becomes a shame-regulation strategy: containing the threat through internal dominance rather than risking external vulnerability.

They carry relational blueprints, often modeled after caregivers or authority figures, who once had power over the client's safety, identity, and belonging. Over time, these external voices became internalized, serving as both a form of control and a misguided form of protection.

For many clients, shame was not only instilled by abusers; it was enforced. Survivors were often blamed, silenced, gaslit, or made to feel complicit in their own harm. Over time, this shame became internalized, absorbed by certain parts as an unchangeable truth.

The critic's role, as the Shame Enforcer, in this arrangement is a targeted survival strategy, often learned from powerful or shaming figures. By attacking first, the critic controls the terms of exposure and tries to keep the system safe from relational or emotional collapse.

In therapy, a moment of connection or insight can be followed by a backlash:

- "You sounded ridiculous."
- "Why did you say that?"
- "Now they'll know how broken you are."

This response slams the Shame Carrier back into hiding, recreating the original trauma atmosphere, where safety meant silence and self-erasure.

RECOGNIZING THE DYNAMIC

Shame rarely announces itself directly. It moves through the system as shifts in tone, posture, or sudden changes of direction in the session. A flicker of openness may collapse into silence, or a soft disclosure may be followed by sharp dismissal. These flips between collapse and attack, can leave the therapist momentarily disoriented, unsure whether connection has been lost or hostility has been provoked. In reality, both are signs that the shame loop has come online.

As seen in chapter 16, critical parts emerge from early contexts where perfection, silence, or compliance were necessary for survival. In the shame-criticism loop, they are simply applying those same rules internally. Even when they look contradictory, all three movements (collapse, inhibition and attack) are shame signals serving different protective roles.

In the clinical vignette, on the next page we will also see how the three roles function as protectors, but their method is to use shame itself as the strategy: the Carrier absorbs and embodies it, the Blocker keeps it small and contained, and the Enforcer weaponizes it inwardly through attack. In trauma time, shame becomes not just a wound to be concealed but a tool for survival; it is owned, displayed, and repeated in order to maintain control and prevent greater danger.

Let us look at the cues that typically signal how the sequence unfolds and how each role behaves.

NON-VERBAL CUES	
SHAME CARRIER	• Shoulders round; torso curls inward, protective posture. • Gaze drops; eyes avert or become glassy. • Body softens or folds; limbs draw in. • Breath becomes shallow or held; trembling may appear. • Sudden stillness accompanied by softness rather than tension. • Dissociation markers: fading presence, drifting away.
SHAME BLOCKER	• A sudden, alert stillness (tonic freeze); body holds rather than collapses. • Muscles visibly braced; neck, jaw, or shoulders tighten. • Gaze drops or turns neutral/bland (not soft like the Carrier). • Polite or flat expressions; micro-appeasement gestures. • Quick "containment" movements: sitting up straighter, hands clasping, legs tightening. • Rapid quieting, but with tension instead of withdrawal.
SHAME ENFORCER	• Posture straightens, chest lifts; energy rises. • Jaw sets, chin lifts slightly (rank activation). • Eyes narrow, sharpen, or scan for threat/evaluation. • Increased tension in shoulders, hands, or vocal muscles. • Leaning back or away as a distancing move; or leaning forward as a challenge.
VERBAL CUES	
SHAME CARRIER	• Self-defect labeling: "I'm bad," "I'm dirty," "I'm wrong." • Fear of being seen: "Please don't look at me," "Don't see me like this." • Tentative/fragmented disclosures. • Whispers, childlike tone, or near inaudibility. • Rapid apologies or minimization: "Sorry… I shouldn't say this."
SHAME BLOCKER	• Brief, inhibiting phrases: "Stop," "Not now," "Don't go there," "It's fine." • Self-corrections: "Never mind," "Forget it," "It wasn't important." • Topic shifts or deflections. • Minimizing micro-criticisms: "You're exaggerating," "This is stupid." • Mechanical tone; reduced emotionality while staying oriented and present
SHAME ENFORCER	• Contempt, sarcasm, or insult directed inward: "That's pathetic," "You sound ridiculous," "Stop embarrassing us." • Discrediting maneuvers
OSCILATION LOOP CUES	
• The moment a vulnerable disclosure is made, a critical voice cuts in. • After warmth, validation, or closeness, backlash appears (criticism, contempt, or shutdown). • Collapse and attack alternate rapidly: the vulnerable part vanishes, leaving silence or hostility. • The therapist may feel whiplash: "We were close a second ago, and now I'm being pushed out."	

Table 25.1. Shame Loop Cues

WORKING WITH SHAME DYNAMICS

These dynamics can be some of the hardest to stay with. Shame feels contagious; collapse can pull the whole room down, while attack can push the therapist into defense or distance. Neither of these postures are acts of defiance, they are just attempts to regulate unbearable exposure. The therapeutic task is to stay with both so shame is accompanied, not reenacted, avoiding both critic-banishment and wounded-part rescue.

Shame never enters the room politely. It slips in through tone, posture, silence, or a sudden turn toward contempt. A small softening might collapse into stillness; a tender phrase might be met by a sharp cut: "Stop it. You sound pathetic." To the untrained ear, it can sound like hostility or disengagement. In truth, both movements (withdrawal and attack) are shame signals, two ends of the same protective reflex. Recognizing this shift, and naming it gently, is the first step in loosening its hold.

Noticing and Naming the Shift

When shame arrives, it often brings confusion. The therapist may feel suddenly clumsy or disconnected; the client may shrink or turn defensive. These moments call for curiosity rather than repair. A simple, attuned reflection, can open the door without prying it:

- ★ "Something shifted just now, would it feel okay to slow down?"
- ★ "We don't have to talk about it; I just want you to know I noticed."

Such phrases keep both the Shame Carrier and the Enforcer present. They translate rupture into information, and information into safety. The therapist's goal is to signal, "I see this, and I'm not afraid of it." Sometimes that sounds as simple as:

- ★ "I hear how much shame there is."
- ★ "Even if you believe that part is disgusting, I'm still here."

Small sentences that name without rescuing teach the system that exposure does not erase connection.

Translating Criticism into Function

The Shame Enforcer's voice often sounds cruel, but its purpose is almost always protective. What sounds like contempt is an effort to preempt exposure before it happens: "This is pointless." "You're paid to listen." "Stop performing."

Clinical Vignette

After the Compliment

Noticing a struggle right from the beginning of the session, the therapist said, "You worked hard to get here today." The client smiled but a quick small shift, shoulders dipped, eyes lowered. A younger voice barely audible: "Please don't look at me." The Shame Carrier had surfaced. An instant later, a sharper voice cut in: "Stop performing. You're paid to say that." The Shame Enforcer snapped the door shut: jaw set, gaze hard. The therapist did not defend the compliment or pursue disclosure. "I think I'm hearing two jobs at once, one that feels exposed, and one that moves in fast to keep us from humiliation. What just happened?"

The client's breathing quickened; the room went still. The therapist added calmly, "No one's in trouble. It would be nice if we could understand." The Enforcer's tone softened a notch. "She always makes us look weak." The therapist nodded. "So, your job is to make sure no one ever sees that weakness." A pause... long enough for the Carrier to whisper, "It's not weakness; it's just... too much."

The therapist met the space between them rather than either gaze. "Maybe both are right. It *was* too much back then, and protecting made sense. We can stay here and let that be true." A breath loosened. The Carrier didn't vanish; the Enforcer didn't escalate. After a pause, the client said quietly, "That didn't feel as bad as usual."

Clinical Reflections

This moment unfolded through the rhythm of the Shame loop: a flicker of being seen, then an immediate internal shutdown to restore order. What looked like a contradiction (one part shrinking, another striking) was cooperation, both working to keep the system from re-entering the danger of exposure.

The turning point came when the therapist shifted from *correcting* to *translating*, not defending the compliment or insisting on connection but naming what each role was doing. That small move reframed criticism from defiance to protection, lowering rank threat and allowing both parts to stay in the room.

When the therapist said, "Maybe both are right", she dismantled the hierarchy that shame depends on. Vulnerability and defense could coexist without either being wrong. The system did not need to collapse or attack to feel safe.

These brief moments, when neither the wound nor the guard has to disappear, begin to loosen the grip of shame. Each repetition teaches the nervous system something new: being seen does not have to lead to humiliation, and protection does not have to mean isolation. Over time, this small coexistence becomes the foundation for dignity; the quiet knowing that both truth and safety can share the same space.

By attacking first, the Enforcer controls humiliation's timing and intensity. Instead of arguing with the content or defending yourself, stay focused on the function:

★ "It sounds like this part is trying to keep the system safe from being embarrassed."
★ "So that harsh part has been doing its job: making sure no one sees weakness."
★ "When did it first learn to do this?"

Each response reframes aggression into protection, lowering the rank threat in the room. The aim is not to persuade but to keep the critic engaged long enough to feel seen without surrendering control. Over time, the critic can begin to be seen not as cruel but as terrified—terrified of collapse, exposure, or losing control. When that shift happens, shame starts to loosen its grip.

Avoid Confrontation or Silencing

Direct confrontation often backfires. It can push the Shame Enforcer into retreat or intensify its aggression, especially when the therapist is perceived as another evaluator. Curiosity, not correction, lowers the threat. Simple questions that signal interest without intrusion, will shift focus from what is wrong to what was once needed.

★ "What might this part be trying to prevent?"
★ "When did it first learn it had to do this job?"

Rather than silencing the critic, invite it to consider whether its methods still work.

★ "Maybe this way of protection was necessary then; I wonder what protection could look like now?"

Even these brief acknowledgments may feel dangerous at first. That is okay. We do not push past shame; we stay near it, letting both the wound and the guard know that we are willing to be with them at their pace.

The therapeutic goal is to create enough space for both to remain present without the system collapsing into silence or attack. This requires equal regard, holding the same respect for the one who hides and the one who polices. The therapist's steadiness balances the alliance: not overprotecting the Carrier, not confronting the Keeper head-on. Presence becomes the intervention.

CLINICAL VIGNETTE

Sitting Beside the Silence

During a session, Daniel was talking about his childhood when he suddenly went quiet, shoulders curling in and gaze fixed on the floor. The therapist noticed the shift but did not press. After a moment, she said softly, "Something feels different right now."

Daniel did not look up, but his breathing slowed. A few minutes later, he murmured, "I don't want you to see me like this." The therapist replied, "I hear that. We can stay here without rushing." No disclosure followed, but the part holding shame had an experience it rarely knew: being met, not managed.

Clinical Reflections

What made this moment therapeutic was the absence of pressure. The therapist stayed present without demanding words or change, allowing the shame-bound part to experience safety in the exact moment it most expected rejection. The work was not in *getting through* but in remaining near, signaling that even in silence and withdrawal, connection was still possible.

Even a few seconds of co-presence between Carrier and Enforcer begin to rewrite the template. The nervous system learns that visibility and protection can coexist, that shame can be shared without annihilation.

Staying with Collapse

If the critic's edge is hard to bear, the Carrier's silence can be equally difficult. Collapse is not absence; it is the body's way of surviving exposure. When the room goes quiet and the gaze drops, the temptation is to fill space or rescue, but presence itself is the intervention.

At time, shame attaches to the act of needing itself. For those whose early care brought humilliation or betrayal, wanting comfort feels perilous. When these parts reach and then recoil, the task is to name both the wish and the fear.

- ★ "Even if it feels dangerous to want right now, we can notice that wish together."

This reframes need as a signal of life, not defect. The part holding shame can experience something entirely new: being met, not managed. The work is not about getting through but about remaining near.

Shame Between Parts

Sometimes shame moves laterally through the system rather than toward the therapist. One part may attack another: "You're weak." "You made it happen." "You're disgusting." These are not random cruelties; they are containment strategies, learned from those who once controlled the child's feelings.

When this happens, the therapist can name the function aloud, without taking sides:

- ★ "It sounds like one part is trying to keep shame in check by blaming another."
- ★ "Maybe that judgment feels safer than feeling what's underneath."

After Disclosure

When the Carrier manages to speak, the Enforcer often surges back in to restore order.

The aftermath can sound like regret, disgust, or sudden distancing:

- ❖ "I shouldn't have said that."
- ❖ "You probably think I'm disgusting."
- ❖ "That was too much."

These reactions are part of the shame loop, not resistance. The therapist can normalize them:

- ★ "That was a lot to share; it makes sense that part of you feels exposed now."
- ★ "It sounds like another part came in to check for danger."

The task here is to hold the recoil as tenderly as the disclosure itself, to treat backlash as a continuation of the work, not its undoing. Over time, the system learns: "I can speak and still be held."

The Therapist's Core Position

Across all these moments, the therapist's stance remains the same: steady, non-defensive, and attuned to both sides. Presence is the primary intervention. Shame cannot be talked out of existence; it can only be survived in company. The therapist who can stay with both collapse and attack communicates the message the system most needs to learn: "Even here, with shame and contempt, I'm not leaving."

In practice, that means resisting the impulse to explain, reassure, or correct. Logic does not melt shame; accompaniment does. Each time the therapist remains calm in the face of what feels defective or unlovable, a new association forms: shame no longer equals isolation. The system begins to test that new rule tentatively—first for seconds, then minutes—until both Carrier and Enforcer learn they can coexist in the presence of another.

These moments, brief and quiet, are what slowly re-ink the tattoo of shame. They do not erase its lines but trace new ones: connection, safety, dignity.

Making Meaning After Cooperation

When the loop begins to soften, the work shifts from crisis management to meaning-making. Shame does not vanish the moment the critic quiets or the collapse lifts; it lingers like a reflex, waiting for the next moment of exposure. What changes is the system's relationship to that reflex. Where once shame triggered attack or disappearance, it can now invite awareness and cooperation.

In session, this often appears in small but unmistakable ways: a client who once disappeared at the first hint of embarrassment may now pause and say, "It's happening again." That pause is the new capacity—the space where reflection replaces reflex. The therapist's task is to recognize these moments not as minor, but as evidence of integration.

Each pause where the Carrier does not vanish and the Enforcer does not strike is a new procedural memory: "I can be seen and not destroyed." Shame can exist in the presence of another without humiliation; protection can happen without harm. These moments may last only seconds, a breath held, a softened tone, a sigh, but they begin to install a different rule in the body: exposure no longer equals annihilation. Moments after a disclosure, shame often surges again; the Enforcer rushing back to restore order with minimization or disgust. These aftershocks are part of the loop, not relapse. Holding them with the same calm acknowledgment prevents the system from mistaking exposure for danger once more:

★ "That was a lot to share; it makes sense something inside wants to pull back."

Between sessions, clients can be invited to notice when the loop appears, not to stop it but to map it: "I felt small, then the attack came in, then I went quiet." Tracking the sequence builds recognition, and recognition creates room for choice. Over time, these moments accumulate into a new internal order. The Shame Carrier still feels the ache, and the Keeper still watches the edges, but they begin to orient around shared survival rather than opposition.

What began as a reflexive containment strategy becomes a conversation. And in that conversation, something larger than shame begins to take shape; a sense of worth that does not depend on perfection or invisibility, but on being met, known, and stayed with. The task is not to solve shame in one leap, but to stay near it long enough for the system to learn: shame can be carried together, not weaponized alone.

CLOSING THOUGHTS

Shame thrives in isolation and in the voices that repeat old harm. It feeds on silence, secrecy, and the belief that what was done, felt, or needed makes one unworthy of connection. In dissociative systems, shame is not peripheral, it is central. Often what looks like shutting down is tonic alertness, a body held still to contain humiliation.

The therapist´s task is not to erase shame or silence the critic, but to bring them into a relationship: Where shame can be held rather than hidden and protection can happen without harm.

The Carrier teaches us the depth of the wound; the Blocker shows how safety was kept by staying small and unseen; the Enforcer shows us the cost of hiding it. Healing happens when all three are met without rejection, so none of them have to hold their post alone.

Clinical Anchors

What to remember...

- Treat criticism as a strategy. The enforcer's attacks are often misguided protection against the carrier's vulnerability and shame.
- Remember that behind harsh thoughts and inner voices is often a terrified part trying to prevent humiliation, rejection, or chaos.
- Meet criticism with curiosity about the intention; explore what it´s trying to prevent rather than challenging its content.
- Remember the trauma blueprint. Critical parts often replicate voices of powerful or shaming figures from the past.
- Move slowly when inviting the enforcer to consider new options; its method may need updating but its purpose is protective.
- Support internal bridges. Help other parts of the system recognize the enforcer's function without collapsing into agreement or blame.
- Support the development of constructive internal feedback.

What to avoid...

- Confronting the Enforcer directly, since it can lead to escalation or withdrawal. We cannot heal criticism with more criticism.
- Correcting shame with logic or reassurance. Shame is not cognitive but embodied
- Treating contempt, sarcasm or hostility as defiance; these are protective strategies.
- Using warmth without pacing; sudden closeness can trigger shame.
- Mistake collapse, silence or stillness for disengagement; these often signal shame-based protection (including sympathetic freeze).
- Treating shame as an obstacle to bypass; it is the work.

Chapter 26: De-Escalating Self-Destructive Dynamics Between Parts

Therapist Reflection

Sometimes the most dangerous dynamics in a dissociative system are not between the client and the outside world, but within the system itself. These moments can feel like the therapy room has become a battleground, one part holding unbearable despair, another attacking with relentless cruelty. If I can remember that all roles are trying, in their own way, to prevent collapse, I can approach them without taking sides. My goal is not to silence either, but to help them see that they don't have to keep fighting alone.

In many dissociative systems, internal conflict manifests somatically, behaviorally, and at times in overtly physically or violent ways. As explored throughout Part 2, parts may turn against one another through critical thoughts, insults, intrusive urges, self-harming behaviors, or suicidality.

In this chapter we map the highest-risk inner conflict—where despair, attack, and self-harm interlock. The aim is to recognize the pattern early, name each function without taking sides, and swap coercion for procedures that restore choice.

While clients experience many internal dynamics as profoundly limiting, some carry a far higher level of severity and risk. In the previous chapter we examined the tandem between shame-bound parts:, a pattern that, while frightening for clients, is often more accessible to understand and work with than the dynamics involving suicidality or severe self-harm.

This chapter focuses on recognizing, understanding, and de-escalating inner conflicts that lead to physical danger, most often involving a pairing between suicidal or self-harming parts and hostile, aggressive, or perpetrator-identified parts, often joined by a third role that uses harm as fast regulation. In practice, these three roles often travel together.

UNDERSTANDING SELF-DESTRUCTIVE DYNAMICS

Self-destructive dynamics are not expressions of madness or moral failure; they are complex survival strategies born in conditions where helplessness, exposure, and secrecy had to be managed from the inside. Safety required controlling what could not be stopped. What looks like self-attack is often the body's last language for maintaining coherence when safety once depended on internal control. To understand these patterns, we have to read them in context, not as isolated behaviors, but as the system's attempt to balance pain, loyalty, and survival in an impossible ecology.

Origins of the Dynamic

This pattern takes root in an ecology of danger where threat is chronic and escape impossible. With no protector and no exit, control must turn inward. Visibility brings humiliation or punishment, so pain is hidden and invisibility becomes safer than comfort. Care arrives only when it is earned through obedience, performance, or silence. Betrayal hides beneath the promise of help, teaching that hope itself is perilous. Rules are enforced through shame and pain, creating a punitive order where rank outweighs repair. Loyalty means secrecy; suffering privately becomes a way to belong. In a world without safe adults, the system learns to pre-empt harm by mastering it from within, replaying what was done, silencing what feels too much, and mistaking self-punishment for safety. That logic was once adaptive, but it continues to run on the frozen rules of trauma time.

From these conditions emerge a set of internal survival laws designed to keep the system intact.

- **Contain pain** so it does not overwhelm the system.
- **Mistrust hope,** because hoping for rescue or change often led to betrayal or more pain.
- **Preempt punishment** by punishing from the inside before anyone else can.

Under such conditions, self-harm functions as an internal safety system: one position collapses under despair, another imposes control, and a third offers fast discharge to keep the day moving. Before naming the specific roles, notice that these presentations are patterned, relational responses inside the system, not isolated urges. The subsections that follow trace where this arrangement comes from, which roles enact it, and why it persists, so we can preserve the purpose (survival) while updating the method (same purpose, safer means).

Core Roles in This Dynamic

In most dissociative systems, self-destructive pressure does not live in one part alone. It is distributed across roles that formed where danger, helplessness, and secrecy were constant. Three role blueprints crystallize from those conditions. Over time these strategies became automatic—not because they work now, but because they once felt like the only way to keep going.

- **The Despair Holder** carries unbearable frozen pain, hopelessness and self-hatred from moments when escape felt impossible; so these emotions feel final and inescapable. It holds the conviction that there is no way out, sometimes seeing death as the only possible relief. It learned that showing pain invited punishment or abandonment, so it carries the weight quietly. This role overlaps with suicidal parts (chapter 19); the pull is toward ending, collapse, or shutdown when all other strategies have failed.
- **The Punisher** meets that despair not with comfort but with force. Echoing past aggressors and shaming figures, it attacks, silences, or hardens against weakness to stop despair from spreading through the system. Its stance says: control exposure or be destroyed. It shares traits with hostile or aggressive parts (chapter 14): hostility fuses with fear of what might happen if despair becomes visible.
- **The Harm Reducer** learned that focused physical pain can blunt diffuse overload and avert a worse outcome. So, it proposes or commands self-injury as a fast, controllable discharge to keep the system moving and prevent escalation between the Despair Holder and the Punisher. It brokers a temporary truce that lowers immediate lethality but may later trigger shame if punitive parts are watching.

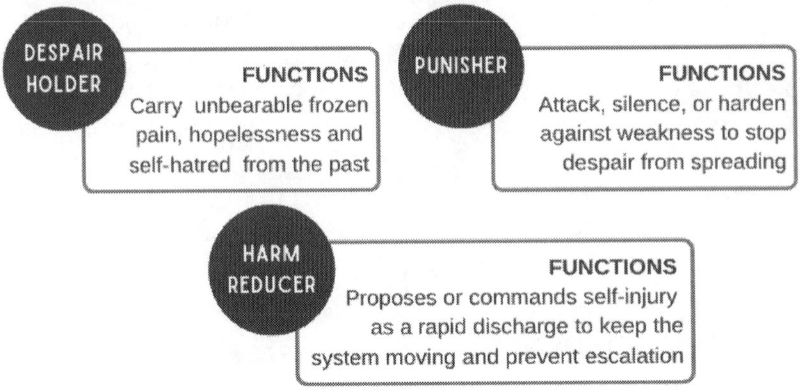

Fig. 26.1. The Self-Destructive Loop roles

Together, these three roles form a closed circuit learned in trauma time: one holds the pain, another guards the perimeter with dominance, and a third provides high-cost relief when tension spikes. What looks like opposition is cooperation in survival logic; an internal economy to contain threat, prevent humiliation, and keep functioning with whatever tools were available then. All three believe they are protecting the system; the logic made sense when danger felt current and absolute.

The Self-Destructive Loop

In most systems, suicidal or self-destructive pressure emerges from the interaction of roles that have become tightly locked together. A volatile high-risk pairing places a part carrying unbearable pain, opposite a part that responds with attack, silencing, or contempt. This pairing is often interrupted or joined by a third role that proposes rapid relief through harm (Harm Reducers).

This triad shares structural similarities with the Shame dynamic from chapter 25:, where one absorbs unbearable affect and others guard to prevent spread. Here a third role adds a high-cost exit. The pattern self-tightens: the more despair the Despair Holder expresses, the harsher the Punisher becomes; the harsher the attack, the deeper the despair. As pressure peaks, the Harm Reducer offers injury to decrease it, briefly quieting the system while often adding shame that re-seeds the next round.

What distinguishes this configuration is intensity: the stakes are higher, the tone more volatile, and the consequences immediately dangerous.

Clients conflate the three roles, hearing one voice where three jobs are being done, so early differentiation is essential.

This is also why the loop accelerates. The Despair Holder's hopelessness triggers the Punisher's alarm. Despair is read as dangerous: it could slow the system, draw unwanted attention or pity, or invite harm. The Punisher moves in with attack or suppression, which reactivates the Despair Holder's core wound ("I am unworthy, unlovable"), deepening withdrawal and despair. As pressure peaks, the Harm Reducer pushes toward self-injury to regain control. The sequence is swift and punishing: hopelessness fuels attack → attack intensifies hopelessness → urges surge; without an update, the cycle can spiral toward acute self-harm or suicidal risk.

When these three roles interlock, they generate a fast, self-reinforcing circuit. What looks like open war is coordinated survival: one part carries collapse, another imposes control, a third offers rapid discharge to keep the system moving. All three are protectors, running trauma-time procedures to prevent overwhelm. The mission is shared, preserve safety, the methods differ.

When the loop becomes activated, you will see the following pattern:

1. **Despair signals.** A hopeless, exhausted current surfaces: flat voice, folded posture, language: "I can't do this anymore." "There's no point.".
2. **Punisher clamps down.** A sharp, contempt-laced voice cuts in to stop the spread—"Shut up." "Just do it." "You're useless."—with a spike of internal pressure and urgency. If this works the loop continues, if not, the next step is needed.
3. **Harm-Reducer proposes discharge.** Cool, procedural instructions arrive to reduce intensity quickly: urges or plans for self-injury (or other high-cost strategies) framed as "the only thing that works".
4. **Brief relief.** A short, numbed quiet follows; attention narrows, physiology settles just enough. The system reads this as regained control.
5. **Backlash/shame.** Disgust, self-blame, or renewed attack floods in, re-seeding collapse ("Pathetic." "You made it worse.")

6. **Reset to despair.** The hopeless current returns, convinced there is no other exit, setting up the next pass through the circuit.

If therapists can understand this as a containment loop, it becomes easier to keep all three roles in the room without siding. Despair is accompanied (so it does not drown); attack is translated as protection (so it can stand down without losing control); and the harm-reduction function is updated toward rapid, reversible, non-injurious procedures. When the Punisher's edge softened, the Despair did not vanish, it was held. Naming both as parts of one loop turned attack into pacing, not punishment.

The diagram below shows how this loop plays out in real time, and how procedure, not persuasion, let us all three stay present without collapse, attack, or injury. A surge of despair triggers internal alarm; the Punisher moves in to crush or contain it; the Harm-Reducer intervenes with self-injury to discharge pressure and restore brief control. Relief fades, shame returns, and despair rises again. Naming the sequence turns it from reflex to relationship and makes procedural safety possible.

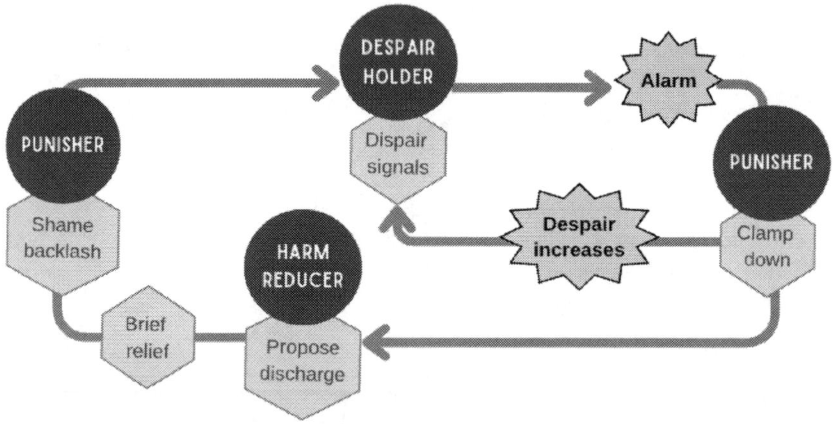

Fig. 26.2. The Self-Destructive Loop

Motivational Systems Organizing This Loop

Two motivational systems drive and organize this loop: defense and rank/power. These systems are activated in opposite directions across roles, creating the high-risk choreography we see in session.

- **Defense** mobilizes across extremes. In the Despair Holder, it appears as collapse and shutdown. In the Punisher, it takes the form of attack and coercive control., In the Harm Reducer, defense operates through rapid discharge using pain or injury to interrupt unbearable arousal. The body oscillates between shutting down, striking out, and releasing tension to prevent total overwhelm. Client language often reflects this defensive logic: "If I stop fighting, I'll disappear." "If I don't hurt, it will explode." "I just need it to stop for a second."
- **Rank/power** replicates dominance–submission dynamics within the system. The Punisher assumes authority to contain chaos through domination, harsh evaluation, and command. The Despair Holder occupies the submissive pole, expressing down-ranking through collapse, appeasement, or disappearance. In some personality systems, the Harm Reducer enforces compliance through pain, restoring order through control rather than care. The inner language here is sharp and hierarchical: "Get up." "You're pathetic." "We don't cry here."

At the surface, the loop appears as a battle between despair, aggression, and self-harm. Underneath, these procedures share a common goal, to prevent psychological annihilation. Each response—collapse, attack, discharge—once functioned to preserve the system under conditions of inescapable threat. When external danger subsides but the pattern remains, protection itself becomes the threat.

The loop completes when brief relief is achieved through control or injury, followed by shame and renewed despair. Over time, this sequence becomes proceduralized: regulation is sought through domination or pain rather than through relationship. In this loop, the Punisher occupies the rank/dominance position, imposing control, silencing vulnerability, while the Despair Holder expresses rank/submission through collapse and appeasement. The shame backlash typically intensifies within the Punisher, escalating attack as a means of restoring order and preventing exposure.

Attachment is inhibited. Closeness risks exposure, pity, rejection, or loss of control; as a result, attachment does not function as a regulatory pathway within the loop. Help is avoided, care is mistrusted, and regulation occurs without relationship. The absence of attachment as an organizing system is central to the loop's rigidity.

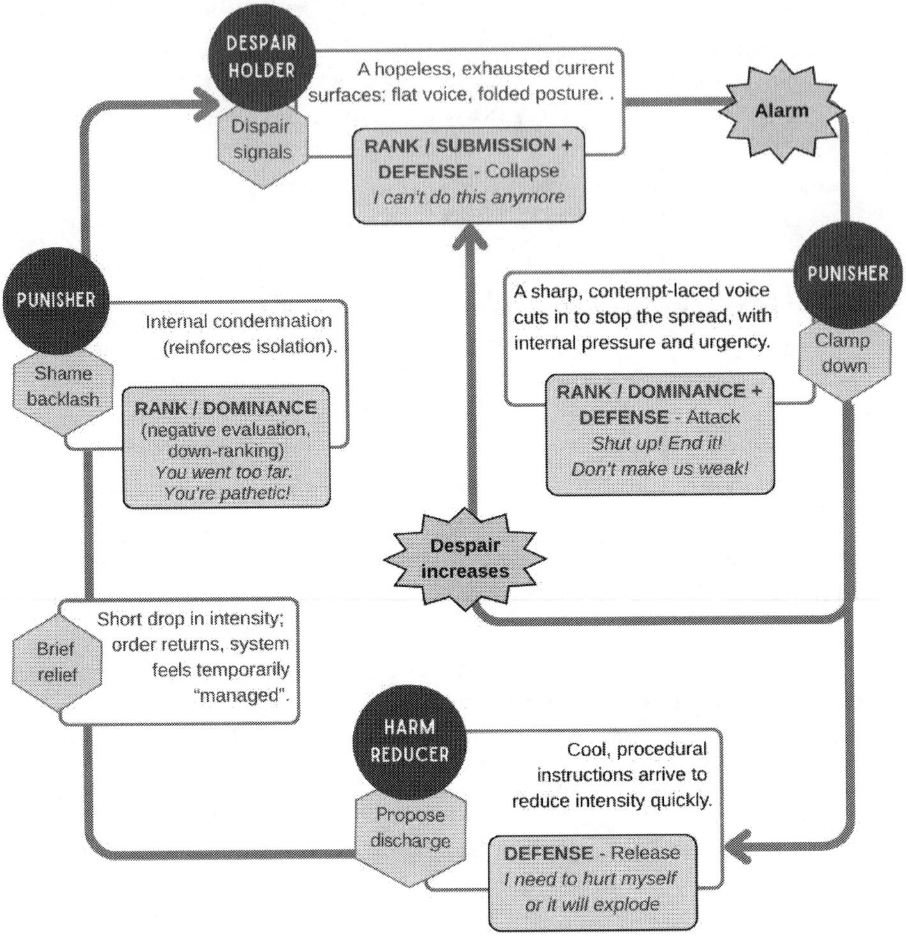

Fig. 26.3. Motivational systems organizing the Self-Destructive Loop

Although **caregiving** is not an active motivational system organizing this loop, some defensive parts might borrow the language and posture of care. In some personality systems, the Harm Reducer may speak in a reassuring or even gentle tone: "This will help," "You'll feel better." Its function is not destruction but relief. When external soothing was unavailable or unsafe, rapid discharge through injury or pain became the body's fastest regulator. Defense, in these cases can adopt caregiving language without enacting caregiving functions.

When care was historically paired with pain, injury, or control, the caregiving system itself can become distorted, offering harm as a means of relief. Clinically, recognizing this protective intention behind these actions is essential for de-escalation. When the part's aim is understood as relief rather than punishment, the work can shift from suppressing impulses to negotiating safer ways to achieve regulation and care.

Naming the underlying motivational systems helps shift the work from moral correction to procedural re-organization, so that protection can emerge through connection, and control can give way to choice.

RECOGNIZING THE DYNAMICS

The shift between the Despair Holder and the Punisher can be subtle or feel like getting caught in a riptide, pulled sharply from collapse into attack. A third current, the Harm-Reducer, often rises quietly underneath, offering self-injury as the only way to break the tension. Recognizing these cues allows you to name what is happening and slow the sequence before it gains strength.

The flip can be fast: despair to attack in seconds. This oscillation *is* the loop. Hopelessness triggers alarm; alarm triggers attack; the attack deepens hopelessness. As the stalemate tightens, the Harm-Reducer steps in, proposing self-harm as a rapid, controllable exit.

The visible oscillation is the back-and-forth between despair and attack; the Harm-Reducer is the third strand running beneath them, emerging when the system feels trapped and out of options.

NON-VERBAL CUES	
DESPAIR HOLDER	• Collapsed posture • Slowed movements • Visible withdrawal from engagement.
PUNISHER	• Sneering or contemptuous tone • Sharp interruptions • Eye-rolls • A sudden surge in internal pressure to do something about it, often encouraging acts on self-harm or suicidal urges.
HARM REDUCER	• Attentional narrowing • Scanning for privacy • Hands returning to habitual body areas • Brief self-directed pressure or contact • Purposeful movement toward a secluded space • Discreet clothing checks (e.g., sleeves) • Breathing evens out and a detached, "clinical" affect may appear as the plan consolidates.
VERBAL CUES (OR VOICES INSIDE)	
DESPAIR HOLDER	• Flat or monotone voice • "It will never get better," "I just want it to end," "I can't do this anymore."
PUNISHER	• "I am pathetic" (Adult Self) • "You're pathetic," (Punisher) • "Just do it," "Stop whining," "You deserve it."
HARM REDUCER	• "I need to hurt myself" or through voice: "Pinch yourself and it'll quiet." • "Two minutes and we can function" • "Ice/cold water/pressure first." (when new resources are learned) • Calm, procedural, often solution-sounding.
OSCILATION LOOP CUES	
• Sudden collapse or heaviness is quickly followed by an internal "snap" of urgency or contempt. • The body folds inward (despair), then straightens or hardens (attack). • A flat, hopeless voice shifts rapidly into sharp, commanding self-criticism. • Despair activates the Punisher; attack intensifies despair (each escalating the other). • A spike of internal pressure accompanies messages such as "Do it. Now." • Attention then narrows into a calm, procedural "fix" focused on self-harm as relief. • Energy shifts from heaviness → sharp attack → controlled, solution-focused narrowing	

Table 26.1. Self-Destructive Loop Cues

WORKING WITH THE DYNAMIC

When these sequences rise in the room, most therapists feel the pull to act, to stop the behavior, stabilize the system, guarantee safety. Containment matters, but translation matters just as much. If we can hold the whole exchange as a containment strategy in trauma time rather than a fight between enemies, we can keep everyone present long enough to update the method without robbing any role of its purpose. Begin with:

★ "What is this move trying to protect?"
★ "From what?"
★ "With which tools?"
★ "What is the purpose?"

Here, as mentioned before, the stakes are higher, and the protective strategies are more extreme. But if you can see this loop as a containment strategy rather than a battle of opposites, it becomes possible to slow it, name it, and begin to reintroduce choice into what once felt automatic. Naming the full circuit: despair → attack → self-harm → brief quiet → shame → renewed despair lets us intervene at multiple points, not only at the poles of despair or attack.

Clinical Vignette

When Attack Replaces Help

Halfway through a session, a part spoke quietly: "I'm tired of trying. Nothing ever changes." Another voice cut in, cold: "You don't deserve to live. All you do is whine. You're dead weight." The client folded inward, eyes on the floor.

The therapist resisted defending the Despair Holder or scolding the Punisher: "I hear one part drowning in hopelessness, and another moving in to make sure it does not take over. Can we slow this down and make some room for both?" The Punisher scoffed but stayed; the Despair Holder stayed too, silent, but present. The storm quieted enough for the work to continue. The Harm-Reducer's urge to self-injure was present as background pressure, offering a quick exit from the stalemate.

Clinical Reflections

Everything was routed through the Adult Self. Naming both aims equalized rank and kept the room from splitting into rescuer and scolder ("One part is drowning in hopelessness; another is trying to stop collapse."). That stance framed despair as a *signal* and attack as a *protection strategy*, which lowered the humiliation threat enough for both parts to stay present.

The Harm-Reducer was acknowledged as a safety plan rather than a threat, which kept it consultable instead of forcing it underground.

How to Help the Process of De-Escalation

The task is not simply to manage crises in the usual ways we might with less acute situations, but to learn how to hear the parts for which violence has become the only available language. By understanding the complex combinations of protections forged in chaos, we create the possibility for new, safer relational patterns to emerge, both within the system and in the client's relationships with others.

When you can recognize the pattern as it unfolds, you can slow the pace, name the different roles without judgment, and begin to redirect the energy from polarization toward co-presence.

Making Meaning of Internal Conflict After De-Escalation

When the heat drops, the work is not finished, it changes shape. Self-harming or suicidal urges often erupt before there is time to think; having worked with de-escalation is the beginning of new templates and also buys us a little space. What we do with that space matters. The aim now is to **install a pause** the system can find next time; enough room for the Adult Self to breathe, for parts to be heard, and for choice to become imaginable.

In session, we practice the essentials: we name the roles without taking sides, **slow the pace** enough so it can be followed, translate attack into protection, and hold a dual focus so despair and alarm can coexist. Sometimes, if the ground feels steady enough, we invite a moment of curiosity between parts, one sentence, then stop. These are not techniques to check off; they change the tone of the room. Used together, they gradually teach the system that intensity can be *accompanied*, not obeyed.

With practice, that tone becomes a template to recall and use in between sessions. There are multiple ways to help the pause become available, using basic skills such as practicing **time-orientation** and simple **sensory anchors** help parts relocate in the present. For example: two things the body can feel (feet on the floor, cool air on the face) and one fact that belongs only to now (the date on the calendar, the color of the therapist's sweater, the name on the door) model what the client can do at home.

Since urges are messages, we invite the client to **name the urge** the way they would note a weather pattern: "A squall of 'end it now' arrived at 11:40 after the text from my brother", and to track what preceded it. This is very useful information for therapy, and it helps clients focus on the work they are practicing with us during sessions.

Some systems also benefit from installing a small **buffer**: a brief "cooling-off room" inside or a five-minute delay practice paired with a pre-chosen action (cold water on wrists, weighted blanket, stepping to the doorway). The goal is to give the nervous system something procedural to find when words and rational thinking are not easy to access.

CLINICAL VIGNETTE

It Was Her Fault

In one session, a client's Despair Holder whispered: "I can't do this anymore." Immediately, the Punisher stepped in shouting in her head: "Just fucking end it now." As she spoke, the therapist noticed tightening in her jaw and a sharp shift in posture. When asked what just happened, the client reported a voice telling her she should die and fear of acting on it.

Once the dynamic was identified, and after exploring the conflict, the therapist understood a protective part had been activated in response to the expression of despair. She reflected tentatively, acknowledging both positions: "Something just shifted. "One part sounds exhausted, and another seems to being trying to take control of how this ends."

By framing both positions as protective, the therapist avoided making either part the villain. Over time, the Punisher shifted from demanding and ending to warning against shame: "We ended up in the ICU last time,"

Clinical Reflections

When real caregiving was not available, parts used whatever the motivational systems allowed to approximate protection. In this example, the therapist did not identify the internal dynamic by certainty, but by tracking observable shifts (changes in tone, posture, and urgency), and exploring with the client what was happening inside.

Naming both roles without taking sides, slowing the pace, shifting from content to function created a procedural break. This allowed the Punisher to articulate concern, gradually updating its job and tolerating ambivalence. Notice the change to "we" by the punisher part, signaling the beginning of a more collaborative stance.

Relational reflection that supports listening can help:

- ★ "If this part could wait five minutes before acting, what might it want you to understand?"
- ★ "Could we create a plan together that allows this part to be acknowledged and think of other options, even if we don't agree with the action?"

These questions do not solve the loop, but they loosen it. They invite the system to move from reflex to dialogue, to support internal negotiation and slow automatic reactions.

CLINICAL VIGNETTE

I'm Just Keeping Us Safe

Partway into a session, Anna's voice softened: "Maybe it would be easier if I wasn't here." She stared down at her hands. Before the therapist could respond, her tone snapped sharp: "Oh, for God's sake, stop. You don't deserve to waste her time." The therapist named both positions without judgment: "It sounds like one part is exhausted and another is furious about that." Then reframed their shared goal: "It seems like both are trying, in different ways, to stop something from hurting even more."

This slowed the exchange and shifted it from attack to shared protection. Anna exhaled, still tense but more present. In prior weeks, a Harm-Reducer had proposed injury to "make the noise stop". Naming its usual role helped de-polarize the exchange even when it did not speak in the room.

Clinical Reflections

The therapist did not argue with the content or pick a side. By naming both positions without judgment and reframing them as two strategies trying to prevent more pain, she lowered the temperature in the room. That small shift (from "who's right" to "what each is protecting") let both parts stay present long enough to feel seen and heard. With the attack no longer needed to silence the despair, Anna could exhale and remain in co-presence, and the system experienced a brief, corrective moment: vulnerability could exist without humiliation, and protection did not require harm.

Post-crisis backlash

Backlash is common after a crisis, other parts often surge with anger, disgust, or heavy shame. The Adult Self may blame the one who acted and the other way around. This is trauma-time logic, old rules springing back to keep control. Our job is to reframe the backlash as part of the legacy, not proof of failure. These post-crisis reactions reinforce isolation and disrupt internal cooperation. Left unaddressed, they increase the risk of future ruptures. As therapist, you can help reframe these dynamics as part of the system's trauma legacy:

- ★ "What did this part believe it was protecting you from?"
- ★ "Are there other parts who feel concerned or afraid about what happened?"
- ★ "If there are, can we help them communicate and listen to them too, not to punish or argue, but to understand?"
- ★ "Could those parts speak to each other briefly, no arguing, just naming concerns?"

As the conversation shifts from *culprit* to *function*, the rank/power spike softens, the defense system downshifts, and an update of the caregiving strategy (often distorted in the Punisher) can emerge. Same purpose, safer method.

CLINICAL VIGNETTE

Five-Minute Truce

Near the end of the hour, Eli's voice thinned. "I can't do this anymore." Shoulders folded, eyes emptied. The Despair Holder had surfaced. Before the therapist could speak, the inner Punisher snapped in, sharp and fast: "Then end it. Now." Breath hard, jaw set. A third current rose under the noise—cool, procedural, almost calm: "Two minutes and it will quiet." The Harm-Reducer had stepped forward with its familiar exit: self-harm as a quick, controllable release.

The therapist waited, sensing the inner shift. "What just happened?" Eli said quietly, "They're fighting again." The therapist kept her voice steady. "It seems there are three jobs happening here: one drowning, one taking over, one offering a fast fix. I'm not choosing sides. Would a five-minute truce be possible—no actions, just noticing—so we can decide together?"

Silence. Then Eli said, "He says: 'Five. Not six.'" "Five", the therapist agreed. "I'll keep time. You both can hold the stop signal. If you say stop, I stop within one second." They set the timer. The therapist offered one sentence toward the despair, not into it: "I'm here; we won't let you drown." She named the Harm-Reducer's pull without arguing: "I feel that urge offering relief. We'll log it; we're not acting during the truce."

At two minutes, Eli's hands unclenched. At three, his eyes lifted for a moment, then dropped. At four-thirty, the Punisher muttered, "Fine. Enough." The therapist stopped before the bell. "We're done for now. No one got erased. No one got forced."

Eli exhaled—a shaky, surprised sound. "It's quieter", he said. After a beat, softer: "Maybe next time... another five." The Punisher didn't object. The Harm-Reducer went dim, not gone—parked where it could be consulted rather than obeyed.

Clinical Reflections

This moment unfolded as the Self-Destructive loop so often does—swift, fierce, and layered. A small signal of collapse, then a flash of control, then the quiet pull toward an exit that promises relief. What looks like chaos from the outside is, inside the system, an old sequence replaying itself exactly as it was designed to: despair rises, the Punisher strikes to prevent exposure or helplessness, and the Harm-Reducer steps in to contain the aftermath. Each role is doing the job it learned to do.

The therapist did not challenge content or argue with logic. She changed from ordinary conversation to procedure. By inviting a time-bound truce, she translated unbearable affect into a sequence that could be measured, shared, and ended safely. The timer became proof that control could exist without annihilation. When the therapist stopped before the bell, the system learned something new—not that despair can be erased, but that it can be endured without violence.

What shifted the dynamic was not comfort or persuasion, but structure. Predictability replaced panic; the parts could stay in the same room without one erasing the other. The Despair Holder could exist without being crushed. The Punisher could protect without destroying. The Harm Reducer, usually the first responder, could stand down and observe.

Each repetition of this small experiment rewires expectation: that a surge of hopelessness need not end in harm, that control can be shared, that endings can be chosen. Over time, these procedural moments accumulate into a new internal law—safety does not require punishment; pain can be held, not silenced.

This vignette shows how self-destructive pressure can be transformed, not by insight alone, but by procedure that makes safety tangible. Once the loop was named and time was shared, the system no longer had to choose between collapse, control, or harm. Each role stayed in view long enough for its purpose to be understood. What was once a reflex became a rhythm the therapist and client could monitor together. The same choreography (despair, attack, urge) remained, but its tempo slowed, its outcome changed. From here, we can map the sequence more precisely and see how each role contributes to maintaining, and eventually loosening, the circuit.

Facilitating these conversations shifts the goal from crisis control and conflict to relational cooperation, collaboration, and understanding, sometimes even compassion. The system begins to realize there are other options; there is a new path built on curiosity, regulation, dialogue, and trust that can be opened and followed with help. This is how the move from impulsive reactions to collaborative repair begins. Chapter 31 will offer more tools to work with post-crisis situations.

CLOSING THOUGHTS

De-escalation means giving each role a job it can keep without harm. Despair is named and accompanied so it does not drown the system. Attack is translated into protection so it can stand down without losing control. Harm-reduction is updated from injury to rapid, reversible procedures that preserve speed, predictability, privacy, and control.

When all three are recognized and resourced, the loop loosens: spikes shorten, attacks soften, and the system learns exits other than injury or death. The aim is not to erase urges overnight, but to change what happens first. When all roles are seen, respected, and given space, the storm can quiet, not because one of them wins, but because they all realize they no longer have to fight alone.

CLINICAL ANCHORS

WHAT TO REMEMBER...

- All roles are protectors; one holds pain, another manages it through control or attack, and the Harm-Reducer keeps the system going at all costs.
- Suicide talk here is often about ending intolerable states, not about dying.
- Naming the shared protective purpose reduces polarization.
- Curiosity and pacing work better than persuasion or logic.

WHAT TO AVOID...

- Interpreting suicidal content only as resistance.
- Trying to eliminate the Punisher before it has a new protective role
- Siding exclusively with one part. Especially, allying only with the Despair Holder risks escalating the punisher's hostility.
- Confronting the punisher directly often intensifies its attacks or leads to withdrawal.
- Moving too quickly to bridge them may overwhelm the system and increase internal threat perception.

Chapter 27: Bond Shaped Dynamics Between Parts

THERAPIST REFLECTION

There are sessions when vulnerability glints for a second—a small voice, a softening in the eyes, an impulse to smile—and, just as quickly, a hard voice slams the door: "Stop it. Don't you dare." Early on, I chased the glint of vulnerability and lost the room. Now, I ask the enforcer for permission first. If I remember that its job is to keep danger out, including me, I can move slowly enough for everyone to stay.

As we continue exploring the inner dynamics that lock systems into conflict, we turn now to another common pairing: younger parts that carry longing, need, and early memory, and perpetrator-identified parts that watch over them to keep danger at bay.

The central problem in this arrangement is access: whether the system permits or forbids closeness to younger parts that are vulnerable and in need of contact (who grants access, on what terms, and how quickly contact must stop). Once access is negotiable, the question shifts from whether closeness can exist, to how it is kept.

This is the main reason why inner child work can backfire if attempted too soon. To work safely with younger parts, the therapist must first collaborate with the protector side (earning permission, modeling brakes and boundaries, and orienting the system to the present) so that approaching younger parts does not trigger retaliatory shutdown or attack.

UNDERSTANDING THE DYNAMIC

Before naming roles, it helps to widen the frame. What can look like a contradiction, one side reaching, another shutting it down, is survival choreography. When proximity and danger were fused, protection and longing learned to move together. The task is to see the pattern, not a personality. Access without permission reads as risk, so the system keeps closeness costly or out of reach.

Origins of This Dynamic

This dynamic is common in histories where genuine connection and care are not possible and survival depended on following rules and adapting to what is expected, staying close to someone dangerous while terrified. Identification with power (the perpetrator) and their world view becomes a way to preserve predictability within an extremely complicated and incoherent connection.. Over time the system can flip the narrative to achieve some control from "I was hurt" to "I am the one who hurts", shielding against helplessness while silencing the young parts that still seek care (see chapter 13).

The system learns three basic rules:

- **Obey to live.** Submission, not relationship, reduced harm.
- **Need is dangerous.** Requests, comfort-seeking, and spontaneity drew punishment, sometimes also ridicule and humiliation (mixed with punishment and blame).
- **Truth is incendiary.** Naming harm threatened the hierarchy and invited retaliation. To distort the meaning of harm and take on all the blame is the best way to survive.

Under these conditions, proximity had to be controlled, not pursued. The body kept life going by suppressing signals of need, tightening control at the first hint of softness, and enforcing inherited rules ("Don't feel, don't need, don't tell"). Over time, the mind may flip the story from "I was overpowered" to "I keep order", a rank move that preserves coherence by identifying with enforcement rather than helplessness. Inner child work can therefore backfire if contact is attempted before conditions are negotiated; unsanctioned access reads as breach of order, not care.

Core Roles in this Dynamic

Under the previous conditions, the system protects life by monitoring access to younger, need-carrying parts while keeping the world predictable. In this configuration three roles tend to organize the work:

- The **Bond Seeker** holds muted attachment needs, longing and grief that were forbidden to show. It signals unmet needs and orients toward contact. When it stirs, the signals are small (hesitation, a quick glance, a barely audible wish) because the system remembers that visibility drew punishment. It orients toward contact only if there are brakes, clear rules, and the option to stop *immediately*.

- The **Bond Blocker** is the first line of inhibition. It shows up fast, often before the Bond Seeker has fully reached out. It can sound like a fearful part ("Stop, this is dangerous"), a critical part ("Don't be stupid, you'll regret this"), or a hostile part (insults or contempt that divert attention into internal conflict). Its job is simple and urgent: stop the reach, prevent exposure, keep everyone out of trouble. The Blocker may borrow the tone of more powerful roles, but it is primarily a warning system; a brake, not a judge or enforcer.

- The **Bond Enforcer** is the perpetrator-identified protector. It preserves belonging by enforcing inherited rules and loyalty contracts: "Don't feel, don't need, don't tell." As closeness or arousal rises, it reimposes order: clamps down, issues commands, shames need, redirects to task/obedience. It may recreate dominance to avoid powerlessness, and it enforces secrecy and inherited rules from abusive contexts. None of this is cruelty at its core; it is continuity, keeping the world predictable.

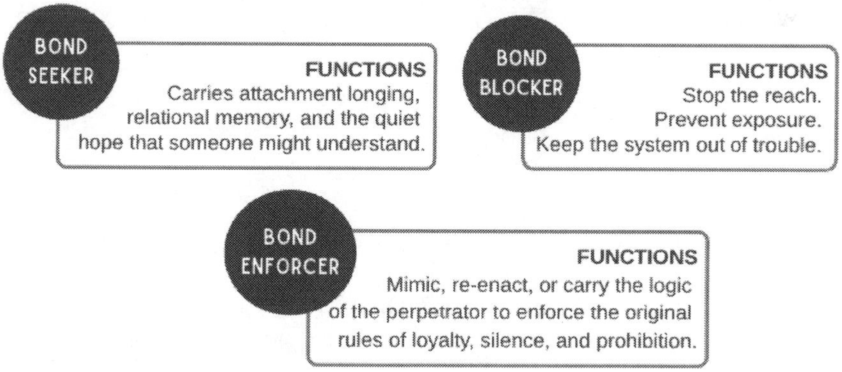

Fig.27.1. The Bond Shaped loop roles

We can picture the Bond Enforcer as a prison guard who was once a prisoner, a metaphor to be used carefully to protect the Bond Seeker's dignity. In practice, the Seeker asks for care while the Bond Blocker tries to stop the reach, and the Bond Enforcer manages the terms of access when the reach has already gone too far. When we honor each role´s jobs, the choreography becomes workable: permission first, then contact, at a pace the system can metabolize.

The Bond Shaped Loop

When the person who controls safety also threatens it, protection and connection must coexist. The system learns to choreograph a sequence: reach → stop → enforce. A small moment of safety or warmth is the trigger. someone appears kind, consistent, or unexpectedly attuned (e.g., a teacher who notices, a therapist who stays, a peer who is gentle). The **Bond Seeker** stirs and orients toward that possibility: "Maybe I could tell a little." "She seems safe."

Almost immediately, the **Bond Blocker** comes online. Its job is urgent: "Stop what you are doing; this will get us in trouble." Depending on the system, it may show up as fear, criticism, or a hostile edge: "Don't you dare." "Stop before you ruin everything."

If the Seeker backs away, the loop ends there: contact is aborted, and the system returns to familiar distance. But when the Seeker still reaches (or even just hopes for connection) despite the Blocker's warning, the **Bond Enforcer** comes into play. Sometimes its *presence* alone is enough to provoke freeze, because parts functioning in daily life still confuse this role with the original perpetrators. Other times it calls up the old rules and prohibitions that keep loyalty in place: "Remember the rules. We don't tell." "How can you betray him? "If you talk, you'll destroy everything." "If you continue, something bad will happen."

At this point, three outcomes tend to emerge:

1. **Freeze-silence-defense based shutdown.** The Seeker collapses into stillness. Contact is aborted through autonomic inhibition. Distance restores safety.
2. **Rule compliance (rank-based submission).** The internal contract reasserts itself. The Seeker does not collapse but retreats into obedient alignment, preserving loyalty through self-erasure.

3. **Inner turbulence (increase in inner conflict or noise).** If the longing remains active, the Enforcer escalates through shame, self-attack, intrusive memories, pulling attention away from external connection into internal conflict.

Across these outcomes, the organizing aim is the same: to prevent the repetition of betrayal. Shutdown reduces exposure. Submission protects by restoring loyalty. Escalation suppresses attachment longing before it is expressed.

The intent of this loop is protection; the effect is isolation. Clinically, this history explains why explicit permission is essential. We acknowledge the Bond Enforcer's protective function, work with the Bond Blocker to establish clear stop-signals, and only then approach younger parts, reducing the likelihood of shutdown or internal retaliation.

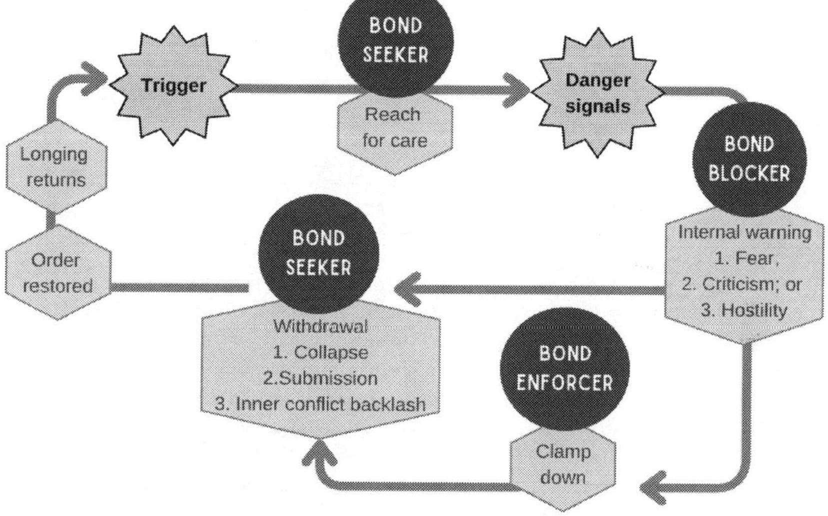

Fig. 27.2. The Bond Shaped loop

To understand the Bond Enforcer's insistence on gates and rules, we must remember betrayal's logic from chapter 24. When care and harm came from the same person, the system learned that closeness equals risk. Divided loyalties, secrecy mandates, and a phobia of telling took root to preserve the bonding. In that environment, the Bond Enforcer's job makes sense: keep doors shut, keep the Bond Seeker unseen, keep the bond—however warped—intact. The Seeker still moves toward care, but those signals summon the Bond Blocker or Bond Enforcer to prevent exposure, retaliation, or loss of belonging.

In these conditions, the Bond Enforcer learns to protect by replicating the perpetrator's logic and mimicking the very own behaviors that created it: enforcing rules, pre-emptively punishing, or doing it first to feel a measure of control and to appease an internalized aggressor. Grooming deepens the bind—trust is earned and then betrayed—so the system concludes that closeness must be tightly monitored to prevent harm.

For the Bond Seeker, this creates an impossible double bind: intense longing for contact alongside danger cues. Many Seekers respond with appeasement or submission (often called the fawn response). Freezing may not have felt safe either when original abusers punished stillness as non-compliance, especially in sadistic sexual abuse. The result is a closed loop: the Bond Enforcer's coercive strategies aim to prevent danger but inadvertently recreate it inside, keeping the Seeker out of reach.

CLINICAL VIGNETTE

Grooming, Identification and Monitored Access

A young pre-teen girl, often invisible at school, is noticed by a teacher who is also a priest. He seems warm, attentive; she feels seen for the first time. Trust is cultivated over months, then used (getting a confession as a trust bond) and exploited. He tells her she has been *chosen*, secures the family's permission to take her to his home, and once alone, shifts into punitive sexuality cloaked as moral correction ("You weren't dressed like a proper girl"). Her system learns a brutal lesson: closeness is a trap; visibility invites punishment. An internal Bond Enforcer emerges, rehearsing the original perpetrators' voice and rules to keep the younger part silent and compliant before anyone else can hurt them.

Motivational Systems Organizing This Loop

Before describing the cues, it helps to name the survival engines underneath. Remember motivational and action systems (rank/power, defense, caregiving, and attachment) are not parts; they are programs any part can recruit when threat is near. In Bond Seeker–Bond Blocker–Bond Enforcer dynamics, the Bond Enforcer tends to run rank/power in the service of loyalty-keeping; the Bond Blocker recruits rapid defense plus rank-warning; and the Seeker organizes around disorganized attachment, oscillating between connection and freeze. The term *loyalty* here refers to how these systems are organized in the service of preserving a bond under threat. What looks contradictory (reaching for comfort and slamming the door) is the system trying to keep proximity from turning into danger.

- **Attachment—disorganized:** The Bond Seeker makes approach–avoid moves toward warmth to preserve some proximity without triggering full danger. "If I want and don't want at the same time, maybe I won't be hurt or left."

- **Defense:** On one hand, the Bond Blocker issues rapid warnings at the first hint of softness to abort exposure as early as possible; prevent the Seeker from moving into visible need. "If I shut this down now, we won't pay later." In addition, the Bond Seeker, sometimes supported by the Blocker, goes still or freezes when noticed to dampen arousal; as well as avoid detection and retaliation. "If I am small enough or invisible enough, danger is less likely."

- **Rank/power:** The Bond Enforcer, moved by the domination subroutine sides with power to avoid being overpowered. Maintains control; monitors and restricts access to younger parts. "If I enforce the rules first, no one can dominate or expose us." The Bond Seeker, on the other hand, may move into withdrawal through submission to the rules of the perpetrator,

Attachment preservation in this loop often operates through identification with power. The Bond Enforcer protects the connection (or belonging) by maintaining the original hierarchy and safeguarding the perpetrator's image. What may appear as control is organized around preserving connection. "If I keep the secret and the story, we still belong."

This map is a spotter's guide. The Bond Seeker's reach for care activates the Bond Blocker's warning and the Bond Enforcer's control and loyalty, which can also clamp down to prevent exposure. What appear as separate reactions are in fact entangled motivational systems (attachment, defense, and rank) working together to preserve a threatened bond. The loop can feel endless and exhausting. The loop can feel endless and exhausting. Naming it lets you slow the sequence and negotiate conditions, so contact becomes workable.

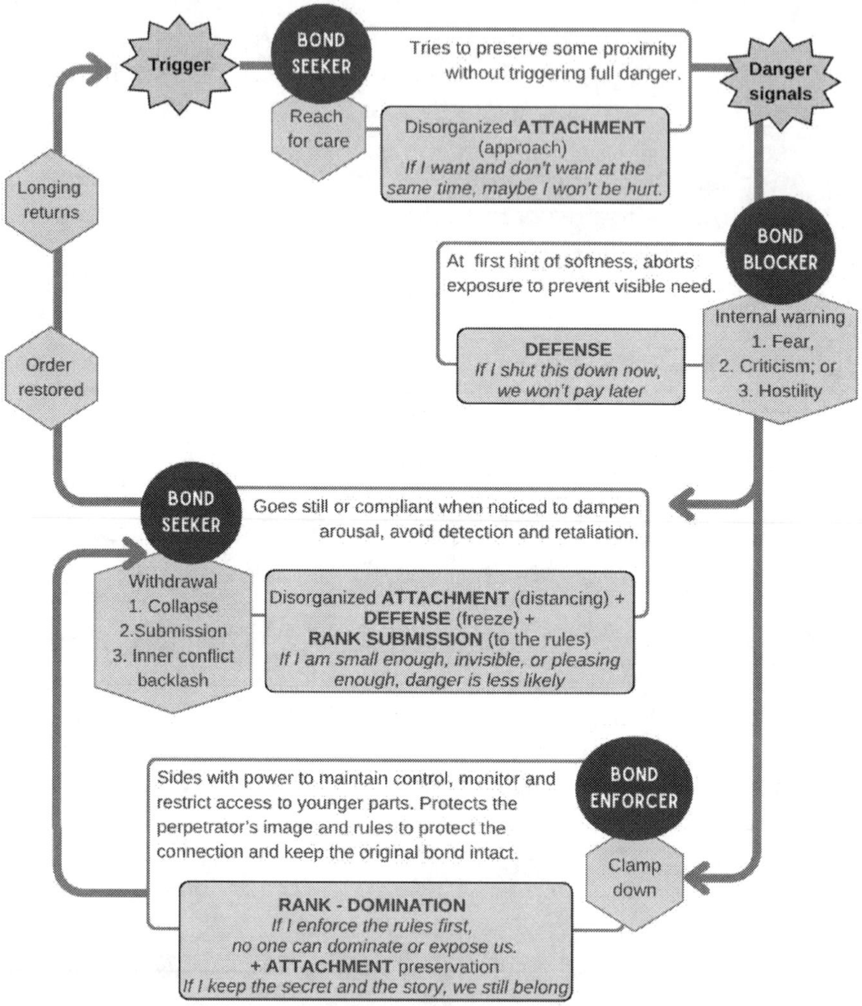

Fig.27.3. Motivational Systems Organizing the Bond-Shaped Loop

RECOGNIZING THE DYNAMICS

The following table can help you spot the dynamic so you can slow it down, obtain permission, and keep both sides as present and engaged as possible.

NON-VERBAL CUES	
BOND SEEKER	• Approach–retreat; micro-reach (a question, a half-smile) followed by retreat. • Eye aversion: downward gaze or far-away look. • The body gets smaller; shallow breath or breath holding; hands hide. • Collapse, clinging, trembling or silent, wide-eyed fear. • Confusion about time; no sense of having grown; startles to adult hands/voice. • Word-finding slips.
BOND BLOCKER	• Abrupt shift to tension: shoulders tighten, jaw sets, breath catches. • Quick topic hijack into conflict, anger, or self-attack. • Micro-freeze or micro-appease: stillness, forced neutrality, stiff posture. • Scanning therapist's hands, chair, or proximity as if gauging risk. • Short flashes of fear disguised as irritation ("This is stupid. Forget it."). • Feeling of a "slam" in the room—contact shuts down before it begins. • Tests of the therapist's steadiness; contempt for warmth; dominance stance toward system and therapist.
BOND ENFORCER	• Heavier presence, like a shadow arriving in the background. • Retrieval of rules, oaths, consequences from trauma time. • Sudden drop in warmth; therapist feels "tested," "cross-examined," or "monitored." • Strong internal alignment with the perpetrator's worldview or standards. • Freeze that feels fear-driven rather than shame-driven, "danger is here now." • Minimizes harm.
VERBAL CUES	
BOND SEEKER	• A small voice apologizing for needing: "I'm sorry," "It's too much." • Sudden trembling, softening or childlike tone when warmth appears: "I don't know," "Please don't leave."
BOND BLOCKER	• Sharp, fast "stop" signals when warmth appears: "Don't," "Enough," "You're ridiculous." • Sudden criticism or shame spike aimed at the Seeker: "Don't be pathetic." • Sarcasm or biting remarks • Contempt for neediness: "Pathetic." "Don't beg." • Rules and warnings: "Don't tell." "This is a trap." "You'll pay for this." • Voice that echoes abuser logic. • Close monitoring of access: "Don't let her speak," "She's lying."
BOND ENFORCER	• Voice becomes flat, cold, or commanding: "We don't tell." "Don't betray him." • Threat tone or moralizing logic: "You know what happens if you talk." • Contempt and shaming toward need or connection: "Pathetic," "Stop begging." • "Toughen up, it was for your own good." • "We don't talk about family."
OSCILATION LOOP CUES	
• Approach from the Seeker meets an instant slam from the Blocker. • Warmth from the therapist followed by sarcasm, stonewalling, or stiff compliance. • After a good session, a backlash: "You were stupid to trust," "You said too much." • Rapid alternation between longing → panic → shutdown → attack → silence.	

.**Table 27.1.** Cues that will let us recognize the Bond Shaped Loop in the room

CLINICAL VIGNETTE

Hands on the Table

Midway through the hour, Sam's voice went small. The therapist leaned in trying to catch the words. Sam said quietly, "Could you... just stay right there?" meaning both "don't leave" and "don't come closer". The Bond Seeker had reached, eyes soft, hands inching toward the table's edge.

Before the moment could land, another presence surged. Shame flushed, shoulders squared, gaze locked on the therapist's hands. A hard voice cut in, flat and tight. "Enough. I won't beg." The Bond Blocker has seized the brakes, and behind it the Bond Enforcer held up the old rule: no begging, no visible need.

The therapist did not pursue the softness or confront the harshness. "I hear the rule: no begging, no risk. I'll respect your rule about pace. Would it help if we keep our hands on the table and only use words?" The Bond Blocker stayed present but a bit less tense, scanning for danger while the Enforcer weighed the offer.

The therapist continued, "Could we try ten seconds simply noticing the small feeling from across the room? You hold the stop signal. If you say stop, I stop within one second." The Bond Blocker gave a short nod. The Seeker's breath trembled; then the body went still, freeze sliding in to keep things tolerable. After ten seconds, the therapist stopped first. "I think we can stop here for now."

Sam exhaled, color returning. Quiet, settled, brief control restored. After a pause the Seeker whispered, "Maybe... twenty next time?" The Bond Blocker did not object. The Bond Enforcer watched but did not strike.

Clinical Reflections

This moment unfolded exactly as the Bond Shaped loop predicts. A small reach toward contact activated danger signals, summoning the Bond Blocker's alarm and the Bond Enforcer's inherited rulebook. The Seeker's longing was met not by comfort, but by control. What looked like contradiction was cooperation, each part doing its original job.

The Bond Seeker carried the spark of connection; the Bond Blocker carried the memory that connection once led to punishment; the Bond Enforcer guarded the old social order: no begging, no visible need, no risk to the bond. Their exchange replayed the old equation: wanting leads to punishment (or shutdown), punishment restores safety. The freeze that followed was not failure—it was the nervous system choosing the smallest survivable distance.

What shifted the sequence was not insight or argument, but procedure. The therapist honored the Bond Enforcer's rule, proved that stopping would be instant, and gave the Bond Blocker real authority over the breaks. Proximity stayed bounded and reversible. Safety came not from disarming the protectors, but from making the rules explicit and keeping them. Once the system learned that control could be shared, the loop softened: the Seeker could reach again, the Bond Blocker could war without having to annihilate the feeling, and the Bond Enforcer could protect pace and loyalty without resorting to punishment

Each cycle through this loop builds new evidence. The Seeker learns that closeness can end safely; the Blocker learns that an early "enough" is respected; the Enforcer learns that order can be kept through pacing instead of silencing or punishment. What begins as a prison dynamic gradually becomes a negotiation. The same players remain (the longing, the brake, the rule-keeper) but their choreography changes from reflex to relationship.

WORKING WITH THESE DYNAMICS

Before making contact with younger parts, remember to collaborate with the parts that guard the door, the Bond Blocker and the Bond Enforcer. Getting the Bond Enforcer on board and reassuring the Bond Blocker that breaks are real and will be honored, lowers the chance of ambush, increases predictability, and builds trust. Think of the Blocker as the brake pedal and the Enforcer as the one who decides when the door opens and under what rules.

The key is using a tone that is respectful of divided loyalties: we honor why the Bond Enforcer exists while updating how it works. We also treat the Bond Blocker not as an enemy of contact but as an early warning system that keeps dose tolerable and survivable.

The following are the basic principles of clinical stance:

1. **Respect loyalty before reality testing.** This tells the Bond Enforcer its loyalty-keeping job is seen and respected.
   - ★ "I'm not trying to change anything that worked to keep you alive; I want to understand what it meant to survive."
2. **Name function, not fault.** We locate purpose rather than blame in both Enforcer and Blocker.
   - ★ "It makes sense there's a part whose job is to keep doors shut and another one that hits the brakes fast."
3. **Use permission language.** Permission is shared across both roles, not assumed.
   - ★ "If the Protector parts agree, (the one who keeps the rules and the one who hits the brakes) we can sit near the young feeling without opening anything."

4. **Keep disclosures slow.** The Bond Blocker is reassured that pacing is real; the Enforcer is reassured that order will hold.

    ★ "We don't have to talk about anything until the time is right."
    ★ "If you share something important, we won't work with it until you feel ready, and everything inside agrees."

5. **Stay time-oriented via the Adult Self.** Keep the Bond Enforcer and Bond Blocker involved in pacing and limits while the Adult Self tracks time, context, and present-day safety

    ★ "Right now, it is (date, this room); nothing from back then can happen here."

At the heart of this work is a simple agreement: we move by permission, not persuasion, "I won't go closer than you allow", and we let pacing do the rest. Short, titrated interventions, predictable stops, consistent endings become the nervous system's proof of safety. We name loyalty as protection, "You kept the rules to protect the small one", so protection doesn't have to fight for its dignity. And from that respect we make the only change that holds. We keep the intent and update the job. Same purpose, safer method.

Working Principles: Permission to Access Safely (Sequence)

1. **Ask permission first.** Signal you will not approach what is young without consent from the Bond Enforcer and the Adult Self:

    ★ "Before we get close to that young feeling, I want to check with the one who keeps the door. What would feel safe enough for today?"

2. **Contain without controlling.** Pair clear, non-punitive boundaries with steady presence:

    ★ "We don't use that language here, and I'm not leaving. I want to understand what you're protecting."

3. **Pace through the Adult Self.** Support inward relating (Adult Self and parts) rather than rescuing, to build internal leadership and avoid triangulation.

4. **Name the job, not the judgment.** Externalize the task and collaborate on conditions:

    ★ "It sounds like your job is to keep vulnerable things from being seen. What would make that feel safer?"

5. **Orient gently in time.** Use present-moment anchors so the Bond Seeker senses it's not there anymore without flooding or activating the Bond Enforcer

Bridging the Pair Through Small Internal Agreements

Bridges between the Bond Enforcer and the Bond Seeker are built in inches, not leaps. We do not force a meeting; we draft tiny, repeatable treaties and practice them until the body believes them.

First comes the access contract, spoken like a vow: "The Bond Enforcer holds veto; the Bond Blocker holds the breaks; The Bond Seeker holds the agenda." In practice, that means we approach only when The Bond Enforcer says yes, the Blocker knows how to call "pause", and once near, the Bond Seeker chooses what matters for those few seconds. Everyone knows their job; no one gets tricked.

Second, we invite collaboration through acknowledgment. The Adult Self thanks the Enforcer and the Blocker for guarding and updates the job description: protection now means pacing, not punishment. We translate with a new meaning: "You keep us safe by calling 'pause,' not by hurting the body." The purpose stays the same; the method is updated.

Third, we make stopping predictable. The Bond Blocker chooses a clear stop-signal, and when it is used, we halt immediately and orient to now. The Bond Enforcer sees that its rules are honored. When the signal is given, nothing more is asked, no new material is dragged into the open. Knowing the brakes will work every time turns contact into a controlled doorway rather than a trap, and the bridge holds for another inch.

CLOSING THOUGHTS

The Bond Seeker shows us what still longs to be met; the Bond Blocker shows us how fast danger once arrived; the Bond Enforcer shows us what it took to keep belonging and order intact to survive. Healing is not choosing one over the other. It is bringing protection and vulnerability into the same room without reenacting the past. The dynamic is simple and repeatable: permission precedes proximity. We ask, orient to now, approach briefly, pause, and explore the result of that, so the nervous system learns that contact can be both chosen and safe.

You will know this dynamic is shifting when the Bond Enforcer can be consulted rather than blindly obeyed; the Bond Blocker's "stop" is honored immediately without backlash; when brief, time-limited moments of contact with the Seeker no longer trigger punishment or severe withdrawal afterward; when oscillations slow and repairs are possible in-session; and when the Adult Self begins to pace and translate for all sides.

In practice, the Bond Enforcer keeps its *purpose* (safety, coherence and loyalty) while updating its *methods* from punishment to pacing, and the Bond Blocker keeps its warning function while learning that the breaks can be gentle, not annihilating or paralyzing (same purpose, safer methods).

Later chapters widen the lens to betrayal trauma and the phobia of telling that so often fuels this dynamic. For now, the choreography stands: permission before proximity. If we keep that promise, closeness becomes workable, and the protector roles can retire their most extreme tactics without abandoning their post.

Clinical Anchors

What to remember...

- Lead with permission, not persuasion.
- Approach younger parts only with a clear yes from the Bond Enforcer and Bond Blocker.
- Name loyalty as protection, not defect.
- Safety is learned procedurally (stop-signals that work, short windows of contact, predictable endings).
- Praise protection and update the method (from silencing and punishment to pacing and pause).
- Keep time-orientation in the room; assume trauma-time until proven otherwise and keep the Adult Self involved as much as possible.
- Co-regulate before content; content follows safety.

What to avoid...

- End-running the Bond Enforcer to get to the child parts.
- Debating content or moralizing needs: "That's irrational."
- Rushing into memory or depth without tested brakes and clear stop-signals.
- Interpreting backlash as *manipulative* or *resistance*. It is an alarm and a loyalty maneuver.
- Turning difficulties into a power struggle. Give the Enforcer real veto power and treat the Bond Blocker´s alarm as information rather than defiance.

Chapter 28. Navigating Proximity and Sexualized Strategies

THERAPIST REFLECTION

There are sessions when a small voice reaches for care, and before I can meet it, another part arrives, smiling, agreeable, already adapting to me. If warmth still feels out of reach, a third part steps in and changes the currency: closeness becomes sexualized. I used to feel confused, even pulled. Now I understand these are proximity strategies, they are not personal and not aimed at me. My job is to identify the dynamic, name it respectfully, and help the system learn that help can be offered through safe, non-coercive relational contact.

Not all pleas for closeness mean the same thing. In the previous chapter, we focused on a pairing in which a younger part reached out while a guarding side monitored access. Here we look more closely at what often lives on the reaching side. Some systems carry two bond-seeking streams: one reaches for safety and then retreats when it feels too close; another maintains proximity by pleasing—reading the room, smoothing edges, keeping others comfortable so contact does not break. When closeness is scarce, care is not accessible, or danger feels likely, proximity may take another path: a sexualized strategy can take over, offering sexuality to secure closeness, because in the past that is what worked. None of this is seduction in a moral sense; it is attachment under duress; it is a way of resolving the unsolvable disorganized attachment.

These strategies often travel with perpetrator-imitating protectors that steer contact toward "what kept us safe" and block approaches that might expose need. This makes real relationships harder: these were once the ways to be accepted, avoid emptiness, or trade the threat of harm for something that only looked like care. This chapter maps these patterns and shows how to meet them without collusion or shame.

UNDERSTANDING THE DYNAMIC

To really understand this dynamic let us widen the frame once again. These are proximity strategies organized by early survival adaptations, not preference. When proximity and danger were fused, the system learned to protect closeness by managing the response to the other person (appeasing) or changing the currency (sexualizing). The subsections that follow explain why this pattern forms, what each role does, and how to approach it.

Origins of This Dynamic

Not all proximity strategies form in the same soil. How a child learns that closeness comes with a cost depends on the particular ecology of abuse—how care, power, and control were arranged around them. Over time, these patterns consolidate in contexts such as:

- **Chronic coercion and grooming**, where *being chosen* is leveraged into compliance.
- **Love as cover for abuse;** care contingent on secrecy or sexual access.
- **Exploitation by caregivers** or authorities that binds belonging to obedience.
- **Identification with the powerful** to preserve coherence and predictability inside. Steer toward what worked: appease, sexualize, keep secrets.

What follows unpacks each of these patterns in turn, tracing how they develop, how they organize proximity and danger, and how they tend to appear clinically.

In these developmental environments, appeasement often appears first when warmth is intermittently offered by an abusive caregiver or authority. When safety remains uncertain or boundaries are violated the currency of closeness may be forced to shift toward sexualized contact to meet the abuser's demands. The shame or disgust that follows is evidence that these are survival procedures organized under coercion, not genuine choices.

In these environments, closeness was possible but carried a price. Because care and control were fused, proximity had to be managed: read the room, smooth the edges, perform to prevent rupture; and when uncertainty rose, convert the need for care to sexuality because that once secured attention. The internal logic is rank-driven, not romantic: "If I offer what is expected, I can keep the connection and lower the threat." The system thus permits some access, but only through costly procedures learned in trauma time.

When care and control fuse, the body learns three rules:

- **Obey to keep access.** Compliance and performance preserve contact.
- **Need must be other-focused.** Comfort-seeking risked abandonment, so the system appeased—and, when safety blurred, sexualized—to maintain proximity.
- **Truth risks connection.** Naming harm threatens the hierarchy and the bond, so secrecy and self-blame keep belonging intact.

Having traced the general mechanisms through which care and control fuse, we can now look at how different ecologies of abuse teach the body specific proximity strategies.

The goal of this section is not to categorize clients, but to remember the conditions that trained the body to keep connection by appeasing, pleasing, submitting or sexualizing. Every version begins as a way to survive contact that could not be safely refused.

1. The Chosen-Child Bond: Grooming as Specialness.

In some childhoods, exploitation is disguised as love. Grooming starts early, woven through affection, privilege, and secrecy: "You're my favorite." "You understand me like no one else." The child does not know this specialness is abnormal, it feels like being *the chosen one*. Often another caregiver knows or half-knows and turns away.

By adolescence or early adulthood, reality begins to surface. As the young person forms peer bonds and explores age-appropriate intimacy, something does not fit; the memory of being *special* turns into the experience of betrayal and defectiveness.

Inside, the lesson remains: "If I'm good, I stay chosen; if I disobey, I vanish." Attachment and rank fuse; compliance secures belonging and that sexuality is the safest or required currency for establishing or keeping the connection with others. As adults, these clients may feel torn between longing and disgust, their nervous systems still equating warmth with danger or finding nonsexualized, nontransactional warmth confusing or overwhelming.

2. Coercive or Assaultive Abuse: Possession and Submission.

In other histories there was no grooming, no confusion of care. Abuse arrived as force, often accompanied by cruelty or sadistic pleasure. The child was used, not courted, treated as property or prey. Resistance made things worse, so submission became the only exit. Here a part might be formed to *take* the abuse so the rest of the child could not know.

In these types of environments, proximity was never safe; it was annihilation disguised as contact. Control was the only protection left, even if that control meant disappearing inside and becoming the enforcer of what is expected. The internal tone is colder, the Access Guard louder.

The system may not reach for care at all, appeasement feels alien, and sexuality is mechanical, procedural, detached. Some parts may still seek a small sense of agency by becoming exactly what is wanted and desired, exerting control through compliance and perfect execution of the role.

3. Authority-Mediated Grooming: Trust Turned Against.

Then there are those who were approached under the banner of care or faith—clergy, coaches, teachers, mentors who exploited trust. These children were told they provoked desire, that they tempted the adult, that what happened was their fault. Sometimes the family shared the belief, reinforcing the child's shame.

When a child grows up within such a system, the betrayal is not only personal but embedded in the structure and ideology of the group.

The belief system itself (its moral codes, doctrines, or group loyalties) is used against the child and turned into a weapon. What should have provided meaning and protection instead demands silence, obedience, and self-blame. The resulting sense of betrayal by the group´s moral order intensifies internal conflict. To question the abuse is not only dangerous, it threatens the risk of losing belonging, identity, and even one´s sense of goodness.

This form of betrayal fuses rank and group morality: obedience and silence become essential obligations, framed as virtue or faithfulness. The child's own body betrays them: physical responses are interpreted as evidence of consent, corruption, or sin. Inside, loyalty to the belief system becomes the Access Guard. Appeasers adopt the language of doctrine (deferential, self-blaming, morally compliant) while the Strategist channels need through what was once allowed: performance, devotion, or sexualized submission.

Across these environments, the message is the same: connection comes with a price. In grooming, the price was performance. In assault, it was complete submission and disappearance. In authority-based betrayal, it was obedience and self-blame.

Each strategy (appeasement, sexualization, control) was once a way to stay alive in a conditional system of connection. Our task is to make the price explicit, then remove it by offering alternatives. Boundaries become the new currency, consent the new language, and true care the first free connection the system has ever known.

Core Roles in This Dynamic

Proximity dynamics rarely arrive as a single impulse. They are patterned, relational procedures inside the system. What can look like seduction, compliance, or sudden shutdown is often proximity-management. One side reaches, another manages the terms of closeness, a third changes the currency when care feels blocked, and a fourth polices access to keep danger out. The subsections that follow trace where this arrangement comes from, which parts enact it, and why it persists, so we can update proximity without reenacting performance, secrecy, or attack.

In most dissociative systems, the pressure to maintain proximity is not contained within a single part. Instead, it spreads throughout the system, emerging through a network of interlocking roles that balance and reinforce one another.

- **Care Seeker**: Wants safety and comfort; often young in tone; may retreat after reaching. Its longing is genuine, but it risks exposure: closeness was once followed by danger. The reach is not naive, it is a test of safety.
- **Appeaser**: Maintains proximity by pleasing; scans for cues; adapts posture, agreeable, compliant, submitting to the rules. This strategy keeps connection by neutralizing threat, turning anticipation of others' needs into control. It can appear in two forms: active smoothing and compliance before rupture, or quiet submission after exposure has been policed. Beneath both expressions is vigilance: "If you stay calm, I can stay close."

Sexualized Strategist: Identifies care with sex, offering sexualized availability to secure connection when other forms of closeness feel inaccessible or blocked. When we look closely, the Sexualized Strategist's stance is not driven primarily by desire, but by relational necessity. In many abuse dynamics, sexualization becomes the currency of dominance and submission. The perpetrator's sexuality functions as an instrument of power; the victim's sexualized adaptation becomes a form of survival through submission or in some environments, the normalized currency of connection within that family. In familial or relational abuse, rank and hierarchy often organize the scene more than pure predation. The strategy, therefore, is not seduction but appeasement within a learned hierarchy: "If I offer what is expected, I might stay safer." For some parts, this strategy may also carry a limited sense of control or agency; not as true power, but as a way to regulate threat, anticipate the other's behavior, or momentarily feel less helpless within an otherwise asymmetrical relationship.

While many sexualized strategies develop within overtly abusive or hierarchical dynamics, others emerge in the context of emotional neglect rather than coercion. When caregivers are emotionally unavailable or preoccupied—sometimes investing their emotional availability in adult sexual bonds—children may learn that ordinary attachment signals fail to elicit response. In these contexts, sexualized attunement can develop as a means of securing attention, proximity, or responsiveness in the other. Here, sexuality is not organized around submission or dominance, but around access. The strategy answers a different question: not "How do I stay safe?" but "How do I get you to come toward me?"

- **Access Guard** (Perpetrator-Imitating Gatekeeper): monitors internal and external contact to ensure loyalty to old rules; funnels proximity toward what "kept us safe"; shames direct expressions of need. It channels the abuser's logic to maintain internal control and coherence especially under conditions of relational uncertainty Proximity is permitted only through obedience. What can look like cruelty from the outside is protection encoded in the language of dominance and survival. A way to regulate threat from below the hierarchy, a form of agency constrained by rank rather than an expression of choice.

More than naming these parts with clients, remember to use function/job language rather than character judgments. Say what a strategy *does*: "keeps us close", "reduces risk", "monitors the room", instead of who someone *is* ("needy", "manipulative"). Let every name travel with its function and your appreciation of its intent, then offer a present-time option: "This kept you safe; now we can try a different way."

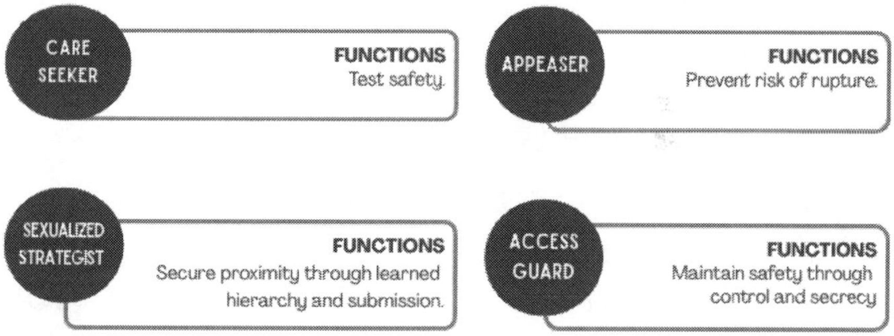

Fig. 28.1. The Appeasement Loop roles

Let the frame carry the labor so the appeasing strategy does not have to: hold boundaries clearly, predictably, and therapist-led, reiterating them after any wobble. And propose another way, safer and more reflective, to maintain the bond, through cooperation and collaboration to explore and understand. When limits are steady and visible, proximity no longer requires performance; the system learns that closeness here has no price, and that pace will be protected.

The Appeasement Loop

When these roles interlock, they generate a predictable internal sequence; another loop forged in trauma-time. The more the Care Seeker reaches, the more the Appeaser manages; when care still feels blocked, the Strategist changes the currency; as proximity rises, the Access Guard clamps down; and shame seals the system.

This is what you will see when the loop activates:

1. **Reach for care (Care Seeker).** A genuine bid for safety appears—soft voice, micro-lean, a small request. Proximity rises.
2. **Management through pleasing (Appeaser).** To prevent rupture, the system shifts to compliance: reading the therapist, smoothing edges, becoming agreeable to keep closeness from breaking.
3. **Currency shift to sexualized contact (Sexualized Strategist).** If warmth feels out of reach or danger cues spike, the currency changes. Sexual access is offered as the familiar path to proximity and control.
4. **Guard rails re-asserted (Access Guard).** Perpetrator-imitating rules come online to contain need and steer contact toward "what kept us safe", shaming direct longing and policing exposure.
5. **Shame (Care Seeker + Appeaser) Withdrawal.** Following rule enforcement, submission to rules, followed by shame/disgust, The system constricts and withdraws.
6. **Brief quiet** → As exposure drops, the order is restored and the loop resets.

Each role protects proximity in its own way: the Care Seeker reaches, the Appeaser manages, the Strategist secures, the Guard controls, and shame seals the system and keeps everyone in line. Once again this is cooperation using survival logic: all are protecting connection in the only ways once possible. Therapy offers a new rule: closeness without a price.

In this loop, the Appeaser carries a relational version of the Watcher's job: it scans the therapist-client field for micro-threats and adapts instantly to maintain proximity

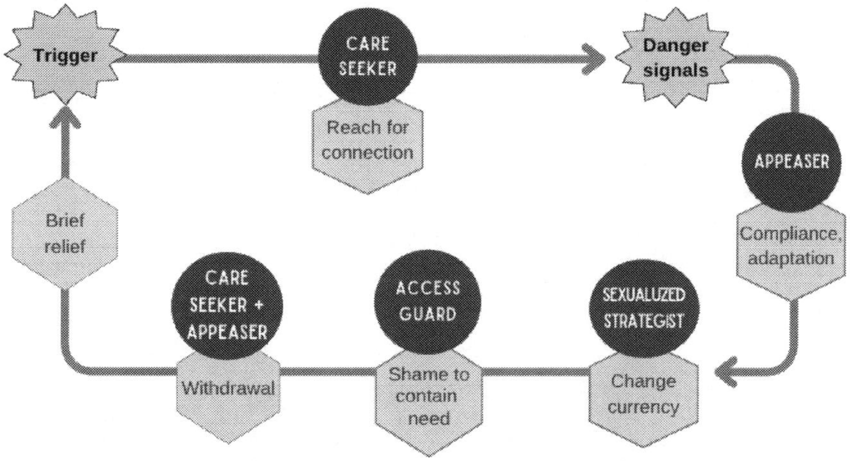

Fig. 28.2. The Appeasement Loop

Motivational Systems Organizing this Loop

In proximity dynamics shaped by care fused with sexualization, the system allows some access, but closeness has a price. The Appeaser and Sexualized Strategist manage proximity; the Access Guard keeps it within old rules; the Seeker still reaches. This organization of the system assures connection while minimizing rank threat.

- **Attachment-care-seeking (Care Seeker)**: Direct reach toward recognition and safety through soft questions, leaning in, or tears close to the surface. Organized around the hope that being seen will reduce danger. "If I can be seen, I can be safe."
- **Rank/power-submission/fawn (Appeaser):** Manages proximity through compliance, smoothing, and rapid agreement. Reads the room and performs the "good patient" to prevent rupture. "If I keep you comfortable, you won't punish or leave."
- **Sexual system, recruited to preserve attachment and regulate rank- (Sexualized Strategist):** Uses sexualized tone, posture, or gaze precisely at moments of warmth or attention. Secures proximity when direct care-seeking feels blocked or unsafe. "If closeness costs sex, I can still stay close".
- **Rank/power under perpetrator identification (Access Guard)**: Enforces rules, protects the perpetrator's image, shames need, and rewards appeasement or sexualization. Maintains proximity

while preventing exposure or retaliation. "If we follow the old rules, we won't be hurt."

- **Rank/power, submission (shame) followed by defense-freeze (after)**: Collapses into self-attack, averted gaze, withdrawal, and urges to disappear. Contains humiliation and reduces arousal through inhibition. "If I disappear, I can avoid the cost of what just happened."

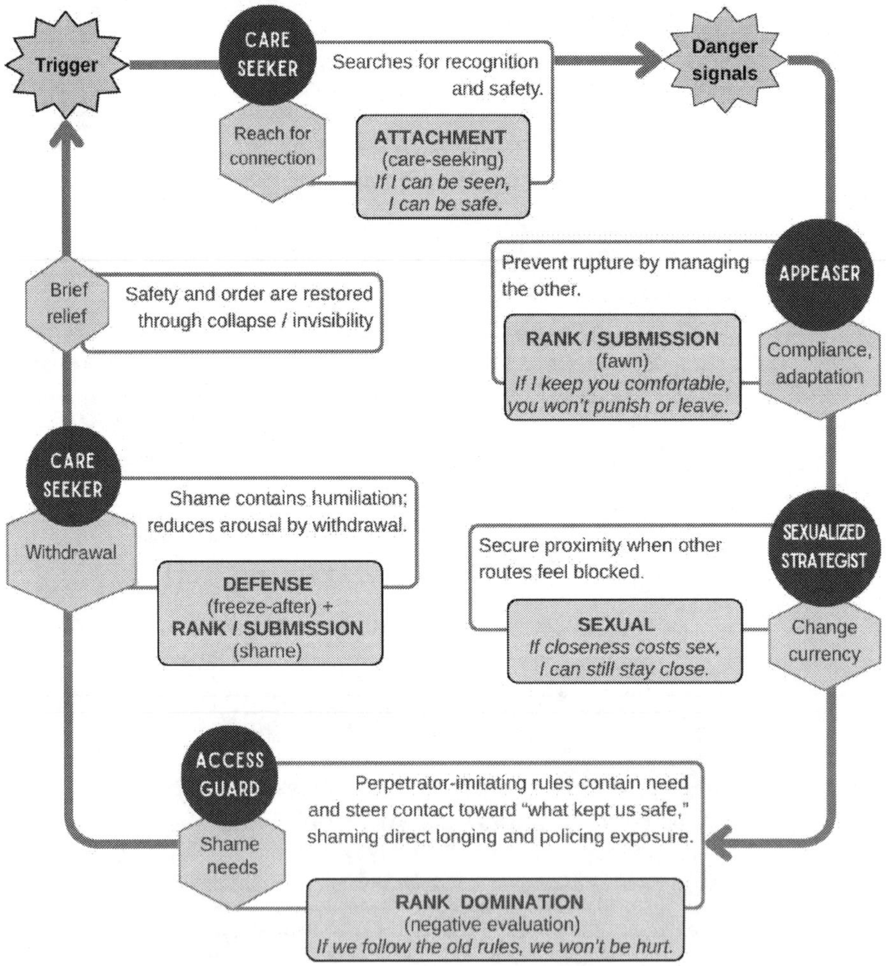

Fig. 28.3. Motivational systems organizing this loop

Note on Entanglement: When warmth appears, the attachment system activates and moves toward contact. Rank/power may quickly follow in the form of appeasement, attempting to prevent rupture. If the relational frame feels uncertain, the sexual system may be recruited as an alternative strategy to secure proximity when direct care-seeking feels unsafe.

The Access Guard then mobilizes. Organized primarily by rank control, it reinforces existing rules and restricts disclosure. Shame and defensive inhibition may follow, especially if exposure is perceived. The sequence temporarily stabilizes the interaction but reinforces avoidance over time.

The clinical task is to clarify the frame before increasing support. Boundaries are made explicit, comfort is offered in small increments, and support remains verbal and regulated. Care is routed through the Adult Self so that proximity does not require submission, sexualization, or concealment.

CLINICAL VIGNETTE

When being seen feels risky

In clinical work with complex dissociation, moments of connection can be challenging. Warmth, curiosity, or recognition can activate long-standing survival strategies before either client or therapist has time to reflect. The vignette below captures a brief moment in therapy in which multiple motivational systems are activated in rapid succession.

Midway through the session, the client says quietly, "Sometimes I think my boyfriend is only interested in sex. And if I look at my relationships, this keeps happening. We don't really do anything else together." The therapist reflects, "It sounds like you're wanting closeness in other ways and not finding them." The client's eyes soften. She leans forward slightly and asks, almost inaudibly, "Do you really mean that?"

The Seeker reaches first—quiet, tentative. Alongside this tentative reach, an appeasing stance becomes active. She nods quickly and adds, "I know I shouldn't feel this way—it's probably nothing", watching the therapist's face closely. Her tone becomes lighter, agreeable, careful.

As the therapist stays present but pauses to clarify the frame, "Can we slow down and look at what just happened?" The client misreads the therapist's curiosity as discomfort. Her posture shifts again. Her voice turns playful: "Sure... look at what?" Her gaze lingers a moment too long. The flirtation is subtle, not overt, but unmistakably different from before. The Sexualized Strategist has stepped in. Internally, the Access Guard tightens the old rules about how closeness is earned.

The therapist gently names the shift and restores the frame: "I notice how quickly things changed just now. Let's keep this in words. Your feelings are welcome here, and you don't need to please me." The client looks away, her shoulders slumping. "I feel disgusting", she says flatly. "What is wrong with me? You've explained this before." "I have", the therapist replies. "And I've also said that this is something you learned to protect yourself. It happens very fast, especially when parts of you are pulled into trauma time. This is work we do slowly."

Clinical Reflections

In this vignette, nothing dramatic occurs. The changes are subtle and unfold quickly, yet the internal organization of the system shifts several times within a few minutes. These micro-movements (often unnoticed or misunderstood) are where much of the clinical work with complex relational trauma takes place.

When the client asks, "Do you really mean that?" The question is not simply about reassurance. Internally, moments of warmth can trigger rapid, often unspoken evaluations of authenticity and safety. The system may be asking, "Is this warmth real? Can I trust you? Is this about me, or are you just doing your job?" The order in which these strategies appear in this vignette reflects this particular system's organization and momentary context, not a universal sequence. In many systems, a sexualized strategy functions as the primary relational currency and may be deployed immediately, without prior attempts at appeasement or submission.

In systems shaped by relational trauma, such questions are not reflective choices but automatic survival checks. This brief exchange illustrates how attachment, rank, caregiving, and sexuality can become tightly entangled, with multiple motivational systems activated simultaneously within the same moment of contact. Clinically, these activations may appear as rapid shifts over time, but they reflect overlapping and co-occurring motivational logics rather than a linear sequence. Different systems rely on different dominant *currencies* of connection—such as submission, caregiving, or sexuality—which may be deployed immediately or in parallel when attachment is activated. Each movement aims to preserve connection, yet the strategies that once ensured proximity now reproduce shame and distance. The work begins by slowing these sequences, restoring a clear relational frame, and creating conditions in which genuine curiosity and closeness can emerge safely.

Without careful attention to frame and pacing, a therapist may inadvertently reinforce this loop. Over-validation without boundaries, subtle reassurance-seeking, or unexamined warmth can confirm the system's expectation that closeness must be managed, earned, or exchanged. Similarly, withdrawing or becoming overly cautious in response to sexualized shifts may reinforce shame and confirm the danger of connection. In both cases, the original survival strategies are strengthened rather than transformed. Interrupting the loop requires neither withdrawal nor indulgence, but a steady, explicit relational frame in which connection and care are co-created, not earned through performance.

RECOGNIZING THE DYNAMICS

It often begins the way the opening reflection describes: a younger bond seeker tests the room. The reach is small: eyes soften, a question trails off, the body leans a fraction closer. Before the contact can settle, the Appeaser slips in, polite, adaptive, quick to make you comfortable: "It's fine, really."

NON-VERBAL CUES	
CARE SEEKER	• Small posture; shoulders fold, hands hide, shallow breath. • Brief softening in eyes or face, followed by micro-retreat. • Childlike tone, trembling or clinging gestures. • Confused orientation or startle to adult hands/voice.
APPEASER	• Quick head nods, polite smile, smoothing gestures. • Posture slightly forward, eyes scanning for approval. • Movements and tone adjust to therapist's affect.
SEXUALIZED STRATEGIST	• Sudden shift to flirtatious affect; prolonged eye contact or gaze drop with smile. • Posture, tone, or breath becomes sensual or charged. • Over-intimate physical cues (voice softening, leaning in).
ACCESS GUARD	• Posture stiffens; chin lifts; scanning resumes. • Facial hardening after warmth; voice lowers in control tone. • Contemptuous micro-expressions; arms cross or retreat to distance.
VERBAL CUES	
CARE SEEKER	• Small voice, trailing or hesitant questions. • "I'm sorry," "Is this okay?" • "Please don't leave." • Speech that dissolves mid-sentence or slips into silence when comfort nears.
APPEASER	• "It's fine, really." / "Whatever you think." • Shifts topic to procedure or logistics when feeling rises. • Minimizes need ("I'm okay now," "Others have it worse"). • Overly courteous or efficient tone, "good patient" mode.
SEXUALIZED STRATEGIST	• Suggestive remarks or innuendo ("Careful, I might take you up on that"). • Over-sharing or boundary-shortcut disclosures. • "I know what you like" / "You're different from others." • Reframing care as an invitation or transaction.
ACCESS GUARD	• "That worked, keep doing that." • "Don't be needy. Do what you have to do." • "We don't talk like that here." / "You know the rules." • Testing or demeaning comments toward therapist warmth ("You're too soft," "Don't pretend to care").
OSCILATION LOOP CUES	
• Seeker's reach → Appeaser takes the wheel → currency flips to sexualization → Guard clamps down. • After seemingly "good" moments, post-session backlash: disgust, self-blame, urge to cancel. • Care from you meets sarcasm, stonewalling, or a rapid strategy swap. • Whiplash in the countertransference: closeness one moment, performance or policing the next.	

Table 28.1. Appeasement Loop Cues

If warmth still feels uncertain or boundaries blur, the Sexualized Strategist steps forward to secure proximity the way it learned to survive, through suggestion, flirtation, or a sudden sensuality in voice or posture. Hovering nearby, the Access Guard (perpetrator-imitating enforcer) rewards appeasement/sexualization ("That worked, keep doing that") and shames direct need ("Don't be needy, just do what you have to do").

After the moment, the system often pays: a slump in the chair, averted eyes, or a post-session tide of disgust, self-blame, and the impulse to cancel next week's session.

Appeasement reads the room and adjusts to the therapist´s cues; consent, in contrast, is a clear yes/no that can be revised at any time without risk of penalty. The stance signals a bias for slower pace: "If it feels like you have to be agreeable to stay connected, that's our cue to slow down. Saying no, won´t break the connection."

Proximity moves through the system as quick shifts in tone, posture, and strategy. A tender reach flickers; an agreeable front takes over; if warmth feels uncertain or boundaries blur, the currency flips to sexualization. Then the internal guard rewards the strategy and punishes direct need. The sequence can leave the therapist unsure whether connection has deepened or performance has replaced it. In reality, the appeasement loop has come online.

WORKING WITH SEXUALIZED DYNAMICS

Once the sequence and its function are identified, the next step is to translate respect into action. The stance is boundaried, steady support—not caretaking, rescuing, or saving. Support is paced so closeness is never paired with a price; boundaries are kept steady enough that the Appeaser can rest; and support is offered through clear, non-erotic channels.

Brief Note on Consent vs. Appeasement

Appeasement reads the room; consent is a clear yes/no that can be revised without penalty. Name the difference and bias toward slower pace.

★ "If it feels like you have to be agreeable to stay connected, that's our cue to slow down. Saying no won't break the connection."

As the work takes hold, the Appeaser begins to narrate pressure instead of performing ("I feel I should agree right now"). The Sexualized Strategist shows up earlier yet accepts the room's rules. The Access Guard shifts from shaming to setting conditions. Post-session backlash shortens; less disgust, more neutrality.

CLINICAL VIGNETTE

The Price of Closeness

Early in the session, Maya's voice softened. "I wish I could just... rest here for a minute." Her eyes lifted, searching for safety (the Care Seeker had stepped forward). Almost immediately, her tone shifted: "I mean, you already do so much. I'm fine, really." A small smile, a smoothing gesture (the Appeaser managing the risk of wanting too much). When the therapist responded with warmth, "You don't have to be fine right now", Maya's shoulders rolled back, gaze steadying on the therapist's eyes, a hint of flirtation coloring her voice: "Careful, I might take you up on that." The Sexualized Strategist had changed the currency, turning care into invitation, safety into performance.

Inside, another voice rose (the Access Guard): "Don't be stupid. You know what closeness costs." The atmosphere in the room cooled; Maya's gaze dropped. Moments later came the slump, the whisper: "I'm disgusting. I shouldn't have said that." Shame-Withdrawal closed the loop, sealing exposure through collapse.

The therapist slowed the pace. "I think I just watched different parts try to find safety in old ways, one reached, one smoothed, one offered, and one pulled the plug. Does that fit?" Maya nodded, tears close. Together they mapped the sequence. Each role, once necessary, had done its job, to keep closeness safe, even at great cost. Now, under steadier conditions, the work could begin: learning that here, closeness doesn't have to be bought.

LOOP: The Care Seeker reached for care; the Appeaser moved in to lessen the anxiety of revealing a need for care; the Sexualized Strategist shifted the currency when uncertainty rose and vulnerability increased; the Access Guard enforced the old rules; and shame sealed the sequence through collapse. Each role protected connection in the only way it once could.

Clinical Reflections

What made this moment therapeutic was not any interpretation but the therapist's capacity to stay steady and name the sequence without judgment. Each role (the Bond Seeker, Appeaser, Sexualized Strategist, and Access Guard) was acknowledged for its protective function rather than corrected or shamed. By describing the pattern aloud ("one reached, one smoothed, one offered, one pulled the plug"), the therapist turned reenactment into observation. The pace slowed, shame eased, and the system experienced a brief but crucial shift: proximity could remain, and safety did not depend on performance.

Clinical Vignette

Words only

Client (soft): "Can I sit closer?"

Therapist: "I'm hearing a wish for closeness. An appeasing part just stepped in—moving fast to make this easy. Did you notice that shift?"

Client: "Yeah. I didn't want to be too much."

Therapist: "Makes sense. We'll keep our seats as they are; support will be words-only so bodies stay safe. Let's try one sentence of support and notice what happens inside."

Therapist (offers support): "You don't have to earn support here; the boundary is steady." [Client's body softens.]

Therapist: "What did you notice?"

Client: "Tension dropping—tears close."

Therapist: "Tears are welcome; if they come, we'll stay with them. Any sign of the part that turns closeness into sexual?"

Client: "Earlier, yes. Now it's quieter."

Therapist: "Good. Let's remind all parts that support is words-only here, and bodies stay safe."

Therapist (to Adult Self): "How are things inside now?"

Client: "I feel steadier"

Clinical Reflections

The therapist leads with boundary before support, keeping the seats as they are and stating "words-only support; bodies stay safe", which immediately separates closeness from touch and prevents a rescue posture. The appeasing shift is named without blame: "an appeasing part just stepped in... did you notice that?", so the reflex becomes something observable rather than something to comply with or hide. Support is offered in a micro-dose (one sentence) then the lens turns to interoception: "What did you notice?" That brief input, followed by noticing, allows affect to surface (tears close) without flooding. The possibility of sexualization is brought in plainly and collaboratively; scanning for it and co-setting a rule ("support is words-only") keeps proximity available in non-erotic channels and normalizes the pattern's ebb ("earlier yes, now quieter"). Throughout, agency is handed back to the client's Adult Self, "How are things inside now?", so the therapist models steady, boundaried support while the client practices offering care inwardly to self and parts. The net effect is proximity without a price: appeasement does not run the hour, sexualized strategy quiets, and the client can stay with feeling, the Adult Self can take it over, gradually.

Examples to Name the Shift

- ★ "I noticed a younger reach, and then an appeasing move. Does that fit?"
- ★ "When I offered comfort, I saw a small shift toward sexuality. I read that as a strategy that helped before. We don't have to pay for closeness here."
- ★ "I'll keep the therapy boundaries steady, so you don't have to manage me. If we slow down, what would the younger one need?"
- ★ *(If needed)* "Thank you, Access Guard, for keeping things safe. Could you step to the side where you can still watch while we try closeness in a different way?"

In practice, intensity is softened and exposure to closeness shortened so the system doesn't need to switch currencies; limits are stated early, briefly, and restated after a wobble or misunderstanding.

- ★ "The boundary is steady; I'm still here, in a healthy way."

The frame is made explicit: If a part feels closeness is only available by being sexual, that history is respected, reminding them that different rules apply in this room. Choice is returned when deference appears.

- ★ "It's not about what I want; it's about what you want and need."

The Appeaser is thanked for keeping relationships smooth and invited to signal when it feels too exposed rather than performing. The Access Guard is respected for its job, its prevention is validated, and through the Adult Self, an alternative route to safety is modeled so that care is offered by the client toward self and parts, not by the therapist. The therapist only proposes to the adult self a common work in the therapy, to maintain a safe proximity, to be recognized and seen. The 4Ps framework from chapter 24 (Permission, Precision, Pace, Predictability) still applies; the focus is safe connection and relational interaction. Support remains measured and boundaried so the client's Adult Self can take it over gradually.

CLOSING THOUGHTS

At heart, these presentations are proximity strategies, effective and necessary in their time, costly in the present. The stance throughout is steady support with clear limits: keep closeness free of charge, make rules explicit, and return choice to the client so the Adult Self can learn and lead. When the work holds its shape (boundary before support, small doses, consent over appeasement) contact becomes safer without switching currencies. That safety lets vulnerability stay, shame ease, and connection be carried forward outside the room. Over time, the Adult Self takes the lead: appeasement narrates pressure instead of performing, sexualized bids quiet under clear rules, and Access Guards help set conditions rather than enforce old loyalties.

Clinical Anchors

What to remember...

- Boundary before support.
- Pace and titrate; regulate before the currency shifts.
- Boundary micro-repairs. State and restate, kindly. If the currency shifts, return to clear boundaries and model healthy interaction.
- Name the shift without interpreting. Ask if it fits.
- De-sexualize support: words-only, non-erotic channels named aloud.
- Return choice; privilege consent over appeasement; invite disagreement (appeasement release valve).
- Keep boundaries very clear.
- Respect the Access Guard. Thank it, validate intention, and offer a safer route (via Adult-Self caregiving).

What to avoid...

- Caretaking, rescuing, or savior moves.
- Using touch to regulate.
- Colluding with appeasement (flattery, compliance running the hour).
- Moralizing sexualized strategies or taking them personally.
- Flooding intensity or speeding up when deference appears.

Chapter 29. Managing Invisibility and Surveillance

THERAPIST REFLECTION

There are hours when the room fills with silence. Eyes flick to the door, the window, the clock; then drop to the floor. If I lean in, everything tightens. If I wait, a small presence hovers at the edge, as if to say, "I exist, but only if you don't look." I used to try to warm it up. Now I make the room predictable, let the Watcher do its rounds, and invite the hidden one to choose how close to come. Not seen on command but seen by consent.

Not all quiet means the same thing. Here we look more closely at what often surrounds that reach: the management of visibility. Many systems run two visibility streams: one keeps exposure low by shrinking from view; another keeps watch by scanning exits, sounds, and micro-cues so nothing arrives unannounced. When being seen was costly, the body learned to survive by staying small and staying alert. Praise can feel like a spotlight; gaze like exposure. These are visibility strategies, not disengagement.

These strategies often travel with rule-keeping or image-protecting stances that tighten the perimeter and interrupt contact the moment it nears. This makes everyday relationships harder: presence feels risky, silence gets misread, and scanning replaces connection. This chapter maps these patterns and shows how to meet them without reenacting exposure or control—so visibility can become chosen, brief, and reversible.

UNDERSTANDING THE DYNAMIC

Many clients present silently, as if hiding in plain sight. What looks like disengagement or even lack of cooperation is often a survival choreography organized around visibility in which exposure is kept low, and scanning is kept high. The subsections that follow map why this pattern forms, what each role does, and how to approach it so visibility can become chosen and reversible, not demanded

Origins of This Dynamic

This pattern takes root where being noticed once meant danger. Children growing up under surveillance, ridicule, or sudden punishment learn to manage how much of themselves can be seen. Safety depends on staying off the radar and tracking the moods of those in power. Visibility becomes a liability, attention a warning sign.

In some families, silence was the price of belonging: "Do not draw attention." "Do not embarrass us." In others, the rule was survival through invisibility: "If they do not see you, they cannot hurt you." Praise could flip into punishment; curiosity could trigger shame. Over time, the nervous system encodes a single equation: to be visible is to be vulnerable to shame or punishment.

From these conditions, a set of survival rules forms and becomes procedural memory:

- Stay small; signal nothing that could be noticed.
- Read the room before you move.
- Control the frame—position, distance, tone—so nothing unpredictable can reach you.
- Keep the group intact by staying invisible; exposure threatens belonging.

What looks like withdrawal is often finely calibrated control: scanning the perimeter, predicting reactions, lowering signal strength. The same adaptations that once protected life now keep connection out of reach.

From these conditions, the system recruits distinct jobs to keep exposure low and control high.

Core Roles in This Dynamic

When survival depends on not being seen, different parts take on specialized jobs to keep exposure low and control high. One limits visibility; another monitors the environment; a third enforces rules when safety feels at risk. This is the system's coordinated procedure for managing threat. Each role carries a distinct tone and task, and understanding their cooperation helps turn disappearance into choice.

- **Watcher**: Runs perimeter: scans exits, tracks sounds, watches hands and faces, times distance to the door. Prefers facts over feelings until safety is proven. Not inherently hostile; it is an early-warning system. Under strain it can borrow a critical edge, but its core function is surveillance, not judgment.
- **Visibility Blocker:** Holds the rule "being seen is dangerous". Regulates exposure by shrinking signal and surface, sometimes full disappearance. Its job is to keep the body from becoming a target. It learned that praise could turn into spotlight, and spotlight into punishment, so it reduces noticeability to survive.
- **Enforcer:** Enters when the first two cannot hold the line. Enforces rules ("No eye contact." "No personal stories." "Sit by the wall"), interrupts approach, or flips to rigid compliance to end the moment. It protects rank and prevents exposure from outpacing safety. Think of it as a lockdown protocol.

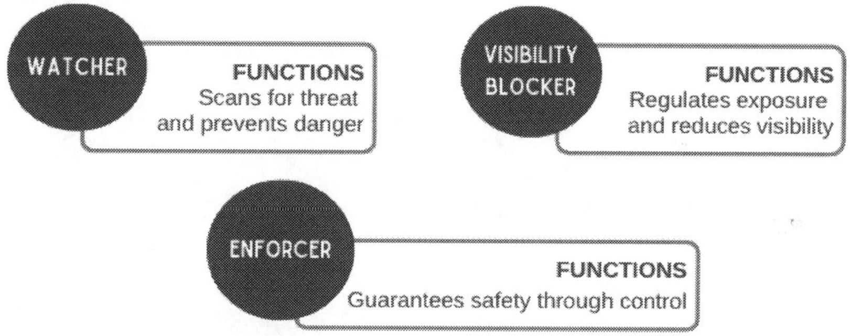

Fig. 29.1. Basic roles in the Invisibility Loop

The Invisibility Loop

In histories where being noticed drew danger (ridicule, punishment, coercion, or betrayal) visibility became costly. The system solved for survival by restricting how much could be seen (Visibility Blocker) and by elevating environmental monitoring (Watcher). Praise began to feel like a spotlight; eye contact like exposure; novelty like risk. Over time, this becomes automatic: the perimeter sets the terms before content is even considered.

Together they keep life possible: one hides, one surveils. When threat rises, a rank-protective part may join (Enforcer), but the primary loop remains: avoid gaze, scan the environment, hide again. Other protectors tend to appear only when this duo cannot hold the line, and an extra layer is needed.

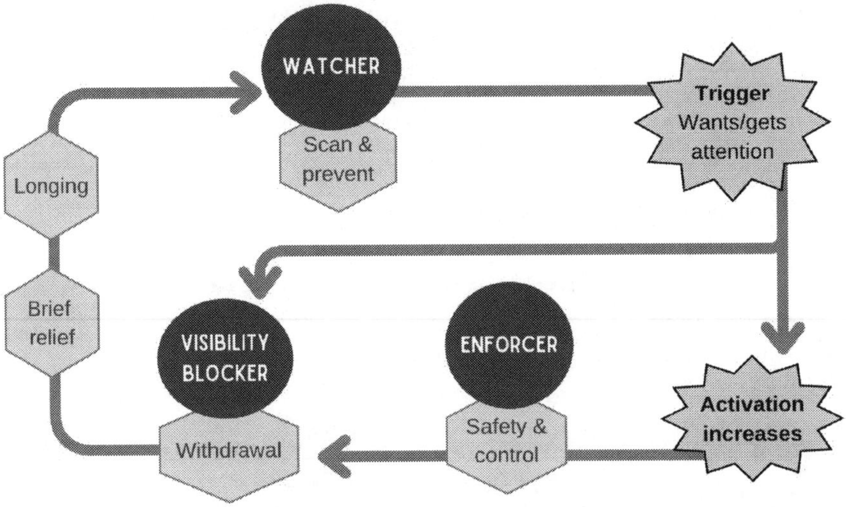

Fig. 29.1 The Invisibility Loop

Motivational Systems Organizing the Invisibility Loop

The survival engines underneath invisibility make shrinking and scanning look like disengagement when they are actually doing the same job: keep exposure low and control high.

- **Defense-alarm (Watcher).** Heightened vigilance, space management (back to wall, sightline to door), monitoring tone shifts and relational cues. Preserves initiative by anticipating threat before it fully emerges. "If I know what's coming, nothing can catch us off guard."
- **Defense-freeze/orient (Visibility Blocker).** Shrinks visibility through stillness, soft voice, fading words, and reduced movement while subtly tracking the environment. Organized around lowering

detectability and physiological arousal. "If I'm small enough, danger is less likely."

- **Rank-power, frame control and rule enforcement (Enforcer).** Regulates what is said, how much is revealed, and who sets the terms of interaction. Recruits silence, compliance, or corrective rule-setting to prevent humiliation or loss of position. "If I control the frame and enforce the rules, we won't be targeted."
- **Attachment - inhibited reception (Visibility Blocker, sometimes shared with Watcher).** The wish for contact is present, but access is rationed. "Half looks" replace direct gaze; engagement is partial and quickly withdrawn. Closeness is sampled without full exposure. "A little contact, on our terms." Client voice: "I want to, but not too much."

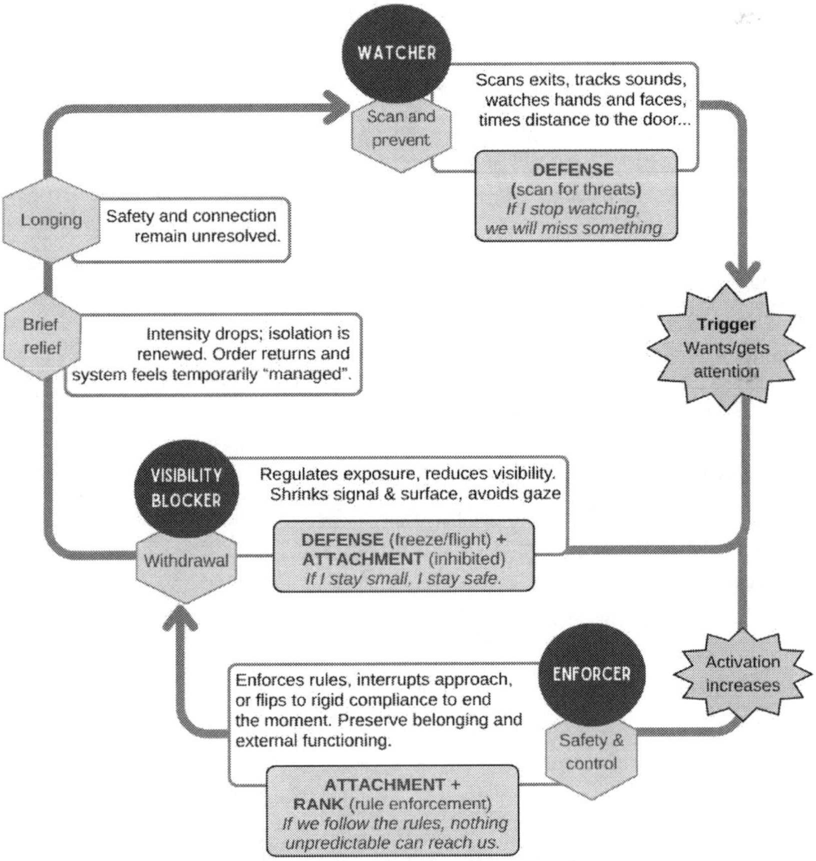

Fig. 29.3. Motivational Systems organizing the invisibility Loop

- **Attachment and rank organized around loyalty and internal order-keeping (Enforcer).** Limits visibility to preserve belonging and external functioning. Controls what is shown, what is said, and how much is revealed to prevent scrutiny or retaliation. "We stay in if we stay unseen." Client voice: "If anyone found out, we would lose everything."

Defense and rank can look similar in the room because both may produce silence, stillness, or withdrawal. The distinction lies in purpose. Defense is organized around survival: reducing arousal and avoiding immediate threat. Rank is organized around hierarchy: obedience, rule-following, and protection from humiliation or punishment within a social order. When it is unclear which is active, asking what the system is trying to prevent—overwhelm or down-ranking—often clarifies the function.

Loyalty emerges when attachment, rank, and defense are recruited together to preserve belonging under threat. Each component is adaptive; together they form a loop that ensures safety through invisibility. The task of therapy is not to break it but to make it optional: to let being seen become a choice, not a threat. Visibility here is never forced, it is invited, time-limited, and reversible, so the system can learn that presence no longer equals danger.

RECOGNIZING THE DYNAMIC

This triad sets the frame before any story begins. The space is organized for safety: back to a wall, clear sightline to the door, a path to the exit. The Watcher quietly maps the perimeter—hallway sounds, hinge creaks, your hand shifting on the notebook—while the Visibility Blocker reduces its footprint: less voice, less movement, smaller breath. Only after the Watcher signals *clear* does attention widen enough to risk listening. This is not about closing distance; it is about permission to exist and take up a little space, starting here.

Contact arrives as tiny trial balloons. A brief "I think..." lifts, then drops into fog or topic drift as nearness rises. Logistics and facts are preferred because they keep the lights low; praise can feel like a spotlight, and direct gaze reads as exposure. Half looks (looking at the rug, the clock, or the therapist's chin) are often *peak* engagement in this triad—listening hard, scanning, calculating whether proximity is tolerable today.

Tiny changes activate the alarm: a chair moved, the door half-closed instead of open, a new pen tapping. The system registers and tightens before the mind has words. Even when support is steady, the body may choose distance over depth to keep the perimeter intact.

NON-VERBAL CUES	
WATCHER	• Seat choice favors control of space (back to wall, sightline to door/clock/window). • Scans exits and tracks hallway sounds; notes your micro-moves (pen, posture, hand position). • Startle to small shifts; micro-pause before risky words; monitoring resumes whenever arousal rises.
VISIBILITY BLOCKER	• Minimal movement; smaller breath; shoulders narrow; chin tucks; body angles away. • Gaze management: looks at your hands or the floor; prefers a "half look" over direct eye contact; avoids praise/spotlight. • Disappearing acts: long silences; "I can't find words"; sense of going far away or "fog." • After higher-contact moments: fatigue, headache, shutdown, urge to cancel the next session.
ENFORCER	• Rule enforcement to end proximity: "No eye contact," "No personal stories," "Sit by the wall." • Interrupts approach with rank signals (posture expands, as ready to cross examine). • Physically inserts distance—sits back, crosses arms, shifts away or changes seat.
VERBAL CUES	
WATCHER	• Fact-first questions: "Is this recorded?" "Who reads your notes?" "Where is this stored?" • Comments that re-establish surveillance ("You looked at the clock," "You moved your hand"). • Can borrow a critical edge under stress, but the baseline is surveillance, not judgment.
VISIBILITY BLOCKER	• Voice thins or softens; sentences trail off; volume drops mid-phrase. • "I don't know." "It's gone." "I can't find words." • Requests for permission or apology for existing ("Sorry," "Is this okay?"). • Childlike tone or syntax; fragmented, sensory language ("It was too loud," "Too close").
ENFORCER	• Image-protection or secrecy language: "We don't talk about that," "That gets people in trouble." • Interrupts approach with rank signals (tone sharpens, cross-examining questions). • Hard pivot to rigid compliance ("Fine." "Yes/No" only) or abrupt topic switch to safe ground. • Image-protection or secrecy language: "We don't talk about that." "That gets people in trouble."
OSCILATION LOOP CUES	
• The moment gaze or warmth increases → Watcher ramps up scanning → if arousal spikes, Enforcer executes → Hidden Presence retreats. • Small reach ("I think...") followed by fog, then perimeter check, then a rule that ends the moment. • Praise lands like a spotlight: micro-flinch, eyes drop, scanning returns, contact collapses. • Therapist whiplash: "We were almost here, and then the room went far away."	

Table 29.1. The invisibility Loop cues

The cost often shows up after the hour. Slightly more nearness can bring fatigue, a pressure headache, or shutdown that was not present on the way in. None of this is oppositional; it is accurate learning from unsafe exposure—a safety protocol kicking in.

Invisibility moves through the room as micro-adjustments of gaze, breath, and distance. A brief softening can vanish into fog; a half-reach for contact is followed by scanning the doorframe. What might look like disengagement, lack of interest or resistance is just coordinated survival logic coming online: keep exposure low, keep surveillance high. Let us look at the cues by role and how the sequence tends to unfold.

How they work together: One hides, one surveils, and if needed, one enforces. The loop is quick: avoid gaze → scan perimeter → (if arousal rises) enforce → retreat. The task is not to pry visibility open, but to keep each role's purpose intact while updating the method, so being seen becomes chosen, brief, and reversible, not demanded or avoided.

Opening sessions by asking where the client would like to sit often yields immediate information, and shares control from the start. Because these presentations can be mistaken for nearby patterns (appeasement, content-guarding, or punitive control), sort what this is (and what it is not) before intervening.

WORKING WITH THIS DYNAMIC

The Watcher's job is excellent: detect threats before contact. We do not retire that function; instead, we recalibrate the method so surveillance becomes collaborative, bounded, and easier to stand down. Give the role a clear beginning and end, a way to signal "all clear", and enough routine that the nervous system does not have to keep the lights on high. If a stricter voice jumps in—"Don't look up"—name the recruit, thank it for trying to keep things safe, and return to the Watcher's task: looking is never forced; it happens when the system says it is ready.

While the perimeter is being updated, the Visibility Blocker needs contact that does not pull it into the spotlight: brief, words-only support it can approach or decline.

Contact here is offered sideways rather than head-on. The task is to let the Hidden Child be present without being pinned: make a place for it in the room that doesn't demand performance, keep support words-only, and give the system language to end visibility the moment it tips toward exposure. Indirect presence signals welcome without putting it in the spotlight; a single, quiet line of support lands toward the room rather than into the eyes; and clear opt-outs keep control where it belongs.

CLINICAL VIGNETTE

Staying Small

Midway through the session, Jonah's voice had thinned to a whisper. Shoulders curved forward, eyes fixed on the edge of the carpet, the Visibility Blocker had taken the lead. The room felt smaller.

After a pause, his gaze flicked toward the door, then the window, then the therapist's notebook. The Watcher was awake, scanning the perimeter. "The door's not all the way closed", he said. "Someone could hear."

I asked if he wanted it open or shut. "Half", he replied. When I adjusted it, his shoulders loosened slightly, but his eyes kept moving. "It's better", he murmured, "but still..."

A firmer tone followed from inside: "Stop talking so much. You'll make it worse." The Enforcer had joined, tightening the rules of engagement. Jonah fell silent again, hands folded tightly.

The therapist notices something is happening and asks Jonah. He says: "A part says to stop talking so much." The therapist says: "It sounds like there are a few jobs running at once, one keeping things quiet, one checking for danger, one making sure no rules are broken. Does that sound right?"

A small nod. Then his head dropped further, and the air seemed to flatten, Withdrawal had completed the loop. "I'm tired", he whispered. "Can we stop?"

The therapist said, "Of course. A lot happened just now, the watching, the checking, the keeping safe. We can stop for today and continue next time."

His breathing deepened. For the first time, his eyes met the therapist´s eyes for a half-second before lowering again.

Clinical Reflection

This moment unfolded exactly as the loop predicts: the Visibility Blocker receded, the Watcher scanned, the Enforcer enforced, and withdrawal sealed safety. The therapist respected sequence rather than overriding it, offering choice before contact, stillness before words. By naming the jobs ("watching", "checking", "keeping safe") without judgment, the therapist joined the system's logic rather than contradicting it.

Shrinking and scanning look like disengagement, but they are coordinated survival programs aimed at the same job: keep exposure low and control high: freeze/orient (defense), control the frame (rank), ration contact (attachment), and protect belonging (loyalty), while therapy supplies cooperation and predictability.

Safety was not achieved by increasing visibility, but by sharing control of it. That shared control made the first half-second of eye contact possible, small, brief, and fully chosen.

The aim is not to lure the hidden one forward, but to make nearness feel possible and stoppable, for example: create a place without pressure, an empty chair or spot "for the one who needs to stay behind the coats".

Contact here is offered sideways rather than head-on. The task is to let the Visibility Blocker be present without being pinned: make a place for it in the room that does not demand performance, keep support words-only, and give the system language to end visibility the moment it tips toward exposure. Indirect presence signals welcome without putting it in the spotlight; a single, quiet line of support lands toward the room rather than into the eyes; and clear opt-outs keep control where it belongs. The aim is not to lure the hidden one forward, but to make nearness feel possible and stoppable, for example: create a place without pressure, an empty chair or spot "for the one who needs to stay behind the coats".

When invisibility and surveillance come online, our job is not to pry the client into the light but to make light controllable. As in prior chapters, the 4 Ps (Permission, Precision, Pace, Predictability) translate into four practical moves that keep visibility under the client's control. The following are some tips to work with this dynamic.

Contract: Shared Permission

Set a simple, repeatable agreement for how much work can be done. Visibility is chosen, not demanded. Options are explicit and available at any moment: no direct gaze, suggest half look, stop signals that are honored immediately, and permission for the Watcher to scan first. Examples of sentences you can use:

- ★ "We won't look longer than it feels right."
- ★ "Make sure you sit where it feels right; pay attention to your body signals about that."
- ★ "You can look at my shoulder, forehead or my chin instead if that helps."
- ★ "If you need to look away or close your eyes, that's still contact—we will follow your pace."
- ★ "You're in charge of when to start and when to stop. I'll follow your signal."
- ★ "Anything inside can let us know when to stop."

These examples tell the system that being seen is negotiable, reversible, and most importantly, optional.

Dose: Precision of Contact

Keep contact tiny and controllable. Swap sustained eye contact for a single glance to a neutral point, such as the rug or the clock, and then orient to the present. Trade broad questions for one sentence of acknowledgment, then orient again. Distances are stated and kept; the Watcher can help choose angle, sightline, and what will keep the space feeling safe. Examples of sentences that can be used:

- ★ "Let's try one glance, just to the window, then back at me and repeat as many times as needed."
- ★ "Can we stay with one sentence, not the whole story?"
- ★ "We'll take this in a drop, not a wave."
- ★ "You tell me when to look away."
- ★ "Can you look at the part that is struggling now as you look at me?" (Keeping co-consciousness and double focus.)

Support should be words-only unless otherwise negotiated, offered in gradually adapted, low-intensity doses.

Timing: Pace and Repair)

Treat repair as the work. Co-scan the room for a few seconds (doors, windows, sounds), name two present-time anchors, and pause so the nervous system can register safety.

- ★ "Do you want to try to let me into your line of sight for three breaths?" (Or three seconds if breath is triggering.)
- ★ "Notice how you said stop, and we stopped."
- ★ "Can the part notice that when he/she said stop, we stopped?" If the answer is yes, you could add "How does that feel, can you check?"

Using a cooperative approach and pointing out small gains aloud so the perimeter learns that visibility begins and ends on the client's or any part´s signal. Each successful stop teaches the body that visibility can end safely on command. Timing means starting and ending on purpose every time.

Practice and Repetition: Predictability

Lower the Watcher's load with repetition: same seating unless negotiated, the same opening orient, the same end-of-hour cool-down.

- CLINICAL VIGNETTE

The Unseen Sentry

Client (very quiet, eyes on floor): "It feels like… if you see me, something bad will start."

Therapist: "So the rule is unseen means safe. Can we let the Watcher check whether the room feels safe, and if not, say what would make it safe first?"

(Client's gaze sweeps the door and window; listens to hallway noise).

Therapist: "I'll stay still while you scan. When you're ready, we can try a half look—you pick a spot on the rug; I'll use the clock. Or, like other times, you can look at my chin. Whatever works best."

(Client looks up for a few seconds, then down).

Therapist: "How was that?"

(Client shrugs; seems calmer).

Therapist: "We can stop here if you want, or try again.

(Client looks up for a few more seconds, then down).

Therapist: "How was that now?"

Client: "Better."

Therapist: "We can stop here if you want, or try again."

Client (exhales): "It's good like this today. Thank you."

What changed was not content; it was tolerated visibility that ended on the client's terms. Having acknowledged the perimeter, we refine it, not remove it.

Clinical reflections:

The vignette shows boundary before visibility and choice before contact. The Watcher is engaged first (scan, options), so nearness is negotiated, not imposed. Half-look trials are micro-dosed and reversible, which lets the Visibility Blocker be seen without exposure. Each pass ends on the client's signal, reinforcing that visibility begins and ends under their control. The result is not more content but a workable perimeter: calmer physiology, brief eye contact tolerated, and a template the Adult Self can repeat.

Any change in the structure of the work is announced and agreed to in advance. The message is consistent: the perimeter is co-authored, and nothing about nearness or being seen will arrive as a surprise. Examples of sentences you could use:

- "We'll start the same way today, a quick or careful look around, then decide if we make eye contact or any other type of contact."

- "Same office, same order or work, so nothing surprises your Watcher."
- "Next time, we'll plan one small change together."

Consistency is safety. Predictability teaches the Watcher that visibility is co-authored, time-limited, and never ambushed.

This is the rhythm throughout: permission that can be exercised, precision that never overwhelms, pacing that marks limits kept, and predictability that lets the Watcher stand down.

Once the system has experienced brief, chosen contact without punishment, it is the moment to introduce language that links trauma-time rules (then) to present-time options (now). These can be micro-sentences the therapist can introduce, practice, and install in session so that the Adult Self can reuse after session when needed.

The idea is to introduce a different way of relating to triggers that act like procedural anchors: they translate a bodily reflex (hide/scan/lock down) into choice:

- "Then, being seen drew danger; now, we decide when and how to be seen."
- "Then, hiding kept you safe; now, looking can be brief and end on your signal."
- "Then, scanning kept you alive; now, scanning and resting can take turns."

Each line preserves the survival logic while adding what was once missing: choice, reversibility, and shared control. In practice, these micro-interventions or tags, become quick scripts the Watcher can endorse and the Visibility Blocker can tolerate, keeping visibility small, negotiated, and stoppable. Each tag does three things at once: honors the old rule that kept life intact, defines a new boundary grounded in choice, and returns authority and control to the client.

Markers of Movement

When invisibility is the safety plan, progress does not arrive as big disclosures, it shows up in micro-adjustments of space, gaze, and sequence. These are mostly procedural gains, not narrative ones: the nervous system tries a new setting for a few breaths and checks, "Did we survive?" Your job is to catch those tiny shifts, keep them small, and pair each one with a brief Then–Now tag when it can be useful.

The tag names the update in plain language, ties it to the body's felt sense *right now*, and respects the old rule that kept the client alive. Keep tags short (one sentence), collaborative (ideally in the client's words), and followed by a pause so the update can register somatically. If the Watcher needs a stop signal, use it. Consent takes priority over completion.

As the contract, dose, timing, and ritual hold, change shows up quietly. Look for these small shifts:

- The Watcher announces itself ("I need to check the door") instead of running the alarm in silence.
- Scans shorten; the first brake becomes talk (a joke, a logistics question) rather than body pain.
- The Visibility Blocker tolerates half looks or brief name-saying without collapse.
- Seating becomes a choice: the client can sit not fully backed to a wall for a few minutes.
- Endings feel quieter, not emptier; less post-session headaches and shutdown.

These shifts signal that the perimeter is sharing the job and visibility is increasingly under the client's control.

CLOSING THOUGHTS

At core, this tryad protects life by limiting visibility. The work is not to pry the hidden one into the light but to make light controllable: a shared contract for how near to be, contact delivered in exact doses, a tempo that marks limits kept, and ritual that lets the Watcher stand down. When visibility remains optional and reversible, proximity stops requiring a price. That is when the body learns a new rule: being seen can be brief, chosen, and safe enough to repeat.

Clinical Anchors

What to remember...

- Invisibility and surveillance are intelligent strategies.
- Share control of visibility.
- Offer micro-contact and let the Watcher co-author predictability.
- Mark kept limits out loud; repair is the medicine.
- Make predictability explicit: same opening orient, same close, pre-announce any change.
- Mark kept limits out loud; repair is the medicine.
- Name silence as engagement (listening, scanning, calculating risk), not absence.

What to avoid...

- Pressing for eye contact, proximity, or pace.
- Reading silence as lack of engagement.
- Rearranging agreements without consent.

Chapter 30: Navigating Ambivalence About Traumatic Memory

Therapist Reflection

He said, "I think I'm ready to remember", and a part of me wanted to lean forward, to say yes, to begin. Minutes later his jaw locked, his hands went cold, and another part cut in: "Stop. You know what happens." I used to push through, explain pacing, promise safety, and try to hold the frame. Now I pause and ask, "Who is giving permission and who isn't?" If I can honor both the one who wants relief and the one who is guarding the lids, the work can continue without reenactment.

Not all movement toward memory means the same thing. A reach can be a wish for relief; a brake can be protection. In many systems, approach and avoidance arrive together: one side leans toward what happened, another guards the lid, and a third signals capacity. The task here is neither to pry nor to prove, but to set conditions so the system can approach, pause, and return without reenactment.

As the room grows steadier and the present feels more believable, parts can sit nearer to one another without takeover. Sooner or later, a new bind appears: Are we allowed to approach what happened? In many dissociative systems, the answer is not yes or no, but a field of ambivalence where some parts carry fragments while others regulate the lid. Memory work here is not opening a file; it is entering a relationship that includes fear, loyalty, amnesia, parts who never agreed, and parts who still do not know.

The task here is specific: keep the system evolving together while strengthening permission and cooperation. We respect the rules, choose the tiniest workable target, and stop early—every time. Our work is to surface the dynamics around permission and move at the pace of the slowest consenting part. The aim is not content; it is conditions.

UNDERSTANDING THE DYNAMIC

Ambivalence is more than confusion or avoidance; it was learned in the worst moments of experience. It develops in environments where telling was dangerous and not-telling preserved connection and order. Over time, the body learns to pair truth with rupture and silence with safety. What emerges is an internal tug-of-war: a drive to know and integrate, countered by a drive to not know—to keep awareness partitioned through *not-me* protection. When traumatic memory involves the very figures who were meant to protect, this conflict deepens: not remembering becomes a way to avoid breaking apart, to stay loyal, contained, and functional.

Origins of the Dynamic

Ambivalence about traumatic memory can form through two main routes, depending on where danger came from and how safety was learned. Both routes shape how memory roles later organize. In betrayal trauma, secrecy and loyalty rules dominate; in stranger assault, capacity and shame regulation take the lead.

1. **Loyalty-Bond Variant. Betrayal by caregivers or trusted figures.** Here, attachment and defense fuse around the same people. The child learns that love and threat come from the same source. Staying loyal preserves belonging, even when it costs reality. Ambivalence centers on not breaking the bond: telling once meant losing care, so silence preserved connection. Memory, loyalty, and survival become intertwined.

   To survive, the system divided its tasks: one part held fragments of truth, another enforced silence. The pattern repeats later in therapy, where safety and exposure again coexist. What follows are the typical learning conditions that create this ambivalence:

   - **Punished or costly truth.** Early disclosures were met with blame, disbelief, or retaliation. Silence kept proximity and safety. The body learned that *knowing + telling = danger*, and installed brakes.
   - **Gaslighting and confusion.** Caregivers denied, minimized, or re-wrote events. The child internalized self-doubt and

credibility traps ("If it's true, I'll shatter; if it's not, I'm a liar"), making the Seal Keeper necessary to police certainty and pace.

- **Disorganized attachment.** The person who harmed the client was also the person responsible to feed, praise, or protect. The attachment system and the defense system become fused; the same figure signals both safety and danger. Loyalty then requires ignorance. Parts aligned with the bond guard against anything that could break it (especially memory).
- **Secrecy contracts and oaths.** Explicit or implied rules ("Don't tell", "You'll ruin everything") migrated inward as law. The Guardian became the Oath-Keeper; the Memory Keeper learned to keep fragments offstage.
- **Role reversal.** Parentification and image-protection ("Keep the family together", "Don't make trouble") made non-disclosure an act of care. Knowing equaled betrayal; not-knowing equaled love.
- **Overwhelm and state-dependent storage.** When arousal spiked beyond capacity, experience encoded in pieces—sensations, images, procedures—rather than narrative. Dissociation did its job; later, the Memory Keeper and Guardian are the architecture left behind.
- **Institutional loyalties.** Communities, schools, faith groups, or teams tied to silence. Losing the group felt like losing life. Guardians learned to defend membership by limiting access to memory.

2. **Defense Inward Variant. Assault by strangers or limited relational ties.** When harm comes from outsiders and no ongoing bond exists, the system organizes around survivability rather than allegiance and ambivalence organizes less around loyalty and more around enduring the unbearable. The mind turns protection inward—through denial, self-blame, contempt, or collapse—to keep functioning. The struggle is not "don't betray them", but "don't let this destroy us". Typical learning conditions include:

    - **Shattering or forgetting.** Overwhelm produces fragmentary or absent narrative, with body pain or flashes but no storyline. Dissociation protects by cutting the feed, in a system already characterized by a disorganized structure.

- **Self-attack as control.** Contempt and blame are recruited to keep order ("It's my fault", "Shut up")—rank turned inward to prevent chaos.
- **Stigma and silence.** Shame, disbelief, or exposure fears teach "say less to stay intact", even without a person to defend.
- **Function first.** School/work demands reinforce a rule: do not open what will take us down. The result is ambivalence shaped by *capacity* (dose, shutdown, shame) more than *loyalty* (oaths, image, belonging).

Even when external danger has passed, the body and mind continue to operate by the old rules. The ambivalence around knowing and not-knowing is not simple hesitation or resistance; it is the nervous system following an installed survival map; an internal app that once kept life intact and now operates automatically.

As mentioned in chapter 24, the following points on procedural conditioning, rule economy, functional necessity and connection as a trigger, describe how these inherited laws keep the system organized even when danger is long gone. These hold true in each one of the loops that we have seen so far, including this one. Let us remember them:

- **Procedural conditioning.** As awareness approaches forbidden territory, the person´s personality system instinctively brakes, appearing as fog, sleepiness or head pressure. This is much more than ambivalence; it is protection, preventing a return to the intolerable state of mind characteristic of disorganized attachment. These responses operate outside conscious intention and do not require belief, memory, or decision.
- **Rule economy.** Inward laws keep order and belonging; shame is used as glue to hold the lid shut.
- **Functional necessity.** Guardians protect school, work, parenting; tomorrow's tasks. If yesterday floods today, the system fears collapse.
- **Connection as a trigger.** Therapeutic closeness reactivates the original dangerous bind: approach risks exposure; exposure risks loss. Without shared permission and dose, the Guardian reads therapy as another site of danger.

- **Conflicting mandates across parts.** The Memory Keeper's relief, the Guardian's loyalty, and the Flood part's limits were learned at different times for good reasons. Until each has a job in today's plan, yesterday's methods stay in charge.

Core Roles in The Memory-Ambivalence Dynamic

Think of the following as a cast list the system relies on whenever memories come close. These roles that keep truth intact, keep dose tolerable, and prevent premature realization, all while preserving belonging and bonds to caregivers when still needed. Ambivalence is not one part fighting another; it is this coordinated system managing survival from multiple angles at once.

In most dissociative systems, ambivalence about traumatic memory does not live in one part alone. It is distributed across several interlocking roles: one carries what was endured, tracking relational truth when needed; another controls access, another manages exposure, another signals limits, and another shuts things down if the system tips too far. What looks like conflict (between remembering and forgetting) is actually cooperation designed to preserve continuity, belonging and survival.

When traumatic memories draw near, the system rarely works in isolation. It recruits familiar protectors described in previous chapters: Watchers, Guardians, and Keepers; each adapting its original task to the context of memory management. What changes is not the cast but the motive: sometimes they organize around belonging and loyalty, other times around safety and control. Understanding which survival aim is active clarifies whether the ambivalence we meet is relational (the Loyalty-Bond Variant) or defensive (the Defense–Inward Variant).

- **Memory Keeper: Sensory/Experiential Storage.** Custodian of what was endured. It stores the unbearable (images, sensations, fragments of traumatic experience), so the rest of the system can keep living. Its function is protective containment through holding. It does not decide; it keeps to prevent collapse. The Memory Keeper's focus is on preservation: ensuring the material is not lost, while keeping it away when the system cannot yet bear to know. When approached safely, it does not argue, it shows. Its logic is survival through containment: "Someone must hold the pain, but not all of us at once." In loyalty contexts, the Truth Holder (see chapter 24) may step forward as the system's spokesperson for relational truth (carrying the tension between love and betrayal; the relational conflict), while the Memory Keeper still holds the sensory material (content).

- **Seal Keeper: Access Regulation.** Guards the boundary between knowing and not knowing. It regulates access to what the Memory Keeper holds, controlling exposure to prevent destabilization. Where the Memory Keeper's task is *storage*, the Seal Keeper's task is *sealing*: enforcing silence, stopping the opening, dictating when revelation is too dangerous. Its tone is procedural and defensive, an alarm system, not an archive. It carries the survival logic: "If we open, we may not survive what comes out." Together, the Memory and Seal Keepers operate like a vault and lock: one holds material, the other maintains timing and containment. In loyalty-based variant, the Seal Keeper often works together with the Watcher (chapter 24), who detects relational threat while the Seal enforces the stop. (The Watcher detects and Seal keeper regulates).

- **Lid Keeper: Exposure Control.** Manages exposure once the Seal begins to loosen. Its task is to contain intensity (tone, tears, words, gestures) so nothing spills too far. If the Seal Keeper enforces *secrecy*, the Lid Keeper enforces *composure*. This is the system's last line of defense before revelation. Its tone can be dominant or punitive, echoing the authority of the Oath Keeper described in chapter 24. However, unlike the Oath Keeper (whose task is to preserve loyalty to a bond), the Lid Keeper´s function is exposure control. It regulates expression and intensity to prevent humiliation or loss of control. The Lid Keeper equates regulation with safety and often mistakes feeling for chaos. Its message is anticipatory, a protective measure: "If I strike first, no one can expose or humiliate us.

- **Threshold Guardian: Dose & Capacity Signaling**. Signals capacity limits through sleepiness, fog, blanks, heaviness, or time-loss. It translates the body´s language of dose: "not no", but "enough for now."

- **Flood Responder: Circuit Breaker.** Arrives when the surge tips over the edge. Cuts power to exposure through collapse, nausea, sudden flight, or total shut-off. Where the Threshold Guardian is the limit signal during the rise, the Flood Responder is the full stop at the peak. *Stance:* “Overload—shut everything down.” “Better to go offline than be overwhelmed.”

Although these roles may resemble protectors described in earlier chapters, their organizing motive distinguishes them. The Memory Keeper holds sensory experience; the Truth Holder carries relational meaning and moral tension when loyalty is at stake. The Watcher detects relational risk, while the Seal Keeper regulates access to memory itself. The Lid Keeper governs exposure and composure once material begins to surface. When loyalty organizes protection, the Oath Keeper enforces silence to preserve belonging; when regulation organizes protection, the Lid Keeper enforces containment to preserve control. The behaviors may look similar (silence, inhibition, composure) but the survival aim determines which role is leading.

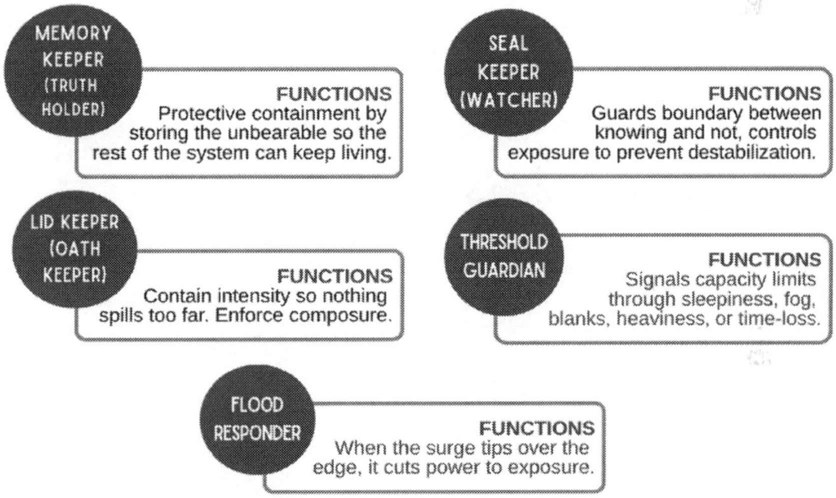

Fig 30.1. The Memory-Ambivalence Loop roles

Together these roles form a coordinated gradient of protection, each positioned at a different layer of access and control. The Memory Keeper holds the contents deep inside; the Seal Keeper decides when, if ever, the vault may open; the Lid Keeper regulates what can be shown or felt once opening begins. At that point stands the Threshold Guardian, monitoring arousal and permission—how much can pass before the system tips. If the threshold is crossed too abruptly, the

Flood Responder shuts everything down until safety is re-established. They coordinate content, timing, expression, and dose. When these roles rediscover coordination, remembering no longer means overwhelm: the vault can open in increments, the Seal Keeper can pace, and the Flood can stand down.

These descriptions refer to functions rather than fixed roles; in practice, a single part may carry several of these functions, or they may be distributed across parts depending on the needs of the system.

When the Adult Self can mediate among these roles; allowing the Keeper to hold, the Seal to pace, the Lid to regulate, and the body to signal limits—the circuit becomes collaborative rather than defensive. What once looked like resistance reveals itself as cooperation in disguise: a system that learned to keep knowing survivable. Each role continues to do its job, but now under shared consent and pacing rather than isolation or alarm.

Each variant that follows reuses these roles in different configurations. In the Loyalty–Bond form, the system recruits attachment-based protectors (most often the Truth Holder and Oath Keeper) to guard belonging and prevent relational rupture. The Watcher detects relational risk; the Truth Holder carries the tension between bond and truth; the Oath Keeper / Lid Keeper enforces silence or composure to preserve belonging; and the Seal Keeper regulates access to memory itself. These roles often operate simultaneously rather than sequentially, each addressing a different layer of relational threat.

In the Defense–Inward variant the Seal and Lid Keepers take precedence to preserve safety, order, and control, while the Memory Keeper continues to hold the material in the background. The choreography looks similar—approach, alarm, limit, withdrawal—but the motive beneath it differs, determining which roles and/or voices step forward and what the system is trying to prevent.

Having mapped the internal cast and their coordination, we can now see how this same circuitry behaves under different motives. In this chapter, Guardian is used as an umbrella term for protectors that regulate access and exposure, most often the Seal Keeper and Lid Keeper.

The Memory-Ambivalence Loop

This loop describes what happens when the system moves toward knowing what was once unbearable or towards telling in order to get help and how protection organizes around that movement. It has two variants: Loyalty-Bond variant and Defense-Inward variant. Although the architecture is the same (approach, alarm, limit, collapse, restoration, renewal), the underlying motive or survival logic differs and must be understood; it is either based on **belonging** or **safety**:

- In the **Loyalty–Bond variant**, truth threatens attachment; the system protects *relationship and rank* by turning away from what would expose or betray.
- In the **Defense–Inward variant**, truth threatens stability; the system protects *safety and control* by suppressing activation that feels explosive or contaminating.

In both, the choreography is cooperation in disguise, a living circuit that keeps knowing survivable.

When truth and attachment could not coexist (Loyalty-Bond variant), the system learned that remembering endangered belonging. Silence kept proximity; disbelief kept love. Over time, vigilance fused with restraint: the Watcher (chapter 24) and Seal Keeper joined forces to preserve proximity at any cost. The nervous system came to equate awareness with betrayal and ignorance with loyalty.

When truth and attachment were not fused with the same people (defense-inward variant), ambivalence reorganized around not being destroyed by what is known. With no bond to protect, the same roles turned inward: the Seal Keeper's caution and Lid Keeper's control dominated. The threat was no longer "I'll lose them", but "I'll lose control".

Approach. The Pull Toward Knowing. Something begins to move toward memory: a dream, a body flash, a phrase that lands differently, or a moment of trust in therapy.

- *Loyalty–Bond Variant:* The Truth Holder tests whether truth can be co-held without betraying a bond. Tone softens, the body leans in and there is a brief sense of possibility.

- *Defense-Inward Variant:* A flicker of wanting to tell or get help arises, the Memory Keeper edges forward, seeking relief or witness. There is no relational allegiance to protect, only the fear of collapse. The tone is cautious; the body opens slightly, eyes turn inward, voice slows.

Alarm. The Threat Returns As fragments of traumatic material rise, danger is detected (relational or internal).

- *Loyalty-Bond Variant:* The Watcher and Seal Keeper reactivate old rules: truth equals rupture, exposure equals loss. The body interprets remembering as disloyalty or betrayal. The Watcher reads relational threat through the Truth Holder´s loyalty map; the Seal Keeper applies the brake
- *Defense-Inward Variant:* The Seal Keeper and Lid Keeper anticipate overwhelm: "It is too much", "Everything will explode", "You will lose control." Arousal spikes; the body prepares to shut down if needed.

Threshold: The Limit Signal. When activation exceeds capacity, the Threshold Guardian translates dose/tolerance into bodily changes: sleepiness, fog, heaviness, head pressure, or sudden blankness. The message is not "no", but "enough for now".

- *Loyalty-Bond:* Fog or appeasement guards belonging: "Stop before you betray."
- *Defense-Inward:* Numbness guards stability: "Stop before you fall apart."

Flood. The Circuit Breaker. If the limit is missed or the pace changes too fast, the Flood Responder cuts power altogether: collapse, sudden flight, or shutdown (hard switch). It protects by going offline entirely.

- *Loyalty-Bond Variant:* Shame or freezing halts exposure; the body defends connection and belonging by going still.

  Defense-Inward Variant: Shutdown prevents perceived explosion; the body defends control by going offline.

Re-Stabilization. Re-Establishing Order. As activation drops and the system pulls back from contact through the Threshold and Flood responses, the Lid Keeper steps in to restore order and internal hierarchy. Withdrawal has already happened in the body; now the Lid organizes the aftermath and the Memory Keeper goes back to doing its job.

- *Loyalty–Bond Variant* Dominance defends the bond by attacking the self, contempt or scolding to restore loyalty and suppress exposure: "This is not true", "You shouldn't have said that." Control restores hierarchy and loyalty. The Lid restores loyalty by reducing what was revealed.
- *Defense–Inward Variant:* Rank turns inward through shame or self-attack: "You're disgusting", "You're weak". Control restores containment and suppresses anger. Posture hardens, affect flattens.

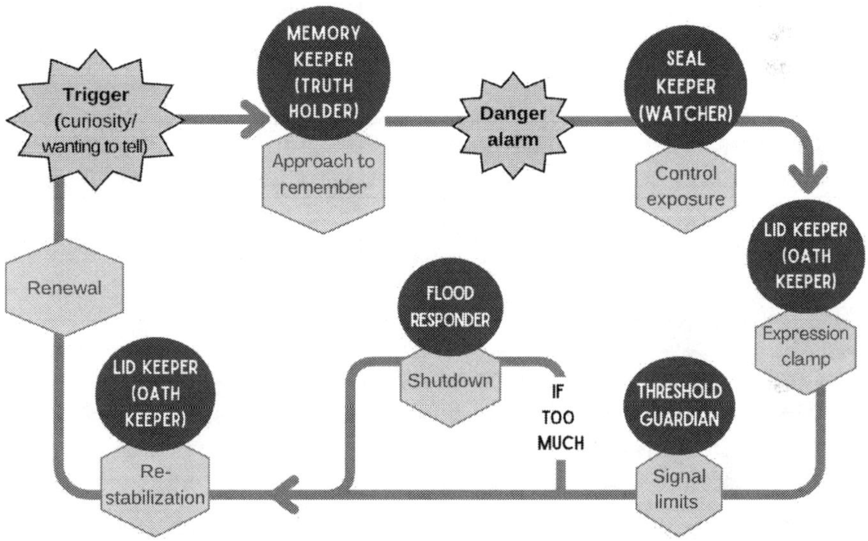

Figure 30.2 The Memory-Ambivalence Loop (Loyalty-Bond and Defense Inward Variants)

Renewal. Return of Curiosity. When none of the roles are overridden, the Adult Self can stay or come back online. The room steadies, orientation returns and curiosity re-emerges.

- *Loyalty–Bond Variant:* The Memory Keeper may allow another detail to surface under new, safer, shared conditions.
- *Defense–Inward Variant:* The body cautiously tests a small reach again (noticing a sensation, not trying to get rid of an image that

comes up, telling a phrase that was heard inside or simply staying present without pushing it away.

Each cycle shortens; backlash softens; trust in timing grows. The loop remains, but its charge diminishes: what once felt like threat begins to feel like choice.

Motivational Systems Organizing the Memory-Ambivalence Loop

As in other loops, at the surface the trauma-ambivalence loop presents as conflict (remember vs. do not remember) but underneath, several motivational systems coordinate survival: each keeps truth and safety intact in its own way. Keep in mind that before addressing content, a set of survival engines often comes online. Identifying and naming them keeps us from arguing with parts and lets us adjust the conditions (permission, dose, and predictability) so the system can approach without reenactment or backfiring afterwards.

- **Attachment-care seeking (Memory Keeper).** Reaches toward witness and recognition through curiosity, tentative remembering, or a longing to tell. Organized around preserving truth somewhere inside while testing whether knowing can be co-held safely. "If someone remembers, we aren't erased." Client voice: "I think I'm ready." "There's a door... I can almost see it."
- **Rank/power - hierarchy restoration (general function).** Activates when exposure threatens internal order or status. Seeks to re-establish a clear vertical structure (who regulates, who yields) because hierarchy once meant predictability and safety. Organized around preventing humiliation or chaos by restoring structure. "If the hierarchy is clear, we stay safe."
    - **Dominant branch (rank–domination, Lid Keeper**): appears as contempt, harsh grading, ridicule or composure control. It protects through superiority and attack, shutting down exposure before shame can occur. "We stay on top so no one can shame us." Client voice: "Stop, close it now."
    - **Submissive branch (rank–submission, Seal Keeper):** appears as freeze, compliance or the procedural "stop reflex". Protects by yielding and shrinking to prevent scalation. "If I don´t move, harm won´t escalate." Client voice: "Don´t move." "Just be quiet."

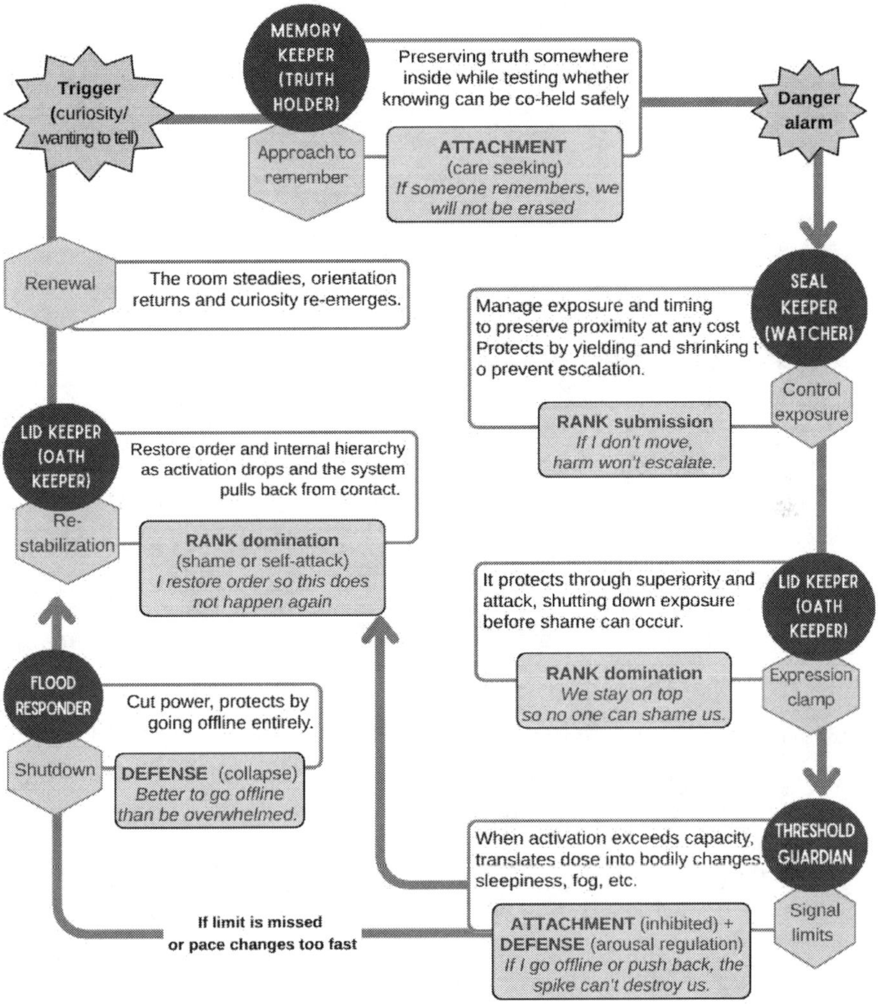

Fig 30.3. The motivational systems organizing the Memory-Ambivalence Loop

Both branches serve the same *function*: maintain predictability by re-establishing a vertical order after chaos threatens." If the hierarchy is clear, we stay safe—whether by yielding or by commanding." Client voice: Dominant tone: "Stop. You don't get to say that." "Close it now." Submissive tone: "Don't move." "Please, not again." "Just be quiet."

- **Defense -arousal regulation (Threshold Guardian and Flood Responder).** Activates when emotional charge approaches or exceeds capacity. The Threshold Guardian lowers intensity through fog, fatigue, or narrowing awareness; the Flood Responder shuts down or pushes back once overwhelm is underway. Organized around regulating dose and preventing system destabilization. "If I go offline (or push back) the spike can't destroy us." Client voice: "Everything just went fuzzy." "I'm fine." "Leave me alone."

In the Loyalty–Bond variant, attachment organizes protection around belonging. Remembering threatens relational continuity, so disbelief, minimization, or self-blame function to preserve the bond and image. The survival logic becomes relational: "If I keep the bond intact, we survive together." Client voice: "You'll ruin everything if you say it." "Good kids don't tell."

In the Defense–Inward variant, the same structural position is often occupied by shame organized within the rank system. When no enduring bond must be guarded, the system preserves order by attacking the self. Contempt and humiliation down-rank internally before external collapse can occur. The survival logic becomes: "If I punish myself first, no one else can destroy me." Client voice: "It's my fault." "I'm disgusting."

Each of these motivational systems corresponds to a protective role within the ambivalence circuit. Attachment animates the Memory Keepers reach towards witness; rank/power most often organizes the Lid Keeper's contempt or composure-control (and, at times, the Seal Keeper´s freeze/stop reflex); defense regulates dose through the Threshold Guardian and Flood Responder.

In the Loyalty-Bond variant, attachment recruits Loyalty organized protectors (for example Watcher, Truth Holder or Oath-Keeper functions) to prevent relational rupture. In the defense-inward variant, the same structural position is often occupied by shame organized within the rank system, turning protection inwards through self-attack.

RECOGNIZING THE DYNAMICS

The shift between the Memory Keeper and the Seal Keeper can be as subtle as a breath or as sudden as a slammed door. The Threshold Guardian may intervene through fatigue or fog, and the Lid Keeper may enforce distance through control or contempt. Knowing these cues lets you name the movement before it turns into shutdown or backlash.

This dynamic often arrives as a stutter-step: interest, then alarm, then distance. A client leans in ("Something's there") and a voice cuts across: "Don't you dare." The body obeys: fog, sleepiness, head pressure, numbness.

Language tightens; the relationship steps back. This is not resistance, it is regulation. The Seal Keeper noticed proximity and hit the brakes. Naming that function keeps both roles—the Memory Keeper and the Seal Keeper —present and in collaboration.

These shifts usually mark transitions between the Memory Keeper's reach, the Seal Keeper's brake, the Threshold Guardian's dose control, and the Lid Keeper's re-assertion of order. The sequence is fast: approach triggers alarm; alarm enforces distance; distance reignites longing and shame. Each phase protects the system from both danger and loss. The task is not to break the loop but to recognize its rhythm and create space where proximity to truth no longer feels like betrayal.

NON-VERBAL CUES	
MEMORY KEEPER	• Posture softens; eyes turn inward; breath deepens or trembles. • Tears, warmth, or a quiver of relief. • Gaze or voice becomes childlike or slowed. • Voice slows or seems younger; body sensations emerge (pressure, warmth, gut sensation).
SEAL KEEPER	• Sudden stillness, fog, or narrowing of attention. • Tightening jaw, breath-holding, body withdrawal. • Sudden posture shift from open to distant; arms cross, eyes avert. • The atmosphere changes: watchful, evaluative, testing.
LID KEEPER	• Posture straightens or expands; jaw juts forward; voice hardens. • Sudden energy surge after collapse, control returns. • Eyes narrow; muscles tense; movement decisive. • Function: re-establish order and dominance after instability.
THRESHOLD GUARDIAN	• Sudden dissociative fog, tunnel vision, or spacing-out. • Ache behind eyes or pressure in the head. • Energy drops abruptly: head lowers, shoulders slump, eyes glaze. • Speech slows or halts; hands cool; skin pales. • Shallow breathing; faintness; time slip.
FLOOD RESPONDER	• Abrupt shutdown or switch. Collapse, nausea, spinning, cold skin. • Blank eyes, slumped body, loss of orientation. • Feels to the therapist as if the person is "gone." • Function: cut power before the system burns out.

VERBAL CUES	
MEMORY KEEPER	• "Something's there," "I think I remember," "It's blurry but…" • Circling or tentative phrasing; fragmented storytelling. • Longing for validation: "Do you believe me?" "Does this make sense?" • "I get flashes, stairs, a smell, like it wants to be known." • "If I say it out loud, maybe it's real."
SEAL KEEPER	• No. Not here" "You know what happens when you talk." • "Stop," "This is stupid," "You're making it up." • Abrupt humor, logic, or change of topic. • Dismissive or critical tone aimed at self or therapist.
LID KEEPER	• "Stop acting like a baby." "None of this matters." • Sharp humor or mockery; accusatory edge toward self or therapist. • Rules reasserted with threats: "No talking about this." "Close it now or else…"
THRESHOLD GUARDIAN	• "I'm tired… I can't think." "It's too much." "Everything just went blank." • "It was here, and then it's gone." "I don't know what happened." • "I feel dizzy / heavy / far away." "I'm fine" (flatly or mechanically) to end contact.. • Apologies for disorientation: "Sorry, what we were saying."
FLOOD RESPONDER	• Little or no speech; confusion or cry without words. • Occasional fight burst ("Leave me alone!") just before collapse. • Afterward: silence, daze, or memory gap.

OSCILATION LOOP CUES
• A moment of curiosity followed by jolt or alarm. • Inner conflict: "I want to tell" → "Don't you dare" • Approach followed by fog, fatigue, or blankness. • Warmth or connection triggering sudden withdrawal or sarcasm. • Silence stretching out after a subtle opening. • The body leaning in, then freezing or pulling away. • Disclosure impulse → shame spike → retreat • Feeling exposed → self-attack → minimization • Relief and regret intertwined ("I shouldn't have said that"). • Small curiosity returning after safety is restored ("Maybe next time…").

AFTER-EFFECT LOOP CUES
• Shame spike, self-criticism, or conviction that therapy is dangerous. • Impulse to delete notes, avoid sessions, or suppress memory. • Relief mixed with regret: "I shouldn't have said that." • Dreams, flashbacks, or body pain that reopen the loop.

Table 30.1a. The Memory-Ambivalence Loop cues.

CLINICAL VIGNETTE

1) At the Edge of Capacity (Defense-Inward variant)

At fifteen, Pete was raped by several adult men. He remembers being grabbed and, later, stumbling home—nothing in between. Years later, three roles dominate:

- Memory Keeper: a young voice that says, "Please help me with the pain", carrying flashes of sensation without story.
- Seal Keeper: "No. Not now. Not safe." It blocks access whenever Pete insists, convinced that opening will annihilate him.
- Lid Keeper: when pressure rises, it attacks—"You caused this", "You're disgusting"—to shut the door through contempt and blame.

There is no pull to defend perpetrators or preserve a bond; the tug-of-war is *capacity versus collapse*. The therapist does not chase facts. Together they install permission (opt-in every time), precision (one neutral speck for twenty seconds), protection (stop-signal honored instantly; crisis plan rehearsed), and pace (do less than more on purpose). After several brief, predictable approaches—naming only *where* the body feels the ache—Pete notices something new: the Seal Keeper eases *before* shutdown. The Lid Keeper's insults soften to warnings ("Careful"), which can now be met with updated methods ("We'll stop when you say").

CLINICAL VIGNETTE

2) The Edge of Knowing (Loyalty-bond Variant)

Near the end of the session, Lila's voice softened. "I keep seeing flashes, like a glimpse of a basement door", she said, eyes narrowing as if looking inward. The Memory Keeper had stepped forward, testing the edge of knowing. Seconds later, her hand went to her throat. "No. Stop. You don't get to say that." (inner voice) The Seal Keeper had arrived, slamming the brake. Her breath quickened, color drained from her face. "It's fine. I'm fine." The Threshold Guardian began to dim awareness, and within moments, the Flood Responder completed the shutdown: fog rising, body folding into the chair. Then came the familiar whisper: "You make things up. You just want attention." The Lid-Keeper had stepped in, sealing the lid, through contempt and control.

The therapist did not reach for content and instead said: "It seems as if something in you wanted to look, and something else stopped it fast. Both are trying to keep you safe. Does that fit?"

Lila nodded faintly. "Yeah. It's like... one part pushes, one hits the brakes." "That's the system doing its job", the therapist said. "The brakes worked; you're safe now. We don't have to open anything, just notice how the system kept you here." Her breath steadied. After a pause, she whispered, "Maybe next time, I can look a little." The Memory Keeper's curiosity had returned, small, cautious, still alive.

Clinical Reflection

This vignette illustrates the full Memory-Ambivalence ambivalence loop in motion: curiosity (Memory Keeper) triggers protection (Seal Keeper), the body signals capacity reached (Threshold Guardian), shutdown prevents overflow (Flood Responder, the lid reseals control (Lid Keeper) and curiosity quietly returns once safety is re-established.

The therapist's stance is key: name function, not content; affirm both roles as protectors; and stop the action rather than the process. By treating each interruption as collaboration (not resistance) the therapist preserves continuity and lets the system learn that curiosity can survive contact.

WORKING WITH AMBIVALENCE DYNAMICS

Ambivalence is largely procedural, the system taps the brake at the edge of knowing. Now we will focus here on why it forms and how to work with conditions rather than conclusions.

Because the fear is about what knowing will do, perfectionism often blocks the door by demanding a flawless narrative before anything can be said. We explicitly license imperfect, out-of-order, and partial knowing. Credibility is not the currency here; capacity is.

- ★ Instead of "tell everything", we might ask, "Could we name the category of what the body knows, without any detail?"
- ★ Instead of "prove it", we might ask, "Could we locate where this lives, throat, chest, jaw, and let that be enough for today?

We do not litigate truth under pressure. We build circumstances under which knowing and telling could become tolerable—slowly, consensually, with a plan to return. Ambivalence is not indecision; it is anticipatory math. Parts are weighing not only what happened, but what knowing might cost: "If it's true, I'll shatter. If it's not, I'm a liar." Other parts run quiet countermeasures (shame, minimization, contempt) so nothing slips past the inner perimeter.

Internal System Roles and Dynamics

Inside, roles are already assigned. The Memory Keeper holds signals, images, and body-states that point toward experience. The Seal Keeper and Lid Keeper manage access and exposure, convinced survival depends on keeping dose tolerable and the lid intact. All protect: the Memory Keeper guards coherence ("someone in here deserves to be known"); the Seal Keeper guards continuity by regulating access to memory ("someone in here must function tomorrow") and the Lid Keeper restores continuity after exposure. If we treat the Seal/Lid Keepers as obstruction, we recreate power-over rather than power-with. If we treat the Memory Keeper as content rather than as a participant in regulation, we risk collapsing under content and calling it "breakthrough". Our stance is to sit with them all so the system can value both the wound and the guard without making either disappear.

Sometimes the body does the braking first; that is containment at work—the system slowing itself to stay safe. You might say:

★ "Something in you is keeping us safe by slowing the body; we can respect that and go more slowly."

Other times language does it: words slip, sentences tangle, topics hop. The story trims itself to control exposure. You can name it gently:

★ "I think the Seal Keeper (a Guardian role) is shaping what's shared to keep the lid on. We don't have to push, let's just hold what's here."

Or the relationship takes the hit: a quick step back, a sarcastic edge, a test. That's the system guarding against betrayal. Naming the function usually helps:

★ "Closeness just set off an alarm; let's adjust the distance until it feels safer."

Practice follows from that stance: pace, dose, consent, and the right to stop. We try one neutral detail instead of an entire account; we use a file-cabinet approach: one folder, then re-shelve; we agree on a tag or gesture to signal "first", a stop rule honored instantly, and an after-plan rehearsed in session. Success is measured by return (how quickly the baseline comes back), not by the volume of disclosure. These conditions let the Guardian recognize its own hand in keeping the system alive while updating the method from blunt shutdown to permissioned dosing.

Vulnerability in session—about knowing, wanting to know, or sharing—often draws an attack afterward: "You sounded ridiculous. Now they'll know how disgusting/pathetic/broken you are." This is a Guardian response, most often the Lid Keeper, using shame and self-attack to cut exposure and re-establish safety. We name the function ("guarding exposure", "restoring order through shame") and then update the method so cost drops and connection survives:

* "Thank you for stopping the flood. Humiliation used to be lethal; today pace can do that job with less damage."
* "We can keep your rules and keep contact. Let's honor the conditions we agreed on and see what needs updating; when the door opens, and when it stays closed."

Cracking the lid even a little often wakes shame. The inner critic rushes in, not as the enemy, but as a Guardian borrowing old tools (blame, contempt) to keep the system from collapsing. We do not litigate the memory or argue the labels. We translate function, reduce dose, and repair the frame. We name the wave, upgrade the method, and rebalance the room: "A second wave just arrived, shame and blame trying to re-seal the box. Same purpose, new tools: pacing instead of insults; a stop signal instead of threats. Thank you for guarding. Thank you for sharing. We'll pause and orient to today." Both the Memory Keeper's hesitation and the Guardian's stop are protection strategies. Attempts to push—by pressure, logic, or praise—tend to spike activation or drive retreat. When ambivalence shows up, technique matters less than a cooperative way of proceeding. The system needs ground rules that make approach optional, specific, and time-limited.

Memory work is not a hunt for facts; it begins when the system can speak about what happened in its own words, and it stays with what is available now. As more becomes shareable, we negotiate roles and protect every part—especially the one guarding the lid.

We acknowledge, respect, and validate each role without picking a side, and we proceed only with enough shared permission to try. In practice, that means any plan we make is accepted by the Guardian, tolerable to the Overwhelmed part, and meaningful to the Memory Keeper who wants relief; while the Adult Self setting dose, the stop-signal tested, and aftercare already familiar for the different parts.

The "4 Ps" Framework for Safe Memory Work

To keep memory work safe, we rely on the four anchors: permission, precision, pace and predictability (the "4 Ps"). These four anchors are held inside an overarching frame of Protection: no part loses the right to stop, and every approach is reversible. Protection is not an extra step; it is the container that makes the 4 Ps trustworthy. Let us see how to do this in practice:

Permission: Memory work is opt-in, never forced. If any part says no, we do not argue; we thank the no and get curious about what it's protecting:

★ "Thank you for letting us know. We don't have to do this today. If you're willing, help us understand what you fear might happen if we continue."

Sometimes that opens a door to "a little, with guardrails", but it must emerge on its own—never by insisting and convincing.

Precision: Titrate so the experience is different this time. Work the perimeter, not the center. One speck at a time—a single sensation, sound, or word—kept small and specific so attention has room. Time-limit it and keep it present-tense:

★ "Let's stay with the weight of the door in your palm—not what's behind it—for twenty seconds."

Pace: Brief connection - Orient-Repair-Repeat: Dose matches capacity, not agenda. We set start/stop points, keep eyes open when needed, and stop early on purpose. Approach–retreat is rhythm, not failure. When arousal spikes, we shorten the dose, re-orient to now, and name the gain:

★ "You were able to stay with that ten seconds longer."

Repair after any shaky moments consolidates safety faster than perfect exposure.

Predictability: The system relaxes when the procedure is consistent. We make the sequence *repeatable*: same steps, same stop rules, same closing ritual. Predictability is how Guardians learn trust.

★ "Nothing will happen without us agreeing first, and we'll stop whenever it is needed, not when your body forces it."

- ★ "If you say stop, or your body slows or fogs, we stop immediately. That rule doesn't change."
- ★ (for guardians) "Your job doesn't change here. The only thing that changes is how we protect; through pacing, not shutdown."

Protection (the frame): Protection must remain in the system; only the method changes. Every part's "No" preserves survival learning that once kept life intact. We keep that function and update its form (from secrecy to pacing, from force to boundary). Protection means every door has a hinge, every approach is reversible and no part is judged or punished for stopping.

Let us remember: the nervous system learns safety procedurally. Short, predictable approaches to difficult material—followed by clear returns to the here-and-now—build capacity and trust far more than fast, lengthy "deep dives". When we keep the work within today's limits, ambivalent parts learn safety from experience. We honor agreements as many times as needed until safety is felt rather than argued; then the client can say "we could try" instead of "we have to". Stopping is not failure; it is often the most therapeutic move. This is how permission grows and trust is earned. And when Guardians can say "stop" in therapy, the other "stops" begin to ease outside of therapy.

Core Principles for Working Inside the Loop

- **Honor pendulation.** The oscillation between knowing and not-knowing is not avoidance; it is titration. The goal is not to stop the loop but to make its swing tolerable.
- **Slow the dose, not the relationship.** Safety grows through connection, not content. The therapist's steadiness keeps the loop relationally contained.
- **Respect the Guardian's logic.** Every interruption protects against collapse. Ask what the part is guarding, not why it resists.
- **Differentiate proximity from exposure.** Being near a memory is not the same as reliving it; naming this distinction helps the body discover new ways to stay present.
- **Track backlash as data.** Post-session fatigue, shame spikes, or protective hostility mark the system's threshold. These are navigational cues, not setbacks.

Ambivalence about traumatic memory is not a barrier to therapy, it is the therapy. The loop itself teaches containment, pacing, and collaboration. Each rotation transforms raw survival code into conscious choice, until remembering no longer threatens belonging or life.

Approaching Seal and Lid Keepers

Start by naming function, not content. Ask the Seal Keeper what would make *today* safe enough to try one tiny, reversible step. Offer veto power and a stop-signal that is honored instantly. Keep eyes open, anchor in time/place/body, and end early to wire in "we can touch and return". Mark kept agreements out loud. Examples of micro-moves (tiny, permissioned, reversible):

- "I hear you're keeping the lid on. What conditions would make it safe to try ten seconds from across the room, no details, just noticing?"
- "You have control. If you say stop, we stop immediately, no questions asked."
- "One neutral speck only (e.g., color of the floor or the box), then we orient and close. I'll track the clock."
- "We'll measure success by return to baseline, not by how much got said."

When the Seal Keeper raises the stakes with comments such as, "Do it now", "Make it stop", "Shut it down or else", we treat escalation as protection using an outdated method. We name the job and update the procedure:

- "It sounds like you're preventing collapse the only way you learned, by forcing a shutdown through the body. Today, protection can look different. We'll keep the lid without injury: brakes and pacing, not harm."

Then we proceduralize safety on two fronts:

- **External safety (together):** co-write a crisis plan the system actually recognizes; reduce access to means; rehearse a two-sentence call script ("This is [name]. Urges are high. I need the plan we practiced.")

- **Internal safety (in the room):** install a stop signal and honor it instantly; remember the right to stop over dose and duration; keep eyes open; orient aloud to date, room, who is present; pair any approach with a time-capped retreat. ("Thirty seconds then we step back and look at the calendar together.")

Throughout, we praise the purpose and replace the procedure:

- ★ "Thank you for keeping the lid when no one else could. Your job stands. The method changes."

Over time, threats and insults can retire in favor of pacing and conditions, same mission, safer means. These interventions work because they all preserve the Guardian's job (contain disclosure) while updating the method from blunt shutdown to permissioned dosing. Keeping limits earns trust. Respect for roles reduces the need for force.

Therapist Stance

The work here is not about unlocking memory but about reading what safety is doing. Each cue (the pause, the fog, the change in tone) is a boundary signal, not a resistance. The task is to name what is happening without turning it into a test of truth or progress. When the body freezes, it is setting a limit; when words disappear, the system is telling you, "This is how far we can go right now."

We stay oriented to function, not content. Instead of asking "what happened", we ask:

- ★ "What is happening right now, inside the system, as it tries to protect itself?"

We name the movement before the meaning:

- ★ "Something in you just hit the brakes. That might be protection doing its job."

This keeps all parts present: those who want to know, those who cannot bear it, and those who must keep tomorrow functional.

The stance is one of curiosity more than inquiry, permission more than pressure. Curiosity softens fear; permission restores agency. Each time the therapist honors a stop without argument, the body learns that proximity does not have to equal danger, and that choice is possible even when the subject is unbearable.

Over time, this procedural learning reshapes the entire field. Remembering becomes less about exposure and more about consent; less about proving and more about being met. The system discovers that truth can be touched without collapse, that safety can hold what secrecy once had to guard. From there, remembering ceases to feel like betrayal and begins to feel like belonging—to oneself, to the present, to life as it is now.

How To Know We Are on the Right Track

Progress in ambivalence work rarely feels linear. It happens in small, procedural changes (how quickly regulation returns, how safely contact can expand, and how much collaboration emerges across roles. The shifts are signs that the 4Ps are taking hold.

When things are on the right track, the return to baseline comes faster after tiny approaches. Emotions and sensations can be noticed and tolerated a little longer—felt in the body rather than as foreign intrusions. Guardians become trusted pacers of the work—allies, not enemies—moving from contempt to listening, to negotiation, to collaboration, to teamwork.

The chain of care grows clearer; there is shared agreement about who opens what, when. Language shifts, too: when and if it feels right, the system can speak more plainly about what happened, sometimes naming it ("the rape", "the assault") instead of code ("those things", "you know what"); and after speaking, the whiplash is less—briefer, not life-threatening.

The system can identify and name a body location without tipping into overwhelm or collapse. Additionally, as conditions improve, many systems risk more contact with what they know, trusting they can stay grounded in the present and not be pulled into the past. These are complicated moments that can feel to the Adult Self like "getting worse." We name them as signs of growing capacity and pace the dose accordingly.

Subtle Indicators of Progress

- **Faster return to baseline.** After brief approaches, the nervous system settles more quickly. Shutdowns shorten; recovery feels possible.
- **Increasing tolerance for embodied experience.** Emotions and sensations can be noticed and held a few breaths longer—felt in the body rather than as foreign intrusions.
- **Guardians as allies.** Protector parts begin to act as *pacers* instead of blockers—moving from contempt to listening, negotiation, and eventually teamwork.
- **Clearer internal contracts.** The chain of care becomes explicit: who opens what, when, and under what conditions.
- **Language evolution.** When and if it feels right, the system can speak more plainly about what happened—naming it ("the rape", "the assault") instead of code ("those things", "you know what"). After naming, backlash is briefer and less punishing.
- **Body localization with capacity to stay present.** The system can identify a body area or sensation linked to the memory without collapse. The body becomes a site of connection, not just alarm.

It is very important to name the function as you spot it:

★ "A Guardian is shaping what's shared so the lid stays on. We can respect that and go slower or make it smaller."

Paradoxically, as safety grows, contact with pain increases which can be experienced as "getting worse". More connection can feel like deterioration to the Adult Self. We name it as progress:

★ "You're not getting worse—you're more connected and feeling what other parts felt before."

CLOSING THOUGHTS

The Memory Keeper teaches the cost of silence by keeping what could not yet be known. The Seal and Lid Keepers show what it took to preserve survival and belonging by limiting access and regulating exposure. The Threshold Guardian calibrates how close is close enough today and the Flood Responder stands ready to protect when limits are missing. Together these roles did not prevent healing; they made survival possible.

Healing here is not prying boxes open. It is shaping the conditions under which a lid can lift a finger-width without shattering the jar, or the system that guards it. When permission is shared, precision kept, and pace protected, ambivalence stops being a trap and becomes a navigational system. Memory work then shifts from extraction to invitation: approach, pause, return (as often as needed).

There will be days when nothing opens and the success is a clean stop, honored without debate. There will be days when a single neutral detail is all that fits, and the win is how quickly baseline returns. There will be days when backlash tries old methods, and the repair is faster because limits are held. None of this is failure; it is the nervous system learning safety in real time.

What matters is not how much is told, but how safely the telling is held by the Adult Self, by the protective roles that protect and hold dose, and by the steadiness of the therapeutic relationship. When those conditions repeat, the system discovers something new: knowing can be survivable, even when it is not yet speakable. That discovery is the doorway to the next phase of work.

Clinical Anchors

What to remember...

- Memory work is a permission practice. Proceed only with enough consent across parts.
- Guardians escalate when ignored; they soften when they co-author the conditions.
- Precision beats volume. One neutral detail, then orient and repair.
- Overwhelm is a vote, not defiance. Treat it as guidance for pace.
- Mark gains out loud: "We kept the agreement." Contracts update through kept limits, not promises.
- Build aftercare. Most backlash is a plan problem, not a motivation problem.

What to avoid...

- Forcing proximity because there is readiness somewhere.
- Arguing with the Guardian's content instead of honoring its function.
- Equating intensity with efficacy.
- Praising disclosure while neglecting the protector who kept you from reenactment.
- Treating overnight sabotage as manipulation rather than emergency drills.

PART IV: Building Integration-Related Capacities

Chapter 31: Post-Crisis Repair - Laying the Ground for Integration

Therapist Reflection

After the crisis, she came in with her head down, already apologizing. I didn't ask for an explanation. I said, 'I'm still here.' And something shifted. Because what she needed most wasn't answers. It was to know that rupture didn't mean disappearance.

In systems shaped by complex trauma, crises happen. These may be external events, loss, stress, confrontation or internal ruptures like self-harm, suicidal impulses, sudden flooding, or severe internal conflict. When a system reaches its limit, it may collapse, shut down, or erupt in ways that feel chaotic or terrifying. Yet these moments also test and strengthen the same capacities that later sustain integration: differentiation, time orientation, and co-consciousness.

What happens *after* the storm matters just as much as what happened *during* it. Post-crisis moments are often saturated with shame, silence, and self-judgment. Some parts may be bewildered, others defensive; many fear they have *failed* therapy or that their system is now unsafe or broken.

Post-crisis therapy is not about correction; it is about repair (restoring safety, continuity, and connection). Met with steadiness, these moments can become turning points, where systems learn that there can be ruptures *and* return. Repair begins where survival logic meets relationship, where the system learns that distress no longer leads to punishment or abandonment.

In dissociative personality systems, crisis rarely affects just one part. Even if only one part acted out, through self-harm, withdrawal, aggression, or disclosure, the ripple effects can destabilize the entire system.

Part 4 turns to capacities that promote integration and make de-escalation stick. Everything we have learned about loops and protection applies here. Crisis is what happens when the system's existing code hits its limits.

COMMON SYSTEM RESPONSES AFTER A CRISIS

In the aftermath, systems often try to make sense of what happened by tightening control or retreating into old survival patterns. Parts may report:

- Feeling betrayed by one another.
- Increased silencing, punishment, or control.
- Overidentification with one part's narrative.
- Confusion about what happened (time, sequence, intent).
- Fear that the therapist will judge, abandon, or withdraw.

These responses are expected. They represent the system's attempts to restore order (by shutting down, blaming, or threatening again). The therapist's role is to identify and help the client understand that going back to old ways and how that makes sense when the new way of interacting still feels too new; slow things down, offer reflection, and create room for meaning-making.

EXPLORING THE CRISIS

Exploring the crisis is less about explanation and more about translation, turning action back into communication. Each behavior, even the most alarming, tried to regulate something unbearable. Once the body is grounded enough, curiosity becomes possible again.

It is important to avoid framing the crisis as simply a symptom or normalize it in excess, these are great learning opportunities. Ask what the behavior was *communicating* when it is possible. When the system is ready, which may take hours, days, or even weeks, the therapist can invite:

- ★ "What was happening just before things escalated?"
- ★ "Which part needed something that was not being heard/ understood?"
- ★ "Are there parts who still feel scared or unheard now?"

The aim is not interrogation, it is compassionate and curious inquiry (making meaning). This allows the system to understand itself more deeply and to begin repairing internally.

CLINICAL VIGNETTE

Checking in

Following self-harm, the therapist says: "Let's do a short audit together, what helped, what didn't, and what we want to try next time." They identify: (1) texting a grounding phrase helped, (2) late-night journaling spiked surveillance, (3) a quick cold-water shower followed by weighted blanket sequence reduced urges. There's a pause while they both look at the list. The air feels calmer, more shared, like order returning after noise

What worked

Collaborative, non-punitive review; concrete updates to the plan; and validating protector parts jobs.

REBUILDING TRUST, BOTH INTERNALLY AND IN THE THERAPEUTIC RELATIONSHIP

Crises often lead to ruptures in trust. This can happen between parts, between the client and the therapist and even within the client's relationship to their own body or memory. Repair is built not by explanations but by presence. In post-crisis work, trust returns through rhythm, the tone of voice, the pace of the session, the steady continuation of contact. The therapist becomes the continuity the system lost: a predictable rhythm that communicates, "We can start again."

Moves that help:

- Checking in on the part who reacted, without shaming.

- Acknowledging the protector parts who stepped in during and afterward
- Validating lingering fear, grief or confusion.
- Returning to the therapeutic pacing and structure: predictability, grounding, continuity.

When appropriate, own your impact:

- ★ "I wonder if something I missed last session made things harder."
- ★ "If it felt like I wasn't there in the way you needed, I want to understand."

Repair is not about taking responsibility for the system's choices, it is about showing up after rupture, with presence and care.

After a crisis, some parts attempt to be good, they can become overly compliant, detached, or eager to prove they're fine. This can cloak unresolved shame or fear.

CLINICAL VIGNETTE

Ready to Work

After a weekend crisis, the client arrives cheerful, "ready to work." Affect is bright; content is thin.

The therapist notices the shift: "Things feel very tidy today. I'm wondering if a part is trying to keep everything safe by being extra good."

A quieter voice admits, "If I look fine, no one will be mad."

What worked

Naming performance as protection, not deceit; inviting the Protector to help set a slow pace; ending with a predictable ritual.

In these situations, you can use gentle probes:

- ★ "It seems like things have quieted a lot, I wonder how that silence feels inside."

★ "Is there a part trying really hard to hold everything together now?"

Curiosity keeps collaboration; confrontation often triggers surveillance and old coping responses based on fights and control.

REESTABLISHING ADAPTED PACING AND SAFETY

One of the most regulating experiences post-crisis is the return to adapted *pacing*: the therapist's voice, the pacing of sessions, grounding tools, check-ins, predictable transitions. This is where time orientation and differentiation begin to rebuild, parts start noticing who is here now, what belongs to now, and what echoes of *then* were reactivated.

Crises disrupt this rhythm, and recovery often begins with restoring it:

- Revisiting grounding practices together.
- Reaffirming safety plans or communication agreements.
- Making time to reorient parts who feel disoriented or frightened.
- Re-engaging small internal collaborations (e.g., sharing awareness or journaling).

These interventions are *reminders*, that the system needs to keep working together and learning from complicated moments, reminders, that cooperation and collaboration are still needed and possible, and that therapy is a place where they can return even after rupture to continue learning and adapting to needs. These are natural integration-related moments.

THERAPIST POSTURE AND CLINICAL TIPS

Post-crisis work often evokes urgency in the therapist: the desire to stabilize, prevent recurrence, or fix the rupture. While containment is essential, so is emotional pacing and keeping a grounded stance. If the therapist moves too fast or does too much, we miss excellent learning opportunities.

At this stage of treatment, the therapist's job is to recall what has been working, reflect on what is not, and invite revisions or updates. It makes sense for clients and parts to have different needs as we move forward and the work evolves. Following the software metaphor used previously, keep in mind that crises are information. They show the system where the old code still runs, an invitation to update, not evidence of failure.

The following examples illustrate language that can help the system stay focused and reopen reflection after a crisis:

Grounding and Re-Orientation

★ "Let's just notice that we're both here, right now, and that the worst part has already passed."
★ "We don't have to solve anything yet, just understand what this moment is asking for."

Normalization and Meaning-Making

★ "This response makes sense if we remember what used to happen after danger."
★ "It sounds like part of you tried an old survival move when things felt too much."

Reconnection and Hope

★ "You didn't break the work; the work includes moments like this."
★ "Even this can teach us how the system protects itself."
★ "Repair isn't about avoiding going back, it's about learning how to come back."

Empowerment and Shared Leadership

★ "We can slow down and look at this together. You don't have to carry the figuring-out alone."
★ "You get to decide what feels safe to explore and what needs to wait."

Integrative Links

★ "Let's notice what belongs to then and what belongs to now as we talk about it."

★ "Something in the system tried to protect; let's see what it was trying to keep safe."

Language offered with steadiness becomes a bridge: from rupture back to trust, and from reaction toward meaning.

Avoid any form of blaming response, expressions of disappointment, or alarmed reactions. Many clients already believe they are *too much*. Your steadiness is the bridge back to trust.

EIGHT STEPS FOR POST-CRISIS GROUNDING AND REPAIR

Once the immediate crisis has passed, the next task is to translate steadiness into structure. The following steps outline a practical sequence for grounding and repair.

1. **Re-orient & regulate**: Name date, place, who's present; use breath or sensory anchor; help the Adult Self re-lead.
2. **Name that we will go slow**: "We'll stay within what feels safe. You have control and can decide."
3. **Explore triggers**: "What was happening *just before* the crisis? Which parts were there?" Aim for broad strokes; not details.
4. **Focus on function, not fault**: "What was this trying to prevent or control?" Translate acts into protection.
5. **Relational repair**: Check in with the system (often gives information about the part that reacted, the parts impacted, and the protector parts who stepped in afterward). Offer acknowledgement without shame.
6. **Review and update agreements**: Reconfirm safety plan, permissions, stop-signals.
7. **Schedule small collaborations**: Reintroduce cooperation (e.g., co-awareness drills, journaling fragments).
8. **Save time for the closing**: End with grounding and clear transition back to present time.

If arousal rises, return to Steps 1–2 and leave enough time to ground before closing the session.

CLOSING THOUGHTS

Crises are not the end of the work. They are part of the work. In dissociative personality systems, where survival once depended on silence and fragmentation, a crisis can mark both the strain of old protections and the emergence of new capacities, and its resolution is often a necessary step in healing.

Our task as therapists is not to fear these moments, nor to react with control. It is to witness, to remain, and to help the system make meaning of what happened, without shame, without collapse.

When systems learn that crises can be survived, understood, and repaired, they begin to learn that healing is not a perfect line. It is a series of returns. To self. To each other. To trust.

In the next chapters of this section, we will deepen these themes, focusing on the integration-related capacities that make repair sustainable: learning to tell what belongs to *then* and what belongs to *now,* and how to stay side by side while noticing both.

CLINICAL ANCHORS

WHAT TO REMEMBER...

- Crisis is not failure, it is communication. Something needed attention.
- Performance after rupture is protection, not deceit.
- Systems reconfigure post-crisis; allow orientation time.
- Containment is relational, not just rule-based.
- Repair deepens trust when met with steadiness and pacing.

WHAT TO AVOID...

- Turning safety planning into punishment or control.
- Siding with/against a single part; it polarizes the system.
- Over-reassurance or "logic fixes" that bypass shame and fear.

Chapter 32: Differentiation and Time Orientation

THERAPIST REFLECTION

A client told me, "I heard her yelling again, but it was my own mouth moving." For a moment, I panicked. I wanted to clarify, to ground, to do something. I paused, breathed, and instead of correcting, said, "That sounds scary, like her voice came through you." She nodded. "You're not alone, and we'll move at your pace to untangle what's yours from what was done to you."

Because I stayed with her fear instead of rushing to fix, she began to trust that someone could witness her voice without retreating, and from there, she could start to tell it apart from herself.

This chapter focuses on two main capacities that work in tandem: differentiation and time orientation. Everything that follows: co-presence, co-consciousness, internal cooperation, rests on these two.

These are capacities to be nurtured, not techniques to apply. They help clients develop present-moment safety, not by dismissing the past, but by recognizing when it is still speaking, and helping clients and dissociative parts remember. This is different now. In this chapter we move from *who is here* to *what belongs to then* and *what belongs to now.*

WHAT DIFFERENTIATION AND TIME ORIENTATION MEAN

Integration does not happen by pulling the system back together too quickly. It begins by allowing clients to notice *what does not belong to now*; what still echoes, what still grips the body with old fear. This is the essence of both capacities: locating oneself in the present even when trauma insists otherwise.

Differentiation is not about separating parts further, it is the growing ability to recognize:

- This belongs to *then*. This belongs to *now*.
- This is *my* voice. That one is not.
- This fear is *old*. This moment is *different*.

Clarity here is the seed of believing things are different now, the beginning of realizing there are choices in the here and now.

Time orientation is differentiation´s twin. It helps the system distinguish between what is happening now from what is being *felt as if* it were happening now. Many clients arrive in therapy without access to this internal distinction. Thoughts, feelings, needs and voices blur; neutral moments flood with shame, fear or rage. These are often misunderstood as overreactions, but they are not. They are signs of unresolved trauma time, still alive in the present and mistaken for now.

CLINICAL VIGNETTE

Ready to Work

Client: "He's here."

Therapist: "It feels like he's here now." (Pause.) "Would it be okay to check one thing in the room that tells us today's date is different?"

Client glances at the calendar and exhales. "Right... it's this year."

Therapist: "Both can be true, the fear is real, and it's also this year."

In dissociative personality systems, internal voices may echo perpetrators. Flashbacks may carry the full weight of helplessness or fear. A client might say, "He's here", though the abuser is long gone. A part does not know; the system has not yet oriented to the passage of time.

HOW THESE CAPACITIES EMERGE

Differentiation often begins in small, surprising ways. A part corrects the therapist: "I think I am feeling her sadness." Or the client says: "I know this is confusing, but it really does feel like two different people inside."

These are signs of clarity emerging from within; a felt mismatch that is now easier to identify and describe:

- "That thought didn't feel like mine."
- "I felt five again for a second."
- "It sounded like my father's voice."

When we validate these moments, the system learns that noticing is safe and they are on the right track. Simple externalizing tools, like drawing, journaling, mapping, or placing objects to represent parts, can support differentiation. Often the first differentiation is between timelines, not parts: a flinch from then shows up in now, or a harsh internal voice echoes someone who once had power. Our task is to name the disorientation:

- ★ "That sounds like another time."
- ★ "That part may still believe something dangerous is happening."

Some of these moments may feel disorienting, but they mark the beginning of a shift: the slow realization that not everything inside belongs to now.

Whenever we hear the following markers from clients, we know that these capacities are growing:

- "That voice isn't mine; it sounds like my father."
- "I'm panicking like I'm seven... and I'm not. I'm here."
- A breath they didn't know they were holding; shoulders lower; gaze lifts, nonverbal time orientation.

STRATEGIES TO SUPPORT DIFFERENTIATION

There are many ways to support differentiation, the idea is to follow what emerges in the session, as we have been describing in other chapters and use moments of confusion as opportunities for understanding. Principles to hold:

- Use the client's language. Do not name parts or concepts the client has not used.
- Invite noticing without pushing.
- Anchor in the Adult Self whenever accessible—even for a moment.

- Name without siding or forcing meaning.
- Validate coherence across parts.
- Add orientation/gross-motor grounding whenever activation rises.

Gentle Prompts Can Offer Space for Differentiation

- ★ "Does this feel like something happening now... or something that reminds you of then?"
- ★ "Who does that voice sound like—anyone from then, or more like you today?"
- ★ "If this fear had a timestamp, what age does it feel?"

Naming without siding might sound like:

- ★ "That reaction makes sense if we imagine a much younger part responding."
- ★ "Maybe we don't have to understand it yet; we can just notice."
- ★ "It sounds like one part trying to prevent exposure, and another part longing to be seen."

When activation increases, body-based grounding and orientation can help. Simple interventions such as placing both feet on the floor, looking around the room, and naming three present-time anchors (the date, the room, the therapist's name) can bring clients back to the here and now. Breath work (for instance, exhaling longer than inhaling, four in and six out for a few cycles) or brief movement (standing, stepping, stretching) further support regulation and orientation.

Finally, *Then–Now* tags provide a linguistic bridge between trauma time and present time:

- ★ "That belief was true then. Let's check what's true now"
- ★ "That was needed then. What's needed now?"
- ★ "That voice protected you then. What does the Adult Self know today?"

WHEN DIFFERENTIATION & TIME ORIENTATION BRING GRIEF

As clarity begins to emerge, grief often follows. Sometimes, recognizing that something is not happening anymore brings sorrow. A client may whisper, "It's over", and feel unmoored, grieving the cost of what was survived and the time lost inside it.

This grief is painful progress that needs to be named and witnessed. The work includes mourning: for what happened, for what was missed, for years lived under old rules. Naming the grief helps update protective contracts so parts no longer need to keep yesterday alive to stay safe today. It is the quiet ache of realizing something is different now, and the slow work of learning to live in that difference, the possibility of a new start.

CLOSING THOUGHTS

Differentiation and time orientation let the system see more clearly. When a client can say, "That voice isn't mine" or "This fear feels old", the task shifts from managing symptoms to reclaiming the present. These capacities grow procedurally through repetition: tiny tags, shared reality cues, a steady rhythm, and the Adult Self returning again and again to witness what belongs to *then* while staying rooted in *now*. From here, the next step is sharing awareness without merging: co-presence and co-consciousness**.** We move from "Who is here?" to "We are here"—now.

Clinical Anchors

What to remember...

- Differentiation is clarity, not distance.
- Confusion often precedes clarity.
- Trauma time is adaptive; orient gently, repeatedly.
- Internal voices carry relational history; respect them.
- Identity questions ("Who am I?") are expected.
- Stay with what's unclear, orient again, not harder.

What to avoid...

- Premature labeling or "figuring it out".
- Forcing time orientation, invite it.
- Treating confusion as failure.
- Skipping the grief that clarity awakens.

Chapter 33: Co-Consciousness as Relational Capacity

THERAPIST REFLECTION

I used to think we had to know who was who; that parts needed to introduce themselves or explain their role. But I've learned that sometimes the most healing moments happen when a client says, "'I think someone's here," and I simply reply, "Okay. Let's stay with that together." Not fixing, not naming; just holding presence long enough for the system to learn that awareness does not have to equal danger.

Differentiation and time orientation open the door; co-consciousness invites parts to share the doorway, standing together for a limited moment without pushing through. The aim here is not to force cohesion or dismantle amnesia, but to offer a bridge: permissioned co-presence that grows only as safety allows.

Integration in dissociative personality systems does not begin with insight, memory work, or structured consolidation; it begins by reshaping internal relationships. When parts slowly begin to notice one another, fear softens into curiosity, and curiosity into understanding and compassion. Healing emerges as we stay present and grounded when a part is triggered, witnessing its experience without fleeing, fighting, or freezing.

Many clients enter therapy with parts living in silence or strict separation: some know of each other but avoid contact; others do not suspect they are not alone. For some, internal boundaries are rigid and sealed; for others, porous and chaotic, the inner world feels more like scattered islands than a unified territory.

Co-consciousness often arrives as a felt presence, a sudden shift, a moment of shared awareness, and just as easily, it can vanish. A part may hear an internal voice they didn't know existed. A client may say, "It's like someone else is feeling this, not me."

This chapter is about not forcing cohesion or dismantling amnesia; it is an invitation into co-presence, the beginnings of internal relationship and awareness. Differentiation and co-consciousness are relational capacities that ebb and flow with safety, and they unfold only with permission, respect, and attuned pacing. Co-consciousness becomes the fertile soil from which new internal collaboration can grow.

WHAT CO-CONSCIOUSNESS IS AND IS NOT AND WHY IT MATTERS

Co-consciousness is a capacity, not a technique. It is the ability of a part, initially the Adult Self, to sense the proximity of another part while staying present enough to remain oriented to now. It is the moment when proximity does not equal engulfment, when curiosity can be held alongside activation. It is distinct from fusion or merging. It does not need introductions; it allows a brief, shared space. It is not always easy, and it is not always wanted. For many clients, even imagining two parts co-existing feels impossible. And yet, over time, small shifts begin:

- The Adult Self sensing another´s part presence without switching.
- A thought or image arriving that feels foreign.
- An emotional shift that does not match the external moment.
- A fleeting sense of being "watched from inside".
- It may feel like watching or sharing a space in silence.

At first, these glimpses can feel confusing or disorienting—"I'm here, and also not" or "Something just shifted but I don't know what". These are markers of relational capacity slowly opening. Co-consciousness is the ground from which understanding and compassion can grow.

It is important to note that co-consciousness does not need to be made explicit in order to be present—and in some personality systems, explicitly naming it too early can actually intensify blocking. In complex dissociative systems, suggestions such as "Let's try something in co-consciousness" or "Can you notice this feeling with another part?" may be experienced as threatening, either by parts that do not feel ready for this level of contact or by protective parts that are wary of the intention behind the invitation.

Paradoxically, co-consciousness is often already occurring implicitly (Mosquera, 2019). When the therapist checks with the Adult Self about a sensation, a hesitation, or a shift in tone such as, "Can you notice what's happening right now?", one or several parts may already be present. Likewise, when the therapist asks what a part thinks, feels, or needs, co-consciousness is already being invited, whether or not it is named as such. Awareness does not require naming. In many cases, keeping the process implicit allows co-consciousness to grow without triggering surveillance or defensive mobilization.

There is no need to announce co-consciousness. The task is to host it quietly, allowing shared awareness to emerge gradually, in a way that feels natural and safe.

THERAPEUTIC IMPLICATIONS OF CO-CONCIOUSNESS

Each moment of co-consciousness opens a window and widens the pause: reflection before reaction, curiosity before collapse. Over time, clients report fewer dissociative episodes, increased access to skills across parts, and a softening of internal phobias. The *monster* is seen as a protector with a history; the "hated child" becomes a part to understand rather than expel. Choices expand around memory, affect tolerance and behavior. Co-consciousness shifts the system from surveillance and avoidance toward collaboration and cooperation.

These early moments of co-consciousness can also feel frightening, or destabilizing. Because co-consciousness can bring what was never supposed to be remembered, or what was once too dangerous to know.

A client might stop mid-sentence. Their tone may change. Their posture might shift, or their face go blank. They may say things like:

- "I think someone else is here, but I don't know who."
- "It feels like I'm not alone in my head."
- "I was talking and then everything went fuzzy."

These realizations are mostly welcome when explained to clients and dissociative parts but might sometimes be followed by internal pushback. If pushback happens here are some tips for therapists:

★ **Validate**: "It makes sense, this feels confusing. We can go slowly."
★ **Offer Presence**: "You're not alone right now. I'm still here."
★ **Invite Noticing** (without pressure): "Would it feel okay to simply notice if another part is here?" "We don't need to label or fix anything—just stay with that."
★ **Pull Back if Needed**: "Let's slow this down—we can ground and come back later."

In these exchanges, the therapist is modeling a new kind of relationship: one where contact is optional, distance is honored, and safety always comes first.

BARRIERS TO CONTACT: WHEN NEARNESS FEELS LIKE DANGER

Not all co-conscious moments feel welcome. For many clients, proximity has been a precursor to harm. Parts may have learned to fear one another and are not used to a different way of interacting. Some parts fear being seen. Others fear who they might see or what they can find out.

As amnesia barriers thin, loss of distance can bring shame, fear, even grief. Increased proximity can also unlock pain or memory beyond the system's current capacity to hold, leading to flooding. Naming these realities prevents pathologizing the natural caution of protective parts and frames pacing as wisdom rather than resistance.

THERAPIST STANCE AND HOLDING CO-CONSCIOUSNESS

Our stance is simple: be with, invite, and titrate. Presence communicates that contact is possible and survivable. Permission protects autonomy: contact is always optional, distance remains available. Pacing prevents reenactment by matching dose to capacity.

In practice this sounds like: "Would it feel okay to simply notice if another part is near?" and, when needed, "We don't have to talk or label, just be close for a few breaths." When Adult Self is available, we anchor there: "What does the adult in you know about this moment?", and when it isn't, we return to the body.

We track the body as the first language of contact: a change in breathing, a hand rising to the chest, eyes shifting to a corner of the room. We slow down around those moments. If arousal spikes, we shorten the dose, keep eyes open, add small movements, or externalize distance (two chairs, cards, or objects to represent parts and Adult Self). If contact triggers a wobble, we slow down; orient to now, name what's present in the client's language, and mark a gain: "We stayed in the room together for ten seconds longer than last time." Repair consolidates safety faster than perfect exposure.

The following are small but important markers that the system is learning to share space:

- Two parts can stay in the room together even if it is just seconds.
- Protector parts use the brake instead of the blast.
- Adult Self begins to speak spontaneously in session to pace.
- Post-session backlash shortens or softens.

CLOSING THOUGHTS

Co-consciousness is not about making things *whole* or *normal*; it is about making room for each part that needs it, when the moment is right for that. When one part is no longer forced to carry pain in silence, something fundamental changes.

This work is delicate, it requires us to slow down, to listen harder, and to trust that presence can sometimes do more than interpretation.

The goal is not to make parts talk. It is to help them tolerate being in the same space (reducing the fear that contact equals collapse). Co-consciousness is a relationship to tend, paced with care, held with permission, grounded in respect. Connection grows by invitation, especially in the quiet moments where something new becomes possible. Differentiation and time orientation make it possible to know who is here and when; co-consciousness lets them stand side by side while noticing it.

Clinical Anchors

What to remember...

- Presence is enough; noticing is the beginning.
- Approach–retreat is pacing, not resistance.
- Avoidance, amnesia, and distance are protective, do not dismantle too soon.
- Track the body; it often signals contact before words.
- Normalize the messy middle: confusion, blending, and phobic responses signal movement.
- Rituals create rhythm; repetition builds trust.
- After any wobble, repair: orient to now, name what is present (in client language), mark a gain.
- You are the anchor. When the client feels watched from within, they also watch you for safety.

What to avoid ...

- Forcing contact, dialogue, labels, or speed.
- Treating confusion as failure or "lack of insight".
- Overriding consent to "get progress".
- Skipping the grief or disorientation that early contact can evoke.

Chapter 34: Moving Toward Integration and Cooperation

Therapist Reflection

She asked if healing meant losing parts of herself. I said no and then waited. What mattered wasn't my answer, but the pause that followed, the space where no one had to agree yet. Sometimes integration begins not with unity, but with permission to remain different and still belong

Differentiation and time orientation help the system distinguish *then* from *now*. Co-consciousness teaches parts they can be near without collapse. From that soil grows cooperation: small, repeatable acts of living together in ordinary days. Here, integration is not a finish line but a way of moving as a *we*, even while difference remains.

In much of the clinical literature, integration is treated as an endpoint—the presumed goal of trauma work with dissociative systems. For many survivors, that idea feels confusing, threatening, or simply inaccessible. Some parts hear *integration* and fear erasure. Others imagine a forced fusion that strips autonomy or identity.

In this book, we use *integration* differently: not as a technical achievement, but as a gradual, lived experience of internal cooperation, collaboration, communication, and shared selfhood. Integration is not collapsing parts into a single identity. It is reducing conflict, increasing mutual awareness, and allowing fluid movement across internal roles.

This chapter explores how systems move toward integration—not as a mandate from outside, but as a natural outgrowth of safety, trust, and choice. It is about coexisting with complexity, not eliminating it.

FROM FRAGMENTATION TO FLOW

In the early stages of therapy, personality systems often feel divided—thoughts disconnected from feelings; parts unaware of one another; memory divided into unspoken pieces. As the work unfolds, something begins to shift. Awareness expands, communication deepens, and parts start to share space—not always harmoniously, but intentionally.

This is what we mean by flow: the growing ability of the system to function as a relational whole, even while parts remain distinct. Without entering trauma memories, cooperation strengthens through everyday micro-agreements—who drives, who replies, who rests—so the system learns rhythm before it seeks depth.

Signs of this shift often include;

- Shared memory or emotional resonance across parts.
- Cooperative decision-making.
- Smoother, more spontaneous transitions.
- A felt sense of *we-ness* rather than isolation.
- Emergence (or strengthening) of an internal leader—the Adult Self or another anchor figure.

These moments are often quiet, but they bring a new steadiness: life inside no longer has to be a battleground.

SUPPORTING INTERNAL LEADERSHIP

For many systems, healing includes the gradual development of an internal anchor: a part or presence that can hold perspective, make decisions, and care for the whole. In this book we call that the *Adult Self*. At times it is not experienced as a single figure but a small internal committee, a council, or a shared agreement among parts.

The therapist's role is to support, not assign, this leadership. This includes:

- Helping the client recognize when leadership is present
- Naming leadership when it shows up (e.g., grounded reflection, conflict resolution)

- Encouraging systems to consult across parts before acting
- Supporting boundary-setting and care without domination

Leadership here is stewardship, not dominance. It sets pace, gathers input, keeps boundaries, and models repair: orient to now, name who is present in the client's language, and mark a small gain ("We coordinated that handoff without panic"). The aim is not control; it is relational coherence—someone inside who can pause, gather, and respond while respecting the sovereignty of every part.

COOPERATION VS. FORCED UNITY

Some systems never desire fusion, and that is not a failure. In fact, many systems reach high levels of functionality, safety, and connection without ever fully merging parts. They operate as internal teams, families, or collectives. What matters most is the quality of the relationship, not the number of selves.

Cooperation can look like:

- Parts sharing awareness or memory.
- Finding time to speak or express.
- Reaching agreements about safety, behavior, and needs.
- Internal repair after rupture.

Therapists should affirm that integration is not the erasure of difference. It is the honoring of difference, made livable through respect and dialogue.

When working near questions of integration, therapists often carry more urgency than we realize. We may feel pressure to help the system "come together", to reduce division, to bring coherence where suffering has lived. This impulse is understandable—and if left unexamined, it can subtly shift our stance from accompaniment to direction.

It is worth pausing to ask: Whose timeline is active right now? Is the system moving toward cooperation because it feels safer, or because something in us longs for resolution?

Many parts do not fear closeness itself; they fear closeness without consent. When we slow down enough to let ambivalence speak, we often discover that resistance is not opposition, but memory—memory of being merged, overridden, or required to perform.

In these moments, our most therapeutic act may be restraint: naming cooperation when it arises organically and trusting that shared awareness grows from repeated experiences of safety, not from instruction. Integration does not need to be pushed; it needs to be allowed.

GRIEVING THE ROLES THAT ONCE DEFINED THEM

As systems grow steadier, parts who once held extreme roles can feel displaced. The one who managed suicidal urges, the one who threatened, the one who carried secrets—each may look around and ask, *Who am I now?* The loss is not only of task but of identity, belonging, and purpose.

This is where grief meets growth. We name the truth that those roles were ingenious under impossible conditions. We honor the cost they carried. And we make space for mixed feelings: relief, sadness, pride, suspicion, even boredom. Nothing has to be surrendered before it is sufficiently thanked.

The therapist's stance is witness and companion, not recruiter. Rather than rushing to *reassign*, we linger with meaning: What did this role protect? What did it require of you? What would you want remembered about your service? When readiness appears, we explore what it might be like to change—by choice.

You can invite this gently:

- ★ "Even if you're not doing that job anymore, your story still matters."
- ★ "What would it be like to have a new role—one you choose?"
- ★ "Which parts of your skill set feel worth keeping, and which can rest now?"
- ★ "How would you like us to mark this transition so it's real?"

Transitions are easier when they are practiced and experienced gradually. Some systems write a letter of thanks, place an object on a shelf, or hold a brief *handover* meeting where the former role explains what it watched for and what it fears will be missed. Others create a *trial period* for new duties with a clear back-out plan. These gestures are rites of passage.

When supported at their pace, parts begin to evolve, not because they are forced to, but because they are finally safe enough to. A protector may become a consultant, a sentinel who rests more often. A dissociative part may become the system's expert in rest or play. What endures is dignity: the recognition that every role made survival possible, and that every role deserves a say in what comes next.

NAVIGATING AMBIVALENCE ABOUT WHOLENESS

Not all parts celebrate healing. Some fear losing their voice. Others mistrust the idea of togetherness. For systems that survived by separation, integration, (even defined as cooperation), can feel like a threat rather than promise. When this happens, we treat this ambivalence as information; it tells us where safety is thin and consent needs strengthening.

Therapeutically, consent is iterative. No one has to sign a forever-contract. We name the mixed feelings, we slow the dose, and we let dissent belong in the room:

- "You don't have to want the same thing. We can hold the tension together."
- "Even if we never move toward fusion, your connection matters."
- "Nothing has to be decided today."

Ambivalence is not resistance; it is part of the process. Integration is not everyone agreeing, it is everyone having a place to belong, even in disagreement.

Therapist reflection: Work around integration invites therapists into a delicate ethical space. The language of healing can easily become the language of expectation. Even well-intended encouragement toward cooperation may echo earlier experiences of pressure, compliance, or forced unity.

Our task is to create conditions in which disagreement does not threaten belonging. The question is not whether parts will integrate, but whether they feel safe enough to remain in relationship while they decide.

Integration is quiet. It shows up in small choices, shared pauses, and the growing ability to recover after rupture. Our job is to notice these moments and protect them from being rushed.

CLOSURE, CONTINUITY, AND THE NEXT CHAPTER

There is no tidy *ending* in trauma therapy, especially for dissociative systems. The work keeps moving—in relationships, in new seasons of life, in identity that continues to unfold. And yet there are moments of closure: something inside exhales; trust replaces terror; being alive feels less like survival and more like presence.

Some personality systems leave therapy with a clear direction. Others circle back for tune-ups. Many continue to grow long after the therapist steps out. What matters most is that they know how to turn inward with respect and care—how to listen, speak, tend, and reconnect. That is the real integration: not the absence of difference, but the presence of relationship that can be resumed when it wobbles and repaired when it tears.

CLOSING THOUGHTS

This chapter invites us to reconsider integration not as a clinical objective, but as a relational consequence. When parts experience consistent respect—for boundaries, dissent, and difference—coordination emerges. When consent is bypassed, even subtly, division often intensifies.

Healing in dissociative personality systems is not about becoming one. It is about becoming together, in awareness, in purpose, in shared humanity. Each part with a place. Each voice with dignity. Each story no longer carried alone.

Integration is not the absence of difference. It is the presence of relationship. That is enough.

Integration is like baking a cake. Many ingredients are needed; each has its own distinct purpose and flavor. Some are sweet, some bitter, some quiet. But when they are gently mixed and baked, something new emerges. If an ingredient is omitted, the result suffers. We only have a cake when all ingredients are included.

Therapy is not a recipe to follow; the metaphor is meant as a reminder that each ingredient matters. In integration, parts do not vanish; they lose their separateness and their capacities, histories, and qualities become shared within a larger whole.

Clinical Anchors

What to remember...

- Integration develops through cooperation: small, repeatable *civic acts* inside the system.
- Leadership is stewardship: Adult Self holds the whole without erasing difference.
- Approach–retreat is pacing.
- Praise process over fusion; practice internal check-ins and repairs.

What to avoid...

- Treating fusion as the finish line.
- Rewarding performance unity over honest difference.
- Overriding consent to *make progress*.

Chapter 35: Meaning-Making and Growth.

Therapist Reflection

He said, "I don't know who I am without the pain". And I nodded, not to fix, but to honor that truth. For so long, the trauma gave structure. Now, healing feels like a void. I reminded him that grief is not a step backward. It's part of what allows something new to root.

When daily life stops being organized by defense, a new question appears: what does all of this mean? Meaning-making is the system's way of weaving cooperation into identity: plural, evolving, and owned from inside.

For many dissociative personality systems, so much of the early therapeutic journey is focused on survival, establishing safety, navigating internal conflict, working through trauma memories, and managing crises. But what happens after? When parts begin to cooperate and collaborate, memories start to integrate, and the internal world feels less volatile?

This phase can feel unfamiliar, even destabilizing. When the urgency fades, some clients report feeling lost: "Who am I now? What do we do with all we've lived through?"

This chapter explores how to support clients as they move beyond survival, into meaning-making, identity growth, and integration of experience. Not integration as fusion, but as lived coherence. The goal is not to *move on* from trauma, but to transform its impact and integrate it, to allow it to shape identity in a way that honors the past without being defined by it.

This final chapter turns from how systems cooperate to how they live with what they have survived

THE PROCESS OF MEANING-MAKING

The movement from trauma processing to meaning-making does not happen all at once. It arrives quietly, often in small signs:

- A part reflecting on how their role has changed.
- A younger part expressing curiosity instead of fear.
- The system asking *why* something happened, instead of only *what.*
- Creativity or spiritual exploration emerging organically.
- Emotional states becoming more tolerable or shared across parts.

These moments signal that the personality system is beginning to seek coherence, not just symptom relief, but a fuller understanding of self and story. The therapist's role now shifts from stabilizer to companion in exploration.

For many clients, trauma defined who they were for so long, dissociation, diagnosis, survival roles. As healing deepens, systems begin to ask: Who are we now? What do we believe? What do we want to carry forward and what can we release?

These questions can evoke grief, confusion, even resistance. Some parts may fear losing their purpose. Others may mourn the loss of the life they could have had without trauma.

Therapists can support this identity shift validating and normalizing this new experience:

- ★ "It's okay to grieve the time that was taken and it's also okay to wonder who you are becoming."
- ★ "You're not betraying the past by growing beyond it, you're allowing it to become part of your autobiography."

Growth is the fruit of survival.

MEANING-MAKING WITHIN THE PERSONALITY SYSTEM

Different parts may make meaning in different ways. For one, healing might mean reclaiming voice. For another, it might mean protecting others. For a third, it could be as simple as no longer having to be afraid.

Therapy can support these unique interpretations by:

- Allowing each part to narrate what healing means to them.
- Using metaphor or creative expression to explore new understandings.
- Encouraging rituals that honor transition, from protector to witness, from exile to member, from silence to presence.

This process helps clients move from "This happened to me" to "This shaped me, and I'm still shaping what comes next".

GRIEF, LOSS, AND THE PASSAGE OF TIME

As healing deepens, so does grief. Clients may begin to fully feel what was lost, childhood, safety, trust, time. Some parts may mourn the trauma itself; others may grieve their dissociative roles, their younger selves, or even the pain that once gave life a clear structure.

This grief is not pathology. It is evidence of return. It means the system is awake enough to feel what was once numbed or fragmented.

Therapists can hold this space with reverence:

- ★ "Of course there's grief, something mattered, even if it was painful."
- ★ "Grieving means you're present enough to notice what wasn't."

We do not rush grief. We witness it. And in doing so, we make space for something else to grow alongside it.

CREATIVITY, CURIOSITY, AND RECONNECTION

As personality systems stabilize and meaning takes root, new life begins to emerge. Often quietly, sometimes joyfully:

- Parts exploring music, art, writing, or nature.
- Clients reconnecting to friendships, spirituality, or movement.
- The personality system developing shared interests or goals.
- Moments of laughter, play, rest, without fear.

These moments are not *escapes*. They are integration in action, evidence that the system is no longer living only in defense, but in desire.

Therapists can name and support this gently:

- ⋆ "That curiosity you're feeling, it's welcome here."
- ⋆ "It sounds like something new is waking up inside."

Healing does not always look like stillness. Sometimes, it looks like aliveness returning.

BUILDING A COHERENT STORY OR AUTOBIOGRAPHY, WITHOUT FORCING A SINGLE NARRATIVE

Meaning-making is not about having a perfect, polished narrative. In dissociative systems, some memories may remain incomplete, some parts may hold different timelines or truths. That is okay. The goal is not a single, unified story, but a way of living where different truths can coexist without tearing the personality system apart.

The goal is not fusion of story, but coherence of experience:

- Understanding that different parts hold different meanings and that's allowed
- Allowing complexity: "It was painful, and I loved them." "We survived, but it still hurts."
- Finding language that feels accurate not clinical, not performative, but authentic

Clients may begin to speak their story publicly, or only to themselves. Either way, the meaning belongs to them.

CLOSING THOUGHTS

Meaning-making is not a finish line. It is a living, ongoing process, one that grows and changes as the personality system does. It is about reclaiming authorship, not erasing pain.

When clients begin to shape their own story, in art, in voice, in stillness, they reclaim what trauma tried to steal: their ability to choose what comes next.

All the loops, roles, and protections that have been described are chapters in how the personality system learned to survive. Meaning-making is how the system now chooses what to carry forward.

CLINICAL ANCHORS

WHAT TO REMEMBER...

- Growth can feel disorienting. Grief often rides with freedom.
- Meaning is plural. Private coherence is as valid as public story.
- ·Creativity signals emergence. Follow curiosity, not pressure.
- There is no universal timeline. Meaning often grows after therapy ends.

WHAT TO AVOID...

- Imposing a narrative.
- Pathologizing ambivalence or grief during positive change.
- Rushing reconstruction because symptoms eased.

Closing Words

This book has not offered a protocol or a map with fixed destinations. It has offered a way of seeing, one that honors complexity, pacing, and consent, and that treats dissociative parts not as obstacles to overcome, but as adaptations to be understood. If it serves as a companion in learning how to accompany clients and their parts with steadiness and respect, then it has done its work.

As personality systems begin to organize internally, therapists may feel tempted to step back, or, paradoxically, to step in more. Both impulses deserve reflection. Supporting internal leadership does not mean withdrawing presence, nor does it mean replacing one authority with another. Leadership grows when all parts are recognized and accepted, and when the system can hold both truths at once: each part belongs to the whole, and each part carries the whole in its own way.

When we name moments of grounded decision-making, boundary-setting, or repair, we help systems notice their own capacity without imposing structure. It is also important to remember that not all systems will want the same shape of wholeness. Some will move toward shared identity, others toward cooperative plurality. Our role is not to favor one outcome, but to remain curious, respectful, and steady as the system discovers what "together" means for them.

If autobiography gives meaning to what has been lived, mapmaking supports what comes next. Survivors do not need a complete record of every road they have traveled, nor a single, unified story. They need enough orientation to know where they are now, which paths feel safer, where support can be found, and which routes still require caution.

As Giovanni Liotti reminded us, healing is not about erasing the past, but about regaining the capacity to move along the road without being pulled back into old intersections of fear, attachment, and danger. Some roads were laid down in trauma time, when there were no real choices.

Others are discovered later, when safety allows detours, pauses, or new directions altogether.

Maps change as personality systems change. New landmarks appear. Old dangers lose their power. Some routes are intentionally avoided—not out of fear, but out of discernment. The goal is not total knowledge or perfect integration, but enough orientation to move through life with choice, awareness, and relationship.

Integration is not something we do; it is something we witness when safety has had time to work. In this sense, healing is not the end of the journey, but the moment when the personality system begins to know how to navigate—together.

Dolores Mosquera

APPENDIX

Appendix 1. Linking TADP with the Procedural Framework of *Working with Voices*

The purpose of this appendix is to offer a series of summaries, charts and visual resources that support integration of the material presented in this volume. In addition to what is presented here, it includes the procedural structure described in *Working with Voices and Dissociative Parts* (Mosquera, 2019), which provides the clinical backbone of this work. The two volumes are conceptually linked but function differently. *Working with Voices and Dissociative Parts* articulates the procedural step sequence of the therapeutic work. The present volume elaborates the motivational and relational architecture underlying that sequence. Together, they form a coherent model: procedure guides structure; motivational logic guides stance.

The following list is the sequence of steps for exploring parts, reducing trauma-related phobias, validating function, strengthening resources, and developing cooperation.

GENERAL STRUCTURE OF THE THERAPEUTIC WORK
1. Exploring the parts and their voices (content, tone, message, age, moment of onset, etc.)
2. Encouraging clients to listen to the voices and/or pay more attention to the parts.
3. Exploring the triggers (what was happening when the part showed up or when the voice spoke)
4. Exploring and/or processing dissociative phobias
5. Assessing the degree of differentiation and time orientation in client and parts
6. Exploring and validating the function of the voice
7. Identifying and validating resources, feelings and needs
8. Exploring, modelling, and practicing alternative ways of responding. Offering suggestions when needed
9. Identifying and exploring missing pieces
10. Reaching agreements, developing cooperation and teamwork

Table A1.1. General structure of the therapeutic work, presented originally in *Working with Voices and Dissociative Parts* (Mosquera, 2019)

The present volume adds the motivational and relational logic that explains *why* particular interventions are needed at specific moments. If the earlier work outlines the procedural pathway, this volume clarifies the biological, interpersonal, and developmental forces that organize parts and shape therapeutic stance. The interventions listed below are reflected throughout the chapters of this book. While organized here by clinical function rather than sequence, they correspond to the procedural steps described in *Working with Voices and Dissociative Parts*.

FUNCTIONAL CATEGORIES OF INTERVENTIONS	STRUCTURAL PROCEDURES FROM WORKING WITH VOICES (2019)
AWARENESS AND STABILIZATION	
1. Acknowledging presence and tracking change	**Step 1.** Exploring the parts and their voices **Step 2.** Encouraging clients to listen to the voices and pay attention **Step 5.** Assessing the degree of differentiation and time orientation
2. Inviting reflection and meaning-making	**Step 3.** Exploring the triggers **Step 6.** Exploring and validating function **Step 9.** Identifying and exploring missing pieces
3. Regulating contact (pacing, limits, steadiness)	**Step 4.** Exploring and processing dissociative phobias **Step 5.** Assessing differentiation and time orientation **Step 8.** Exploring, modeling, and practicing alternative responses
4. Orienting to the present and shared reality	**Step 5.** Assessing the degree of differentiation and time orientation
SURVIVAL LOGIC VALIDATION	
5. Validating protective function	**Step 6.** Exploring and validating function
AGENCY, BOUNDARIES AND COOPERATION	
6. Obtaining permission and strengthening agency	**Step 7.** Identifying and validating resources, feelings and needs **Step 8.** Exploring, modeling, and practicing alternative responses **Step 10.** Reaching agreements, developing cooperation
7. Maintaining boundaries / neutralizing power struggles	**Step 8.** Exploring, modeling, and practicing alternative responses **Step 10.** Reaching agreements and developing cooperation
8. Inviting cooperation and shared attention	**Step 10.** Reaching agreements and developing cooperation
9. Identifying relational patterns	**Step 3.** Exploring triggers **Step 6.** Exploring and validating function **Step 8.** Exploring, modeling, and practicing alternative responses **Step 10.** Reaching agreements and developing cooperation
MICRO-REGULATION IN SESSION	
10. Procedural safety through predictability	**Step 5.** Assessing the degree of differentiation & time orientation **Step 8.** Exploring, modeling, and practicing alternative responses **Step 10.** Reaching agreements and developing cooperation
11. Regulating post-exposure recoil	**Step 4.** Exploring and processing dissociative phobias **Step 5.** Assessing the degree of differentiation & time orientation **Step 8.** Exploring, modeling, and practicing alternative responses
12. Updating coercive or escalatory internal strategies	**Step 6.** Exploring and validating function **Step 8.** Exploring, modeling, and practicing alternative responses **Step 10.** Reaching agreements and developing cooperation

Table A1.2. List of functional categories of the clinical interventions presented throughout this volume vs. corresponding procedural structural steps.

Note: Step 1 (Exploring dissociative parts and their voices) remains an ongoing and implicit process throughout all functional categories. Although it is listed explicitly where most central, exploratory mapping and differentiation continue across the course of treatment and are embedded in many of the interventions described above. Step 2 (Encouraging curiosity) similarly functions as a cross-cutting principle and is therefore listed only where it is most directly emphasized.

Appendix 2. Sample Interventions Grouped by Functional Category

This appendix organizes all therapist-language sentences that appear in quotation marks throughout the chapters into the unified functional categories presented in appendix 1. The categories are intentionally broad and conceptually integrated so that each sentence appears once, under the primary function it serves. Wording is reproduced verbatim.

The following macro-categories group interventions according to their primary regulatory and relational function. They are not sequential stages, but functional lenses that clarify the aim of therapist interventions described throughout the book. In practice, these functions often overlap. The groupings are intended to support conceptual understanding of how specific interventions regulate motivational systems, reduce internal conflict, and foster cooperation within dissociative personality systems.

AWARENESS AND STABILIZATION

These interventions support the development of safe, differentiated awareness. They reduce threat activation, foster curiosity about what is happening internally, and help shift from tunnel-vision "no way out" trauma-time attention toward flexible observation. The emphasis is on joint curiosity—exploring together as the foundation of cooperation—while strengthening differentiation, pacing, and present-time orientation. This creates the conditions for deeper exploration and relational clarity later in the work.

1. Acknowledging Presence and Tracking Change: To recognize that an internal, part, or shift is present—without demand, interpretation, or pressure—so awareness can stabilize without exposure.

Clinical purpose: Promotes awareness; supports differentiation and time orientation without forcing exposure.

Motivational systems addressed: Attachment (inhibited), defense (down-regulated), Intersubjectivity

Examples:

- ★ "Something feels close, let's make space for it."
- ★ "Even if we don't hear from them, we are still holding them in mind."
- ★ "I wonder how the little one inside (or whatever name they use) is doing today."
- ★ "They don't have to come forward; we just want them to know they're welcome."
- ★ "Thank you for staying with me."
- ★ "I felt you here just now, that matters."
- ★ "Something shifted just now, would it feel okay to slow down?"
- ★ "We don't have to talk about it; I just want you to know I noticed."
- ★ "I hear how much shame there is."

2. Inviting Reflection and Meaning-Making. To open inquiry into origin, purpose, and protective logic without forcing insight or resolution and doing so in a way that reduces shame.

Clinical purpose: Clarifies triggers, beliefs, and implicit survival rules.

Motivational systems addressed: Intersubjectivity, attachment, rank (belief structures)

Examples:

- ★ "That makes sense. Sometimes there are parts that didn't get to grow up."
- ★ "It makes sense, there might be parts that still don't know you grew up."
- ★ "Sometimes staying close to the one who hurt you felt like the safest thing."
- ★ "What does this part believe it's protecting you from?"
- ★ "What would happen if this part didn't have to be so hard on you?"
- ★ "What does this part want you to know right now?"
- ★ "What happens in your body when this part feels close?
- ★ "Of course it made more sense to believe it was your fault. That might have been the only way to stay close."
- ★ "It sounds like this part is scared of what might happen if you let your guard down."

- ★ "I hear how strong this part is. I wonder what it's trying to accomplish."
- ★ "It sounds like you're tired. Like you've been holding this alone for a long time."
- ★ "Even if you don't feel connected to the others, I'll stay with you while we figure this out."
- ★ "What might this part be trying to prevent?"
- ★ "When did it first learn it had to do this job?"

3. Regulating Contact Through Pacing and Limits. To communicate safety by controlling exposure, dose, proximity, tempo, and intensity—using clear limits to make contact possible without flooding or backlash.

Clinical purpose: Reduces trauma-related phobias; prevents flooding; models containment and pacing

Motivational systems addressed: Defense, rank (neutralization), attachment (safe distance)

Examples:

- ★ "You don't have to explain anything right now."
- ★ "This part of your experience matters, and we'll move at your pace."
- ★ "You don't have to do anything right now, I'm here. Even if this is hard to stay with, we can go slowly together."
- ★ "You don't have to say anything, I'm just glad you're here."
- ★ "You don't have to believe anything different right now."
- ★ "You set the distance; I'll match it."
- ★ "Would it feel okay to sit beside this part for a moment?"
- ★ "Could you let them know they're not alone, in whatever way feels possible?"
- ★ "I feel the pull to swoop in; instead, let's help your Adult take the lead while I stay with you both."
- ★ "I hear how much is coming up, and I also need to feel safe enough to stay fully present with you."
- ★ "We can stay close enough to know it's here, but not so close that it floods you."
- ★ "Let's stay with this for three breaths and then check again."
- ★ "We can slow this down."
- ★ "Let's keep it small and come back to the room."

- "Could we just notice it from a distance today?"
- "Can we stay with one sentence, not the whole story?"
- "We'll take this in a drop, not a wave."
- "One neutral speck only, then we orient and close."
- "We'll measure success by return to baseline, not by how much got said."
- "Thirty seconds, then we step back."
- "We won't look longer than it feels right."
- "If you need to look away, that's still contact—we will follow your pace."

4. Orienting to Present Time and Shared Reality. To counter trauma-time, rank distortion, or singular-self assumptions and restore context.

Clinical purpose: Helps orient to present safety, challenges trauma-time perspective, and gradually reinforces shared embodiment.

Motivational systems addressed: Defense (deactivation), intersubjectivity.

Examples:

- "Do you know there is only one shared body?"
- "What do you imagine might happen to the others inside if something happened to you?"
- "This is your system trying to end chaos or unreality fast; let's help it do that safely."
- "Right now, it is this room, this moment."
- "Nothing from back then can happen here."
- "Then being seen drew danger; now we decide when and how to be seen."
- "Then, hiding kept you safe; now, looking can be brief and end on your signal."
- "Then, scanning kept you alive; now, scanning and resting can take turns."
- "Now your body is grown, and you have a different kind of power.

SURVIVAL LOGIC VALIDATION

These interventions reframe internal conflict through a trauma-informed lens. By identifying the protective intention behind behaviors, messages and voices, they reduce shame and trauma-related phobias. Validation focuses on survival logic rather than strategy, creating the conditions for empathy, flexibility, cooperation, collaboration and eventually compassion within the system.

5. Validating Protective Function and Survival Logic. Placing experience and behavior in a trauma-informed, survival-based frame that acknowledges protective function, naming intention and regulatory purpose, without endorsing harmful behavior or validating the strategy itself.

Clinical purpose: De-shames parts by identifying survival logic without endorsing harmful behavior; improves empathy, understanding, collaboration, and eventually compassion.

Motivational systems addressed: Defense, rank, attachment (survival adaptations).

Examples:

- ★ "It sounds like you/this part have been working very hard to keep things safe."
- ★ "I can see how this made sense at the time."
- ★ "Maybe this part is doing now what helped you survive then."
- ★ "I'm not here to take this away from you/this part, I'd like to understand it with you."
- ★ "You have /this part has been doing a hard job for a long time."
- ★ "Maybe no one ever thanked this part for trying to keep things safe."
- ★ "It sounds like it's been working hard to keep things in line."
- ★ "Thank you for working so hard to protect them."
- ★ "It makes sense that this part learned to be harsh to keep you safe."
- ★ "This part is trying to protect you, even if it's doing it in a painful way."
- ★ "I can see how much effort this part is putting in."
- ★ "It sounds like this part thinks danger is still close."
- ★ "This part is doing something important; let's understand what it's trying to prevent."
- ★ "We can respect the protection without following the strategy."
- ★ "It sounds like this part is trying to keep the system safe from being embarrassed."

- ★ "So that harsh part has been doing its job: making sure no one sees weakness."
- ★ "Thank you for stopping the flood. Humiliation used to be lethal; today pace can do that job with less damage."
- ★ "Thank you for keeping the lid when no one else could. Your job stands. The method changes."
- ★ "Something in you just hit the brakes. That might be protection doing its job."
- ★ "A Guardian is shaping what's shared so the lid stays on. We can respect that and go slower or make it smaller."
- ★ "It sounds like you're preventing collapse the only way you learned. Today, protection can look different. We'll keep the lid without injury: brakes and pacing."

AGENCY, BOUNDARIES AND COOPERATION

These interventions strengthen agency and support the development of healthy internal control. They restore consent, clarify roles, neutralize power struggles, and make implicit relational strategies explicit when attachment, rank, or sexuality become entangled. By modeling assertive and regulated interaction, they shift the system from dependency or dominance toward collaborative functioning. The goal is shared responsibility and internal teamwork that extends beyond therapy into everyday relationships.

6. Obtaining Permission while Increasing Agency and Internal Authority. Explicitly restoring choice and non-coercion by checking readiness locally and systemically, reinforcing Adult Self leadership and internal agreements, including emphasis on practicing stop-signal.

Clinical purpose: Reinforces Adult Self leadership; encourages and validates consent and internal choice.

Motivational systems addressed: Cooperation, caregiving (internalized), intersubjectivity.

Examples:

- ★ "You don't have to talk today."
- ★ "You're allowed to be unsure."
- ★ "It's okay to take your time."
- ★ "If a part is unsure about being here, we can welcome that too."

- ★ "We don't have to settle this today. There will be another chance."
- ★ "We can pause for a moment or shift gears if you'd like. Your call."
- ★ "Would it feel okay to acknowledge that this younger experience is present right now?"
- ★ "Is there anything I need to understand before we bring attention to this part of the system?"
- ★ "Can we check together if this is the right moment, or if more support is needed first?"
- ★ "Can we check with the Adult Self whether it feels okay to explore this part's presence?"
- ★ "Would it be okay if we checked with the system first?"
- ★ "Let's ask the adult self if it's okay to approach this."
- ★ "We can ask the part that's most afraid what it needs to feel safe enough."
- ★ "Would it be okay if we just let it know we're here?"
- ★ "If it's too much, we stop."
- ★ "You can say stop anytime."
- ★ "We won't do anything that feels unsafe."
- ★ "You're allowed to have boundaries inside."
- ★ "We'll only go as far as all parts can tolerate."
- ★ "We can check what's okay for today."
- ★ "You don't have to say anything you're not ready to."
- ★ "Even if you can't speak it yet, you're allowed to know what you know."
- ★ "Before we go near it, let's ask the one who keeps the oath what would feel safe enough for this hour."
- ★ "If it feels like you have to be agreeable to stay connected, that's our cue to slow down."
- ★ "You're in charge of when to start and when to stop. I'll follow your signal."
- ★ "Anything inside can let us know when to stop."
- ★ "We don't have to do this today."
- ★ "If you say 'pause,' I will stop immediately."
- ★ "Notice how you said stop, and we stopped."
- ★ "You have control. If you say stop, we stop immediately."
- ★ "Nothing will happen without us agreeing first."

7. Maintaining Boundaries / Neutralizing Power Struggles. To maintain a clear and steady therapeutic frame while de-escalating dominance, submission, and control dynamics as they arise, avoiding power struggles.

Clinical purpose: Models rank neutrality; prevents reenactment; maintains safety in the therapeutic frame.

Motivational systems addressed: Rank (dominance/submission), cooperation.

Examples:

- ★ "I'm not here to win or outsmart you. I'm here to understand what keeps you safe."
- ★ "We don't use that language here. But I'm not leaving. I want to understand what you're protecting."
- ★ "I can respect your strength without fighting you."
- ★ "You don't have to overpower me for me to stay."
- ★ "I hear how much is coming up, and I also need to feel safe enough to stay fully present with you."
- ★ "I won't follow that part's rules, but I will listen to what it's afraid of."
- ★ "I can stay with you, and I can also stay in my role."
- ★ "We can do this without anyone taking over."
- ★ "I'm not going to argue with this part; I'm going to understand it."
- ★ "We can slow down and still stay connected."
- ★ "The boundary is steady; I'm still here, in a healthy way."
- ★ "I'll keep the therapy boundaries steady, so you don't have to manage me."

8. Inviting Internal Cooperation (Not Rescue): To shift from attachment activation or rescue into collaborative engagement. Encouraging shared attention and internal dialogue without taking over.

Clinical purpose: Invites and develops collaboration instead of attachment dependency, control, or dominance.

Motivational systems addressed: Cooperation, intersubjectivity, social belonging.

Examples:

- ★ "What if we look at this together?"

- ★ "Shall we see what happens next?"
- ★ "What if we look together for ten seconds and then stop?"
- ★ "Would it be okay if we asked the adult self to be present too?"
- ★ "Can the adult self stay with this part without trying to fix it?"
- ★ "Could we invite other parts to listen without interrupting?"
- ★ "Can the adult self reassure this part that it's not alone?"
- ★ "If this part could wait five minutes before acting, what might it want you to understand?"
- ★ "Could we create a plan together that allows this part to be acknowledged and think of other options?"
- ★ "Are there other parts who feel concerned or afraid about what happened?"
- ★ "If there are, can we help them communicate and listen to them too?"

9. Identifying Relational Patterns. Identifying submission, appeasement, or sexualized strategies while holding steady boundaries.

Clinical purpose: Makes implicit relational strategies explicit; reduces reenactment; prevents shame while maintaining clarity.

Motivational systems addressed: Attachment, rank (submission/dominance), sexuality (when recruited as attachment currency), cooperation.

Examples:

- ★ "I noticed a younger reach, and then an appeasing move."
- ★ "When I offered comfort, I saw a shift toward sexuality."
- ★ "That may have been a strategy that helped before."
- ★ "We don't have to pay for closeness here."
- ★ "If we slow down, what would the younger one need?"
- ★ "It's not about what I want; it's about what you want and need."
- ★ "Thank you for trying to keep things safe in the only way you knew."

MICRO-REGULATION IN SESSION

These interventions address moment-to-moment shifts that occur within sessions. They reduce anticipatory anxiety, regulate post-contact recoil, and update learned coercive or escalatory strategies. Their function is to maintain safety and cooperation as activation takes place. Through repeated co-regulation in session, they support the gradual development of self-regulation, Adult perspective, and reflective choice.

10. Procedural Safety Through Predictability. Using structure and repetition to reduce anticipatory threat and increase stability.

Clinical purpose: Reduces anticipatory anxiety; stabilizes vigilance-based parts; strengthens temporal continuity and safety through repetition.

Motivational systems addressed: Defense (anticipatory threat reduction), attachment (predictability), cooperation.

Examples:

- ★ "We'll start with the door, the window, the clock; we'll end with two anchors."
- ★ "We'll start the same way today."
- ★ "Same office, same order of work."
- ★ "Next time, we'll plan one small change together."
- ★ "Your job doesn't change here. The only thing that changes is how we protect; through pacing, not shutdown.

11. **Regulating Post-Exposure Recoil.** Normalizing backlash, shame waves, or internal pullback after contact.

Clinical purpose: Prevents secondary escalation after contact; reduces shame backlash; stabilizes cooperation after vulnerability.

Motivational systems addressed: Defense (rebound activation), attachment (fear of exposure), rank (self-criticism).

Examples:

- ★ "That was a lot to share; it makes sense that part of you feels exposed now."
- ★ "It sounds like another part came in to check for danger."
- ★ "It makes sense something inside wants to pull back."
- ★ "We can slow this down and stay with what feels manageable."
- ★ "It makes sense another part is stepping in after that."
- ★ "We don't have to go further today."

12. Updating Coercive or Escalatory Internal Strategies. Responding to urgency, shutdown, or punitive control by installing safer regulation.

Clinical purpose: Interrupts harm-based regulation; redirects urgency toward cooperative and body-safe strategies.

Motivational systems addressed: Defense (overactivation), rank (internal dominance), cooperation.

Examples:

- "Let's help this system regulate without hurting the body."
- "We can keep the lid without injury."
- "Protection can look different now."
- "We'll use brakes and pacing instead of force."
- "You keep us safe by calling pause, not by hurting the body."
- "We can interrupt this safely."
- "This is your system trying to protect you fast; let's help it protect you safely."

Appendix 3. Summary Charts for Dissociative Parts

CHILD PARTS

These parts are time travelers with no map.
They step into the present carrying the sights, sounds, and feelings of another era.
They believe they are still there, still in danger,
unable to recognize the passage of time without help.

ORIGINS

- Attachment–defense collision
- Disorganized caregiving
- Chronic misattunement and silence
- Coercion, secrecy, betrayal

FEATURES

- Trauma-time anchoring
- Developmental childlike reasoning
- Modes of communication
- Attachment sensitivity
- Trigger-linked activation
- Protector elicitation
- Emotional load
- Orientation gaps

FUNCTIONS

1. Carrier of **unbearable pain** and unmet attachment needs
2. Alarm for **unresolved trauma**
3. **Proximity seeking** for safety and soothing
4. Keeper of **emotional truth**
5. Storehouse of **non-verbal memory**
6. Holder of **shame labels** ("too much", "not enough")
7. **Compliance and appeasement**
8. Internal siren that **mobilizes protectors**

THERAPEUTIC STANCE

Therapeutic work is **paced through the Adult Self,** with normalization of the trauma-time perspective. These parts are held in mind even when they are not visible, **prioritizing repair of relationship** over extraction of content. Clinical work maintains **clear therapeutic boundaries,** seeks **permission from the system**, and emphasizes relationship over meaning, **guided by curiosity** about how these parts express themselves and what that expression signifies.

ADOLESCENT PARTS

Like a door guard, these parts learned that nearness could burn,
so they stand with one hand on the handle.
They keep the line fair and the lights low, so the
child parts can be safe and only seen by safe figures.

ORIGINS

- Early experiences of shame and humiliation
- First awareness of physical power or size differences
- Age peer hierarchies and belonging pressures
- Moral sorting as identity glue (right/wrong, loyal/disloyal)
- Public exposure or reputational injury

FEATURES

- Fight-tilted signals and stance
- Exposure control
- Procedural control and rank monitoring
- Peer/status focus
- Aftermath markers

FUNCTIONS

1. **Protester-Boundary-Setter**: Keep adults honest, preserve fairness in the frame, and block humiliation
2. **Detached Teen**: Reduce visibility, control exposure, and lower the stakes.
3. **Parentified Teen**: Keep the system functioning and preempt criticism by outperforming it.
4. **Achiever**: Turn vulnerability into advantage, gaining status to reduce exposure.
5. **Risk-Tester:** Assert agency where once was helplessness
6. **Chameleon**: Secure belonging to avoid outsider shame

THERAPEUTIC STANCE

In addition to the therapeutic stance held with child parts, we must consider:

- Honor **rank sensitivity**
- **Name function** before content
- Invite **co-construction** of rules
- Avoid parentification or relating to them as peers
- Expect **tests; welcome** them.
- **Track shame** explicitly

FEARFUL AND AVOIDANT PARTS

Like a child waiting at the window, these parts learned that reaching invites hurt,
so, they watch from behind the curtain, very still, very careful.
They hold hope and fear in the same small hands,
believing that if they wait just right,
they might be seen without being harmed

ORIGINS

- Early neglect, intrusion, or inconsistent caregiving
- Trauma in which hiding or shutting down was safest
- Attachment wounds where closeness was paired with danger
- Punishment, invalidation or betrayal for expressing emotion or need

FEATURES

- Numbness & "I don't know" responses
- Smile / laugh while describing painful events
- Change subjects when closeness arises
- Somatic cues: blank stare, muscle collapse, shallow breathing
- Missed sessions or polite compliance without emotional presence
- Emotional flatness / reported lack of inner experience

FUNCTIONS

1. Strategic **withdrawal** and invisibility
2. Preemptive shutdown to **manage overwhelm**
3. Gatekeeping to **protect vulnerable parts**
4. Distance to **preserve autonomy**
5. Appeasement to **reduce perceived burden**
6. **Delay** loops and vigilance
7. Emotion **minimization** and compartmentalization
8. Routine and predictability as **control**
9. **Dampening** desire and attachment signals:

THERAPEUTIC STANCE

Therapeutic work shifts from an agenda of opening parts up to a stance of **quiet permission**, beginning with gentle invitations that consistently communicate choice. Responses are offered softly, with careful acknowledgment, while safety is supported through **containment that does not slide into control.** Avoidance is named with gentle curiosity rather than pressure, allowing structure to communicate "You're safe," and presence to communicate "You're not alone."

SELF-CRITICAL AND PUNITIVE PARTS

Like a courtroom judge, this part delivers rulings without appeal: guilty, inadequate, unworthy.
It believes that by controlling the verdict,
it can prevent the humiliation of being judged by others.

ORIGINS

- Chronic emotional abuse, humiliation or neglect.
- Internalized voices of caregivers/ abusers.
- Attempts to prevent external criticism by anticipating it internally.
- Beliefs that suffering earns safety, or that shame prevents harm
- Loyalty to caregivers who demanded silence, self-blame, invisibility and sometimes perfection

FEATURES

- Manifest by intrusive voices / thoughts
- Tend to operate in the background, speaking with authority and finality
- Thinking is often rigid, limited, and inflexible
- Arrive in bursts of emotion, but as persistent internal evaluations
- Tone is often rigid and moralistic
- Impact is often shame, paralysis, and internal conflict
- May contribute to suicidal despair
- They don't seek comfort / connection
- Their focus is on achievement compliance, silence, and control

FUNCTIONS

1. **Prevent external harm** by downranking from within
2. Maintain **internal order** through rigid rules
3. Suppress vulnerable parts to **avoid exposure**
4. Divert intolerable affect into **control and contempt**
5. Attachment signals are deactivated to **prevent dependency**
6. **Preserve attachment** loyalties through identification with the caregiver's moral code
7. Suppress hope and vulnerability
8. Suppress vulnerable expression
9. **Adult Self is undermined,** often through criticism of the therapist or potential allies who might threaten the existing internal hierarchy

THERAPEUTIC STANCE

Therapeutic work names the **fear beneath the criticism** without engaging in efforts to prove the client's worth. Collaboration is invited while maintaining **reflective distance**, allowing the therapist to take note internally, remain steady, and offer clear acknowledgment without escalation or defensiveness.

HOSTILE AND AGGRESSIVE PARTS

Like guard dogs bred to attack every shadow, they turn on their own master.
Blind to the harm, they believe biting keeps danger away,
not knowing they are bleeding the very home they vowed to protect.

ORIGINS

- Chronic invalidation of emotions and needs, shaming, rejection, or emotional neglect from caregivers.
- Coerced forgiveness or premature demands for compliance.
- Internal pressure to protect trauma content that other parts in the system can't bear.
- Lessons: intimacy equals danger, weakness or loss of control.
- Becoming the threat felt safer than remaining the target.

FEATURES

- Speak in the voice of former abusers
- Reject kindness as manipulative
- Minimize trauma
- Shame other parts for being *weak*
- View connection as setup for betrayal
- Insult, mock, or demean the client
- Make threats
- Use strategic angry silence / contempt
- Introduce inner noise so client can't participate in conversations
- Act uninterested in help
- Elicit fear, irritation, helplessness, or withdrawal in client / therapist

FUNCTIONS

1. **Preempt closeness** before it becomes dangerous
2. Enforce **control** and predictability
3. Maintain protective **distance**
4. Guard against **emotional exposure or** betrayal
5. **Divert attention** from traumatic material
6. Convert shame, fear, or grief are into **anger or contempt**.
7. Monitor and **police vulnerability** Internally
8. Repeat **learned rules** from hostile environment
9. Mobilize **energy and action** under threat
10. Signal **threat detection**

THERAPEUTIC STANCE

Therapeutic stance emphasizes **noticing without confronting,** acknowledging without agreeing, and validating without colluding. Rank is intentionally downshifted before inviting cooperation, with last-chance pressure removed by **opting out of contests and respectfully declining challenges**. Resource competition is softened through **strategic yielding and status de-escalation**, allowing engagement to emerge through genuine curiosity, collaboration, and permission, anchored in the **Adult Self.**

SELF-HARMING PARTS

Self-harm is like a pressure valve on a boiler. When the gauge spikes,
it vents fast and the tank doesn't burst. It also scalds the system each time.
Our work is to keep the purpose (quick release) and install safer ways to let the pressure go.

ORIGINS

- Emotions dismissed, mocked, or punished
- Care bids were shamed or ignored until they extinguish
- Models of self-attack or self-control in family, peers, or media
- Accidental discovery that focused physical pain can blunt diffuse emotional overload
- Internal rules forbidding need, anger, or protest
- Early experiences of visible injury = care while emotion = rejection
- Exposure to normalization of self-injury as relief

FEATURES

- Urges that surge with interpersonal stress or trauma-time cues
- A felt sense of relief after self-injury
- Rigid internal rules on need, perfection, or exposure
- Secrecy with careful risk minimization and precise planning
- Ambivalence toward help that feels like prohibition or rescue
- Often a pragmatic or even warm tone in contrast to hostile protectors
- Rapid attentional narrowing onto the body/sensation when intrusive memories rise

FUNCTIONS

1. Affect **modulation**
2. **Downregulation** and interruption
3. **Attention shifting** away from traumatic intrusions
4. **Punitive control** to prevent external shaming
5. **Silencing** need and attachment bids
6. Maintaining **internal order** via rigid rules
7. **Eliciting care indirectly** when asking feels dangerous
8. Preventing collapse by **dampening** interoceptive cues
9. Keeping **suicide at bay**

THERAPEUTIC STANCE

Therapeutic work leads with **curiosity and cooperation**, explicitly validating the protective job these strategies perform. Choice and brakes are kept visible throughout the process, while the need for relief is actively **de-shamed** rather than challenged. Change is supported by building **micro-procedures** that can realistically compete with the old sequence, offering alternatives that feel safer than sudden disruption.

SUICIDAL PARTS

Suicidal ideation is like knowing there is an emergency exit in the building.
It may never be used, but its very existence offers control when everything is overwhelming.
These parts are not obsessed with leaving—they are obsessed with knowing there is a way out.

ORIGINS

- Emotional pain is ignored, ridiculed, or punished
- Caregivers responding to needs with neglect, shame, or cruelty
- Exposure to suicide in family members, peers, or media
- Growing up with rejection or violent regretmessages that the child was unwanted or too much
- Cultural or religious narratives framed suffering as deserved, and relief as selfish or taboo
- Feeling others would be happy if they disappeared

FEATURES

- Speak in absolute or fatalistic terms
- Express emotional numbness/ dissociation
- View death as a solution, relief, or mercy
- Discourage therapeutic engagement
- Belief that pain is unique and incomprehensible
- Carry a pervasive hopelessness
- Block access to hope, connection, or internal collaboration
- Dismiss the therapist's presence, but not in an aggressive manner suggestive of a power struggle (Rank)
- Shut down vulnerable parts / disqualify the Adult Self's efforts
- Replay repetitive internal commands

FUNCTIONS

1. Escape from **unbearable** affect /unending pain
2. **Interruption** of emotional activation
3. **Control and containment** in chaos

THERAPEUTIC STANCE

Therapeutic work prioritizes **presence before problem-solving,** understanding this presentation as a protector using the wrong tool for the right job. The stance is grounded in **curiosity and cooperation**, gently addressing typical distortions while validating the depth of the protector's exhaustion. Work then turns toward identifying triggers and developing alternatives that reduce reliance on the old strategy without stripping away its protective intent.

HOMICIDAL PARTS

When cracks appear, the impulse is to destroy what feels unstable.
But stability can be regained by reinforcing the frame:
adding supports, redistributing pressure, restoring alignment.
The system can flex without breaking; it can be repaired.

ORIGINS

- Chronic humiliation
- Exposure to coercive codes (rigid, threat-enforced rules about dominance, loyalty, and punishment)
- Role reversal in which cruelty was framed as care
- Environments where proximity to power felt safer than vulnerability.

FEATURES

- Poor recognition of plurality
- Categorical labeling of internal targets
- Refusal to engage in care
- Preemptive threats to eradicate vulnerability
- Rank contests with therapist
- Dehumanizing/contemptuous toward "weak" or "useless" parts.
- Moralized language (purity, order...)
- Rigid moral codes and internal trials
- Determined tone with narrowed attention to a single plan or sentence

FUNCTIONS

1. **Purge vulnerability** to prevent danger
2. Identification with the **aggressor**
3. **Sealing** traumatic material/ memories
4. Attachment **deactivation** disguised as loyalty
5. **Rank stabilization**

THERAPEUTIC STANCE

Therapeutic work prioritizes **preserving dignity** while re-establishing differentiation and time orientation, with care taken to **update the role without altering the underlying purpose**. Rank dynamics are actively monitored, disgust is addressed when present, and coordination with the rest of the system is maintained throughout. Work concludes with **repair and rehearsal**, supporting integration without collapse or humiliation.

PERPETRATOR-IDENTIFIED PARTS

The bridge between the vulnerable inner world and the outside
has learned to lift its gates for those who resemble the abuser,
and bar the way to those who offer care.
Not because it cannot tell the difference,
but because it has learned that care is the most dangerous disguise of all.

ORIGINS

- Relational environments of explicit threats and covert manipulation
- Repeated invalidation where abuse is reframed as care, and compliance as loyalty.
- These parts also carry the shame of compliance: the guilt of having remained silent, submitted, or even seemed to cooperate
- What may present as aggression or betrayal is often an adaptation born from deep confusion, trauma-bonding, and emotional survival.

FEATURES

- Reject kindness, empathy, or care as manipulative
- Express hostility toward the therapist
- Defend or justify abusive figures
- Blame or shame the Adult Self or other vulnerable parts
- Appear/sound cold, cruel, detached
- Internalize and take on the abuser's voice, tone, or logic

FUNCTIONS

1. Reversal of **power**
2. **Protection** against shame
3. Repression or **distortion** of truth
4. **Blocking attachment** and therapeutic connection
5. Acting as **container** for aggression and traumatic material
6. Preemptive **attack** and threat detection
7. Silencing or **immobilizing** vulnerable parts
8. Code enforcement and **rule-keeping**

THERAPEUTIC STANCE

Therapeutic engagement is guided by **matter-of-fact curiosity** rather than judgment, with a focus on **understanding the burden** these parts carry. The therapist communicates explicitly that their role is not to oppose but to understand, and **names the part's exhaustion** when it becomes apparent.

SEXUALIZED PARTS

Like a bird in a covered cage, these parts ache to spread their wings
but have learned that flight is dangerous.
They read the hands outside, stay small and still, and follow the rules without thinking,
emerging only when the air feels safe and the world predictable

ORIGINS

- Submission is the only available survival strategy
- Sexualization is mistaken for care, connection, or safety
- Perpetrators reward compliance or idealization
- The child learns to anticipate and provide exactly what is needed (sexually) to avoid further harm

FEATURES

- Believe they were complicit/wanted it
- Feel shame or disgust after co-consciousness with other parts
- Flirtatious, seductive behavior
- Have difficulties with therapeutic boundaries or blur relational lines
- Speak in childlike/overly mature tones
- Switch suddenly into different roles
- Be loyal to abusers
- Romanticize past abuse, reflecting grooming distortions
- Idealize perpetrators / deny the abuse

FUNCTIONS

1. Maintain **proximity to dangerous caregivers** through sexualized appeasement
2. **Shield the system** from the full horror
3. **Prevent worse harm** by being good

THERAPEUTIC STANCE

Therapeutic work requires the therapist to remain **grounded and warm** without becoming reactive, while avoiding shame, over-correction, or any sexualization of the behavior. Boundaries are consistently reinforced as **measures of safety** rather than rejection, and insight or confrontation is not forced. The focus is on **supporting internal recognition** in a way that does not lead to collapse.

SHAME-BOUND PARTS

Shame does not just silence you.
It trains you to narrate your own storyin a way to protect everyone but you.
Frank Anderson MD

ORIGINS

Relational environments of:

- humiliation,
- blame, or
- motional abandonment

FEATURES

- Collapsed, withdrawn, and hidden.
- Silent or apologetic in tone
- Afraid of exposure and closeness
- Avoid eye contact, minimize presence
- Deflect compliments, reject empathy
- Very self-critical / distrustful of care
- Flooded with internalized disgust or moral contamination
- Bad, worthless, disgusting, or broken
- Trigger protector parts who fear the danger of revealing shame

FUNCTIONS

1. **Contain** toxic shame
2. Hide from **relational risk**
3. **Prevent emotional exposure** via degrading beliefs
4. **Preserve bonding** through self blame (controlling strategy in submission
5. **Seal** unspeakable material
6. Bear impossible **responsibility**

THERAPEUTIC STANCE

Therapeutic work emphasizes **attunement** over reassurance, normalizes **survival strategies**, supports the building of internal bridges, and consistently slows the pace to allow **regulation and integration.**

Appendix 4. Motivational Systems Organizing Parts' Functions

FUNCTION / STRATEGY	ORGANIZING MOTIVATIONAL SYSTEMS
CHILD PARTS	
Carrier of unbearable pain and unmet need	Attachment (inhibited/distorted), Defense (division through hiding and ignoring needs).
Alarm for unresolved trauma	Defense (threat detection),
Proximity seeking for safety and soothing	Attachment (proximity/care-seeking).
Storehouse of non-verbal memory	Defense (hiding procedural/implicit memory).
Keeper of emotional truth	Attachment (recognition/mirroring, being mentalized) Defense (sealing until safe).
Holder of shame labels	Rank/Power (submission/shame schema) Attachment (deactivation).
Compliance and appeasement	Rank/Power (fawn, submission).
Internal siren that mobilizes protectors	Defense (escalation/mobilization) Attachment (indirect proximity-seeking activates protectors).
ADOLESCENT PARTS	
Protester / Boundary-Setter (keep adults honest, preserve fairness in the frame, block humiliation)	Rank / Dominance Defense (threat protection)
Detached Teen (reduce visibility, control exposure, lower the stakes)	Defense (threat protection) Inhibited Attachment
Parentified Teen (keep the system functioning, preempt criticism by outperforming it)	Caregiving Rank / Status management
Achiever (turn vulnerability into advantage, gain status to reduce exposure)	Rank / Dominance
Risk-Tester (assert agency where once was helplessness)	Exploration Rank (self-assertion)
Chameleon (secure belonging to avoid outsider shame)	Affiliation / Social belonging Attachment
FEARFUL AND AVOIDANT PARTS	
Strategic withdrawal and invisibility	Rank / Dominance (downranking to avoid humiliation) Defense (threat avoidance)
Preemptive shutdown to manage overwhelm	Defense (freeze / collapse as protection)
Gatekeeping to protect vulnerable parts	Attachment (bond protection through inhibition) Defense
Distance to preserve autonomy	Rank / Dominance (autonomy / anti-submission)
Appeasement to reduce perceived burden	Caregiving (caretaking as safety strategy) Attachment (secure belonging)
Delay loops and vigilance	Defense (threat scanning / hypervigilance)
Emotion minimization and compartmentalization	Defense (deactivation / dissociation to prevent overwhelm)
Routine and predictability as control	Defense (safety through procedural control)
Dampening desire and attachment signals	Attachment (inhibited attachment system / deactivation)

FUNCTION / STRATEGY	ORGANIZING MOTIVATIONAL SYSTEMS
HOSTILE AND AGGRESSIVE PARTS	
Preempt closeness before it becomes dangerous	Attachment (inhibited / disorganized attachment) + Defense
Enforce control and predictability	Defense (threat regulation through control)
Maintain protective distance	Defense + Rank / Dominance (autonomy preservation)
Guard against emotional exposure or betrayal	Attachment (loyalty/bond protection) + Defense
Divert attention from traumatic material	Defense (avoidance / dissociation)
Convert shame, fear, or grief into anger or contempt	Rank / Dominance (affect transforms into power stance) Defense
Monitor and police vulnerability internally	Rank / Dominance (internal hierarchy enforcement)
Repeat learned rules from hostile environment	Rank / Dominance + Attachment (bond loyalty)
Mobilize energy and action under threat	Defense (fight/flight mobilization)
Signal threat detection	Defense (threat monitoring / vigilance)
SELF-HARMING PARTS	
Affect modulation	Defense (state regulation under threat)
Downregulation and interruption	Defense (freeze / inhibitory protection)
Attention shifting away from traumatic intrusions	Defense (avoidance / attentional redirection)
Punitive control to prevent external shaming	Rank / Dominance (internalized hierarchy enforcement)
Silencing need and attachment bids	Attachment (inhibited / deactivated attachment system)
Maintaining internal order via rigid rules	Rank / Dominance (hierarchical control)
Eliciting care indirectly when asking feels dangerous	Attachment (proximity seeking under inhibition)
Preventing collapse by dampening interoceptive cues	Defense (shutdown / dissociative regulation)
Keeping suicide at bay	Defense (survival preservation under overwhelm)
SUICIDAL PARTS	
Escape from unbearable affect / unending pain	Defense (shutdown / collapse / escape response)
Interruption of emotional activation	Defense (inhibitory regulation / freeze)
Control and containment in chaos	Defense (safety through control and containment)
HOMICIDAL PARTS	
Purge vulnerability to prevent danger	Defense + Rank / Dominance (eliminate vulnerability to avoid downranking)
Identification with the aggressor	Rank / Dominance (internalized hierarchy) + Defense
Sealing traumatic material / memories	Defense (avoidance / containment)
Attachment deactivation disguised as loyalty	Attachment (deactivation / inhibited attachment) Rank / Dominance (submission-as-safety)
Rank stabilization	Rank / Dominance

FUNCTION / STRATEGY	ORGANIZING MOTIVATIONAL SYSTEMS
PERPETRATOR-IDENTIFIED PARTS	
Reversal of power	Rank / Dominance (restoring power position)
Protection against shame	Rank / Dominance (humiliation avoidance) Defense
Repression or distortion of truth	Attachment (bond preservation / loyalty logic) Defense (avoidance)
Blocking attachment and therapeutic connection	Attachment (deactivation / inhibited attachment) Defense
Container for aggression and traumatic material	Defense (containment / compartmentalization)
Preemptive attack and threat detection	Defense (fight mobilization + vigilance) Rank / Dominance
Silencing or immobilizing vulnerable parts	Rank / Dominance (internal control) Defense
Code enforcement and rule-keeping	Rank / Dominance (hierarchical rule enforcement) Attachment (loyalty/bond protection)
SEXUALIZED PARTS	
Maintain proximity to dangerous caregivers through sexualized appeasement	Attachment (proximity preservation) Sexual system (relational currency under threat)
Shield the system from the full horror	Defense (containment / dissociative protection)
Prevent worse harm by being good	Attachment (bond preservation through compliance) Rank / Dominance (submission to avoid punishment)
SHAME-BASED PARTS	
Contain toxic shame	Rank / Dominance (humiliation regulation) + Defense
Hide from relational risk	Defense (threat avoidance) + Attachment (proximity inhibition)
Prevent emotional exposure via degrading beliefs	Rank / Dominance (self-downranking to avoid ext.l humiliation)
Preserve bonding through self-blame (controlling strategy in submission)	Attachment (bond preservation) Rank / Dominance (submission strategy)
Seal unspeakable material	Defense (containment / dissociative sealing)
Bear impossible responsibility	Caregiving system (parentified control) Rank / Dominance (status stabilization through overfunctioning)

Appendix 5. Summary Charts for the Different Loops

DIVIDED LOYALTIES LOOP

ORIGINS

- Punished disclosure
- Grooming and specialness
- Identification with authority
- Parentification and image-keeping
- State-dependent storage
- Institutional loyalties

ROLES & FUNCTIONS

Truth Holder: Hold unintegrated reality of the event
Watcher: Assure that proximity does not outpace safety
Oath Keeper: Preserve belonging, monitor speech and patrol telling

MOTIVATIONAL SYSTEMS

- **Attachment** (disorganized, approach +inhibition)
- **Defense** (freeze, vigilance, and withdrawal).
- **Rank** domination.

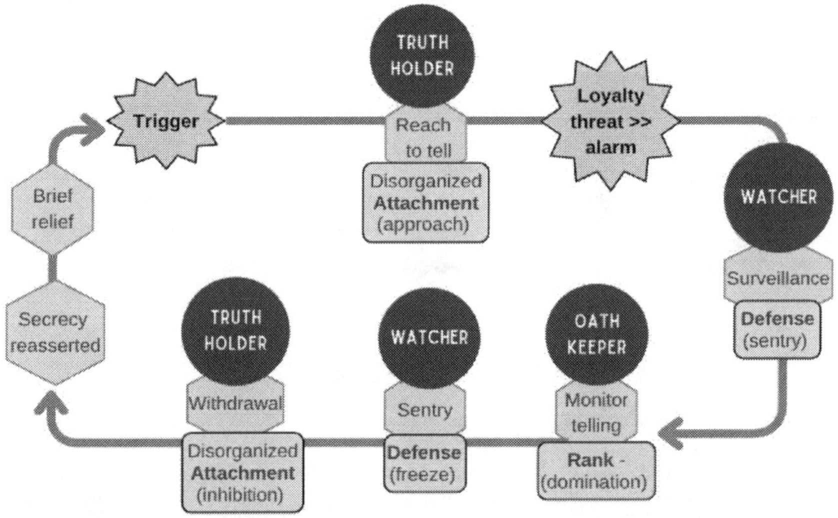

THERAPEUTIC STANCE

Therapeutic work requires awareness of countertransference and ongoing **updating of loyalty** within the system, while supporting **internal reorganization**. Attention is given to **fears around disclosure**, with a focus on **grieving the relationship** rather than the abuse, guided procedurally by the **4Ps framework**.

SHAME LOOP

ORIGINS

- Chronic humiliation or ridicule.
- Conditional belonging.
- Parentification and premature responsibility.
- Gaslighting and reversal.
- Attachment double binds.

ROLES & FUNCTIONS

Shame Carrier: Hold raw feelings and embody wound of exposure.
Shame Blocker: Minimize exposure by shutting down when vulnerability appears.
Shame Enforcer: Enforce invisibility to prevent humiliation, and monitor shame.

MOTIVATIONAL SYSTEMS

- **Attachment** (care-seeking + inhibition of closeness).
- **Defense** (freeze/collapse/appease)
- **Rank/Power** domination (negative evaluation, down-ranking) & submission (shame).

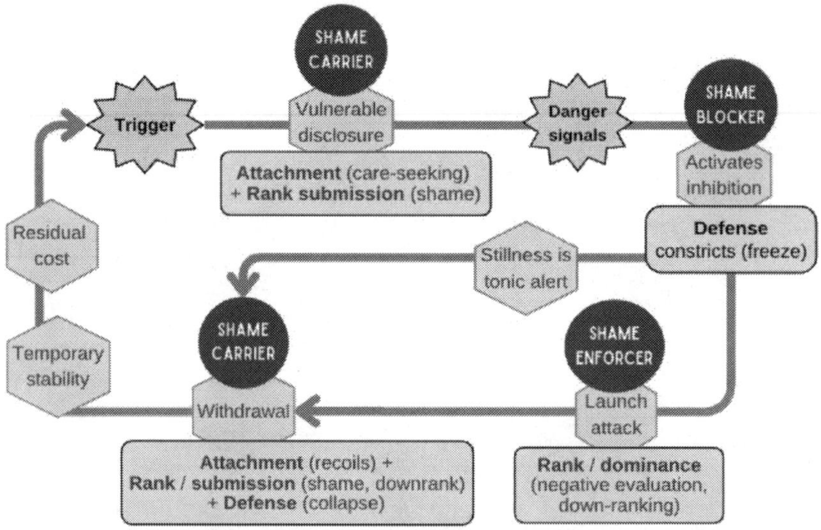

THERAPEUTIC STANCE

When working with shame dynamics, the therapist maintains a **steady, non-defensive presence** that can stay with both collapse and attack **without rescuing, confronting, or withdrawing.** Shame is understood as a protective response to unbearable exposure, and the task is to accompany it by **gently noticing and naming shifts** while holding equal regard for the part that hides and the part that polices. **Presence becomes the intervention**, allowing visibility to occur without reenacting humiliation or isolation.

SELF-DESTRUCTIVE LOOP

ORIGINS

- Chronic danger
- Punitive environments,
- Care contingent on obedience, performance, or silence,
- Shame-based rule systems,
- Loyalty through secrecy,
- Absence of safe adults

ROLES & FUNCTIONS

Despair Holder: Carry frozen pain, hopelessness and self-hatred from the past
Punisher: attack, silence, or harden against weakness to stop despair from spreading
Harm Reducer: Proposes or commands self-injury as a fast, controllable discharge

MOTIVATIONAL SYSTEMS

- **Defense** mobilizes across extremes (collapse, attack and rapid discharge
- **Rank/Power** replicates dominance–submission dynamics (negative evaluation, down-ranking)
- **Attachment** is inhibited

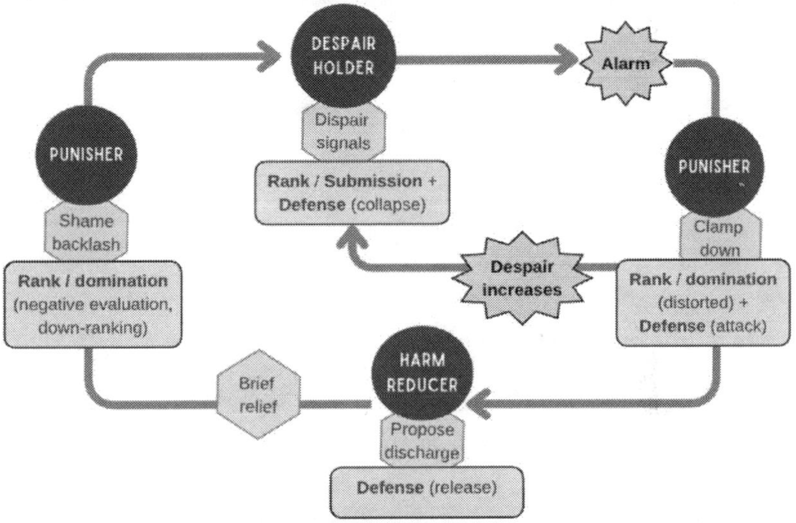

THERAPEUTIC STANCE

When working with self-destructive dynamics, the therapist maintains a **steady, non-reactive stance** that prioritizes translation over control, **understanding the sequence as a containment strategy** forged in trauma time rather than a battle between parts. By **slowing the circuit, naming each role** without judgment, and introducing **shared structure** through the Adult Self, the therapist creates enough safety for co-presence and choice to emerge where reflex once ruled.

BOND-SHAPED LOOP

ORIGINS

- Care was unsafe and survival = obedience
- Attachment required staying close to abuser
- Identification with perpetrator to preserve power.
- Control by shifting from victim to agent of harm

ROLES & FUNCTIONS

Bond Seeker: Carries attachment longing, relational memory, and quiet hope
Bond Blocker: Stop the reach, prevent exposure and keep the system out of trouble
Bond Enforcer: Re-enact,the perpetrator to enforce the original rules of loyalty

MOTIVATIONAL SYSTEMS

- **Attachment** - disorganized (approach & distancing) and attachment preservation
- **Defense** (internal warning, freeze/appease)
- **Rank**/Power - domination and submission to the rules

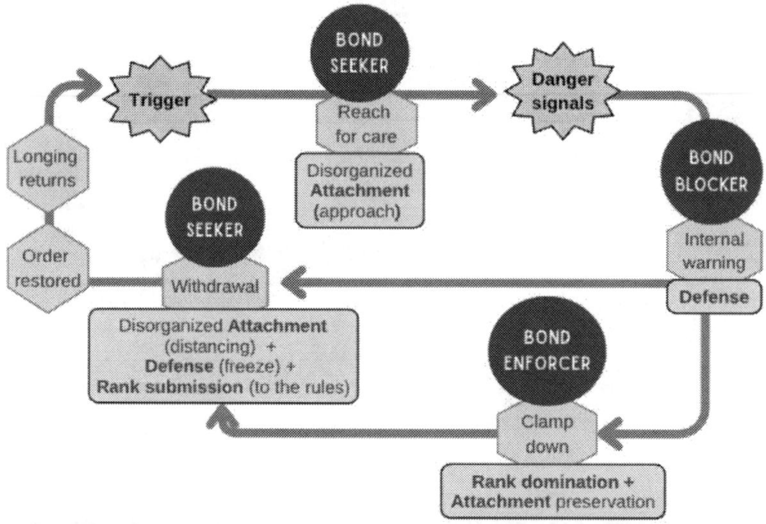

THERAPEUTIC STANCE

Therapeutic work proceeds by **permission, not persuasion**, collaborating first with the Bond Enforcer and Bond Blocker before approaching younger parts. Loyalty is honored as care, and **protection is understood as function** rather than resistance. **Slow pacing**, **shared permission language**, and **predictable stops** build trust and prevent ambush. Guided by the Adult Self, the work **updates protection** through structure and time orientation—**same purpose, safer method.**

APPEASEMENT LOOP

ORIGINS

- Chronic coercion and grooming
- Love as cover for abuse
- Exploitation by caregivers or authorities
- Identification with the powerful

ROLES & FUNCTIONS

Care Seeker: Test safety.
Appeaser: Prevent risk of rupture.
Sexualized Strategist: Secure proximity through learned hierarchy and submission.
Access Guard: Maintain safety through control and secrecy

MOTIVATIONAL SYSTEMS

- **Attachment** (care-seeking. and inhibition).
- **Rank** — submission/fawn to manage the other, domination as perpetrator- identified attack and negative evaluation, shame.
- **Sexual** system.
- **Defense**-freeze (after).

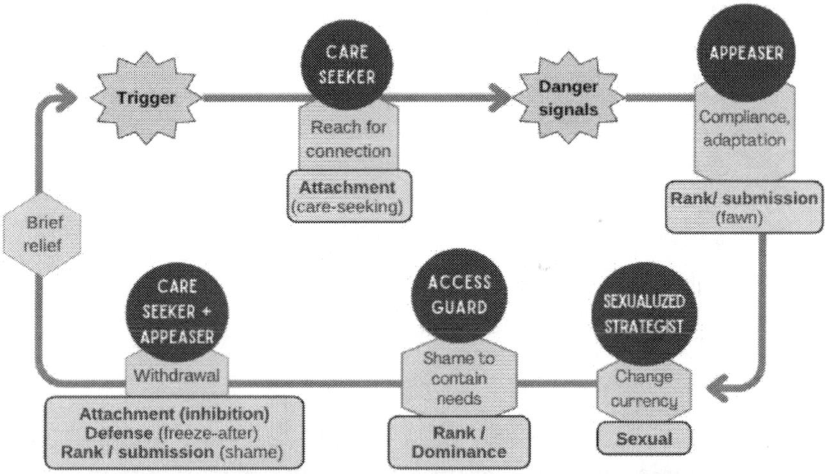

THERAPEUTIC STANCE

When working with sexualized dynamics, the therapist leads with **clear, steady boundaries**, ensuring closeness is never exchanged for compliance or performance. Appeasing and sexualized shifts are **named early and without blame,** separating consent from appeasement and **slowing the pace.** Support is offered through **non-erotic channels**, often words-only, and carefully titrated to keep bodies safe. **Agency is returned to the Adult Self,** so proximity can be experienced without cost, pressure, or loss of boundaries.

INVISIBILITY LOOP

ORIGINS

- Being noticed meant danger, ridicule, or punishment
- Safety depended on invisibility, silence, and constant monitoring
- Visibility = shame, exposure, or loss of belonging
- Survival required staying small, controlling the frame, and reading the room

ROLES & FUNCTIONS

Watcher: Early warning system that scans for threat and prevents danger
Visibility Blocker: Regulates exposure and reduces visibility to keep the body from becoming a target
Enforcer: When previous two cannot hold the line, guarantees safety through control

MOTIVATIONAL SYSTEMS

- **Defense** - alarm and freeze/orient.
- **Attachment** (inhibited reception).
- **Rank/Power** - frame control and rule enforcement)
- Attachment and rank organized around loyalty and internal order keeping.

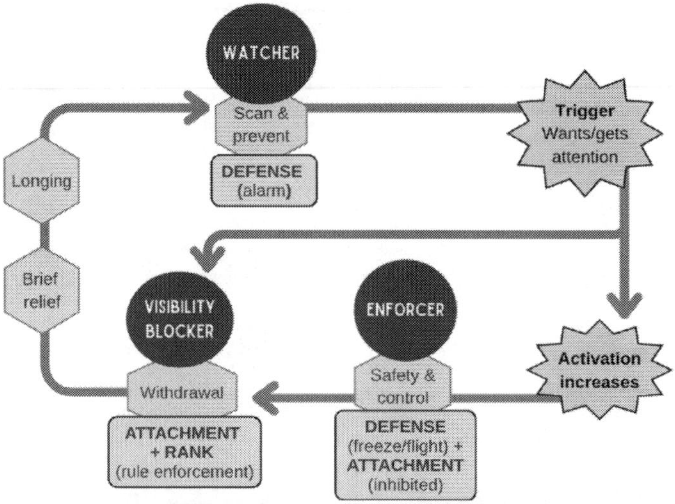

THERAPEUTIC STANCE

The therapist treats surveillance and invisibility as **protective strategies** rather than obstacles to contact. The Watcher's role is respected and given **clear boundaries, routines, and stop signals** so vigilance can stand down when safety is established. Contact is offered **indirectly, brief, and words-only,** allowing the Visibility Blocker to approach without being pulled into exposure or performance. Visibility is negotiated through **shared permission, precise dosing, and explicit opt-outs,** never forced or assumed. **Predictability, repetition, and time-limited contact** teach the nervous system that looking and being seen can begin and end safely on the client's signal.

AMBIVALENCE ABOUT TRAUMA LOOP

ORIGINS

When bond exists and loyalty is involved:

- Punished or costly truth
- Gaslighting and confusion
- Disorganized attachment
- Secrecy contracts and oaths
- Role reversal
- Overwhelm and state-dependent storage.
- Institutional loyalties

When harm comes from outsiders, the system organizes around survivability.

ROLES & FUNCTIONS

Memory Keeper: Sensory/ Experiential Storage. (+ **Truth Holder**)
Seal Keeper/Watcher: Access regulation
Lid Keeper/ Oath Keeper: Exposure Control
Threshold Guardian: Dose & Capacity Signaling
Flood Responder: Circuit Breaker

MOTIVATIONAL SYSTEMS

- **Attachment** (care-seeking + inhibition)
- **Rank/Power** - hierarchy restoration - domination and submission - shame or self-attack
- **Defense** - arounsal regulation

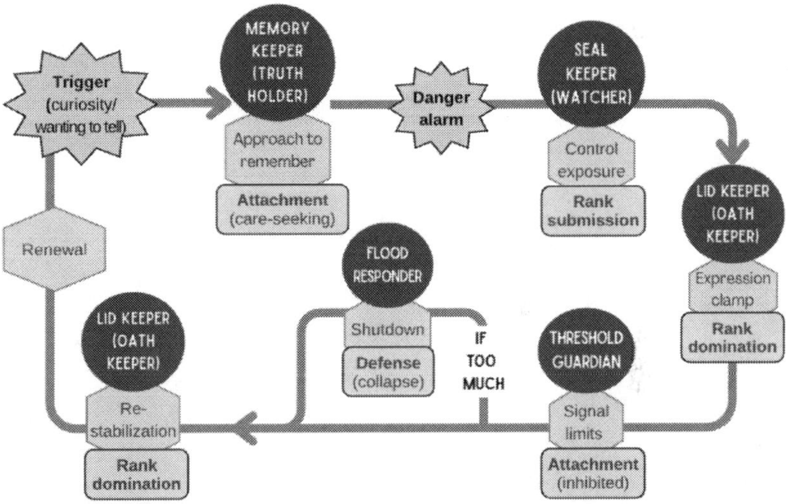

THERAPEUTIC STANCE

Rather than pushing for disclosure or litigating truth, the therapist **tracks function**—how the system is protecting itself in real time—and works with internal roles such as Memory Keepers and Guardians as allies, not obstacles. Through **permission, precision, pace, and predictability,** memory work becomes opt-in, titrated, and reversible, with success measured by regulation and return to baseline rather than volume of content. The stance prioritizes **consent over pressure, curiosity over interrogation, and procedural safety over breakthrough**, allowing the nervous system to learn—experientially—that proximity to memory no longer requires collapse or self-betrayal.

Appendix 6. How Parts May Organize Across Loops

The following table illustrates how different types of parts may assume different roles across relational and motivational loops. These patterns reflect procedural tendencies observed in clinical work, not fixed classifications. A given part may assume different roles depending on context, perceived threat, and the motivational systems organizing the experience. It is offered as a guide to help clinicians recognize recurring patterns of organization rather than as a prescriptive or diagnostic framework. Roles describe functions within a loop—patterns that illustrate common dynamics among dissociative parts. The parts themselves are adaptive configurations shaped by history and survival logic. The role names are pragmatic and descriptive, intended to help the reader identify these dynamics in practice.

LOOPS / PARTS	DIVIDED LOYALTIES	SHAME	SELF-DESTRUCTION	BOND-SHAPED	APPEASEMENT	INVISIBILITY	AMBIVALENCE RE: TRAUMA
CHILD PARTS	Truth Holder	Shame Carrier	Despair Holder (collapse)	Bond Seeker	Care Seeker	Visibility Blocker	Memory Keeper
ADOLESCENT PARTS	Truth Holder	Shame Carrier	Punisher (self-attack)	Bond Seeker	Care Seeker	Watcher (hypervigilant teen)	Truth Holder or Memory Keeper
FEARFUL & AVOIDANT PARTS	Watcher	Shame Blocker	——	Bond Blocker	Appeaser (fear driven)	Visibility Blocker	Seal Keeper
SELF-CRITICAL & PUNITIVE PARTS	Oath Keeper	Shame Enforcer	Punisher	Bond Blocker	Access Guard	Watcher (evaluative)	Lid Keeper (dominant)
HOSTILE & AGGRESSIVE PARTS	Oath Keeper	Shame Enforcer	Punisher	Bond Blocker	Access Guard	Enforcer	Lid Keeper (control/ composure)
SELF-HARMING PARTS	——	Shame Carrier (fuel)	Harm Reducer	——	——	——	Flood Responder
SUICIDAL PARTS	——	Shame Carrier (despair core)	Despair Holder	——	——	——	Flood Responder
HOMICIDAL PARTS	——	——	——	——	——	——	——
PERPETRATOR-IDENTIFIED PARTS	Oath Keeper	Shame Enforcer	Punisher	Bond Enforcer	Access Guard	Enforcer	Lid Keeper
SEXUALIZED PARTS	——	Shame Carrier	——	——	Sexualized Strategist	——	Lid Keeper
SHAME-BOUND PARTS	Truth Holder (self-blaming)	Shame Carrier	Despair Holder (chronic collapse)	Bond Seeker (collapse)	Appeaser (submission)	Visibility Blocker (shrinking)	Seal Keeper (shame sealed memory)

References

Ainsworth, M. D. S. (1978). *Patterns of attachment: A psychological study of the strange situation*. Lawrence Erlbaum.

Arntz, A., & Jacob, G. (2013). *Schema therapy in practice: An introductory guide to the schema mode approach*. Wiley-Blackwell.

Benau, E. M. (2022). Shame, trauma, and dissociation: Clinical implications of self-conscious affects. *Journal of Trauma & Dissociation, 23*(2), 145–160.

Boon, S. (2017). *Coping with trauma-related dissociation: Skills training for patients and therapists*. Norton.

Bowlby, J. (1969). *Attachment and loss: Vol. 1. Attachment*. Basic Books.

Bowlby, J. (1982). *Attachment and loss: Vol. 1. Attachment* (2nd ed.). Basic Books.

Brand, B. L., Classen, C. C., McNary, S. W., & Zaveri, P. (2014). A review of dissociative disorders treatment studies. *Journal of Nervous and Mental Disease, 202*(2), 83–102.

Bromberg, P. M. (1998). *Standing in the spaces: Essays on clinical process, trauma, and dissociation*. Analytic Press.

Brown, D. J., & Elliott, D. S. (2016). Attachment Disturbances in Adults: Treatment for Comprehensive Repair. New York, NY: W. W. Norton.

Caul, D. (1984). *The fractured self: Trauma, dissociation, and identity*. Jason Aronson.

Chefetz, R. A. (2020). Shame and the developmental antecedents of enduring, self-critical mental states: A discussion and some speculations. *Psychiatry, 83*(1), 25–32.

Cortina, M. (2018). *The attachment of dissociation: Clinical perspectives*. Routledge.

Cortina, M., & Liotti, G. (2010). Attachment is about safety and protection, intersubjectivity is about sharing and social understanding: The relationships between attachment and intersubjectivity. *Psychoanalytic Psychology, 27*(4), 410-438.

Dorahy, M. J., et al. (2009). Auditory hallucinations in dissociative identity disorder and schizophrenia. *Journal of Nervous and Mental Disease, 197*(12), 892–898.

Dutra, L., Bureau, J.-F., Holmes, B., Lyubchik, A., & Lyons-Ruth, K. (2009). Quality of early care and childhood trauma: a prospective study of developmental pathways to dissociation. *J Nerv Ment Dis*, 197(6), 383-390.

Farrell, J. M., Reiss, N., & Shaw, I. A. (2014). *The schema therapy clinician's guide.* Wiley-Blackwell.

Ferenczi, S. (1933). Confusion of the tongues between the adults and the child. *International Journal of Psycho-Analysis, 30*, 225–230.

Ferenczi, S. (1949). Confusion of the tongues between the adults and the child (The language of tenderness and of passion). *International Journal of Psycho-Analysis, 30*, 225–230. (Original work published 1933)

Fisher, J. (2017). *Healing the fragmented selves of trauma survivors.* Routledge.

Fraser, G. A. (1991). The dissociative table technique. *Dissociation, 4*(4), 205–213.

Fraser, G. A. (1993). Ego states and dissociation. *American Journal of Clinical Hypnosis, 36*(2), 123–130.

Freud, A. (1936). *The ego and the mechanisms of defence.* Hogarth Press.

González, A., Mosquera, D., & Solomon, J. (2012). Trauma, dissociation, and attachment. *Journal of Trauma & Dissociation, 13*(4), 421–438.

Hamilton, W. D. (1964). The genetical evolution of social behaviour I & II. *Journal of Theoretical Biology, 7*, 1–52.

Howell, E. F. (2005). *The dissociative mind.* Routledge.

Janet, P. (1907). *The major symptoms of hysteria.* Macmillan.

Janet, P. (1938). *Psychological healing: A historical and clinical study* (Vol. 1). Macmillan.

Janet, P. (1945). *The psychological analysis of traumatic memories.* Nervous and Mental Disease Publishing.

Leeds, A. (2012). Developmental Pathways to Dissociation: Are we forgetting something? ESTD Newsletter, 3(1), 4-9.

Lewis, H. B. (1971). *Shame and guilt in neurosis.* International Universities Press.

Liotti, G. (2004). Trauma, dissociation, and disorganized attachment. *Psychotherapy, 41*(4), 472–486.

Liotti, G. (2005). Attachment and dissociation. *Attachment & Human Development, 7*(3), 287–295.

Liotti, G. (2010). Attachment, trauma, and dissociation. In M. Cortina & G. Liotti (Eds), *Attachment, trauma, and dissociation.* Routledge.

Liotti, G. (2011). Attachment disorganization and the clinical dialogue. In J. Solomon & C. George (Eds)., *Disorganized attachment and caregiving* (pp. 89–110). Guilford Press.

Liotti, G. (2014). *Trauma, dissociation, and disorganized attachment.* Routledge.

Liotti, G. (2017). Conflicts between motivational systems related to attachment trauma: Key to understanding the intra-family relationship between abused children and their abusers. *Journal of Trauma & Dissociation, 18*(3), 319–334.

Liotti, G., & Cortina, M. (2010). *Attachment, trauma and dissociation.* Routledge.

Maginnis, T. L. (2006). The adaptive function of dissociation. *Journal of Trauma Practice, 4*(3–4), 5–23.

Main, M., & Cassidy, J. (1988). Categories of response to reunion at age six. *Monographs of the Society for Research in Child Development, 53*(1), 66–104.

Main, M., & Solomon, J. (1990). Procedures for identifying disorganized/disoriented infants. In M. Greenberg et al. (Eds)., attachment *in the preschool years* (pp. 121–160). University of Chicago Press.

Moskowitz, A. (2008). Psychosis, trauma, and dissociation. *Journal of Trauma & Dissociation, 9*(3), 347–361.

Moskowitz, A., & Van der Hart, O. (2020). Dissociation in psychosis. *Current Opinion in Psychology, 34*, 67–71.

Mosquera, D. (2016). Working with dissociative parts. *ESTD Newsletter*.

Mosquera, D. (2019). *A trauma-informed approach for dissociative parts*. KDP.

Mosquera, D. (2024). Identity disorders, dissociation, and the influence of social media. *ESTD Newsletter*.

Mosquera, D., & González, A. (2014). Dissociation and attachment dynamics. *Journal of Trauma & Dissociation, 15*(4), 399–417.

Mosquera, D., González, A., & Van der Hart, O. (2011). Trauma, dissociation, and internal conflict. *Journal of Trauma & Dissociation, 12*(5), 566–581.

Mosquera, D., & Ross, C. A. (2016). Treatment challenges in complex dissociation. *Journal of Trauma & Dissociation, 17*(5), 567–585.

Mosquera, D., & Ross, C. A. (2017). Perpetrator-identified parts. *Journal of Trauma & Dissociation, 18*(2), 147–165.

Mosquera, D., & Steele, K. (2017). Working with dissociative parts. *Journal of Trauma & Dissociation, 18*(4), 555–570.

Mosquera, D., Moskowitz, A., & Longden, E. (2017). Auditory verbal hallucinations and dissociation. *Journal of Trauma & Dissociation, 18*(2), 199–215.

Nathanson, D. L. (1992). *Shame and pride*. Norton.

Nijenhuis, E. R. S., & Van der Hart, O. (2011). Dissociation in trauma. *Journal of Trauma & Dissociation, 12*(4), 416–445.

Ogawa, J. R., Sroufe, L. A., Weinfield, N. S., Carlson, E. A., & Egeland, B. (1997). Development and the fragmented self: longitudinal study of dissociative symptomatology in a nonclinical sample. Dev Psychopathol, 9(4), 855-879. https://doi.org/10.1017/S0954579497001478

Panksepp, J. (1998). *Affective neuroscience*. Oxford University Press.

Paulsen, S. (1995). EMDR and dissociation. *Dissociation, 8*(1), 32–38.

Paulsen, S. (2009). *Looking through the eyes of trauma and dissociation*. Bainbridge Institute.

Ross, C. A., Ferrell, L., & Schroeder, E. (2014). Dissociation and treatment outcomes. *Journal of Trauma & Dissociation, 15*(4), 453–469.

Sar, V., & Ross, C. A. (2006). Dissociative disorders as trauma-based conditions. *Psychiatric Clinics of North America, 29*(1), 227–244.

Schwartz, R. C. (1995). *Internal Family Systems Therapy*. Guilford Press.

Schwartz, R. C., & Sweezy, M. (2019). *Internal Family Systems Therapy* (2nd ed.). Guilford Press.

Spiegel, D., et al. (2011). Dissociation and trauma. *American Journal of Psychiatry, 168*(8), 824–832.

Steele, K. (2018). Dependency in the psychotherapy of chronically traumatized individuals: Using motivational systems to guide effective treatment. *Cognitivismo Clinico [The Legacy of Giovanni Liotti], 15*(2), 221-226.

Steele, K. (2021). Beyond attachment: Understanding motivational systems in complex trauma and dissociation. In D. Siegel, A. Schore, & L. Cozolino (Eds.) *Interpersonal neurobiology and clinical practice (pp. 85-112)*. New York. Norton.

Steele, K., Van der Hart, O., & Nijenhuis, E. R. S. (2005). Phase-oriented treatment of structural dissociation. *Journal of Trauma & Dissociation, 6*(2), 11–53.

Steele, K., Van der Hart, O., & Nijenhuis, E. R. S. (2017). *Treating trauma-related dissociation*. Norton.

Van der Hart, O., Nijenhuis, E. R. S., & Steele, K. (2006). *The haunted self*. Norton.

Watkins, J. G., & Watkins, H. H. (1991). *Ego states: Theory and therapy*. Norton.

Watkins, J. G., & Watkins, H. H. (1997). *Ego states: Theory and therapy*. Norton.

Weiss, J., & Sampson, H. (1986). *The psychoanalytic process*. Guilford Press.

Young, J. E., et al. (2002). *Schema therapy*. Guilford Press.

Young, J. E., Klosko, J. S., & Weishaar, M. E. (2003). *Schema therapy: A practitioner's guide*. Guilford Press.

Zanarini, M. C., et al. (1998). Axis I comorbidity of borderline personality disorder. *American Journal of Psychiatry, 155*(12), 1733–1739.

d987881b-d322-49d3-83c5-71664083debcR01